EGYPT:
MILITARY SOCIETY

EGYPT:
MILITARY SOCIETY

BY *Anouar*

Abdel-Malek

THE ARMY REGIME, THE LEFT, AND
SOCIAL CHANGE UNDER NASSER

Translated by *Charles Lam Markmann*

 RANDOM HOUSE   *New York*

First American Edition

Library of Congress Catalog Card Number: 68–14511

To the fraternal memory of

Shohdi Attia el-Shafei
(Alexandria, 1911–Abu Zaabal, 1960),

*who brought honor to our generation
and who was my friend*

Preface

Two "BLACK FRIDAYS" define the boundaries of Egypt's national revolution, during its last stage, under the military regime. On the morrow of Friday, January 25, 1952—when British armor took its heavy toll of Egyptian lives in Ismailia—Cairo was set on fire by select activist groups, which were later identified in the (unpublished) trial proceedings as belonging to the extreme Right in league with the various forces intent on blocking the path of the rising United National Front, while more than one and a half million persons, the people of Cairo, watched in the streets, chatting or sipping drinks in silence. At 5 P.M. on January 26, senior army and police generals, dismissed by the ex-king as if from a banquet, started their action: to restore order, impose curfew and on the next day suspend the (1923) Constitution, dismiss the elected government of the land, disband the guerrilla groups active in the Suez Canal Zone against the British military base there and put their members in jail, together with all the leading cadres of the national and progressive movements. Less than six months later, during the first hours of July 23, 1952, the "Free Officers" seized power.

And yet, on the morrow of that first "Black Friday," the people of Cairo stood away from the political scene: they saw no connection between what was put to flames—the modern center of Egypt's capital—and their own destiny. In their fatherland the Egyptians felt alien. Cairo, the nerve center of power and culture, of tradition and renaissance, the successor of the Pharaonic Memphis and the Christian Babylon, the city of Al-Mo'ezz, Saladin, the Fatimids and Mohammed Ali, the nerve center of Islam, where Bonaparte and Cromer had failed, after the Turks—Cairo, "the victorious," lay open, its wounds bleeding, humiliated by the defection of its inhabitants, ready for strife and slaying. For on that day Cairo was viewed by the Cairenes, and by the Egyptians at large, as no more than the common meeting ground of foreign imperialism and local despotism. A day of shame and mourning. A day that meant the end of everything "normal."

Fifteen years later came another "Black Friday," better known to foreigners. At 6 P.M. on Friday, June 9, 1967, Gamal Abdel Nasser addressed the people of Egypt, and beyond them, the peoples of the whole Arab world. Egypt's armed forces had been severely hit; the Sinai occupied; the Suez Canal paralyzed; the air force practically wiped out as an operational unit; acts of treason, felony and conspiracy were open and rampant throughout the land; fifteen years of hard-won achievements were severely endangered; the military power élite had lost, at one stroke, all pretension of being recognized as a possible political leadership for Egypt; inflated hopes and real achievements were seriously called in question. The people of Egypt were awakening to a nightmare, by very far the worst in their tragic history. One man stood at the helm, a man who had held undisputed power—or so it seemed at the time—for fifteen years. This man had been reaping the glory and abuse in Egypt's name from 1952 to 1967. As Egypt crumbled he frankly recognized the fact, admitted full responsibility and resigned from the Presidency and all political offices. While he was speaking, antiaircraft batteries were turned toward the skies over Cairo—with no Israeli planes above; armed gangs moved toward the Soviet embassy, since the USSR was held responsible for the military failure; officers met all over Cairo with groups of the ex-ruling classes, ready for the takeover. And on the east bank of the Suez Canal, the most powerful invading army that ever set foot on Egyptian soil was preparing for the final count. All was set. Nothing had been neglected. Egypt would have to pay for "Suez." And the man at the helm would have to go, his myth shattered, his anti-imperalist national-radical course dismantled, his policies denied. The Middle East could then be brought to reason, oil could easily be made safe, and Egypt, under a "reasonable liberal government"[1]* could go forward with the blessings of the West, accompanied, to be sure, by huge financial support, perhaps even a face-saving "evacuation" of the Sinai on certain conditions, and by a swift and radical suppression of the radical and left wings of the national movement.

Then things started moving. But this movement did not follow the prescribed course. After a few moments of hesitation the whole country swang into action: the streets of Cairo were flooded with more than two and a half million; the whole population of Tantah, the center of the Delta, was marching on the capital; the same in Port Said, where, however, the people were recalled in a desperate move not to empty the city; from every city, town and village, from Alexandria to Aswan, from the Western Desert to Suez, a whole nation marched. And its slogans could not be misunderstood: *"No imperialism! No dollar!"*[2]; *"No leader but Gamal!"* Ever since the May 1967 crisis, the people of Cairo and Alexandria had instinctively taken up the 1919 revolution's popular battle hymn—*Biladi, biladi, fidaki dami!* (My Fatherland, O Fatherland, Yours Is My Blood!) —and now it exploded like a thunderstorm and a shield, broke through intrigues and conspiracies and found its way to the national broadcasting station, asserting Egypt's nationhood and national resolve. "There was a moment, at the cease-fire," wrote Isaac Deutscher in his last document, a moving political testament, "when it looked as if Egypt's defeat would lead to Nasser's downfall and to the undoing of the policy associated with his name. If that had happened, the Middle East would almost certainly have been brought back into the Western sphere of influence. Egypt might have become another Ghana or Indonesia. This did not happen, however. The Arab masses who came out in the streets and squares of Cairo, Damascus

---

* This and subsequent numerals refer to Source Notes following the end of the text.

and Beirut to demand that Nasser should stay in office, prevented it from happening. *This was one of those rare historic popular impulses that redress or upset a political balance within a few moments. This time, in the hour of defeat, the initiative from below worked with immediate impact. There are only very few cases in history when a people has stood by a defeated leader in this way* [my italics]. . . . For the time being, neocolonialism has been denied the fruits of Israel's 'victory.' "³

Gone were the days of passivity. Gone was the feeling of not-belonging. Gone was the lack of identification between a people and its fatherland. The time had finally come for the people of Egypt to come on stage, as full-fledged actors, and directors-to-be, of its own destiny.

"Bilad Miçr kheirha li gheirha" (The land of Egypt, its riches belong to others)—so runs an ancient Egyptian proverb. And another one, deeply ingrained in Egyptian hearts: *"Miçr omm el-donya"* (Egypt, mother of the world). When Cairo was put to flames, it looked as if the malediction embodied in the first proverb was to prevail. Fifteen years later, on June 9, 1967, the people of Egypt hoisted their national will at high mast. Objectively, "Nasserism" must be held responsible for that, too.

Fifteen years. The history of what will in the future be recognized as the final stage of Egypt's national revolution has come full circle, and the stage has been set for social revolution.

For good and bad, for better or worse, Egypt is now on the move: *"On s'engage, et puis on voit,"* as Bonaparte directed during the Italian campaigns.

This book deals, specifically, with the people of Egypt—the national movement, and the economic and social transformation in relation to the ideological struggle—between the two "Black Fridays." And the analysis provided stems from an interpretation of Egypt's seventy-century-old history, within the same geographical and geopolitical framework.

Contradictions abound, whatever angle one chooses to start from, for contradiction lies at the very heart of this singularly complex ensemble of tradition and modernity. It would of course seem even more complicated and contradictory if one chose to observe Egypt from outside its long history. Without steeping oneself in its history, one could not possibly understand anything of Egypt's national being, its essence, so to speak, of which the history of these fifteen years is but *one* of the potential expressions.

II.

At this point a "preliminary guide" to the Egyptian maze might prove useful, for the military regime in Egypt since 1952 has been analyzed in remarkably divergent terms. Observers and specialists alike have tended to emphasize two main aspects: nationalism and dictatorship. In spite of many differences, the European Left has come close to the general and mostly adverse conclusions agreed upon by the leading political scientists of the West. The main difference is that whereas the Right has felt, and still feels, a deeply rooted hatred of "Nasserism," the Left is still seeking a way out of its confusion while deploring the political repression against the Egyptian Left.

In Egypt itself, these past fifteen years are looked upon as a revolutionary and empirical transition from feudalism to socialism. Such informed opinion as is permitted to find an outlet in the press appears divided among a wide range of descriptive categories: "state capitalism," "the welfare state," "Arab socialism," "scientific socialism," "democratic and co-operative socialism"—to list only the main ones. Thus the analytical problems involved are not only those of the hitherto West European-centered social sciences; the same difficulties and the same uncertainties confront the Egyptian theoriticians. This book makes no claim to a final, dogmatic solution to the questions, for such an attitude would be fundamentally opposed to the author's view of scientific research in general.

A first approach may be attempted at the infrastructure level, i.e., the economic, political and sociological aspects of the regime. The problem of fixing specific dates lies mostly outside the scope of this essay, but it is possible to distinguish three main stages since the coup d'état of July 23, 1952.[4]

Until then Egypt, though enjoying a large degree of formal independence, had in fact been a semidependent state, ruled by the agrarian wing of the Egyptian bourgeoisie in alliance with foreign capital, under the aegis of the Palace. Its colonial-type economy can be characterized as an underdeveloped capitalistic one, with a predominantly agrarian structure. The confusion between agrarian capitalism and feudalism which existed in most political circles in Egypt led to the political developments initiated by the Free Officers and described as anti-feudal. In fact, as all serious research has shown, the Egyptian economy has been predominantly of the capitalistic type since the last quarter of the nineteenth century—with large-scale production for the market, especially of cotton, and a growing use of wage-earning labor—although there remained many, often deep-rooted features of (Oriental) feudalism, in human and social relations alike, especially in Upper Egypt.

From the 1919 revolution to the coup d'état of 1952, the Wafd was allowed to rule for a bare seven years, though holding an undisputed electoral majority. This gave more than twenty-five years to the minority parties, representing the right wing of the Egyptian bourgeoisie: especially the Liberal-Constitutional party, mouthpiece for the big landowners (since 1923); the Saadists, closely linked with the industrial and financial fast-growing sections of the Egyptian bourgeoisie (since 1937); the Independents, who mainly represented the Palace, foreign vested interests and sections of big capital. This arrangement was imposed on the Egyptian people by military occupation, and the British gave support to whatever forces opposed the militant national-liberation movement. This policy worked because of the inefficiency of the Wafdist leadership, especially after 1945, as well as the repression of the Left since the early thirties.

However, it was clear to all that the unsolved and growing problems of Egypt were bound to provoke a more radical solution. This was attempted in the violent national upheaval of 1935, which brought the Wafd back to power and led to the Anglo-Egyptian treaty of 1936; and also immediately after World War II, when the re-emergent Marxist Left, together with the trade unions, the Wafdist youth and Liberal wing, created a National Committee of Workers and Students (1946) as a new center of leadership for the liberation movement. It was this alignment of forces which, after the repression of 1946 and then of 1948–50, brought back the Wafd to power in 1949, encouraged its reluctant leadership to denounce the 1936 treaty (in 1950), and launched guerrilla action against the British base in the Canal Zone (October 1950 to January 1951). The stage was thus set for a United National Front government, based on popular action and inspired by the Left, and under the benevolent patronage of Mustafa el-Nahas, the aging leader of the Wafd.

On January 26, 1952, Cairo was in flames. Then, on July 23, the Free Officers seized power.

1. The *first stage* of the military regime (*1952–56*) was aimed at modifying the structure of power in order to create a modern national, independent, industrialized society. This was achieved, at the top of the sociopolitical structure, by the abolition of the monarchy and the establishment of the Republic of Egypt, the dissolution of all existing parties and organizations (except the Moslem Brotherhood, until 1954), the elimination of the traditional political élites, largely influenced by the European, mainly French and British, liberal tradition (*ahl al-kafa'a*, the capable men), and these were gradually replaced by a new type of officials—officers, economists, technocrats and engineers, mostly with American, German and British backgrounds (*ahl al-thiqa*, the trusted men). At the bottom of the pyramid, this policy was tackled by agrarian reforms which sought to weaken the economic basis of the land-owning capitalists while greatly increasing the number of small landowners, as well as redirecting capital investment to industry. It also aimed at the elimination of Communist influence in the countryside, which was already in ferment by 1951. Then the Liberation Rally party emerged, a paramilitary formation ideologically parallel to the Moslem Brotherhood. It was hoped that local capital, mostly invested in land, would accept the official enticement, backed by a mass of new legislation, to invest in industry with the help of the newly established Industrial Bank and the Permanent Council for the Development of National Production. However, 70 percent of all new investment went into the building industry and the

military regime was unable to persuade the industrial and financial sections of the Egyptian bourgeoisie to support it in the task of social transformation.

2. The *second stage* (*1956–61*) started with the Suez crisis. Having succeeded in obtaining Britain's agreement to the gradual but complete evacuation of the Canal base (October 19, 1954), the military government launched its offensive against the Baghdad Pact (1955–56), and then switched to the economic problems facing Egypt—first of all the Aswan High Dam. This conjunction of political-military-economic issues brought about John Foster Dulles' refusal to extend financial aid for the High Dam project. This was followed by the nationalization of the Suez Canal Company and the three powers' aggression against Egypt.

The result, to the outside world, was unexpected. Fifty-five French and British-owned firms were either "Egyptianized" or nationalized under the aegis of the Economic Agency, which came to represent state-owned firms as well as the initial state participation in firms. Thus the Suez aggression inaugurated the public sector of the Egyptian economy and provided a further incentive to economic planning. The state was endowed, by imperialism, with the necessary resources for it to become a senior partner with the most important groups among the Egyptian bourgeoisie.

The second stage of the military regime thus appears as a coalition between the military apparatus and the financial and industrial sections of the bourgeoisie (and especially the Misr group). But this coalition, according the the Free Officers' view, was to work mainly in the economic field: political control, the "power of decision," should continue to rest entirely in their hands.

During the early years (1956–58)—the Bandung period— the regime appeared ready to grant a certain amount of United National Front concessions and measures, especially after the release of Communists and leftists in the middle of 1956. The publication of the leftwing daily, *al-Missa,* the promulgation of the 1956 Constitution, the elections to the Council of the Nation, and the establishment of the National Union as the only permitted political party, in which the nominees of the military apparatus and their bourgeois allies found their place, are the main new political facts of this period. In foreign affairs, the doctrine of positive neutralism proved an inspiration to many countries who were similarly opposed to military pacts.

By the end of 1958 the situation was changing rapidly. There was Communist opposition to organic unity with Syria and a preference for federalism; the Communist movement itself, after a generation of factional strife and struggle, had established the (second) Communist party of Egypt (February 28, 1958). The emergence of a National Front regime under General Kassem after the Iraqi revolution of July 14, 1958, was looked upon as an "alternative" in Egypt. There was repression against the Communists and the Left (January–March 1959), and there was also penetration in depth of the Syrian administration and economy by the military group and by leading sections of the Egyptian bourgeoisie.

On the home front, however, the military group continued to wield a monopoly of political power, and the Egyptian bourgeoisie again displayed a conspicuous lack of enthusiasm for the economic policy of the regime. In particular it showed a marked reluctance to invest in the industrial sector. Something had to be done to restore some degree of harmony to the alliance.

3. The *third stage* (*July 1961–June 1967*) started with the laws of nationalization. The military regime had earlier shown its hand by nationalizating the National Bank of Egypt and Bank Misr (February 11, 1960). By the beginning of 1962 all banks, all heavy industry, insurance and the key economic enterprises were state-owned, and all medium-sized economic units had to accept a 51 percent state participation in their capital ownership and therefore in their administration. There was, further, an extensive medium and light sector of economic activity in which the state's participation was enforced, and the whole network was made to fit into the newly created "public agencies," of which, in the beginning, there were thirty-eight. This constituted the public sector as against the private one. Economic planning had begun with the first of two Five-Year Plans (1960–70), whose aim was to double the gross national product in all fields of the economy.

The "third revolution" of August 12, 1963, brought a new wave of legislation which nationalized 228 companies in industry, transport and mines. Former shareholders were to receive compensation in the form of government bonds bearing 4 percent interest, payable in fifteen years. Another 177 companies (including all internal transport and three arms factories) followed on November 11, 1963; then came the turn of six land corporations (November 18, 1963).

This profound modification of the key sectors of the Egyptian economy had to find resonance in the sociopolitical field, and it was the task of the National Congress of Popular Forces (made up of national capitalists, peasants, workers, the professions, civil servants, university teaching staffs, students, women—the armed services were added later as one of these "forces") to discuss the draft of the *Charter of National Action,* presented to its members by President Nasser on May 21, 1963. This important document proclaimed *inter alia* that "socialism is the way to social freedom" and that "scientific socialism" was the suitable style for finding the right method leading to progress. The Charter was adopted despite fanatical opposition inspired by the Moslem Brotherhood. A new organization, the Arab Socialist Union, was established as the central organ of political activity; it was intended to represent all popular forces, the workers and peasants being entitled to 50 percent of the seats in all the committees of the Arab Socialist Union, as well as in the future Council of the Nation.

It is not difficult to understand why these developments have led to intellectual and political confusion and why there has been a marked tendency to oversimplify the definition of the new society that is emerging in Egypt. It has been variously evaluated as socialism at one end of the scale, and at the other, as leading to the establishment of a new bourgeoisie which will become the tool of neoimperialism. In the field of economics, the following facts can be established:

1. The controlling position of imperialism has been uprooted, and both the economic resources of the country as well as the power of political decision are now entirely in Egyptian hands.

2. Until 1963, private ownership was still the dominant mode of production in the Egyptian economy as a whole, but particularly in the landholding sector and in the building industry. The estimates of the 1962–63 budget put the private sector's contribution to the national income at 65.8 percent, thus leaving only 34.2 percent to the public sector. Naturally, the proportion of private and public, measured by national-income contribution, varied widely between different parts of the economy, private being represented by 93.8 percent in agriculture, 87.5 percent in building, 79.1 percent in commerce, and 56.4 percent in industry. However, the new wave of nationalization measures of August 1963 brought 80 percent of industry into the public sector, and the November decrees aimed at making the public sector a majority influence in commerce, transport and armament factories. But agriculture remained relatively untouched, as did building.

It is therefore clear that the strategic sectors of the national economy have been taken away from the Egyptian bourgeoisie and brought under the ownership and control of the state.

3. The state controls the objectives, the priorities and the methods of growth of the national economy as a wohle, through the planning organs and within the framework of the Ten-Year Plan. As the state also provides about 90 percent of new capital formation, it can obviously impose its own priorities on economic developments, such as large-scale industrialization, the High Dam, prospecting for new sources of energy, and desert-land recovery. Economic planning, however, is still based on private enterprise and is loosely regulated by market requirements. This is well demonstrated by the much-publicized data relating to the profits of the nationalized firms.

4. Thus the considerable industrial build-up, although it lays primary emphasis on the heavy and strategically important industries, still encourages the consumption pattern of a welfare-state type of economy, and through the "demonstration effect" it permits a pattern of imports with a bias toward durable consumer goods, such as television sets and household equipment. Voices are being raised in Egypt itself against the dangers of this situation, and at the same time it is recognized that Egypt's rate of economic growth during the decade 1952–

62 has been somewhat inferior to that of other countries. Clearly the creation of new industries, even though accelerated, will not, on this pattern, lead to a rate of economic growth which will transform Egypt into a predominantly industrial society within a reasonable period of time.

5. Although there are considerable difficulties in assessing, with a high degree of accuracy, the extent to which different leading social groups are reaping benefits from the new economic course, two groups stand out: the medium and large landowners (but not the old landed aristocracy), and the new "power élite."

It must be noted here that this new power élite, or managerial class, is not comparable to the entrepreneurial class which has come to the fore in Europe and the United States since the late eighteenth century, and it has nothing in common with the leading strata of the socialist (i.e., Communist-controlled) countries. This, in itself, does not constitute a weakness; it only does so when leadership by a mass political organization is lacking.

6. The repression of the Marxist Left (1952, 1954–56, 1959–64) has given considerable encouragement to economic cooperation with, and reliance upon, West Germany and the United States. By mid-1963, half of the wheat supplies were coming from America, while West Germany received a record number of Egyptian students, especially technologists, and at the same time a growing and very expensive network of loans and joint enterprises was being built up. The year 1963 brought some unexpected developments, among them the attempt to curtail Egypt's commitments in Yemen by a thinly disguised wheat blackmail threat by the United States; growing complaints about the stringent conditions of West European (mainly German) financial and economic assistance; and above all, by the opposition to Egyptian influence in Middle East politics as a whole.

7. To sum up: the Egyptian economy appears to be a mixed economy. It is still, in many ways, capitalistic: the land remains nearly untouched by nationalization; the public sector, though under the direction of managers (technocrats), is still regulated by the market demands and (public) profit incentive;

planning, and foreign aid particularly, tend to strengthen this pattern, at least in the short run. It is a relatively fast-growing economy with a central state-capitalistic sector (the public sector) of unusual proportions, but although every new wave of nationalization weakens the power of private capital, it only provides more solidly entrenched positions and power to the technocrats.

The transition to socialism may be considered under way when the delegates of the "popular forces" direct the political and economic life of the country. At present Egypt is ruled by a powerful state apparatus—dominated by the military—and an economic technocracy. Socialism further requires that economic development and planning develop the capital-goods sector, and that it not concern itself, as is true at present, with the building of a welfare society (which is now the main support of the military-technocratic power élite). These are the two main economic prerequisites for socialism—and for the rest we must turn to a consideration of the political situation.

In the sociopolitical field, the following appear to be the main features:

1. The dismantling of the (traditional) Egyptian bourgeoisie was accomplished, as already noted, in two stages.

2. The bourgeoisie has been replaced by an establishment controlling the strategic, dynamic sectors of the economy and of society as a whole—that is, the public sector of the economy, the state apparatus (the armed forces and the security service), and the political and ideological organizations and institutions (civil service, foreign affairs, publishing, the arts and the mass media): in fact, a new state capitalist class.

These new leading cadres have been recruited mainly from the lower- and middle-bourgeois strata, but they include some from the old ruling groups: senior officers, technical experts (economists, engineers, university professors), administrators and organizers.

3. The officers' corps is now organically integrated with the leading economic, administrative and political groups. All those who had to leave the armed forces, or who elected to do so, have been appointed to the upper ranks of the nonmilitary

establishment. About fifteen hundred officers came within this category between 1952 and 1964.

4. The new power élite can be defined more as a technocracy, largely under German and American influence in their attitudes and approach, rather than a mere bureaucracy. This technocratic élite is superimposed on the huge traditional Egyptian bureaucracy, which is still growing fast but which today wields less power than it did under the inefficient ministers of the former regimes. The press is continuously engaged in campaigns to improve the efficiency of this passive bureaucracy and to try to force it to adapt itself to the needs and pace of the technocratic élite.

The dangers of the situation, with this highly concentrated technocratic establishment sitting astride the bureaucratic pyramid, become more apparent when we analyze the structure of manpower and the labor force in Egypt. In 1960, 77 percent of the population could be considered within the manpower category, although only 32.6 percent were in the labor force. This labor force, moreover, apart from those in agriculture, was heavily concentrated within the tertiary sector. The broad divisions are: 21.7 percent in the infrastructure and services; 10.6 percent in commerce; 54.3 percent in agriculture; 10.6 percent in manufacturing; and 2.8 percent in construction. These figures clearly show the extent to which the dynamic sector—manufacturing—is limited in the Egyptian economy today. Under such conditions, the overconcentration of economic, political and ideological power in the hands of the technocratic-bureaucratic establishment could only prove harmful to Egypt's future development.

5. The new power élite gathered strength in the struggle against the Egyptian Marxist Left (the Communist party and the large fringe of progressives and militants). The anti-Communist repression continued, with different degrees of severity, between 1952 and 1964. While a general state law prohibits all political parties, there is a specific anti-Communist law, dating from the late 1920s, which has been strengthened by the military regime. No such law applies to any other organized ideology. Yet the general line of Egyptian Marxism, despite its persecution, has been one of critical, but not conditional, sup-

port of the regime, and its objectives have been the promotion of a popular-democratic, independent national state.

It is not surprising, therefore, to discover that the leading cadres of the regime are recruited from two ideological groups: the German-American and the Moslem Brotherhood. At the end of 1963, the Arab Socialist Union was under the direction of Major Hussein el-Shafei (from the Moslem Brotherhood wing of the Free Officers); Dr. Abdel Kader Hatem, Minister of Culture and National Guidance (typical of the American cadre); and Kamal Rifaat (an enlightened technocrat with Titoist sympathies). The Union had absorbed those who belonged to the Moslem Brotherhood but only a few leftists, and these in their individual capacity. The overall direction of the economy was in the hands of Vice-President Abdel Latif el-Boghdadi (a former manager of Misr Airways, and known to represent the alliance between the officers' corps and big business) and Dr. Abdel Moneim el-Kayssuni (a capable economist of the Liberal school). The president of the Executive Council, Ali Sabry, a highly efficient administrator, had, until 1952, a conspicuous pro-American past, to such an extent that Ahmed Baha'Eddine, the editor of the daily *al-Akhbar,* could write, in 1962, that "what we discover first, inside the UAR, is that the Revolution has concentrated its efforts on building the 'material characteristics' of socialist society without concentrating on its 'human characteristics,' i.e., the socialists! There can be no socialism without socialists! . . ." This integration was then sought, within the framework of the Arab Socialist Union, through the creation of an inner core of educated political cadres, which was to comprise a larger proportion of the Left.

6. Overcentralization and anti-Marxism—in a state whose official philosophy and policy are described as "scientific socialism"—impart a highly autocratic flavor and style to present-day Egyptian society. Every step forward comes as a decision of the state machine from above, never as an initiative from the people. While no other political parties have been allowed, the regime has proved itself unable to inspire and organize its own party. The result has been a growing and widespread political apathy, in a country that hitherto was notably ebullient. If the

state insists on doing everything by itself, and by order, then why not watch from afar?

It must be emphasized that this political apathy is a new phenomenon. It did not exist before 1959. And it came to an end on June 9–10, 1967. Even the crisis of the spring of 1954 did not stop political activity, contacts or discussion; and this was followed by the period of the opposition to the Baghdad Pact, the Suez crisis and the Bandung period. Between 1939 and 1959, Egyptian Marxism had succeeded in attracting the best of Egyptian youth to its philosophic ideas and to its vision of an Egyptian renaissance, and it had become the intellectual dynamic force both for the intelligentsia and for the working class in the main cities. Because of the lack of contacts with the international Communist movement in general, and the Soviet Union in particular, Egyptian Marxism was compelled to make its own way by developing a theoretical position within a distinctly national framework (and this long before the theory of "polycentrism" was formulated). Its ideas and theories met with the respect of the non-Marxist sections of the intelligentsia and informed patriotic opinion. The severe repression of 1959 therefore deeply affected not only the Marxists but progressive groupings in general. The attempt to destroy this body of thought and action was to bring about a general crisis in all fields of intellectual and political life. The intellectuals were singled out, but they were only the symbol of a far wider crisis of Egyptian society, and one which involved the gravest dangers for the whole course of Egypt's future.

Much can be gained, at this point, by turning our attention to the problem of the superstructure of Egyptian society.

1. Egyptian history throughout the ages illustrates certain special characteristics involving overcentralization in the administrative structure from its earliest days. The struggle of the Egyptian people to live and work amid deserts meant that there must always be a central authority responsible for artificial irrigation, regulation of the Nile level, drainage and allocation of water. Since this could not be supervised by some regional authority, the land of the Pharaohs came to be the seat of the oldest centralized and unified state in history,

and "the most compact of the 'hydraulic societies.'" In more recent times, the regulator of water supply was to be the main controller, or owner, of economic resources and activity. This has happened twice in modern history; first, under Muhammed Ali, and then, today, with the military regime led by Gamal Abdel Nasser. Private ownership is but a recent development in Egyptian economic history and was only introduced in the late nineteenth century.

This centralized control and management, and sometimes ownership, in the economic field under a single state authority was bound to enhance the role and importance of the state apparatus to an unusual degree. Further, if we take into account the geopolitical vulnerability of Egypt, the need to build a strong army was a logical consequence. It is, therefore, no coincidence that army leaders should wield economic power during many periods of Egyptian history: after the eviction of the Hyksos, during the Mameluk era, under Muhammed Ali, and today, in the form of the present military regime, with its control over the public sector.

These developments in the economic sphere were inevitably reflected in matters of ideology, and from the Pharaohs to Nasser, the master of temporal power has been the center of a unified spiritual power. This is the source of the long tradition of theocracy in Egypt, and we should remember that even before Coptic (i.e., Egyptian) monotheism came to the fore, the Pharaonic pantheon showed a clear tendency toward unity; this trend was also powerful behind the Sunnite Islam of Egypt.

2. This last point may serve as an introduction to the general analysis of ideology.

Let us consider briefly the development of the modern intellectual situation from the time of the cultural renaissance introduced by Mohammed Ali's envoy to Europe, Rifaa Rafe' el-Tahtawi (1801–73). Two main trends can be distinguished— Islamic fundamentalism and liberalism. The first, initiated by Gamal Eddine el-Afghani, took shape with his reluctant disciple, Sheik Mohammed Abdu. Their aim was to promote a new renaissance in the Islamic countries by criticizing decadent tradition in the light of common sense and reason, but still within the framework of religion, which must continue to hold the central position in social life and politics. All factors leading to disunity, such as political parties, should be proscribed, although discussion would be allowed within a unified and centralized organization. The religious education of the people would gradually prepare the way for representative government, but, Abdu proclaimed, only a benevolent despot "could promote the renaissance of the East," and he added, "Fifteen years would be enough." This trend came to have its right wing —the Salafiyya—with the *al-Manar* publishing group of Rashid Rida and, above all, the Moslem Brotherhood. Its radical wing, however, continued its search for a reasonable degree of liberalism within the framework of Islam, and this was the work of Ali Abdel Razzek, his brother Mustafa, and, later, Mohammed Khaled Khaled.

The second main trend, liberalism, was launched toward the end of last century, under the impact of Tahtawi's thinking, by a group of Lebanese émigré thinkers and writers who had found refuge in Egypt (the *al-Muktataf* group and above all Shibli Shumayyil as well as Farah Antun), and about the same time, by a number of prominent members of the new bourgeoisie and intelligentsia, who were also searching for the conditions which would lead to a national renaissance. Among these were the *al-Garida* group of Ahmed Lutfi el-Sayed, Kassem Amine and Ahmed Fathi Zaghlul, as well as Saad Zaghlul, who was to create the Wafd party and lead the revolution of 1919. On the left of this group stood the Socialists, Shumayyil and Antun and, particularly, Salama Mussa and Abdel Rahman Fahmi. It was this broad trend that was mainly responsible for the development of modern Egyptian culture and politics from 1919 to 1959. The central figures were Taha Hussein and Tewfik el-Hakim, and they were accompanied and followed by large numbers of active intellectuals. On the left of this main group were the Egyptian Marxists, who first appeared in 1920, but whose influence became more powerful after 1939. Finally, on the right of this liberal trend, another group was developing under German-American influence and it was closely linked with the Egyptian bourgeoisie (the *Akhbar el-Yom* group, with Abbas el-Akkad as its intellectual leader).

Some of the Free Officers who carried through the 1952 Revolution belonged to the Moslem Brotherhood, and only very few to the Marxist groups. The majority, under Gamal Abdel Nasser, were at first naturally inclined to radical Islamic fundamentalism. This was their intellectual tradition and it provided a respectable justification for their professional emphasis on authority, as well as contempt for discussion and factions. Moreover, they believed that their traditional faith would help to unite the nation behind them, and that as an ideology it was not only more efficient than the vague ideas of the Wafd, but even more important, that it would provide an effective counter to the ideas of Marxism, potentially the only serious opposition. At any rate, this was their position until the 1954 clash with the Moslem Brotherhood. It was, however, the process of grappling with the many difficult problems of the immanent independence that forced a change upon the Egyptian leadership. Its central problem was the creation of a modern society in Egypt. This was first attempted during the second main stage of the Revolution—between the years 1956 and 1961—in alliance with the upper bourgeoisie, and excluding the landowner class. Although in the end the alliance turned out to be a failure, one important result was that Islamic fundamentalism came to develop a virulent anti-Marxist orientation.

This failure provoked a major crisis of ideas and policy. It was a serious blow to the establishment, and even more to the right-wing elements in the political leadership. Nasser himself had for years been moving slowly toward a pragmatic vision of the future, and he was gradually becoming aware of the need for a revision of fundamentals. This became the task for the 1962 Congress: "The socialist solution to the problem of social development in Egypt—with a view to achieving progress in a revolutionary way—was *never a question of free choice*. The socialist solution was a *historical inevitability imposed by reality*, the broad aspirations of the masses and the changing nature of the world in the second part of the twentieth century"—so reads Section 6 of the Charter, entitled "On the Inevitability of the Socialist Solution." And Section 9, on "Arab Unity," following as it did the famous speech of self-criticism of October 16, 1961, came very close to an abandonment of the policy of organic and centralized unity, put forward in the years 1956 to 1961. It began, moreover, to approach the policy advocated by the Egyptian Marxists. This may be summed up as, first, the need for unity in the struggle against imperialism; second, an emphasis on the oneness of culture and historical traditions of the Arab world; and third, the necessity for international policies which would further the reunification of the Arab world in ways that would respect the traditions and needs of each individual country. Paradoxically, it was just these ideas of the Marxist Left which were used as a pretext for the repression beginning in January 1959.

III.

A closer look at the role of the army—more precisely, the army officers' corps—in society and politics, since 1952,[5] should be added here. Meanwhile, one should bear in mind that the term "military society" does *not* apply to Egypt as a sociological unit, but to a recent and still-current image of Egypt under the military regime. Therefore, "military society" applies specifically to the hegemony of the power élite of the officers' corps, and the impact of this hegemony *upon* Egyptian society.[6]

1. The political action of the officers' corps in this first phase (1952–1956) can be characterized in the following way:

(i) Complete seizure of the state apparatus (armed forces, police, prisons, and to a lesser degree, the courts) from the very first hours of the coup d'état. It was then that Gamal Abdel Nasser became Minister of the Interior and Colonel Zakaria Mohieddine took over both the political police and the intelligence service, thus inaugurating his long proconsulate of the state and repressive machinery.

(ii) Formulation of the elements of a radical national program, whose economic and social components remained sketchy at this point, the main emphasis being put on the objective of independence and the reconstitution of a sovereign state endowed with genuine autonomous power.

(iii) However, considerable ambiguity and imprecision were evident in the definition of an overall political line, both internally and in foreign relations. This has been variously attributed either to the political inexperience of the new leadership or to their Machiavellianism. Both elements were involved, though it is difficult to assess which predominated.

(iv) Important shifts in the structure of political power and decision-making as a result of two new elements: the hegemony exercised by the Executive Council of the Revolution, the real center of political life, and the creation on January 23, 1953, of the first unified political party, the Liberation Rally, of which Nasser was named Secretary-General on February 6.

2. The political action of the officers' corps during the second phase (1956–1961) can be characterized in the following terms:

(i) Conquest of the totality of political power of decision, and not merely the control of the state apparatus;

(ii) assertion of hegemony over decision-making in the economic, social and ideological fields, accompanied by a tighter grip on the whole of public life;

(iii) a striking retrenchment in the conception of political alliances, notably a rupture in the front with the industrial and banking sectors of the upper bourgeoisie, which had long been maintained at any cost;

(iv) confrontation with the Communist and Marxist Left with a view to reducing it psychologically and politically, and then, in the second repressive wave, to destroying its organization and cadres. By this act the state and its military leadership were left alone to face the only political force which had been tolerated by the regime since 1954: the Moslem Brothers, with their fundamentalist, integrist ideology and their Secret Organization, which was geared toward direct action.

3. The political role of the officers' corps during the third and last phase under study can now be characterized as follows:

(i) After the launching of the Charter of National Action and the Arab Socialist Union, President Nasser divided the military cadres into two categories. Officers active in politics had to turn in their uniforms and were stripped of all privileges that came with their rank. In return, they received key positions in the state, constituting the great majority of senior diplomatic personnel; a considerable proportion of presidents, directors and board members of public agencies, etc.; a very large number of Ministers, Vice-Ministers, Undersecretaries of State and directors of the various ministries; and a significant proportion of the key posts in culture, the press, information, radio and television.

A second category comprised officers who continued their military careers. They received a higher training than what had been available before 1952: an Institute of Higher Studies of National Defense was created, and a new rank (*fariq awwal*, army general), following the Yemen war, thus permitting a considerable inflation of the general-officers' caste. Staff officers were afforded greater weight in military and political decision-making, and these better-qualified senior officers blended well with a group of technocratic cadres capable of authoritatively challenging their civilian counterparts.

Progressively the role of the officers' corps became more clearly defined, exactly along the lines envisaged by part of the activist wing of the old Free Officers organization. Not only the highest state position, in the person of the President of the Republic, but also the whole of the overall direction of the state apparatus (notably the Ministries of War and of the Interior) and of the government are in military hands. In the Cabinet of Sidky Soliman, which was installed on September 10, 1966, the Prime Minister himself was an engineering colonel of great competence, three of the four Vice-Presidents of the Council were senior engineering General Staff officers (Abdel Mohsen Abul Nur and Mahmud Yunes, and Sarwat Okasha, who also had a doctorate in literature from the Sorbonne), and the fourth, Dr. Mahmud Fawzi (Foreign Affairs), had a counterpart on the strictly ministerial plane—another officer, Mahmud Riad. Half the Council of Ministers was composed of senior and staff officers. Furthermore, this domination and control over the power of decision extended to the key area of the public sector and of the two linked zones of culture and information.

The principal characteristic of the reshuffle installing the Sidky Soliman government lay in the fact that for the first time since the seizure of power in 1952, it was the *radical wing* of the

Free Officers group and of the attached civilian cadres which obtained governmental power, once the pro-Western super-Ministers had been dislodged (Dr. Abdel Moneim el-Kayssuni for Economics and Finance; Abdel Kader Hatem, Culture and Information; Sheik Ahmed Abdu el-Shorabassi, Social and Religious Affairs, etc.). Certainly several Ministers representing this tendency kept their posts. But the center of decision—at the government level—shifted into the hands of a new group. "At the *government level*"—a necessary qualification, because *state power* remained the prerogative of the President of the Republic.

Furthermore, the Arab Socialist Union itself, conceived as the crucible of all socialist forces, was basically run by dominant members of the officers' corps, former members of the old Revolutionary Command Council or simply functionaries in the ruling politico-military apparatus. Out of an Executive Committee of one hundred, it is possible to discover only two who belonged to the "historical" non-Communist Left. All the others were named by the ruling nucleus of officers, in particular by Ali Sabry, the current Secretary-General, the leading proponent of a dialogue with the West and notably with the Americans in 1952. Sabry has been radically yet subtly opposed to any alliance with the Marxists, and emerged as the leader of the official Left after isolating Kamal Rifaat, member of the Secretariat for Ideological Affairs, while Major Khaled Mohieddine was restricted to the Peace Movement. This tendency naturally increased at all levels in provincial and urban committees, section committees, committees at cell or base level, and so on, but it has been the leading committees which experienced to the greatest extent his invasion of the military into the political process.

Everything proceeded as if the political cadres drawn from the military were applying to their civilian opposites the rule which the state leadership applied to the Marxist Left: "*Collaborate with them, absorb them, but at all costs keep all decision-making power in our own hands.*" On the political level the Arab Socialist Union, unwieldy and inflated (5 million members out of a 30 million population), is inevitably afflicted by paralysis due to its lack of cadres and effective powers, since all Communists, Marxists and Socialists historically known as such, have been pushed aside. Elsewhere, in other domains of public life, the domination of political elements from the officers' corps has generally made for greater efficiency (the Suez Canal Company, the Aswan High Dam), although it is still difficult to predict the long-term effects this structure of management may have on social life.

In the last analysis, *everything* in Egypt will depend on the creation of a genuinely popular Socialist party, equipped not only with proper *means of action* but also with the power of *critical reflection*—not just in the cultural and aesthetic field, but above all in the domain of social science and political theory.

There are numerous examples to prompt thought, most notably that of Atatürk. A national revolution notwithstanding, precipitated by an independence war which lasted four years and mobilized an entire nation with millennial traditions around the new slogans of liberty, modernity and renaissance, less than a generation later Turkey was caught in the vice of religious reaction—pushed back but still tolerated and, in fact, deeply entrenched in the countryside—and of the bureaucracy, but above all of the security apparatus itself, resolutely hostile to any further social transformation. The renovation set in motion by Atatürk affected culture and daily life in the countryside, but without any ulterior socialist project. This process was halted in the absence of any effective instruments for mobilizing the people around the military leader and national hero. Evidently there was a crucial difference in timing, as the Charter notes, with regard to the espousal of socialism. Yet the *central* problem is identical: *How can the "national" revolution be transformed into a "social" revolution? How can the social dialectic be revived, both at the theoretical level and at the practical level as well?*

In Egypt the process of national revolution has attained the most advanced stage experienced in the present history of the "Three Continents." Its originality resides, basically, in its initiation of a genuine and deep transformation of the economic and social structure of the country, including the countryside. To effect this transformation, two instruments were deployed:

first, the officers' corps, "this national-radical and cross-sectional force," whose social roots lie in the lower bourgeoisie, and which has converted itself, along with its fringe of technocratic personnel, into a new class—in the sociopolitical as well as in the economic sense of the term. Secondly, an empirical and statist ideology was developed, reinforcing the ancient traditions of Egyptian pyramidal centralism, now endowed with the label of socialism.

The critical factor—namely, the "popular masses," in whose name all this functions—still remains at a distance from the political power of decision, even if called on as a participant in the discussions. The fact is that the process of transformation of social life now makes possible a rapid and real takeoff, not merely on the "developmental" plane, but in the creation of a socialism which would be genuinely Egyptian in style and form. Hence the co-ordinated resistance from the governing apparatus and the bureaucracy—the ruling class, in short. Egypt's multiple problems, and their inevitable consequences, stem from this situation.

At present, solutions are still being sought within the old framework: via state action through the apparatus and the administration—and through a party which exercises no real power. The Soliman Cabinet, which came to power in the autumn of 1966, was on the whole technically, and to some extent politically, adapted to bring about this transition.

Then, on the morning of June 5, 1967, Israel launched into war and obtained a lightning military victory. But the political objectives—the overthrow of the Nasserite regime and the ensuing removal of the Syrian regime—were not achieved. Analysis of the present conjuncture enables us to highlight the key elements in the struggle that is a consequence of the aggression:

(a) The pretension of the *army*, as a corporate force, to occupy a hegemonic position in Egyptian politics is now profoundly rejected by all popular classes and groups. Already in his July 23, 1967 speech Gamal Abdel Nasser implied that the whole High Command, notably the commander in chief of the air force, refused to follow political directives. At the same time, however, he completely exonerated the people's army;

the aim was to try to rally the middle and lower cadres against the generals, and to reconcile them with popular feeling as a whole.

(b) The *apparatus* seemed, at first, deeply shaken, its military wing thoroughly discredited and now undergoing a complete reorganization, its political wing using powerful influences to work for an opening to the right. The former War Minister, Shams Eddin Badran, who was responsible for the exclusion of all the officers trained in the Soviet Union from operational commands (given instead to "safe" officers, whose loyalty was secured by favors received), was replaced, first, by A-W. el-Bizry, and then, on July 21—two days prior to the speech marking President Nasser's apparent personal takeover—by Amin Hameh Huweidi, whose task it is to re-establish the political loyalty of the armed forces. At the same time another ascendant name is that of Abdel Mohsen Abul Nur: Minister for Agrarian Reform (after having been one of the Vice-Premiers in the Cabinet of September 1966), he was named Commandant of the Popular Resistance movement (June 21), then Assistant Secretary-General of the Arab Socialist Union (July 9)—the Secretary-General no longer being Ali Sabry, but the President of the Republic himself.

(c) The *party* is incapable of functioning, according to the best-qualified observers. A new Central Committee has to be chosen, and its precise composition will enable us to make some assessment of the Left's position in the leadership of a party which aims to be Socialist. But in any event, it is hard to see how the center of gravity of state power can be shifted from the ruling apparatus, which has evolved in the direction of a markedly anti-Marxist nationalitarian ideology toward a Socialist party, led by socialist cadres. At present the party organization installed by Ali Sabry remains static: functionless local organizations; a "political organization" (cadres) whose time is spent in discussion and the drawing up of reports; and the paramilitary Arab Socialist Youth Organization, some three hundred thousand youths trained for street action, and openly anti-Marxist.

(d) The *popular masses*, whose action on June 7 and 8 was decisive not only in keeping Gamal Abdel Nasser in power but also in imposing the establishment under his authority of an armed people's resistance organization, have not been neutralized by the apparatus. Instead of forming popular militias to protect the country, back up the political power against any plots, and in so doing, promote the advance of new political cadres from the base, the apparatus—personally led by Zakaria Mohieddine—refused to distribute arms, except grudgingly to certain key factories at night. The presidential address of July 23 stated that the country did not have the means to arm the people. From this withholding of arms to demobilization, to disaffection, the way has been opened for a consolidation of the rightist apparatus, neutralization of the radical and leftwing tendency, and ultimately for a renewal of the political operation checked *in extremis* by popular action on June 9–10, 1967.

The kernel of the crisis which affects the Egyptian national revolution and inhibits its development may now be formulated in two propositions:

1. It is impossible to build a modern state in the absence of a "political class" in the Gramscian sense of the term; yet this is precisely what the military regime has tried to eliminate since 1952.

2. It is impossible to initiate a socialist revolution and to build a popular state in the absence of socialists, without a mobilization of the popular masses, rural and urban, and the revolutionary intelligentsia; certainly not by relying on a political apparatus committed to a fight against the Left, and by that fact open to all forms of penetration.

To speak of "renewal" after the discrediting of the military leadership means little—unless its aims are specified in the sense mentioned. But the most important thing to recognize is that the thesis which explains everything in terms of the retardation and lack of development of Egyptian economy, society and technology is *fundamentally* erroneous. Vietnam, where the most modern military machine in the world is bogged down, is there to prove the contrary. A country that is much more backward in many respects than Egypt can maintain its independence, can strengthen its position and advance along an authentically national-socialist path, *provided* it has a political force, a genuine political leadership, armed with a radical and scientific social philosophy wielded boldly and creatively. Egypt's future is at this price.

Although this book stops formally on the morning of June 5, 1967, I felt that some indications about the resulting situation should be given, as above. In fact, these lines were written on the eve of defeat. In the autumn of 1967 the real culprits came to light: not only important elements of the General Staff and High Command but Marshal Abdel Hakim Amer himself, and also—as the key element in the conspiracy that brought President Nasser to his feet just as he started to lead a deep radicalization of his political course (the new Soliman Cabinet of 1966 following, as it were, in the purge of former landed aristocrats after the Kamshih affair*)—the leaders of the apparatus, in fact the *real shadow government, i.e., the state*, in Egypt. For the men who are now tried publicly finally reveal the problem of the nature of state power: Salah Nasr, head of the political secret service (*al-mukhabarat al-'amma*); Shams Badran, former Minister of War; Abbas Radwan, former Minister of the Interior and acting head of the secret service; and their activist military colleagues. Indeed, this trial should be pushed to its logical consequence, i.e., the true nature of power in Egypt, since the burning of Cairo . . .

IV.

This book revolves around a central thesis: the military experiment in Egypt is a specific one; i.e., the path followed by Egypt to win back its independence, break the chains of archaism and move forward to modernity since 1952 is fundamentally, historically Egyptian. This *nationalitarian* path was ushered in by the military regime under Gamal Abdel Nasser, whose personality, action and role have been submitted to varied waves of adulation, hatred, appreciation or contempt, and have sometimes been explored by brilliant journalists or

---

* In the spring of 1966 a young militant of this town investigated land reform in his district. He was killed on orders by the powerful family of the Fikys. Immediately, a Higher Council for the Liquidation of Feudalism was set up, under Marshal Amer. Revolution was finally the order of the day in the countryside.

talented Orientalists. Until 1962, it must be admitted, very little had been submitted to the searching lenses of theoretical analysis combining history and sociology. And yet, problems raised by Egypt's national revolution under the military regime should have drawn more serious attention.

It will become evident to the reader why I have tackled this task with Marxist methodology combined with that "sociological imagination," so aptly termed by C. Wright Mills, which seems to me to be illuminating in any attempt at a significant exploration and probing of a complex dynamic social reality so deeply grounded in history.[7]

The guideline, throughout, has been the search for the Marxian *principle of historical specificity* in the case of Egypt. There are multiple statements relating to this principle, and more specifically, in Chapter 11, which is devoted to this problem. I should like to draw attention to a concept, here introduced and expounded for the first time through the case study of Egypt's national revolution, i.e., the concept of *nationalitarianism*.

Around 1945–47 many of us were struck by the inadequacy of the traditional concept of "nationalism" as applied to the rising expectations of the colonial, ex-colonial and dependent countries. For in the terminology of sociology and politics within the Western framework, "nationalism" immediately points to two sets of notions. A first, negative set of notions, such as the negation of the other, an isolationist attitude, the refusal of universalism; and a second, positive and even directly activist set of notions, such as territorial expansion and frontier hostilities that have led to the European wars during the past four centuries, of which the two last were termed "world" wars, inasmuch as they drew other countries and peoples into the struggle for world domination, led by the Western powers. Hence the prevailing opinion in liberal and progressive Western circles today that "nationalism" is both outdated and debased, that the time has come for regional and continental arrangements, and that interdependence, rather than independence, should be the motto, etc. And yet, observers could not fail to notice the rising tide of national feelings and achievements in the West itself, as well as in the developed socialist countries. Asia, Africa and Latin America, where national revolutions are intermingling with social revolutions, do not appear nowadays to be ambling down a lonely path, dominated by the question of nationalism.

Hence my concern to draw lines. In the case of Europe and North America—and particularly in the case of the highly developed capitalist countries of those parts of the world—"activist" nationalism can be seen as the privilege of nations long established in their modern (i.e., bourgeois-capitalistic) form, of independent and sovereign national states struggling for the control of riches and resources in Europe and all over the world. And because of the fact that this struggle led directly to the two world wars, "nationalism" can logically be condemned as synonymous with aggression, chauvinism, inhumanity and opposition to internationalism.

On the "Three Continents"—of which Egypt is a nodal point —the process is historically different. For the struggle against imperialist occupation, penetration and hegemony aims fundamentally at reconquering the power of decision in all fields of national life, as a necessary prelude to the "reconquest of national identity," which lies at the very heart of the national-renaissance process. In this light, evacuation of national territory, the independence and sovereignty of the national state, and the eradication of the ex-imperial power's positions are but means to an end. And this end—national renaissance—which unfolds via policies and paths that are specifically national, is assaulted unceasingly, with all available weapons and from all possible angles—more so, perhaps, within the country itself. This phenomenon—historically different—is, however, structurally and specifically different, at the present stage, from Western "nationalism." This is why I have proposed to call it *nationalitarianism*, or the *nationalitarian* phenomenon. Every action, every idea, every development can be seen as converging toward the constitution, the re-constitution, the mastery of both the nation itself and the national state by the people of that nation, and in the case of old nations, as a specific national renaissance. For a time the negative aspects may prevail—but only apparently so. What is at stake is wholly different. It belongs to the sphere of construction, of social positivity. And its aggressive character, its polemical self-affirmation, should not lead observers, practitioners and students astray.

Though this book does not deal specifically with the theory of *nationalitarianism,* it has been conceived and launched as a spearhead for this theory, of which here only the general traits have been touched upon.[8] But it was necessary to indicate the central role of this concept in the analysis propounded, lest it be parked in the marginal reserve of "case studies."

Why, then? And how?

The burning face of Egypt has, as I said, led many observers and specialists to either contempt or superficial descriptions. There have been very few interesting books on Egypt since 1952, and serious works are even less numerous, though they are, happily, beginning to emerge. In Egypt itself the "crisis of the intellectuals," announced in 1961, is not yet over, although much progress has been accomplished after 1965, and even more after September 1967. Serious studies, articles and some books are being published, amid literally hundreds of volumes filled with empty talk—variations on the common theme of Agitprop literature.* And if 1961 was the apex of the process of estrangement of the Egyptian intelligentsia, it was only fitting that this book should have been launched in 1962 to speak out and clarify, in the name of a whole persecuted generation—not in a formal sense, but based on the life experience of one member of this generation—its odyssey from state office to prison, camp and exile, despair and romanticism, psychological reconditioning and strategic realism. Only this way is it possible to put an end to the "school of liberal Eurocentrism," i.e., paternalism and contempt, about Egypt: the time has come to make it clear that if they are to emerge, the "Three Continents" do not necessarily have to lose their identity in the cosmopolitan molds of Western industrialized societies; and the role of theory, and of theoretical development about itself by the intelligentsia of the "Three Continents," must be recog-

---

* Agitprop—short for Communist Party Bureau for Agitation (spoken word) and Propaganda (written word), responsible for guiding public opinion in the USSR.

nized through work actually done, as leading to more understanding, as more significant than the hitherto descriptive
"phenomenological" books and pompous papers of contemptu-
ous para- and post-Orientalists.[9]

From "Why?" to "How?" The foundations of this book lie in
the author's life experience, particularly between 1939 and
1959. During that period I was intimately connected with the
national and progressive movement at work in Egypt. And life
was merciful enough to let me share in the responsibilities and
molding of the Egyptian Left during those fateful years. From
1959 onward I have been living in Paris, engaged in academic
scientific research in the field of comparative sociology and
social theory. It was thus possible to combine life and research, action and theory, the past of Egypt's national revolution with our people's future. Technically this volume is based
on Egyptian books, theses and dissertations, newspapers and
periodicals, reports of congresses, documents, etc., but the
only true access to the events is to live through them, day by
day. Official sources, mostly of doubtful accuracy, but becoming less so as we advance in time, have been amply used, as
have all available material and published works in European
languages.

The main source of this book is, however, my direct and
never-broken organic link with Egypt, its national movement,
its cultural renaissance—and our people. When writing, I
would never feel alone: friend and foe, comrade and opponent
never abandoned this ship, but this is true, above all, of the
warm, tormented, crystal-clear, humane, courageous company
of those with whom I shared, share and shall always share the
burden, suffering and promise of Egypt's national renaissance
toward socialism. They alone, collectively, can take pride in
whatever achievements this book may point to, and in whatever positive appreciation it may enjoy. For in propounding,
in theoretical terms, the broad vision of Egyptian Marxism—
as a genuine school of thought and action, a "collective mind,"
as Gramsci put it—I am only doing so on behalf of my companions, in the light of their experiences, always bearing in
mind the principled body of the Egyptian people's will, their
hearts and minds, their right to emerge and be recognized as

the prime architects of Egypt's destiny. And it goes without saying that all shortcomings are the author's and his alone.

A new generation is rising in the land of Egypt, our inalienable fatherland. This study is primarily aimed at them. Lest we forget. Lest we err. Lest history remain a curse when it can be a promise. Lest we accept that the people of Egypt, having saved their nation's independence, liberty and, indeed, its very being, on June 9 and 10, 1967, should now be torn away from its own fatherland.

Should the truth be harsh, I would want to recall Spinoza: ". . . the truth which is to itself its own evidence." The truth which can hurt—but remains the only path to rationality, the one and only path that shall lead the people of Egypt to fulfill Tahtawi's will: "Let the fatherland be the place for our common happiness, which we shall build through liberty, thought and the factory."

Acknowledgments would run, literally, into hundreds of names. I have mentioned the main ones, while talking about the sources of this work, and singled out the fraternity of my friends and companions whose book this is. I now wish to acknowledge the fact that were it not for the perceptive hospitality of the Centre National de la Recherche Scientifique, and its department of sociology, to which I am proud to belong since 1960, this research work could not have been completed in the way it has. Lest we forget.

I would also like to extend my gratitude to the directors and librarians of the following institutions: Bibliothèque Nationale; Bibliothèque de l'Ecole Nationale des Langues Orientales Vivantes; Fondation Nationale des Sciences Politiques; Bibliothèque de la Documentation Internationale Contemporaine; Bibliothèque de la Faculté de Droit et des Sciences Economiques (Paris); the British Museum Library; the Public Records Office; the University of London Library; the Library of the School of Oriental and African Studies, University of London; the Middle Eastern Centre Library, St. Antony's College, Oxford; the Bodleian Library (Oxford); Dar al-Koutoub (Cairo); Bibliothèque Nationale (Tunis); etc.

Were it not for the amiable and perceptive patience of my editor, Alice E. Mayhew, and Barbara Willson, and the pains-

takingly accurate work of my translator, Charles Lam Markmann, this book would have found a most uneasy way to the
English-reading audience. For which I heartily thank them.

ANOUAR ABDEL-MALEK

*Centre Nationale de la
Recherche Scientifique
Paris, February 1968*

Glossary

ardabb—unit of capacity=198 liters, or 5.45 bushels.

bey—Ottoman rank below that of pasha.

caliph—lieutenant of the prophet Mohammed; in principle, leader of the Islamic community (*umma*).

diwan—Council; sometimes ministry.

feddan—unit of measure=4.201 square meters, or just over one acre.

fetwa—legal-religious consultation delivered by a mufti in answer to a demand.

fida'iyyin—guerrilla.

fiqh—canonic law of Islam.

firman—order, decree.

'hadiths—traditions, a collection of tales relating the words and deeds of the Prophet, and having a normative value.

iltizam—responsibility to exact taxes, usually on land holdings, imposed by the government.

imam—religious leader.

kantar—unit of weight=44.9 kg., or 99 lb.

mu'tazilites—rationalist school of philosophy (eighth to ninth centuries), fought and destroyed by Caliph Al-Mutawakkil.

multazim—holder of *iltizam*, enjoying the privilege of collecting taxes on behalf of the government.

nahda—renaissance.

omdeh—village mayor.

pasha—highest rank in Turkey and in the provinces of the Ottoman Empire.

saniyya—pertaining to the sultan or king.

shari'ah—religious law of Islam.

sheik—elder.

sheik el-balad—town mayor.

souq—market.

Sunna—majority trend in the Islamic faith which considers itself to represent orthodoxy.

ulema—men learned in religion, the nearest to a Moslem "clergy."

umma—community of believers; Islamic "nation."

wakf—endowment in favor of religious or charitable institutions.

watan—fatherland.

Contents

part one

Egyptian Society
Before the Coup d'Etat

To abandon the struggle for private happiness, to expel all eagerness for temporary desire, to burn with passion for eternal things—this is emancipation, and this is the free man's worship.

—BERTRAND RUSSELL, *The Free Man's Worship*

"MY FATHER had left me two *feddans* [acres] as an inheritance . . ." So begins the story of Shehata Ragab, a *fellah* like any other, lost in the mass of the 21,473,000 Egyptians on that January 26, 1952, when Cairo burned, six months to the day before Faruk was dethroned by the action of the army.

Shehata Ragab, a fellah, lived then on the *ezbeh* (farm) called Ezzeddine (from the name of its owner) in the village of Kafr Da'ud, in the province of Beheira, southeast of Alexandria. "My father had left me two *feddans* as an inheritance. But the pasha sent his thugs after me, and they started to beat and threaten me, so that I finally gave up the land to their master and left the village . . . No, I'll never forget what Daramalli, the pasha, said (he was known for his cruelty and his hunger to seize the land of the *fellahin*). It was his custom to call together the *omdehs* [mayors] of the villages and make them take off their shoes and walk on thorns . . ."[1]

Shehata Ragab was not alone in those days. In the throng that grew bigger from hour to hour, itinerant food sellers and merchants of every kind crowded the silence of the city. More than a million Shehata Ragabs, in motionless silence, watched Cairo burn all morning long and all afternoon long on that Saturday, January 26, 1952,[2] a key date, a central date in the evolution of Egypt after the Second World War.

For several years, and especially after 1957, on the initiative of the evening newspaper, *al-Missa*, the Egyptian press published a mass of reports and interviews that became, in a way, a poignant epic of everyday life. In them the reader could watch the procession of the characters with their everyday clothes, their faces marked by poverty, their budgets, their family histories, the memories of their loves, the graduation certificates wrested out of long nights of toil, their hopes, their vast weariness, but also that amazing vitality, charitable and ironic, that is the warp and woof of man in the land of Egypt. They had names: Abdel Hamid Ali Ibrahim, once a soldier, once a policeman, now a messenger for a newspaper;[3] Fuad Mustafa Ibrahim, peddler and great lover of literature—"the writers in this world are of three kinds: those who write for money, those who write for reputation, those who write for truth"—who protested: "What? My philosophy? What philosophy? Life has nothing to do with philosophy. The art of living is a difficult thing, and most people these days have very soft bones. As far as I'm concerned, I treat people decently and want them to do the same with me. That's all!"[4]; Abdel Hamid Mahmud, coffee vendor and student in the School of Law, who used to dream of "doing something for the future."[5] Dandaraui Abdel Moneim Hassan left his hungry village in order to become a dynamiter in the new Aswan High Dam project.[6] And there was the blind popular poet, Sayed Makkaui, with his disturbing speech.[7] Or that anonymous functionary of the ninth category, the father of four children, who had stopped going to the coffee house fifteen years earlier, who never dared to send for a doctor because of the abject poverty in which he lived out his endless months ("At home none of us thinks any more about the first of the month"), who always, out of habit, took the same sidewalk day after day, who sat up all night with his eldest son, a student at Cairo University, balancing the future against the burden of the life of every day.[8]

Why that everyday life rather than another?

Why, on that Saturday, January 26, 1952, the burning of Cairo?

Why, six months later, the coup d'état of the "Free Officers"?

On the History of Capitalism in Egypt

The history of landownership in Egypt is yet to be written. But meanwhile the history of Egyptian capitalism, even in its broad outlines, may clarify the position of the average Egyptian in 1952.

There is general agreement that Bonaparte's French invasion (1798–1800)—that is, the armed irruption of the ideas of 1789 and the methods of government of the French Revolution —was the tocsin for the overthrow of the old structures of Oriental feudalism, the omen of the end of the reign of the Mamelukes, to whom the Sublime Porte* had given Egypt in fief.[9] The proclamation of June 27, 1798, challenged the Mamelukes' right to seize land for themselves, and promised the ulemas,† most of them rich landed proprietors, the creation of a central civil government in Cairo. The merchants in the cities profited by the growth of trade and looked forward without sorrow to the prospect of a rise in the volume of foreign commerce. The law of September 16, 1798, established land prices, recognized the right of the fellah to inherit, organized the recording of land titles—in a word, established the foundations of private ownership of land in Egypt for the first time in history.

On what was done by Mohammed Ali Pasha‡ there are varying views. Must his drive to eliminate, then exterminate the Mamelukes, which began with his accession to power in 1805, be regarded as the signal for the creation of the first bourgeois state in Egypt?

According to Fawzi Guergues, "while Mohammed Ali established many factories, they were not the result of the natural evolution of the merchant middle class; there was no elimination of artisan production or any replacement of it by the large factory, financed by the capital accumulated by that middle class and affording employment to hundreds of workers," so that the "destruction of the Mamelukes' rule was essentially the work of a foreign military power and not at all that of the internal evolution of Egypt. That is why feudal rule itself was not damaged as such, it merely changed form, and feudal power was thenceforth concentrated in the hands of Mohammed Ali, who then set up a centralized feudal state."[10]

Ibrahim Amer, however, is less categorical: "The system of agricultural exploitation," he says, "was a temporary tran-

* The Ottoman court and government in Turkey.
† Doctors of Moslem religion and law.
‡ Viceroy of Egypt 1805–48.

sition system between feudalism and capitalism, a system during which Egypt went through a phase of ambivalent evolution. This was an Oriental feudal system in the stage of
disintegration and collapse, and bearing within it the elements
of a capitalist system based on a merchant economy and
oriented toward the establishment of the private ownership
of land"; besides, he adds, "the reasons for the emergence of
the middle class in Egypt antedated any foreign intervention;
it was a matter of the evolution of the Egyptian agricultural
economy from the stage of a natural (barter) economy to
a market economy, as well as the growth of industrial and
commercial cities and of their needs in products of the soil."[11]

For the moment, at least, the lack of detailed studies makes
it impossible to resolve the discussion. Let us observe by the
way that the historians of the Egyptian economy, particularly
Mohammed Fahmy Leheita and Rashed el-Barawi, do not
even raise the problem, leaving this task to the Marxists.

In 1809 Mohammed Ali abolished the system of the
*iltizam.** Between 1813 and 1818 he brought about the creation of the first Egyptian land register, and he distributed,
either in fee or in life tenancy, two million *feddans* among
the great men of the kingdom (military leaders, members of
the reigning family), the former *multazimin* (buyers of the
right to extort), the village sheiks and the Bedouins. The
movement thus begun was never to halt: the recognition of
a limited form of private property in land (1846); the right
to lease land for three years, to mortgage it, to sell the use
rights to a third party, and finally to bequeath land (1858);
the introduction and rapid intensification of the cultivation of
cotton under Ismail Pasha† in order to supply the English
factories deprived of raw materials by the American Civil
War; the conveyance of land in fee to a tenant against payment of six years' taxes in advance, in a lump sum (1871);
then, after the English occupation in 1882, the legalization

* *Iltizam*: a system of land tenure in Moslem countries, whereby influential senior officials, officers and favorites of the central government
held the land, for which they paid a fixed amount of revenue, exacted
by violence and abuse from the fellahin (a system similar to the French
fermiers généraux).
† Khedive (viceroy) of Egypt 1863–79.

of private ownership of tax-exempt land (1883), and of land under cultivation (1891); and finally the abolition of corvée except in cases of public need (1893).

Less than a century after Bonaparte and Mohammed Ali, a class of landed proprietors owned the soil of Egypt under a system of private property and sold its products on world markets as well as on local markets. The Egyptian bourgeoisie was born.

The Penetration of Imperialism

The invasion of modernism was to be accomplished through the constant increase of debt and the establishment of foreign capital, companies and banks in Egypt during the second half of the nineteenth century.

The vestiges of Ismail's resistance, after the inauguration of the Suez Canal—an undertaking that typifies the great epoch of international imperialism in Egypt—was soon to give way to an organized national movement that found its instrument of action in the Egyptian army, its leadership in the colonels headed by Ahmed Arabi, its clearest expression in the movement of ideas exemplified by the Islamic reformism—fundamentalism—of Mohammed Abdu and the nationalitarian liberalism of Abdallah el-Nadim.

The revolution of 1881–82, directed against the European grip on finances and the economy, and at the same time against the absolute power of Khedive Tewfik,* was answered by British military occupation in 1882. Sir Evelyn Baring (later Lord Cromer)† defined its economic objectives as follows: "The policy of the government may be summed up thus: 1) export of cotton to Europe subject to 1 percent export duty; 2) imports of textile products manufactured abroad subject to 8 percent import duty; nothing else enters into the government's intentions, nor will it protect the Egyptian cotton industry, because of the danger and evils that arise from such measures . . . Since Egypt is by her nature an agricultural country, it follows logically that industrial train-

* Eldest son of Ismail Pasha; Khedive of Egypt 1879–92.
†As British consul general, governed Egypt 1883–1907.

ing could lead only to the neglect of agriculture while diverting the Egyptians from the land, and both these things would be disasters for the nation."

A quarter-century later Cromer himself, in his report for the year 1905, was to draw up the balance sheet of this policy: "The difference is apparent to any man whose recollections go back some ten or fifteen years. Some quarters [of Cairo] that formerly used to be veritable centers of varied industries—spinning, weaving, ribbonmaking, dyeing, tentmaking, embroidery, shoemaking, jewelry making, spice grinding, copper work, the manufacture of bottles out of animal skins, saddlery, sieve making, locksmithing in wood and metal, etc.—have shrunk considerably or completely vanished. Now there are coffee houses and European novelty shops where once there were prosperous workshops."[12] The wretchedness of city and country was countered by the enrichment of the large landed proprietors, who had finally found a regular customer in the occupying power. It was able to guarantee them incessantly growing wealth, since Egypt had become from end to end a gigantic cotton plantation for the factories of Lancashire. Thus was born the political alliance between Great Britain and the large landowners, headed by the royal family, which was to dominate Egyptian political life for three quarters of a century.

From 1882 to 1914 the invasion of Egypt by large European capital, especially British and French, was to reach its full height.

The year 1898 proved crucial: in February came the signing of the contract for the Aswan Dam, which was to endow all Egypt with permanent irrigation for the huge cotton plantation; Sir Ernest Cassel* guaranteed its financing. On June 21 an agreement was made for the sale of the properties of Daira Saniyya to Rafael Suarès.

On June 25 the National Bank of Egypt was founded by Sir Ernest Cassel, Rafael Suarès and Constantino Salvago.† An issuing bank as well as a deposit bank, the NBE was in fact to become the central bank, which held all the state's

---

* British international financier (1852–1921).
† Prominent financiers of the Jewish colony in Egypt.

receipts, as well as the deposits of the large landowners, and which issued Egypt's currency, whose gold reserve soon found the way to London. The NBE extended its control to the Agricultural Bank set up by the government in 1902 to assist the small landowners (the so-called five-*feddan* law).[13] Foreign capital invested in Egypt rose from 21,280,000 Egyptian pounds (£E)* in 1902 to £E100,152,000 in 1914, exclusive of the Suez Canal Company. Between 1900 and 1907, 160 new companies were founded, with aggregate capital of £E43 million. In 1907 it was noted that 51 percent of the foreign capital was invested in land companies and 24 percent in mortgage companies. In the same year there were 143,671 foreigners among Egypt's population of 11,287,359. In 1892 the public debt owed by Egypt to her European creditors had reached £E106,098,000.[14]

The Egyptian ally too—the large landed proprietors—was growing rich and increasing its share in the country's income. From 1894 to 1914, in fact, the number of large holders (possessing more than fifty *feddans*) went from 11,220 owners of 1,997,000 *feddans* (that is, 1.3 percent of the owners and 44 percent of the land) to 12,480 owners of 2,397,000 *feddans* (.8 percent of the owners and 43.9 percent of the land). And this concentration of large landownership was taking place at the very time when the Egyptian population—80 percent of which then lived in the countryside—was rising from 9,714,000 in 1897 to 12,292,000 in 1914 and when the cultivated acreage was growing negligibly, from 5,327,000 to only 5,652,000 *feddans*.[15]

The Two Wings of the "National" Bourgeoisie

The First World War was to give a new impetus to the process of social differentiation. The merchants made fortunes by supplying the British forces; many factories employing more than fifty workers each were established, especially in spinning and weaving, oil pressing, tanning, grain

* Egyptian pound (100 piasters). Since 1885 one pound sterling has been equivalent to 97.5 piasters, and this figure has been kept after the de facto devaluation of 1962.

milling and metalworking, as well as numerous mercantile firms, but in relation to 1914, prices had risen 211 percent by 1918 and 312 percent in 1920.[16] A major development was the creation of a Committee for Commerce and Industry in 1917 by Ismail Sidky, Talaat Harb, and others, who were calling for the establishment of Egypt's own industry.[17] It was up to the new bourgeoisie of the cities—merchants, businessmen, members of the professions, especially lawyers and engineers —to create a theater of action for the modernist wing of the rich landowners and an area of investment for their idle funds. In 1920 Talaat Harb set up the Bank Misr with a capital of £E80,000. The appeal that he made to the big proprietors was heeded, although rather feebly, since deposits rose to only £E296,000 during the first year.[18] Two years later, in 1922, the Wafd party* decided to boycott English products and banks, and issued a call to the people: "Egyptians should deposit their money in the Bank Misr. They should count it a duty to buy the bank's stock so that its capital may reach a level that accords with the economic situation of the country and enables it to assist in getting national projects under way, as well as Egypt's industry and commerce. We must buy products manufactured in Egypt, give them publicity, encourage others to buy them. Preference must be given to Egyptian merchants; as for English merchants, they must be boycotted . . ."[19] And in 1924 the Egyptian Federation of Industries was created by a group of industrialists and financiers, most of them Europeans.

It was from this time that it is possible to speak of two wings of the Egyptian bourgeoisie: what was generally called the "national bourgeoisie" (which meant the Wafd) and the upper bourgeoisie. Fawzi Guergues offers a striking analysis: "Confusion must be avoided," he writes, "between the national wing of the bourgeoisie, represented by the Wafd, which itself represented the rural rich, the merchants and the intellectuals on the one side, and the industrial wing of the bourgeoisie on the other. The latter . . . had a complex structure. In part it remained closely bound to the land, and its relations with industry were recent; what is more, they

* See page 18.

were only in their initial stage. The essential thing here is that this industrial wing did not work in any genuine way in the realm of industry either before or after the war, but that it had invested its money in corporations whose total capital had reached £E8 million by 1914, composed of money belonging to Egyptians and to foreigners resident in Egypt— companies of which the majority, as Crouchley shows, were land companies and in no way industrial. An industrial consciousness had been born among the large landed proprietors; this consciousness was to develop as foreign capital infiltrated into the country and yielded huge profits there. So it was that the class of large landowners began to create industry from above, with thousands of pounds, in collaboration with the foreign funds then invested in Egypt. The owners of these foreign funds themselves, in spite of the fact that their wealth was invested in Egypt, had an ambivalent outlook: on the one hand they retained firm bonds with their countries of origin, but on the other hand, the very fact that these funds were invested in Egypt impelled them to commit their futures through the acquisition of guaranties as to the evolution and progress of Egyptian industry."[20]

What is striking in this differentiation is the fact that the "modern" industrial and technocratic wing of the Egyptian bourgeoisie was not born out of private enterprise, following the classic path of the European middle classes (commerce– manufacture–industry), but that it was formed, so to speak, within the very womb of the imperialist invasion of Egypt by foreign capital, as the ally and junior partner of that investment. Whence the paradox for this "modern" industrial and technocratic wing of the bourgeoisie: instead of being the spokesman of a more effective parliamentarianism, of a rationalization of society, of a philosophy more concerned with real progress, of a political intransigence that, would, moreover, have been justified by its function as a vanguard within an Egyptian society in mutation, it was to be the chosen instrument of political reaction, notably in the parties of its choice, the Saadist (founded in 1937), the Independents (which contained the principal leaders of the Egyptian Federation of Industries—Ismail Sidky, Hafez Afifi, Hussein Sirry,

Ali Maher, Sherif Sabry, Ahmed Abbud, Ali Yehia, Mohammed el-Farghaly, et al.) and its allies representing large
landownership in the Liberal-Constitutional party. The main-
stay of the most rigid reaction on the domestic level, it was to
be, in foreign policy, the ally of the imperialists: first, of Great
Britain, but then, and particularly, of the United States after
the victory in 1945.[21]

Essentially the Wafd remained a representative of the autochthonous forces of the Egyptian bourgeoisie—these included a section of the big landowners which was to become
preponderant only after the Second World War; the average
rural middle class, the urban middle class, the professions,
the intellectuals, the lower middle class and especially the
government employees and the merchants, to whom must be
added a substantial number of agricultural workers and a
certain category of urban workers, especially those employed
by the state. The Wafd brought together forces whose ties
with the occupant were not organic, but resulted essentially
from the entanglement of the whole of the Egyptian economy
with the dominant British interests; and that is why it was
to be the genuine expression of the entire nation, asserting
itself as the authentic, disturbing, tenacious, noisy and stead-
fast representative of the national will to be. In spite of the
ouster from power enforced on the Wafd by the collusion
between the occupant and the Royal Palace (the Wafd governed during only seven of the thirty years between 1922 and
1952), the party of Saad Zaghlul and Mustafa el-Nahas was the
basic political force in the country for thirty years. As we shall
see, the industrial and technocratic upper bourgeoisie later
took revenge, overthrew the Wafd, which had become increasingly divided and afflicted with ineffectiveness, and took over
the execution of the objectives of the national middle-class
revolution at the cost of the destruction of the democratic
freedoms so laboriously evolved by the Wafd, which, in this
area, was always assured of the tenacious and active support
of the Left.

From 1919 to 1939, but especially after 1939, the Egyptian
bourgeoisie made giant strides. Here too it is important to
note the specifically Egyptian character of this progress: it

is not, indeed, the creation of a new bourgeoisie that we shall observe, but rather that of a very highly concentrated upper bourgeoisie of a frankly monopolistic character,[22] in which the Misr group was to play a preponderant part.

On December 28, 1914, the date when Egypt was declared a British protectorate, foreign investments amounted to £E92 million, of which £E67 million were invested in land, against £E8 million in Egyptian capital; in addition, at that time Egypt owed £E94 million abroad. In other words, foreigners were the owners of 92 percent of the capital then invested.[23] The Egyptian Federation of Industries was representative of this division. In 1930 Ismail Sidky, president of the Federation —a towering and highly complex top figure of the new "Establishment"—became Premier, abolished the Constitution of 1923, and installed a government of harsh terror that lasted until 1935; but above all, he was concerned with regulating the Egyptian economy in the face of the world depression: tariffs for the protection of local products; flexibility of duties on imported products; duty-free imports of machinery and raw materials; settlement of disputes between employers and workers. There was an obvious concern to protect the Egyptian market against the effects of the competition among the various capitalist countries, and hence to preserve it as the fief of Great Britain; efforts were also made to cut down the multiplicity of jurisdictions that at that time encouraged salaried employees of British firms to seek employers less narrowly governed by the rulings of the Mixed Courts* which were predominantly French, Belgian and American.[24]

New investments were to mark the rise of Egyptian capitalism. Between 1934 and 1948, £E36,718,614 of new capital was to flow into Egyptian corporations; of this figure, £E21,041,566, or 78.7 percent of the new investments, was Egyptian. In 1948 the total capital of all the corporations operating in Egypt had reached £E117,935,000, of which

---

* Until Ismail Pasha introduced the Mixed Courts, resident Europeans had been exempt from any Egyptian court action. See Capitulations (Chapter 5).

£E71,624,177 belonged to foreigners (that is, 61 percent) and £E46,308,823 (or only 39 percent) to Egyptians.[25] In 1943 the old national debt was converted into a government loan; out of a total of £E86,670,000, nonresidents' share in it amounted to £E33,100,000 or 38.1 percent; but it must be added that a good part of the remaining 61.9 percent belonged to foreign companies, groups and individuals resident in Egypt.[26]

The monopolist character of the Egyptian industrial economy was visible everywhere: in the sugar and cement industries, in distilleries, in chemical fertilizers, but above all within the group of industrial companies set up or brought together by the Bank Misr through a system of holding companies which became the main body of the whole economy. The Bank Misr alone represented 28 percent of the total of Egyptian banking capital, or £E120,285,000, at the end of 1960. Its managing group—Talaat Harb, then Hafez Afifi, Ali Yehia, Mohammed el-Farghaly, Ahmed Abbud, followed by the great families of the Allubas, the Abazas, the Badrawis, the Serag Eddines, the Kolalis, the Lozis, the Wakils, the Manzalauis—controlled everything available, from aviation to printing, from the film industry to the mines and quarries, from textiles to ocean shipping; in certain sectors (dyeing and processing, aviation, films and navigation especially), foreign (that is, British) participation was substantial.

There was also rapid growth in the distribution of the new investments. Land exploitation, irrigation and mortgage loans dropped from 76.06 percent of all investments in 1912 to 46.97 percent in 1942; during the same period, investments in industry rose from 8.99 percent of the total to 22.49 percent, and those in the banking and commercial sector from 6.09 to 17.63 percent.[27] The Second World War was like a whip to the development of Egyptian capitalism: the total amount invested in industrial and commercial corporations rose from £E86 million to £E106 million; textile production from 100 million to 142 million yards, fiber output from 17,000 to 41,000 tons (these last figures are for the year 1947); similar increases could be cited for all branches of industry (cement, petroleum, sugar, vegetable oils, alcohol, etc.). On the basis of the 1930 index, total industrial output rose from £E13 million to £E18 million, while agricultural production fell from £E54.1 million to £E43.6 million during the same period. Factory payrolls rose perceptibly, from 247,000 to 756,000 in 1947; there were at that time 1,042,277 workers in the cities and 1,410,000 on the land. The concentration of workers in the large factories rose as well: in 1947, 53 big factories employed 129,900 workers, while 263,900 worked in 3,400 plants employing from 10 to 50 persons each.[28]

A Moat of Injustices

Why then, at the same time as this spectacular growth, did one still encounter a Shehata Ragab, an Abdel Hamid Ali Ibrahim, a Fuad Mustafa Ibrahim, an Abdel Hamid Mahmud, a Dandaraui Abdel Moneim Hassan, and those thousands of minor officials of the lower categories? How can one account for this misery that seemed to grow in step with the curve of investments, with the surge of hope?

The fact is that the war, the source of gigantic profits for the Egyptian bourgeoisie, brought ruin to every worker's family. Certainly the national income had risen, from £E168 million in 1939 to £E860 million in 1950. But the cost of living had gone from the 1939 index of 100 to 329 in 1950. On the basis of statistics it might seem an improvement. Had not savings risen from £E8 million in 1939 to £E132 million in 1944—that is, from 5 percent to 29.1 percent of the national income? Indeed they had . . . but the rise in prices put things back into their proper place: the real annual income of the average Egyptian was £E9.5 in 1950–53, whereas it had been £E10.2 in 1939—in other words, it had declined by 7 percent.

Why this rise in the cost of living?[29] For one thing, it was true, there were the facts of nature, of an agriculture that did not grow at the same rate as the population: in 1897 a population of 9,715,000, of whom 80 percent were fellahin, lived on 5,000,000 *feddans*, and there was a cultivated area of 6,800,000 *feddans*; in 1937 a population of 15,933,000, of whom 75 percent were fellahin, lived on 5,300,000 *feddans*, and the cultivated area amounted to 8,400,000 *feddans*. In 1952 the population had reached 21,472,000, of whom 68 percent were fellahin, and it had to live on the products of 5,600,000 *feddans,* or 9,300,000 cultivated per year.[30]

But at the other end of the scale, the profits distributed by corporations to their stockholders rose from £E7.5 million to £E20 million between 1942 and 1946, while the rental value of the lands leased by the large proprietors to the fellahin went from £E35 million to £E90 million. In 1952, 6 percent of the landowners held 65 percent of the land under cultivation, a little knot of 280 lords—in the forefront of whom stood the royal family—owning 584,401 *feddans.* But 2,760,661 peasants had to share 5,962,662 *feddans.* The average holding of a large proprietor was 3,765 *feddans,* that of a small holder was 1.5 *feddans* . . .[31]

A millennial pyramid of injustices was crushing the daily life of the Egyptians.

On January 8, 1952, President Harry Truman of the United States and Winston Churchill, the British Prime Minister, held a conference. Their interest was to dam the revolutionary nationalist tide in Egypt and Iran, sharing the burden. The American government announced a few days later that it was suspending the help that it had been giving to Egypt for some time.

On January 25 the British armor and field artillery stationed at the Suez Canal base converged on Government House in Ismailia, the Canal station halfway between Suez and Port Said. A full-scale battle raged throughout that Friday between the British forces and the local police, who had entrenched themselves in the building. By evening the Egyptians had lost more than 150 men.

On the following day, Saturday, January 26, the popular demonstrations that broke out in Cairo, Alexandria and every city in the kingdom were very quickly taken over by arsonist teams that set fire to the whole commercial, modern center of the capital. On the same evening the army went out into the streets and a curfew was imposed; the next day the Constitution was suspended, a state of siege was proclaimed and

Prime Minister Nahas' government was dismissed. At once, and even before the beginning of any investigation into the source of these events, thousands of young patriots—Wafdists, Communists, nationalists, trade unionists—were arrested and interned, the popular militia groups that had been conducting guerrilla warfare against the Canal base since October 1951 were dissolved and disarmed, and the press was muzzled.

How was that point reached? Why that Saturday, January 26, 1952? Who burned Cairo?

The real masters of Egypt were haunted by the ghosts of two revolutions, quite dissimilar in both timing and political content: the Egyptian revolution of 1919 and the "Long March" of the Chinese revolution that culminated in the foundation of the People's Republic of China in 1949.

The National Movement from 1919 to 1952

The Egyptian revolution of 1919–23, almost entirely ignored by Western political thinkers, had certainly ended in a partial defeat, and the Wafd, the ruling party, even though it enjoyed the overwhelming confidence of the people, was thrown out of power in 1927. But the year 1919 had seen the peasants go into action by whole regions, cutting lines of communication, seizing land, and, under revolutionary lawyers and intellectuals, proclaiming ephemeral "republics" in several areas, following the example of the republic of Ziftah, one hour away from Cairo, under the Wafdist deputy, Yussef el-Ghindi.

In the cities this insurrectional rising of the countryside was matched by a strong movement of national unity. There was unity between Moslem and Copt, too often divided by the ruses of the occupant, especially Cromer's successor, Sir Eldon Gorst, but also by a past that was still alive in their minds. There was unity between the workers—whose trade unions took on a character at once economic and political under the influence of young Wafdist lawyers as well as that of the Socialists, especially Antun Marun, who later became secretary-general of the Federation of Egyptian Trade Unions and died in prison—and the lower middle class, composed of ruined merchants, minor officials and, chiefly, lawyers, engineers and physicians. Along with the university and high school students, they would become the representatives of an intelligentsia inflamed by the writings of Mustafa Kamel and Mohammed Farid, aware of its uniquely Egyptian character thanks to Ahmed Lutfi el-Sayed, and finding in Saad Zaghlul the symbol of its strength and pride. There was unity, at least in the beginning (1919–23), between these popular forces and a very important part of the urban rich and the large landed proprietors, eager to become the exclusive masters of the country's wealth in the general movement. There was unity between the people and the police forces, the officers and soldiers of the army, only a small group of whom, headed by Mohammed Heydar—later director general of prisons and then Minister of War at the time of the burning of Cairo—was willing to march against the revolution. There was unity among the writers, the poets, the artists, the men of religion, the philosophers and the illiterate masses thirsting for liberty. The formal declaration of independence, heavily mortgaged by the four special clauses (1922)*; the proclamation of the Constitution of 1923, which gave a disproportionate place to the powers of the king; the creation of the Bank Misr in 1920; the emergence of the Wafd as the dominant political party, but also that of the Socialist party (1920) and the Egyptian Communist party (1920), the substantial reinforcement of the labor movement and the creation of the first Federation of Egyptian Trade Unions—each event was a victory, each was a symbol.

What Was the "Wafd"?

But the revolution did not reach the rural areas, and in the cities the coalition between the Palace and the upper bourgeoisie held the Wafd in check and incited it to

* The four "Reserved Points" were: 1) The security of communications of the British Empire; 2) the defense of Egypt against foreign aggression; 3) the protection of foreign interests and of minorities; and 4) control of the Sudan.

turn against the Left, to become part of the system in which, in short, the Egyptian middle class had expanded its own share.

Between 1923 and 1952 the Wafd majority was to govern for only seven years. The Palace parties—Hilmy Issa Pasha's Ittihad and Ismail Sidky Pasha's Shaab (1930)—those of the great landed proprietors (the Liberal-Constitutional party, founded in 1923 by Mohammed Mahmud, second only to the king in his landholdings), of the industrial upper middle class (the Saadist party, founded in 1937 by Mahmud Fahmy el-Nokrashy and Ahmed Maher), supported in various ways by the self-styled "Independents," representing the banks, big business, big industry and the technocratic managerial staffs, were to govern the country in close agreement with London and then, after 1945, with London and Washington. Egypt continued to be the cotton plantation of Lancashire, but there was more and more desire to see her become the major political and military base of imperialism at the intersection of three continents, in that meeting place of Africa, the eastern Mediterranean and the Middle East, which commands the approaches to the colonial world, and for which in those days (1919–45) the label of "Third World" had not yet been invented.

To be exact, although the Wafd was dedicated to parliamentary democracy, to the promotion of greater justice in the daily life of the country—and the evidence of this lies in the great work achieved in the area of education under the direction of Taha Hussein,[32] the establishment of the right to a job,[33] the creation of the Farm and Co-operative Credit Bank in 1930 to provide assistance to the small landowners, in particular— it had nothing of a revolutionary popular party. At no time did its leaders envisage carrying revolution to the heart of the social structure, of achieving a better distribution of the land, of doing any damage to the upper middle class that was despoiling the poor in close co-operation with British and international high finance.

This tendency toward social conservatism, which in the end became outright political reaction, was to be accentuated with the rise of Fuad Serag Eddine Pasha, one of the largest landholders, who became secretary-general of the Wafd in

1952 and adopted a course in direct contradiction to that of his predecessors, Makram Ebeid and Sabri Abu Alam, both of whom were genuine representatives of the lower-middle-class urban intellectuals, both profoundly liberal and democratic, both dedicated to the great ideals of 1789 and to the revolution of 1919. Agrarian revolution was therefore inconceivable, and so was any conjunction between the peasantry and the national middle class of the cities, between the people and the national armed forces. It is in this, rather than in the persistent campaign against the Left since 1924, that one must recognize the underlying cause of the failure of the 1919 revolution to attain the objectives of the Egyptian national bourgeoisie revolution: the control of political power—domestic and foreign policy—and the democratization of the life of society in the cities and the countryside through the exercise of the whole range of economic power by the national bourgeoisie in alliance with the people.

In 1952, when Cairo was burning and the Free Officers were preparing to seize power, it was still the rich landed proprietors who dominated the political scene and blocked the road to any change in structures, to the annihilation of anachronism.[34]

Now, to be precise, it was in the Chinese revolution that Egyptian political thinking in the years 1945–52 found, little by little, the example of what the Egyptian political revolution of 1919 might have been if it had given birth to a revolution of the fellahin, if it had created a popular national front, if it had been endowed with an insurrectional army. More and more the "Long March" seemed the alternative, the only possible alternative, to long servitude for a country of an ancestral civilization, a country of poor peasants, where the upper bourgeoisie in power proved impotent to renew in depth the lives of millions of men who thirsted for their renaissance.

Such is the double backdrop against which the increasingly revolutionary developments of the Egyptian national movement would be set off after the end of the Second World War.

The Nationalist Right

For a long time even before the war, the propaganda of the Axis powers had sought to detach the Egyptian upper middle class from its alliance with Great Britain and to seduce the nationalist elements which had arisen among the lower classes. Mussolini, "the protector of Islam," acted through the intermediary of the royal family, linked by tradition to the house of Victor Emmanuel. Hitler, on the other hand, was the hero of a group of young Egyptian nationalists in violent reaction against Great Britain, especially in the wake of the Anglo-Egyptian treaty of 1936, which itself was the result of a compromise arrived at between the Wafd and the British government after the new revolutionary wave of 1935.[35] Fathi Raduan, Nur Eddine Tarraf and their group of young men from the old National party, and Ahmed Hussein, the leader of the Green Shirts of the Misr al-Fatat (Young Egypt) party—the future National Islamic party (1940) and then the Socialist party (1946)—attended the Nazi party Congress in Nuremberg in 1936 in search of an ideal and methods of action.[36]

To Egyptian public opinion the Second World War seemed a quarrel between the Allies (the possessors of colonies and other dependent countries, including Egypt) and the new powers that challenged their pre-eminence. The agents of the Axis in Egypt took full advantage of the crisis in food supply,[37] the increasingly sharp irritation aroused in the man in the street by the state of siege, and the transformation of the country into a military base for the British Middle East Command. In January and February 1942, Marshal Rommel's drive to El Alamein, some fifty miles west of Alexandria, was viewed by many people as the prelude to a "liberation" of Egypt by the Italian and German soldiery. Demonstrations against the food shortages degenerated into anti-British explosions with cries of *"Ila'l-amam ya Rommel!"* (Forward, Rommel!) and *"Hiza Farouk fawka ra'sak ya George!"* (Faruk's foot on your head, George!).

On the morning of February 4, 1942, British tanks encircled Abdin Palace and forced Faruk to accept a government headed by Mustafa el-Nahas, who agreed to return to power "on the points of English bayonets," as it was to be told later.[38] By apparently legitimatizing this brutal British intrusion on Egyptian sovereignty, the leadership of the Wafd brought itself into great discredit with the masses. The Saadist party and the Independents turned toward Washington, which seemed to them to be destined to take over the shaky power of Britain. The fascist parties—Ahmed Hussein's Young Egypt, but above all the powerful secret society of Hassan el-Banna's Moslem Brotherhood—recruited and organized in secret, in spite of legal prohibitions.

Rebirth of the Marxist Left

But it was principally on the Left that the essence of the new direction of the Egyptian national movement took form. Groups of intellectuals, foreigners as well as Egyptians, created the four Marxist organizations which, surviving multiple vicissitudes and repeated internal divisions, were to provide the key men of the future unified (second) Egyptian Communist party in 1958. In an early period these organizations launched a campaign to win over the Egyptian intelligentsia, more particularly the students and graduates of the university. This was the period when centers of political and cultural training were set up, notably Dar al-Abhath al-Ilmiyya (Institute for Scientific Research), Lagnat Nashr al-Thakafa al-Haditha (Committee for the Propagation of Modern Culture), and "Etudes," from 1941 to 1946. Very soon there was a Marxist press: *al-Fagr al-Gadid, Omdurman, al-Tali'a* (1945–46) and, later, *al-Gamahir* (1947–48). The second stage was that of the junction with the worker movement, which was accompanied by a radical Egyptianization of the leading cadres.[39] Two labor union centrals were established at the end of 1945 by the militant leftist workers: the Preparatory Committee for the Congress of Egyptian Trade Unions and the Congress of Egyptian Trade Unions.[40] At the same time, across from Shepheard's hotel, a National Popular University began evening courses for the training of working-class leaders; more than six hundred workers were to take courses there in political economy, history, philosophy, literature and international affairs during the six months of this university's life. Egyptian trade unionists of both trends took part in the congress that brought into being the World Federation of Trade Unions in Paris (October 1945).

The year 1945 marked the end of the hegemony of the Egyptian bourgeoisie in the leadership of the national movement. The two wings of the Egyptian middle class separated as soon as the war was over, preparing for the negotiations for evacuation: the Wafd was thrown out of office on October 8, 1944, to the benefit of Ahmed Maher, the leader of the Saadist party, who was, however, assassinated on February 24, 1945, because he planned to declare war on the Axis powers (this was done two days later), but the Wafd continued to accept the whole responsibility for the nation's destiny; against it, Ahmed Maher had created a Political Institution, composed of the leaders of the anti-Wafd parties and the Independents and charged with advising the government in matters of national demands.[41]

On the "National Committee of Workers and Students"

Almost at the same time a new entity was created by Wafdist, nationalist and Communist intellectuals and the trade unions: the National Committee of Workers and Students, whose direct and daily influence extended to the two universities of Cairo and Alexandria, to the students in the secondary and technical schools all over the country, to the whole of the intelligentsia, to major sections of the professions and to all Egyptian trade unions without regard to allegiance or geography.

Earlier, on February 17, the Joint Student Committee had published a National Charter with three points: total evacuation of every square inch of the Nile Valley by British land, sea and air forces; internationalization* of the Egyptian problem; liberation from economic subjection. The NCWS's

---

* Putting the problem before world public opinion and, more specifically, before the newly founded UN, instead of submitting it to direct bilateral Anglo-Egyptian negotiations.

manifesto-program, announced in the huge auditorium of the School of Medicine in Cairo, addressed the people in these terms:[42]

"The Egyptian trade unions and the students of the Egyptian universities, of Al Azhar, of the Higher Institutes, of the private and secondary schools, all have resolved to make February 21, 1946, the Day of Evacuation, the day of a strike by all bodies and groups of the people—

"A day of renewal with the sacred national movement that has the participation of all elements of the Egyptian people united around their right to total independence and complete freedom—

"A day that will make it clear to British imperialism and to the whole world that the Egyptian people has completed its preparations with a view to active combat until the nightmare of imperialism that has crushed our hearts for sixty-four years has vanished—

"A day that will be a document in the hands of the Egyptain negotiators so that they may present it to the imperialists as proof of the fact that the Egyptian people is resolved not to give up, even for a moment, the evacuation of Egypt and the Sudan—

"A day that shall be a universal awakening of the Egyptian people, which will thus make it plain that it will accept no deviation, no relinquishment of its right to independence and freedom—

"A day when public services, means of communication, commercial and public offices, institutions of learning, and factories will halt all activities throughout the country.

"The majesty of this day summons us all to keep our sacred cause from being diverted into riots, destruction, or impairment of the public safety.

"Let us all raise aloft the banner of our country, let us reaffirm our unity without divisiveness—workers and artisans, students, merchants and officials, our whole people standing solidly together to tear off the infamous badge of humiliation and slavery."

The methods were those of mass action: national committees of industries, district committees, committees of professions, directed by the NCWS; mass demonstrations; strikes; contacts with the international anticolonialist and democratic movement; and finally, in the future, an armed struggle against the forces of occupation.

The two groups of the middle class prepared to negotiate under the double slogan of "evacuation" and "unity of the Nile Valley under the Egyptian crown . . ." While the coalition of the Wafdist left and the Communists brought the idea of democracy to the urban masses and gave the people a desire to take the fate of the whole country into its own hands, the minority anti-Wafdist coalition, which clung to power,[43] allied itself with Great Britain in order to control the situation better while concentrating the fire of its operations against the national democratic group. On February 9, 1946, under the orders of Premier Mahmud Fahmy el-Nokrashy, the Egyptian police surrounded and then raised the Abbas Bridge in order to break the tide of student demonstrations flowing in from Giza to the center of Cairo; several dozen were killed or vanished and several hundred were wounded. The Cabinet was compelled to resign. Ismail Sidky succeeded to power; he feinted, so that it seemed as if he would permit the demonstrations. On February 21, 1946, huge demonstrations were held simultaneously, at the call of the NCWS, in Cairo, Alexandria and all the other cities; the machine guns at the garrisons of Kasr el-Nil claimed many victims. Sidky saw that the new popular movement had to be broken if he wanted to be able to negotiate the joint defense treaty proposed to him by Ernest Bevin, then Foreign Secretary. On March 4 there was a new demonstration, one of mourning, which was also a protest against the Premier's attitude: he spoke of the people as "the crowd." On July 8 al-Ahram published an appeal by the NCWS to make the day of July 11, the anniversary of the bombardment of Alexandria in 1882, a tremendous manifestation of the national will. On July 10 the representatives of fifteen popular movements announced their support for this appeal. That night the police under Sidky, who was also president of the Egyptian Federation of Industries, arrested almost two hundred political and union leaders, students, professors, journalists and writers on charges of "Communism," ordered the dissolution of eleven political, cultural and labor organizations, and suspended the leftwing newspapers as well as the great Wafdist daily, *Sawt al-Umma,* headed by Mohammed Mandur.[44] Taking advantage of the respite thus gained, Sidky left for the negotiations in London, where he completed the so-called Sidky-Bevin plan of October 26, 1946. Under mass pressure, seven members of the negotiating committee publicly disassociated themselves from the affair, and Sidky was constrained to resign in December 1946. Nokrashy returned to power; this time he tried to win a decision from the Security Council, relying on the support of the United States (August–September 1947). The result, of course, was negative: the bourgeoisie demonstrated its incapacity to resolve the national problem even formally.

It became necessary to put a real stop, which, it was hoped, would be decisive this time, to the emergence of the Left. Indeed, in spite of the dissolution of its own organizations and the disappearance of the NCWS, the Left was broadening its influence in the universities[45] and, above all, was becoming more and more active within the Wafd, particularly through the voice of Aziz Fahmy, lawyer, poet and champion of civil liberties and democracy in Parliament and the country at large, and through the pen of Ahmed Abul Fath, editor in chief of *al-Misri,* which became the leading Egyptian daily. There would have to be a battle against the de facto coalition between the Wafdist left and the Communists, the workers and the students, and—a new development—penetration by the national front, especially after 1945, into the working-class centers of Shubra el-Kheima, near Cairo; Mahalla el-Kubra; Sharqiya, opposite the military base at the Suez Canal; and Beheira, south of Alexandria.

The Moslem Brotherhood and Imperialism

This battle was to be the mission and the function of the Moslem Brotherhood. Its "Supreme Guide," Hassan el-Banna, was satisfied in the beginning to hold himself in readiness, to refuse any clear-cut commitment, although he emphasized the indispensable presence of Islam in the core of political life. But the creation of the NCWS in 1945 had forced him to unmask his guns: he sent his troops into battle against the Wafdist-Communist front, created his own centers of popular organization—in the universities, the labor movement and the press—denounced the new popular movement in the name of religion, and spread confusion. Hassan el-Banna's publications of this period and the editorials of *al-Daawa* were subjected to analysis by Mohammed Hussein, spokesman for the Dar al-Abhath al-Ilmiyya group, in his book *The Moslem Brotherhood in the Balance,* which appeared in 1945 and cannot be found today; but it constitutes an unchallengeable record: the powerful secret society, whose leader maintained close relations with Brigadier Clayton, then Oriental counselor to the British embassy in Cairo, did nothing against the occupant; on the contrary, its propaganda and action against the national front were extremely violent. At the same time the secret network of the Moslem Brotherhood set out to prepare the country. It was the direct organizer of a series of murderous acts: the attempted assassinations of Mustafa el-Nahas (December 6, 1945; April 25, 1948; then November 1948); the assassination of Amin Osman by Hussein Tewfik (January 5, 1946); the dynamiting of the Metro film theater (May 6, 1947); the assassination of the deputy president of the Court of Appeals of Cairo, Ahmed el-Khazindar (March 22, 1948); the repeated dynamitings of Jewish businesses and residential quarters (Cicurel and Oreco, the Ades stores, in July 1948; Benzion, Gattegno, the Me'adi Company, in August; but above all the dynamiting of Haret el-Yahud, the Jewish quarter in September (twenty dead, sixty-one injured); the explosion in Galal Street (November 1948), and the discovery of a jeep loaded with explosives in Cairo (November 5, 1948).[46]

On December 4, 1948, General Selim Zaki, the police chief in Cairo and the key figure of the repressions, was killed in his armored command car under the walls of the School of Medicine, which the police were besieging. The wave of terrorism unleashed by the Moslem Brotherhood finally attained its objective: to provide the government with an excuse for suspending civil liberties and striking a new blow at the national front. But the very excesses of the terrorists forced the government's hand: in order to protect itself, it had to strike the clandestine organization as well.

Why the Palestine War?

Let us go back a little further, to the spring of 1948. A gigantic script, as big as the whole of the Near East, was being filled out step by step but inexorably.

It was on May 15, in fact, that the British troops left Palestine, where Britain's mandate had run out. Civil war had begun there several months earlier. On May 15 it was real war; the Arab League countries intervened in order to keep Palestine Arab. From a long-range point of view the operation was to be of inestimable value to the Western powers, supported in the very heart of the Arab East by an ally who— as 1956 and 1967 would show—did not hesitate to launch a military action against an Arab country guilty of anti-imperialism. But that is another story. At the moment the war in Palestine aimed to make it possible for the reactionary governments in the Arab countries to open a new campaign against the Left, which was accused this time of treason, since the various Communist parties, conforming to the Marxist-Leninist principle of the right of peoples to self-determination, called for acceptance of the state of Israel within the limits laid down by the UN in 1947, the creation of an Arab state of Palestine, the indemnification of the refugees, and the conclusion of a peace treaty with Israel. A state of siege was proclaimed in Egypt on May 15, and thousands of Communists, unionists, progressives and left-wing Wafdists were interned in the concentration camp of El Tor, on the Red Sea. On December 8 Nokrashy announced the dissolution of the Moslem Brotherhood. On December 28 he was killed by Abdel Meguid Ahmed Hassan, a member of that fraternity. On the same day Ibrahim Abdel Hadi succeeded Nokrashy as head of the Saadist party and of the government. He ordered the arrest and internment of the Moslem Brotherhood's militants, but Hassan el-Banna remained at liberty. Finally, on February 12, 1949, the Supreme Guide was assassinated in his turn.

El Tor provided a new respite but no solution to the basic problem. On November 3, 1949, Hadi had to step down, yielding to a transition government headed by Hussein Sirry. Two months later, on January 3, 1950, Egypt had her last general election: the Wafd remained the leading party in Egypt, but it did not win an absolute majority, since it received only 1,135,643 of the 2,859,741 votes cast—in other words, 39.6 percent—in spite of the massive support of the Left, which had resolved to put an end to openly reactionary governments. Thirty-two independent deputies were elected on the basis of the manifesto issued by their group in November 1949: it called for the limitation of landownership, the abolition of the wakfs,* the accelerated industrialization of the country, a rise in protective import duties, social insurance for workers, the closed shop, administrative decentralization and universal free education. This was the group representing the industrial bourgeoisie and the intellectual circles that were dependent on it for their means of action (notably the press group of the Amin brothers' Akhbar el-Yom). One Labor deputy and one Socialist deputy were also elected.

More than ever the Wafd appeared to be what it had never in actuality ceased to be: an electoral front for the various sections of the national middle class, dominated by the large landed proprietors who held the controls, thanks to Fuad Serag Eddine. Nahas announced his intention to negotiate with Great Britain, and he signed a Point Four agreement with the United States on May 5, 1950, a gesture that was to be followed by negotiations with a view to concluding a treaty of friendship, trade and navigation between Egypt and the United States. In the cities, worker agitation was resumed— forty-nine strikes in 1950—and the Communists swiftly broadened their influence, momentarily dammed by massive internments. The Peace Movement rallied a great number of intellectuals around its newspaper, al-Katib. A Preparatory Committee for the Federation of Egyptian Trade Unions was

---

* In Moslem law, property held in perpetuity for religious or charitable purposes.

working on the reconstruction of the labor movement. The students' Executive Committee resumed its activities under a leadership two thirds of which belonged to the national front (Wafdist-Communist). Finally, the feminist movement undertook to establish a national union of women.

From Negotiation to Guerrilla Warfare

For twenty months the Wafd negotiated stubbornly. "We should not forget," Mohammed Salah Eddine, the Wafd's Foreign Minister, told the English negotiators, "that the most important weapon in the hands of Communist propaganda in Egypt and in every country occupied by foreigners is just that very fact of occupation, as well as the economic and social effects that flow from it. This propaganda falls in favorable soil in the minds of patriots concerned with the independence of their country, to such a degree that it becomes possible to fear the insensible spread of confusion between patriotism and Communist propaganda."[47] At home, while the forces of the National Front were increasing their pressure on the Nahas Cabinet, the right wing of the Wafd, led by Serag Eddine, was busy ensuring a defeat for the revolution: the state of siege was abolished only five months after the Wafd had returned to power; a law was promulgated that prevented any action in opposition to the consequences of the suppression of 1948–49; finally Serag Eddine strove, in vain, to weaken the resistance of his own deputies in order to get them to adopt the law on political suspects . . . Twenty months of ceaseless struggle, during which the right wing of the Wafd vainly sought to avoid or shift the battle. Twenty months that culminated in the rupture of negotiations and the denunciation of the Anglo-Egyptian treaty of 1936 and of the convention of 1899 on the Sudan, on that evening of October 8, 1951, which marked the victory of the forces of the National Front over the Wafdist right—in other words, the theoretical victory of the new popular leadership of the national movement over the old leadership exercised by the upper bourgeoisie.

Thenceforth it was no longer the leadership of the Wafd

that held the initiative in Egypt. Five days after the memorable proclamation of Mustafa el-Nahas to the Chamber of Deputies, the Wafdist government rejected the proposals made to it by the United States, Great Britain, France and Turkey for its adherence to a collective treaty for the Middle East (October 13, 1951), thus officially burning its bridges not only with the occupying power but, this time, with the whole NATO.

On the day after Nahas' proclamation to the Chamber of Deputies—that is, on the morning of October 9—popular demonstrations began to break out in the cities. In Ismailia, provocators tried to make the demonstrators attack the storehouses of the English NAAFI;[*] shots were exchanged, and armored vehicles invested the city. This was the signal for the guerrilla warfare that was to be extended to the whole Suez Canal base from October 9, 1951, until that January 26, 1952.

At an appeal from the government, eighty thousand Egyptian workers and office employees left their jobs, thus paralyzing the administrative level and the logistical substructure of the base.

In Cairo and Alexandria the students' executive committees organized the recruiting of volunteers, who, grouped in *katibas* (battalions), left quickly for the province of Sharqiya, the vestibule of the Canal. Who were the members of these *guerrillero* formations? Students, workers, many of whom had formerly been employed at the base, fellahin of the locality, many intellectuals. They belonged to the Communist organizations, the Wafdist youth groups, the old National party, even Young Egypt; many were from the MB. A group of young officers instructed the volunteers in the use of arms. But the army and the police were held strictly in reserve. Every night the volunteers who had come from the cities went off to the base. They had four clear objectives: to destroy supply dumps, to cut lines of communication, to prevent any resupply, to make life impossible for the soldiers at the base. There was no unified command, each group obeying its own leader. There was no co-ordination: often, conse-

[*] Combined post exchanges of the British navy, army and air force.

quently, because the alarm had been give by one attack, another attempt in the vicinity by a different group resulted in a bloody defeat somewhat later. But above all, there was no root in the local population; the groups of volunteers were primarily city men who had come, arms in hand, to carry out the mission formerly assigned to all Egyptians by the National Committee of Workers and Students; they did not see, at least for the moment, the imperative necessity of converting their revolutionary activity into a true peasant revolution, and it did not occur to them to link the problem of land with that of independence. And yet the political programs of the Left at that time placed this question at the center of everything. But the organizations were divided, and there was no stable and effective directing body of the tacit National Front.[48]

As it proceeded, the military action became more precise and spread into the villages. Resistance committees were formed in all sectors of Ismailia and among the peasants of Birket Abu Gamuss, Ezbet Atwa and Nefisha. Pitched battles took place between the British forces, supported by artillery and armor, and the *fida'iyyin*,* especially at El Korein and El Tell. At El Korein, for the first time, British armor came up against a whole village in arms, and it had to retreat.[49]

In the British camp, troops from the island of Mauritius refused to fight and were put under arrest by the hundred; heavily indoctrinated by Communist propaganda since the years 1939–45 and by the Peace Movement, the contingent's soldiers grumbled and wished for the end of this wearying and useless war. The *Times* of London echoed this state of affairs: "The nerves of the British soldiers," it said, "are subjected to a harsh ordeal. They wonder what interest there can be in retaining a military base that has lost all its usefulness because of an opposing national feeling . . ."[50] Almost six hundred *fida'iyyin* fell in the struggle.[51] Every province, every city furnished its contingent of heroes fallen splendidly on the field of honor: from Sharqiya, Mustafa Ahmed, Mahmud el-Mardanly, Mohammed Rashad Greish, Salama Ibrahim, Sayed

* Volunteers; members of the guerrilla movement.

Abu Sheesha', Mohammed Abdel 'Al Hodhod; Abbas el-A'ssar, whom Alexandria University honored in a gigantic silent demonstration; Omar Shahine, Ahmed el-Menissi, Ahmed Esmat, the pilot—all from Cairo; and young Nabil Mansur of Port Said.

In Cairo the Wafd was overwhelmed. On the day after British artillery had destroyed the village of Kafr Abdu, the government had to act: it seized the Gezira Sporting Club and expelled the English members, it began consideration of a diplomatic and trade rupture with London, and the recall of its ambassador from the Court of St. James's, the highly Anglophile Abdel Fattah Amr, as well as the punishment of any person collaborating with foreign military forces in the country, and above all the right of all citizens to bear arms (December 15, 1951). In addition, the government was studying the possibility of replacing its economic and commercial relations with Great Britain by treaties with the USSR and the socialist countries (i.e., Communist-controlled). It even considered creating an anti-imperialist alliance among the countries of the Arab League. On the popular level, the organization of the armed struggle progressed swiftly. In the beginning of 1952 the organizations that were directly engaged formed a federation in order to compensate for deficiencies learned through experience and dearly paid for. The problem was that of transforming the struggle of the *fida'iyyin* into a peasant war of national liberation, both by distributing arms to the peasants and by creating a unified command for the *katibas,* as well as a political-military newspaper, a communications organ among all sectors. The Preparatory Committee for the Federation of Egyptian Trade Unions was on the way to building an effective group. The Communist organizations became reconciled with one another in action. In spite of the assassination of Aziz Fahmy by the political police (May 1952), the left wing of the Wafd held Fuad Serag Eddine in check and controlled the whole party press. From Moscow, Peking and all the socialist capitals, messages of solidarity and promises of help poured in.

On November 29, 1951, Bulletin No. 35 of the occupation

forces declared, for the attention of the Wafd: "It was the imperative duty of the Egyptian government to strike down the heads of this criminal movement with an iron hand . . ."[52]

On December 18 the king declared void the election held by the Officers' Club, which had shown a nationalist majority headed by Major General Mohammed Naguib. This was contrary to the wish of the Palace, which intended to keep the army under its thumb, available for the maintenance of order.

On December 25 the king appointed Hafez Afifi Pasha head of the Royal Cabinet. Former chairman of the board of directors of the Bank Misr and one of the chief directors of the Misr complex, this was the man who, in midsummer of 1951, had publicly rebuked the Wafd for its nationalism and proclaimed his pro-British sentiments. The *New York Times* immediately hailed this act as "the first ray of light that has come to pierce the incandescent atmosphere of Egypt since the rupture of relations with Great Britain."[53]

On January 8, 1952, the Truman-Churchill conference was held.

On January 13 the weekly paper *Akhbar el-Yom*, well known for its hatred of the Wafd and the entire Left, said: "The British embassy in Cairo [it was headed at that time by Sir Ralph Stevenson] has come to see the necessity of finding a solution based on the evacuation of the British forces from Egypt, given the fact that the military men themselves think that such a solution has become inevitable, since it is now impossible to reinforce the military base in the present circumstances and in the midst of the popular resistance that is steadily increasing."

Who Burned Cairo?

On January 25, on the order of Fuad Serag Eddine, Minister of the Interior, the *buluk nizam* (provincial police), entrenched in Government House at Ismailia, joined battle with British tanks and artillery, which fired point-blank for twelve hours. The massacre of the peasant policemen aroused all Egypt, but this time even the forces of order decided to go over to action.

At dawn on that Saturday, January 26, 1952, the weekly issue of *Akhbar el-Yom* came off the presses in El Sahafa Street. It contained these predictions: "Among those measures under study by the government in response to the British aggression in Ismailia, one suggests that the British ambassador be declared *persona non grata,* and others envisage the closing of British consulates throughout Egypt and the rupture of diplomatic and economic relations with Great Britain." On another page there was a dispatch from Ewer, the paper's London correspondent: "London expects that the Egyptian army will join the battle of the Canal . . ." The next day was to be the initial session of the first organizing meeting of the General Federation of Trade Unions. It was also the expiration date for the ultimatum issued by a number of officers, which would mean their collective resignation for lack of concerted action by the army and the people.

In the morning of that Saturday, January 26, 1952, a general strike closed all the factories. The students of Fuad and Ibrahim universities and of Al Azhar marched on the center of Cairo, where they were joined by workers coming from the suburbs. From the balcony of the Premier's office the Minister of State, Abdel Fattah Hassan, addressed the crowd: he promised an immediate rupture with Great Britian and the conclusion of a friendship treaty with the USSR. The king invited all general officers of the army and the police to a banquet in Abdin Palace. The political police, whose chief, Brigadier Ibrahim Imam, could not be found, was mobilized in Cairo and Alexandria, but many of its officers closed out their bank accounts . . .

Shortly before noon the arsonist teams went into action. They carried lists showing, in order of priority, the buildings to be burned. Who were they? Militants of Ahmed Hussein's old party, the Green Shirts of Young Egypt, now called the Socialist party; fanatics of "Shabab Mohammed," who preached the "return to the desert"; but also, and mainly, militants of the Moslem Brotherhood secret organization. These, in large part, had been held in reserve all through the battle of the Canal. By fostering a psychosis of fear, they made every effort to create out of nothing an anti-Jewish sentiment hitherto unknown in Egypt. While Wafdists and Communists were going off to the Canal, the Moslem Brotherhood launched its campaign of destruction against the bars and amusement places of Cairo and Alexandria, firing on lovers in dark suburban streets, preaching religious fanaticism, aggression and hatred . . .

By noon the business district, the modern city in the heart of Cairo, was burning, and the fires spread in the early hours of the afternoon. The demonstrators, who were now spectators, stolidly watched the exploits of the incendiary fascist bands surrounded by hundreds of young thugs without jobs, the wretched, deformed *Lumpenproletariat* of Cairo. They watched as they did because the splendid capital belonged not to them but to the rich whose businesses were burning. So they let it go . . .[54]

Who burned Cairo?

Ten years afterward the question was still unanswered on the judicial level. Strange things occurred. Certainly the investigation was conducted by the Attorney General himself. Ahmed Hussein, the leader of the Socialist party, was accused, arrested, then set free by the military government at the very time when Lieutenant Colonel Gamal Abdel Nasser was Minister of the Interior. Ahmed Hussein even published a thick book on the trial, in which he appears as a hero. Seven arsonists were sentenced to long terms at hard labor, but in January 1959 they were absolved by a high military tribunal and quietly released at the same time when the political police were hunting down progressives. The official investigation never led to anything. The case was closed. One day the files will certainly have to be opened again . . . Until then, for lack of facts, there is only political analysis or eyewitness testimony at our disposal.

The men who burned Cairo were the same men to whom that fire provided a pretext for crushing—this time decisively —the national struggle that was on the point of turning into a genuine popular revolution with the massive support of the peasants. These forces have names: imperialism; the wealthy landed proprietors rallying around the king; the industrial upper bourgeoisie. For a long time these forces had supported and armed the clerical-fascist organizations that sowed terror and provocation, in order to discredit the national movement and divert its strength against fictitious enemies.

On that same evening of January 26, while Cairo was still burning—a vision of horror unforgettable to all who lived through that day of sorrow—Fuad Serag Eddine ordered the arrests of 250 people, most of them Wafdist and Communist members of *fida'iyyin*, and imposed a curfew.

The following day Nahas decreed a state of siege. Immediately the Wafd was turned out of power, and Ewer could write in the next issue of *Akhbar el-Yom*: "There now exists a viewpoint of optimism that is greater than ever before by reason of the change of government in Egypt. What is most important, as His Excellency, Ali Maher Pasha, has said, is to create the best possible atmosphere for the negotiations. In order to do this, calm and order must first be re-established and aggression must be halted . . ." Thousands of militants once more took the road to the concentration camps. The Constitution was suspended. Censorship was imposed on the press. The military courts sat without interruption. In a few weeks the dissolved *katibas* found themselves cheek by jowl in the camps.[55]

Its vanguard destroyed before it could even move, the Egyptian people lost its revolution.

For that purpose, Cairo had to burn.

Between the fire and the coup d'état, six months went by in which the reactionary forces sought to bring the situation under control by means of curfew and mobile machine-gun teams that regularly plowed through the streets of the burned capital. Six months, four Cabinets: Ali Maher's, Naguib el-Hilaly's, Hussein Sirry's, and once again Naguib el-Hilaly's. What was happening?

The Egyptian bourgeoisie, until now incapable of accomplishing the dual task of the national revolution—independence and, above all, the modernization of the economy and the society—through the traditional parties, was trying to find its way. Its industrial wing, in particular, intended to establish its predominance in the government against the back-ward and outmoded agricultural wing. But in order to do this, it had to be wary of the popular movement, whose massive support would very quickly outrun the limited objectives of the Misr complex and the Egyptian Federation of Industries. Finally, to complicate matters, a key part of the state apparatus —the Egyptian army—could not be counted on (whence the recourse to armored teams of the security police).

The Anger of the Big Industrialists

Let us look more closely. The industrial wing of the Egyptian upper bourgeoisie had grown rapidly after 1945. Thus the funds invested in industrial corporations rose from £E28.5 million in 1945 to £E56.8 million in 1950, to which £E7 million in new investments was added in 1951, plus £E3 million in 1952. In 1950 the nonagrarian sector represented 56 percent of the national income. But the cotton export declined in the first half of 1951, while importation of wheat and flour went from 531,000 tons in 1950 to 1,110,000 in 1951—in other words, a disbursement of £E37.6 million in the latter year.[56]

And yet every effort was made by the big landowners, who continued to dominate the political scene, to curb industrial production and, consequently, the political power of the in-dustrial and technocratic group of the Egyptian bourgeoisie.

Three documents offer the keys to the crisis and foreshadow its climax: the Preface to the *Yearbook* of the Egyptian Federation of Industries for 1951–52; the *Yearbook* of the National Bank of Egypt for 1950; and the Federation's *Yearbook* for 1952–53. These three publications appeared during the transition between the two systems, that crucial time when Cairo burned. They reveal the essence of what the basic forces in the capital were thinking in confrontation with the problems of Egyptian society in crisis.

In the first document the EFI brings up a number of "truths": "The first truth is that while industrial production con-tinued to grow during the year in spite of concomitant troubling factors, it is nonetheless below the productive capacity of the factories because of the weakness of the local market and the difficulties of export . . . The second truth is the frightening drop in new investment: £E9 million in 1951, while funds accumulated in deposit accounts have risen to £E37 million; this has taken place in a country with a high birth rate which, in order to maintain its economic level, needs to invest several tens of millions of pounds every year . . . This makes it imperative to act quickly to eliminate the causes of this state of affairs, all the more in that the majority of them arises, we believe, out of the administrative obstacles that have been erected against economic activity . . . The third truth consists in the atmosphere of incomprehension that continues to exist between the state and industry . . . and that owes its origin to the vestiges of that agrarian mentality that we know so well . . . We all believe [however] that Egyptian industry is our only road to the future, a road that we intend to surround with a meticulous network of safeguards . . . Above all we must face the facts of life in our country: the inexperience of the governmental staffs, the need for capital, the necessity to encourage investment in industry, the abolition of restrictions that necessarily results from this, and the creation of a propitious atmosphere . . ."

The National Bank of Egypt, for its part, points out that "the increase in income derived from agriculture continues to be employed, as in the past, for the purchase of land, the construction of rental buildings, and the purchase of luxury goods. . . ."

The EFI's report for 1952–53 amounts to a veritable cry of alarm: "Stagnation has prevailed in cotton spinning, especially on the home market, because of the many price reductions imposed by the authorities, the consequent disturbances in the markets, the difficulties of export . . . The silk industry has faced a real crisis . . . Flax has suffered especially from the measures taken by the Ministry of Agriculture . . . the government still refuses to change the customs duties on linseed oil, thus aggravating the shortage of raw materials . . . With the exception of gold and salt, the mining industry has been active. Exports, however, have declined, except for phosphate . . . Over the past few years the petroleum industry has shown a certain regressive tendency for reasons that are generally administrative . . . , the strictness of the terms of the new law on mines and quarries, particularly the right reserved to the government to requisition in the event of imperative need . . . The electrical industry and the battery industry have been the major victims [of administrative difficulties] . . . The food industries are still exposed to the difficulties created for them by the policy followed in this respect by the authorities. Sugar production is still hampered by the exorbitant excise duty imposed on it . . . The crisis that has beset the tomato-and-vegetable-canning industry since the end of the war continues with the same intensity . . . The rice industry has also had a bad year . . . The problems of the vegetable-oil industry are a typical example of the harmful effects that can ensue from government intervention in matters of production . . . Soaps have had to take heavy losses . . . The pharmaceutical industry has suffered a decline in output . . . The slump in our cigarette exports is still the most impressive feature of that industry . . . Never in the annals of Egyptian tourism has the season gone through such a dead calm . . . The lack of co-ordination remains the chief obstacle to the development of river navigation . . . The construction industry has once more fallen into almost total inertia . . ."[57]

Undoubtedly the governments that followed one another in office after February 4, 1942, really attempted a certain rejuvenation of the economic and social conditions, only to make way for new forces: the creation of the Council of State* by the Sidky Cabinet (1946) in order to make government operations more efficient; the acceleration of reimbursement by Great Britain for the sterling debts to Egypt contracted during the war and amounting to £405 million by English reckoning and £600 million by Egyptian (agreements of 1947 and 1948);[58] the reactivation of the project for the electrification of the Aswan Dam by the Nokrashy Cabinet (1945); then the creation of the Industrial Bank by the second Nokrashy

* The supreme administrative Court of Justice, modeled after the French *Conseil d'Etat.*

Cabinet, and the promulgation of the law that required every corporation to have an Egyptian participation amounting to at least 51 percent of its capital (1947); and the new agreement on the sterling debts (March 1949). The policy of the Nahas government, in 1950–51, was characterized by a timorous reformism that did not prevent the large landowners from maintaining their domination of the state; Fuad Serag Eddine was then the head of the party's apparatus and the strong man of the government.

In May 1951 the government distributed 1,000,000 *feddans* to the poor peasants in small parcels and announced its intention to increase the number of small landowners, though without any agrarian reform. It promulgated a number of labor laws that improved conditions for the workers (the collective labor-contract law of July 31, 1950, the workmen's compensation law of August 17, 1950, the law of February 21, 1950, granting cost-of-living increases; but against these, the curb on the right to strike of February 8, 1951). But in September 1950 the government took a whole series of measures that amounted to as many brakes on the growth of the industrial sector: the imposition of taxes on rental income, commercial and noncommercial profits, industrial profits, professional income; then, on September 11, surtaxes on commercial and industrial profits.

There was now, in the opinion of the industrialists, clear proof that the traditional parties hardly had the strength or will to act in aid of the transition between agrarian Egypt, enslaved to one-crop agriculture and the grip of the past, and industrial Egypt, oriented toward modernization, efficiency and power within the Arab world. The largest of these parties, the Wafd, had fallen into the hands of the big landed proprietors, while its left wing, which understood the needs of the economic and social evolution, was dangerously linked to the Communists. The Liberal-Constitutional party, which was the party of the large landowners, remained true to itself, in spite of the fact that it was now led by one of the most brilliant of modernist Egyptian writers, Dr. Mohammed Hussein Heykal, instead of that great feudalist, Mohammed Mahmud Pasha. The Saadist party itself, although linked to industrial capital and bound to execute its policies, lacked the necessary trained men to make the breach.

The industrial bourgeoisie would try to find a political expression for itself. Certainly the Saadist party was still its favorite. But it was necessary to regroup the forces which, for one reason or another, hesitated to join it. Just after the Second World War, Ali Maher had founded the Gabhat Misr (the Egyptian Front), which he hoped would become the brain of the Independent group. At the same time—which, let us not forget, was that of the reinforcement of the national front and the Communist ascendancy—Dr. Ahmed Hussein, sometime ambassador in Washington, created Gam'iyyat al-Fellah (the Peasant Organization), which hoped, with a program aimed against the excesses of rural inequalities, to lure the small and medium landowners tempted by the Wafd. This was the time when the Misr al-Fatat party became the "Socialist party" in order to profit by the allegiance of a large part of the intelligentsia to Marxism and by the obvious sympathy for the Soviet Union. The Moslem Brotherhood, while continuing to work for its own aims, made rewarding alliances with big capital and set up a whole series of companies, especially in commerce and finance.

From the Philosophy of History . . .

This was also the period when the industrial bourgeoisie would try for the first time to equip itself with the elements of a coherent ideology. In 1938 Mirrit Butros-Ghali published his programatic work, *The Policy of Tomorrow,* which commingled the realism of business circles with generous ideas of reformism; in 1939 Mahmud Kamel published the first edition of *Tomorrow's Egypt,* in which reformism turned for support, this time to the pledge of national socialism and the ideas of European fascism. But in 1950 there appeared a philosophic interpretation of the whole Egyptian history by a talented economist, Dr. Sobhi Wahida, at that time secretary-general of the EFI. It was entitled *On the Bases of the Egyptian Question.*

After an analysis of the impact of the Arab conquest on an

Egypt that had remained pharaonic, and then of the disastrous effects of the Turkish conquest, he presented the Egyptian renascence, which began early in the nineteenth century, as the basic work of the nation under its own leaders, who undertook to integrate the contribution of Europe into the old Egyptian stock. The "European tide" proved to be both fertilizing and a stimulus to "symptoms of puberty," among the very foremost of which must be recognized the disorganization of the European-educated Egyptian intelligentsia. Since the intellectuals knew little of the history of their own people, they were unable in fact to become the agent and symbol of that necessary resurrection of the national heritage, enriched by the contributions of the technical civilization of middle-class Europe. The result was a multiplicity of "inferiority complexes" that were the prelude to capitulation, to renunciation of selfhood.

From one end of Egyptian society to the other, confusion reigned everywhere, and the spectacle offered by daily life was that of a contradictory chaos on all levels. Whereas the people was not yet in a position to act, it was "the Egyptian governing class that had the means of action, above all time and money." To increase efficiency, to modernize, though in harmony with the profound nature of the nation, was therefore to be the government's task. Above all, the governing class should block the economic hemorrhage caused by the Mamelukes.[59] Dr. Wahida's whole study, nourished on a solid historical foundation, amounted to an effective argument for the primacy of economics, of economic action, in political and intellectual life. Hailed by his chiefs, the leaders of Egyptian industrial capital—Ismail Sidky, Abdel Kawi Ahmed, Tewfik Doss, Hassan Nash'at, among others—the author seemed to be the first theoretician of Egypt's history and her future, a philosopher of history, and, to boot, an economist of talent and a technocrat by vocation.

After the Palestine war the situation became daily more confused. The Wafd, as we have seen, returned to power. But the bloody clash between the Saadist party and the Moslem

Brotherhood in 1948–49 and the division of the industrial wing of the upper bourgeoisie had no counterpart except in the Communist party. The two groups—the big industrialists and the Communists—both champions of a radical modernization of Egypt, though with basically different conceptions of the future, demonstrated their inability to act in time: the industrialists because they did not yet possess the instruments of action indispensable to the elimination of the hegemony of the landed upper bourgeoisie, the Communists because of their internal divisions, their weakness in the countryside among the peasants, the repeated persecutions of which they were the target, the burden of their ally, the Wafdist mass, which could not drastically alter the character of its political leadership, and, above all, the Palace's exploitation of the burning of Cairo.

. . . . to the Army Movement

One force was still in the field, its mass proudly deployed and surrounded by respect and popular sympathy, which regarded it as Faruk's victim, while its spearhead was hidden in clandestinity: the army. The Egyptian army of 1952 was no longer the army of 1882. The high command was still under the king's control. But the Wafd and especially its War Minister, Hamdi Seif el-Nasr, were ceaselessly busy in the creation of a national army; in 1936, on the pretext of the military obligations imposed on Egypt by the Anglo-Egyptian agreement, Mustafa el-Nahas took the opportunity to open the doors of the Military Academy to young cadets from the middle classes, whereas the earlier regulations had made the academy the fief of the sons of the wealthy.

The young leaders who received their second-lieutenants' insignia from 1938 to 1940 were all deeply imbued with nationalist ideas. For the most part Wafdists, or members of the Moslem Brotherhood and thus faithfully reflecting the tendencies that divided the Egyptian middle class, they included a minority that was drawn to Marxism; some were to be disciples of Ahmed Hussein and would try to lend the force of their arms to General Aziz el-Masry, the Chief of Staff who was removed by the British for his collusion with the Axis in 1942. In every heart the hatred of the occupant was twinned with the determination to do everything for the rebirth of Egypt.

What was striking in this group of young leaders, from which the Free Officers would soon be recruited, was the fact that they remained in complete harmony with Egyptian social reality. Recruited by their training to the ideal of the efficacity of the industrial society, ideologically they remained, especially in matters of politics and religion, within the orbit of the doctrines that expressed the thinking of the landed section of the Egyptian middle class: the Wafd and, in part, the Moslem Brotherhood. Whence the general character of their demands, the lack of a program, the poverty of doctrine that would mark Egypt ten years later. They were alone, however, in enjoying a credit that was still new in public opinion. The scandal of the sale of defective weapons, cleverly exploited by Ehsan Abdel Koddus, editor in chief of *Rose el-Yussef*, Egypt's leading weekly, and by Ahmed Abul Fath in *al-Misri*, was to make them the victims of a conspiracy that aimed, through them, at the whole Arab movement of national liberation. This conspiracy was compounded by the king, his advisers, the arms traders, the military high command loafing in the villas of Abbassia; moreover, it seemed to be more widespread, and its presumed leaders—Premier Ibrahim Abdel Hadi of Egypt, Premier Riad el-Solh of Lebanon and King Abdallah of Jordan—fell to the avenging bullets of the young nationalists.

After having taken part in the national revolutionary movement of 1935–36, most of them had endeavored to act against the British troops during the Second World War, chiefly at the time of Rommel's drive, and then, after having participated in the political agitation of 1945–47 and suffered the defeat of Palestine, they served as instructors toward the end of 1950 for the guerrilla warfare against the Canal base.

But in any event their action was of secondary importance. Military service had hardly allowed them the leisure to share in the redirection of the national movement between 1936 and 1952. At no time did they provide its theoreticians, its political staff or its militants. The efforts and sacrifices that made for progress in the liberation and in the democratization of the country received from the Free Officers no more than marginal help, which was practically negligible and of which the people as a whole knew virtually nothing.

There was one force that the young officers could utilize for the benefit of their reputation, the only force that had emerged morally intact from the chaos of the Palestine war and the burning of Cairo: the army. The king still believed that he could make it the tool of the Palace with impunity. He intended to force the dubious General Hussein Sirry Amer on the leadership of the Officers' Club while making him the commander of the infantry. And the king's brother-in-law, Colonel Ismail Sherin, was to be made Minister of War and the Navy, regardless of the counsels of prudence lavished time and again on the king by Mortada el-Maraghi, the government's head of police and security in 1950–51.

At dawn on July 23, 1952—three o'clock in the morning— the leadership core of the Free Officers, seven men, occupied the army's General Headquarters at Abbassia. The high command was arrested and the seizure of power was over. Three days later King Faruk had to abdicate and left Egypt forever.[60]

Was this revolution?

The Social Character of the Military Regime

To analyze a nut is to crack it.
—HEGEL, *Science of Logic*

THREE MAJOR STAGES have thus far marked the road of the Egyptian military regime. It is the general custom to regard them from a political standpoint, as can be seen from a review of the works on Egypt that have appeared since 1952. Very soon, however, such an approach to the problem turns toward the psychological, toward the portrait gallery, and seen through these lenses, the event becomes colored by them, even causally.

Already from the outset of the coup d'état, fundamental realities imposed their presence and their rhythm. What I shall seek to bring out is the basic constituent elements, the substructure, so to speak, that would determine even the situation of the problem—the social character of the military regime in Egypt—and the solution that was proposed for it here.

In the beginning there was neither a detailed program for, nor a theoretical vision of, the future Egypt. But Egyptian society, roweled to the core by the imperative need to become modernized, to become effective and active—in sum, to industrialize itself in independence—was to give meaning and coherence to endeavors marked with the seal of an empiricism tainted always with suspicion and occasionally even with adventurism.

"The chief factor that brought on the revolution," Nasser was to say later in his preface to M. M. Ata's book *Misr bayna thawratayn,* "lay in the need to increase our living space in the face of the growth of the population, which could be counted in millions in the past years and which afflicted the productive apparatus with a paralysis that was virtually total, thus presenting serious dangers for the country . . ."

Three stages—the land problem, industrial development and, finally, the destitution of the old bourgeoisie—were the preludes to the inauguration of the new leadership.

CHAPTER 1

THE LAND PROBLEM

MOST CERTAINLY there is the problem of key dates. The burning of Cairo was one in relation to the army's coup d'état. The uprising at Kafr el-Dawwar on August 13, 1952, was one in relation to the promulgation of Law No. 178 on September 9, 1952, relating to land reform.[1]

Let us remember these two dates. It is not unprofitable to go back to the history of the agrarian question in Egypt. Then everything becomes clearer—the status of the fellah and the power of the landed aristocracy—and then one can understand the need to prevent by reforming while there is still time.

Many investigators have tackled the history of the agrarian question in Egypt, notably Yacub Artin, Révillont, M. Saleh, Mohammed Kamel Mursy, J. Anhury, Sadek Saad, G. Baer. But it is to Ibrahim Amer that we owe the first complete study, at once clarifying and creative, of the history of the agrarian question—embracing simultaneously the system of landed property, its exploitation, rural social structures and the peasant movement—in his book *Al-ard wa'l-fellah, al-mas'ala al-zira'iyya fi Misr*.[2] We shall follow his analysis here in its essentials.

Brief Sketch of the Agrarian Question

We know that the ancient Pharaoh was one with the deity, or with the gods, at least until the end of the Old

Kingdom. A highly centralized bureaucratic government assured him of political and ideological control of the nation; his
domination of the water system—the digging of irrigation
canals, the construction of dikes against floods, the regulation
of the level of the Nile—made him the absolute master of
everyday life. This was because "irrigation and drainage work
absorbed a large part of the labor force that was not actually
employed in agriculture . . . It was not possible to carry out
this *hydraulic* task in an effective manner on the local level
alone; that is why the central government was always concerned to assure the administrative and political unity of the
country in order to bring its great irrigation projects to a successful conclusion while at the same time it exercised a real
positive power and controlled a substantial labor force . . .
So, then, as a god and as the actual master of the sources of
irrigation and of labor, the Pharaoh was the sole owner of the
land of Egypt."[3]

As the sole owner the Pharaoh was progressively led to surround himself with agents, if not with allies. These were
ministers, administrators of districts and priests, who were
joined by "servitors of souls" and then by "servitors of the
gods"—as many functionaries as the properties that the
Pharaoh made available for religious services or for burial
grounds. Little by little the central government found itself
stripped of part of its monopoly, in proportion to the steady
rise in the quantity of land turned over to the functionaries,
the temples and the beneficiaries of all kinds of *wakfs* before
that word even existed: the eclipse of the Old Kingdom was
at hand. Toward the end of the Sixth Dynasty in the twenty-
first century B.C., the district governors were also, as a rule, the
high priests of the major temples—that is, the principal tenants
of the Pharaoh's land. The struggle against the Hyksos invaders in the eighteenth century B.C. and the conquests of the
Ramses' made it necessary to establish an army of mercenaries,
whose chiefs also received lands. This is perhaps the source of
the statement that under Ramses II, there was a three-way
division of land between the king, the priests and the warriors.[4]
A first manifestation of private ownership of land occurred
under the Middle Kingdom, but it seems certain that it was of

short duration, for the triumph of the Theban dynasty restored the Pharaoh's monopoly of landed property.[5]

"Under the Lagides,* more than under the other dynasties," wrote Mohammed Kamel Mursy, former rector of Cairo University, "the king seems to have been the leading owner of most of the land of Egypt."[6] The conquest of Egypt by the Arabs in the seventh century A.D. made hardly any change in the structure of landownership. "Property in Egypt," Yacub Artin tells us, "was set up on very different bases from those in the other countries conquered by the arms of Islam . . . No land was distributed to the Mussulmans who had helped in the conquest; no parcels were taken away in order to form the one-fifth that was part of the plunder belonging to the Caliph under the law. On the contrary, the conquerors, having confiscated the lands belonging to the Greeks who were killed during the war, or exiled and dispossessed after the capture of Alexandria, redistributed them among the existing communes and then shared them out among the Christian Egyptians, who would work them." Then, having cited the accounts of Ibn Abdel Hakim and Al-Siyuti describing the procedure for the distribution of taxes, the author concludes: "It becomes quite clear that property as we understand it did not exist in Egypt, and we see that from the very beginning of the conquest, the inhabitant of the country, the Egyptian, the cultivator, did not really own the soil, which belonged to the commune and, by extension, to the sovereign, which means to the state."[7] And the state meant the *beit el-mal*, the Ministry of Finance. The institution of *wakf*, which was private and religious, took root in Egypt and acquired more and more marked importance, which it was to retain until 1954.

It is necessary to modify this description. In fact, while the state was indeed the sole owner of land in Egypt—both under the Pharaohs and after the Arab invasion in the seventh century A.D.—it did not exclude the practice of a kind of life tenancy, which took three main forms.

The first was the land allotted for exploitation to the clergy and the religious institutions in return for their support. Later there appeared the allocation of land to military chiefs and

*The Lagid (or Macedonian) dynasty, 332 B.C. to 30 B.C.

lords of whose services the royal house wanted to be assured
during periods of external expansion or internal disturbance.
Finally there was the land allotted to some wealthy farmers
in exchange for fiscal obligations and payments in money and
in kind, which were officially and strictly defined; this last
form appeared toward the end of the pharaonic era and at the
beginning of the Middle Ages, at the time when the state was
in pressing need of money and when agriculture could obviously be further developed only at the price of a certain
autonomy on the part of the peasants, a certain "interest" in
the land that they were working without rights of any kind.

On two occasions, under the Middle Kingdom and under
the Mamelukes, the life tenants, particularly the military chiefs
and the clergy, exceeded the limits and even went as far as
to bequeath their land or give it to a third party. But the
central power lost no time in regaining the upper hand, and
the majority of the peasants knew nothing of landownership
well into the seventeenth and eighteenth centuries.[8]

If such was the case, to what extent is it possible to speak of
"feudalism" in Egypt?

When he had disposed of the arguments based on religious
inspiration—the centralization of land and of power having
been as characteristic of the Egypt of the Pharaohs as it was
of the Egypt of Islam—Ibrahim Amer forcefully restated the
thesis advanced earlier: "The form taken by landownership
in Egypt differed from that of Europe. In the first case it was
a matter of state property, whereas in the second, it was a
question of private property. The principal reason for this
difference lies in the difference in the irrigation system of
Egypt and Europe: artificial irrigation in the first case, but
natural irrigation, based on rainfall or on limited irrigation
projects, in the second."[9] And he cites his sources: Adam
Smith, Richard Jones, John Stuart Mill, and then Karl Marx in
his letter of June 2, 1853, to Friedrich Engels: "Bernier is
right in ascribing the basic form of all the phenomena of the
Orient—he speaks of Turkey, Persia and Hindustan—to the
fact that there is no private ownership of land. There is the
real key even to the sky of the Orient." Engels replied on June
6 in these terms: "How is it that the Orientals never attained

to private ownership of land, even in feudal form? In my opinion, the major reason is the climate, in combination with soil conditions, especially the vast desert areas . . . There artificial irrigation is the first condition of agriculture, and this is the business of the communes, the provinces or the central government. In the Orient the government always has only three departments: finance (looting at home), war (looting at home and abroad) and public works (which is concerned with reproduction . . .)"[10]

Two factors, however, threatened to change this picture: one was the Mamelukes and the other was the system of *iltizam* (literally: obligation).

On "Oriental Feudalism"

The Mamelukes can be compared to the feudal lords of the Occident only by distortion and in a purely formal fashion. In fact, the system of artificial irrigation in Egypt has always required the presence of a strong, unified central power which needs major agents, officials and administrators more than it needs local governors. This explains why, whenever the Mamelukes attempted an uprising, they turned quite naturally and immediately toward the central authority in Cairo, as was the case at the time of the revolt of Ali bey el-Kebir in 1769. From the Pharaohs to our own time, Egypt has always constituted a single entity, a single national unit.

The case of the *multazimin,* the upper tax collectors, is illustrative. These powerful officials, put into office by the central authority when it was weak, were supposed to pay for their posts by remitting each year the total sum of taxes due from their clearly defined territories. Hence they had to collect this sum by all available means, imposing great burdens on the peasants in order to end the year with a profit. It is true that the post of a *multazim* gradually became hereditary through the bestowal of many gifts on the central authority. But that authority alone remained the master of the land, and it alone could confer the privilege of *iltizam,* which it could also revoke by way of reprisal.

Hence it is not a feudal system of the European type with

which we are dealing here, but rather with an "Oriental" feudalism.

"The system of landownership and the social system that was superimposed on it in Egypt before Mohammed Ali . . . were those of an 'Oriental feudalism' the bases of which, in contrast to those of European feudalism, were the absence of private property [in land] and the centralism of the state's power in the domain of agriculture. There were, however, certain points of resemblance to European feudalism: namely, the system of tribute and that of a natural economy in rural areas."[11]

Bonaparte's French expedition (1798–1801) and then the accession of Mohammed Ali, as we have seen, struck grievous blows against "Oriental feudalism." In fact, the law of September 16, 1798, inaugurated land prices, recognized the peasant's right to inherit and regulated the recording of landownership.

In 1809 Mohammed Ali abolished the *iltizam* system. In 1811 he massacred the Mamelukes in the Citadel. Between 1813 and 1818 he established a registry of land titles and distributed the communes' land among the peasants and certain categories of functionaries. The two million *feddans*—that was the cultivated area of Egypt at that time—were distributed as follows:

(a) *ab'adiyyat* (land exempt from registration) and *tshiflik*,* or *gafalik* (farms), bestowed by Mohammed Ali on members of his family and his court, on military chiefs and high officials, amounting in all to 200,000 *feddans*, exempt from taxes; "it was the pasha's intention," Artin says, "to create a hereditary landed aristocracy";[12]

(b) *awsiya*, or 100,000 *feddans* given to the former *multazimin* by way of compensation;

(c) *masmu'h al-mashayekh* or *masmu'h al-mastaba*, land given to the village sheiks, amounting to 154,000 *feddans;*

(d) *al-rizka*, tax-exempt land turned over to foreign functionaries, amounting to 6,000 *feddans;*

(e) *el-'erban*, land bordering on villages and given to the Bedouins.[13]

---

* Turkish word, meaning large estate donated by the ruler to his dignitaries.

M. H. Eleish and Rashed el-Barawi offer an analytical description that is slightly different from Ibrahim Amer's. According to them, in fact, the land was distributed at that time in this fashion:

(a) *al-kharajiyya*, land given in life tenancy to the peasants, in parcels of three to five *feddans;* the statute of 1846 was intended to allow the life tenant to transfer his rights to a third person, thus making the land *gharuka* (the drowned land);

(b) *awsiya*, especially in Lower Egypt, the *multazimin* arranging in fact to preserve the enjoyment of these lands to their descendants by means of the *wakf;*

(c) *al-rizka*, land exempt from taxes but not liable to being turned into *wakf;*

(d) *ab'adiyyat wa gafalik*, land which, in 1842, Mohammed Ali allowed to be fully owned in order to make the large proprietors directly interested in the advancement of agriculture;

(e) *masmu'h al-mashayekh* or *masmu'h al-mastaba*, also tax-exempt.[14]

The major difference between this system and that of the "Oriental feudalism" of the Arab and the Turkish periods is this: before Mohammed Ali, the state monopolized the land under the dual aspect of ownership and exploitation, whereas Mohammed Ali preserved only the ownership aspect, leaving the task of exploitation to individuals under his vigilant and cruel supervision.[15] That is why it is possible to accept Ibrahim Amer's conclusions, according to which "the system of agricultural exploitation in Mohammed Ali's time was a temporary system of transition between feudalism and capitalism."[16]

The trend toward the establishment of private property in land was never again to be halted. The abolition of monopoly, forced on Mohammed Ali by the European powers in 1940, led to the law of 1846 that recognized a limited form of ownership and permitted mortgaging and conveyance to a third party. In 1858 his son, Said Pasha, promulgated a general regulation that instituted private property: the right to lease land for three years, to mortgage it, to sell the rights of use to a third party and to bequeath title. The reign of Ismail

(1863-79) brought rapid introduction and intensification of the cultivation of cotton in order to supply the English mills cut off from their supplies of raw materials by the American Civil War.[17] In 1871 a law allowed the conveyance of title to land against the lump-sum payment of six years' taxes in advance. Then, after the British occupation in 1882, private ownership of tax-exempt land was legalized (1883), as it was for cultivated land (1891), and finally tribute was abolished except when it would benefit all (1893).[18]

The private ownership of land gave birth to the Egyptian bourgeoisie, the evolution of which is traced from various points of view at a number of places in this book.

The Social Classes in the Rural Areas

What picture was presented by the rural social forces? What was the composition of the landholding wing of the Egyptian bourgeoisie, which, in concert with the occupant, was to dominate Egyptian life from 1882 to 1952?

Some recent statistics will make it possible for us first of all to gain a general view of the distribution of landed property between 1894 and 1952:

	SMALL HOLDINGS (fewer than five feddans)		MEDIUM HOLDINGS (five to fifty feddans)		LARGE HOLDINGS (more than fifty feddans)	
YEAR	% of owners	% of land	% of owners	% of land	% of owners	% of land
1894	83.3	21.7	15.4	34.3	1.3	44
1914	91.3	26.7	8.5	30.4	.8	43.9
1930	93.1	31.6	6.3	29.7	.6	38.7
1952	94.3	35.4	5.2	30.4	.5	34.2

But within the first group—the small proprietors owning fewer than five *feddans*—two subgroups must be distinguished: that of the peasants owning fewer than two *feddans* and therefore incapable of assuring their own subsistence, and that of the small holder properly so called, who had two to five *feddans* and could meet the material needs of existence. The first group numbered 2,308,901 peasants sharing

1,230,062 *feddans:* 84 percent of the landowners (owners, not peasants) held 21 percent of the land.

At the other extreme, in the group of large owners, the sub-group of the landed aristocracy must be clearly distinguished: 280 owners held 583,400 *feddans:* thus .01 percent of the owners held 10 percent of the land.[19]

Let us go back to the comparative table above: While the proportion of large landed proprietors has dropped to one third of what it was fifty years ago, the land that they own has remained more or less at the same level (with due regard to the fact that cultivated land has risen from 4,000,000 *feddans* at the end of the nineteenth century to almost 6,000,000 in 1952). At the same time, the proportion of medium proprietors has fallen to almost one third of what it was fifty years ago, without any corresponding reduction in their actual holdings; it is probable even that these holdings have grown by reason of the expansion in areas under cultivation. Finally, the proportion of small owners has risen substantially, but without any great increase in the land that they own. "In the case of the small holders," Ibrahim Amer says again, "let us note that 70 percent of them—that is, 2,000,000 people— own less than half a *feddan* each, so that they are virtually destitute. Almost 8,000,000 peasants own no land at all; their only means of existence is either to rent scraps of land and pay for them in kind or to find salaried work on big farms, such as maintenance jobs on canals, water courses, etc."[20]

Let us take a closer look.

The landed upper bourgeoisie (more than fifty *feddans*), often better referred to as the "landed aristocracy" but also most inaccurately called "feudalists," was itself divided into two groups, according to the method of exploiting the large holdings.

The first group—the largest owners—was composed of those magnates who managed their property by leasing it to third parties, or *compradores.*[21] Before 1952 such a lease was made in either of the two following ways: a lease to one person, who in turn subleased small parcels of one to five *feddans* to working small holders; or a lease made through a succession of intermediaries in such a way as to enforce the best price. The tendency to lease became widespread after the Second World War, rising from 1.73 percent of the land in 1939 to 60.7 percent in 1949 and then to 75 percent in 1952. In fact, the average yield per *feddan* was £E17 in 1947–48, while the average rental was £E40! The result, of course, was a skyrocketing of rentals—472 in 1950–51, based on an index of 100 for 1938–39—and of land prices, the *feddan* rising to £E800, although its real value was in the neighborhood of £E200. There was a host of supplementary means of exploiting the peasant: multiple taxes and tolls, a rise in rentals to match the rise in the price of cotton, short-buying of crops at prices below those of the market, the sale of fertilizer, the rental of machinery, and usurious loans to the peasants.[22]

The most important nucleus of this group was made up of Faruk and the royal family: 159,000 *feddans* of the best land for the family as a whole, and an annual income of £E750,000 derived from the king's holdings.

Another important element of this group was the state itself: more specifically, the department of state properties. This department held title to all fallow land, as well as large areas leased to individuals. Under this category, in fact, the state cleared a profit of £E824,264 in 1949–50, while the distribution of state land that had been reclaimed—182,623 *feddans* between 1935 and 1950—was accomplished to the profit of the large owners, who received 90.7 percent of it, the medium owners getting 7.6 percent and the small holders only 1.7 percent. Thus it is easy to see the extent to which, before 1952, the state was one of landed aristocracy.

The second group was that of the rich cultivators. This was the minority fraction of large landed proprietors who themselves worked their land, either in order to produce raw materials for sale to processing industries, notably in cotton, or to sell consumer goods to both the domestic and world markets.[23]

Having constituted the backbone of the Islamic reform party, Al Umma (1907–14), and then of the Liberal-Constitutional party from its foundation in 1923, these two groups enhanced their representation and indeed their grip within the Wafd, on which little by little they impressed a conservative attitude, especially under the influence of Fuad Serag Eddine.

The medium landowners (five to fifty *feddans*) were composed of men who, having enough land for their needs, worked it themselves with the help of a small number of farm hands.

Here again it is possible to distinguish two groups. First of all there was an upper level (owning twenty to fifty *feddans*) of relatively comfortable proprietors, whose ideal consisted in working their way into the class of the large owners and who were for that very reason deeply conservative (they provided the Moslem Brotherhood with cadres, hiding places and money). Then there was a lower level (five to twenty *feddans*), whose situation was one of constant deterioration. The whole of this subgroup was an integral part of the national, liberal and democratic middle class that found its expression in the Wafd. It was within this group that the intellectuals of independent Egypt were born—Taha Hussein, Abbas el-Akkad, Ahmed Amin, Ibrahim Abdel Kader el-Mazni, Dr. Mohammed Hussein Heykal, Salama Mussa, Ahmed Hassan el-Zayat, Ali Mustafa Musharrafa, Hussein Fawzi, Tewfik el-Hakim, and so many others—as well as the political leaders of the Wafdist movement. Many were to turn to socialism.[24]

Below this class there was the rural lower middle class, composed of small holders of one to five *feddans* and of poor peasants who worked their own bits of land, occasionally even subleasing a parcel on which they worked in order to supplement their scanty incomes. The principal concern here was the rental rate for land, and this innumerable class wanted that rate made to correspond to the income from land. The market for farm products governed these men's very lives, since only a rise would make it possible for them to exist on even a minimal level.

This group traditionally constituted the left wing of the Wafd in the countryside, and it provided many points of support for the Communists. Certain elements, exacerbated by suffering and imbued with religious ideology, joined the extreme-right movements (especially the Moslem Brotherhood, the variably named party of Ahmed Hussein, and later the National Union and the Arab Socialist Union).

Thus far, let us not forget, we have been dealing with owners. Now, the majority of the Egyptian peasants had no land at all. How many were they? Eight million, according to Ibrahim Amer; ten to fourteen million, according to the calculations of the IEDES.[25] In 1947 they outnumbered the labor needs of agriculture by 47 percent, and it seems probable that only one third of them were actually employed in farm work, at subsistence wages of 8 to 15 piasters per day. A silent, exploited mass, surrounded by hunger, disease and death—but also, and especially after 1945, a mass stirred into life by the flow and ebb, often daily and always weekly or seasonal, of those among them who went off to the cities and there became factory workers or students. New ideas came from the cities. A phrase, a slogan: *"Al-ard li man yafla'huha!* (Land to those who work it!)"* Land meant—who could tell?—the end of the endless wait to die. The peasants were going to rise . . . but let us not anticipate.

Under the Thumb of the Banks

To complete the picture there should be some mention of the part played by the banks in rural areas. In fact, the one-crop cultivation of cotton, introduced under Ismail and then becoming one of the chief characteristics of the imperialist exploitation of Egypt by the English under Cromer, stimulated the creation of a whole banking and mortgage system which, hand in hand with the tax department, reaped an annual harvest from the Egyptians farmers.

The Egyptian Land Bank was founded in 1880 with French capital. In 1905 the English set up the Land Bank of Egypt, which came to the support of the predominantly English interests in the Agricultural Bank of Egypt, established in 1902 by the National Bank of Egypt and liquidated in 1936. In consequence of the disastrous effects of the world depression of 1929–30, the Wafd decided in 1930 to create the Banque du Crédit Agricole d'Egypte in order to provide help for the small and medium landowners; but under the pressure of the prominent families, the Wafd had to step down and Ismail Sidky, who succeeded to power, promulgated the law of 1931: the minimum holding for every prospective borrower was raised from fifty to 200 *feddans*, so that only the large proprietors could get help from this bank. In 1949 it became the Crédit Agricole et Hypothécaire d'Egypte, and the loan procedures were eased.

Throughout this period the grip of these banking groups on Egyptian land, mostly in the hands of French and English financiers, was colossal. In 1907, for instance, the value of the cultivated acreage was £E120 million, while mortgages amounted to £E60 million! A considerable amount of Egyptian land thus fell into exploitation by the credit banks instead of by the owners.[26]

The Egyptian peasant's struggle for the land of Egypt has not yet found its chronicler. A great mass of paternalistic prejudices about the passivity of the fellah—the good, the poor, the unhappy Egyptian fellah—has made him the subject of pitying or exotic studies. Folklore has taken the place of politics, and history is made to fit the dimensions of social economics. Since 1945 there have been a few attempts to reconstruct the history of the peasant movement, notably in the works of the Marxist historical school (Sadek Saad, Shohdi Attia el-Shafei, Fawzi Guergues and Ibrahim Amer in particular, as well as Ahmed Rushdi Saleh).[27] These are its principal stages:

The Struggle for the Land

Throughout the nineteenth century there were three objectives: the legalization of the right to private ownership of land; the struggle to free the peasant from the obligation of unpaid labor; and the rationalization of the fiscal system by making it uniform. Toward the end of the nineteenth century there was an awakening of national consciousness of the peasants. The Egyptian officers' movement, led by Colonel Ahmed Arabi in 1881–82, was a profound expression of the small and medium owner's resentment of the European powers' financial grip on the Khedive, and therefore it attracted the spontaneous and enthusiastic participation of the peasants in the revolution and in the armed resistance against the landing of the British forces in 1882, especially in the northern Delta region.[28]

At the beginning of the twentieth century, Mohammed Farid, who had succeeded Mustafa Kamel as head of the National party in 1908, became the spokesman of the rich landowners and championed their aspiration to be the major political force against the Anglo-French banks even as he supported the desire of the small and medium holders to be protected against the disastrous effects of the farm-credit policy. Whence the National party's program: a reduction in land taxes, the creation of "agricultural unions"—this meant corporations, not trade unions—to defend the farmers against the government and the big proprietors, the defense of subtenants against usurers, and, under the influence of Omar Lutfi, the creation of agricultural co-operatives (1912).

After the First World War, the Egyptian revolution of 1919 under the leadership of the Wafd headed by Saad Zaghlul represented two phenomena: on the one hand, the drastic crisis among the medium and poor classes of the peasantry because of the increases in taxation during the war, and on the other, the consolidation of the commercial middle class of the cities and its aspirations to sovereignty over the market and the national state. The revolution lasted from 1919 to 1921 and sporadically thereafter until 1923. The peasants took part in it massively, most often under their own leaders: they sabotaged railroads, made armed attacks on British troops and police, destroyed storehouses, and also occupied land and proclaimed independent republics in many *mudiriehs* (provinces) of Upper and Lower Egypt. A few years later the peasants came to be in the vanguard of the popular struggle against the dictatorship of Ahmed Ziwer (1925) and especially of Ismail Sidky (1930–35).

The principal demands of the Wafd's program in the field of agriculture were: the organization of the poor peasants into unions, and the establishment of relations with trade unions and international labor organizations; the abolition of the *ezbeh* system, whose similarity to feudal exploitations was striking; the forgiveness of debts for peasants owning fewer than thirty *feddans;* total tax exemption for peasants with fewer than ten *feddans;* the imposition of special taxes for irrigation on owners of more than 100 *feddans;* and the establishment of co-operative banks for the small proprietors. But until the end of the Second World War there was no mention of agrarian reform within the Wafd.

We know the upheavals that the Second World War produced within the economy and society of Egypt. The considerable reinforcement of the industrial group, the Egyptian upper bourgeoisie, the influence of the Chinese revolution, and above all the growth of the Communist movement in the cities and after 1945 in the countryside, were all factors that would force the agrarian question to the top of the list of domestic problems, which themselves were subordinated to the struggle for independence and the evacuation of the national territory.

As early as 1944 Mustafa el-Nahas, once again Premier, admitted in the Chamber of Deputies that "the most serious defect, the fault that is responsible for the poverty of the majority of our people, is the great number of large estates." In the same year Senator Mohammed Khattab, under the influence of the initial studies made at that time by Marxist groups,[29] proposed in the Senate the first project for the limitation of landownership. The ceiling, originally set at fifty *feddans,* was raised by the Senate's Social Affairs Committee to 100 *feddans,* which Khattab accepted; but the Senate as a whole defeated the plan on June 16, 1947.

In 1945–46 the National Committee of Workers and Students gave agrarian reform first priority in internal reforms and adopted the slogan *"Al-ard li man yafla'huha!"* It set a peasant rising as the first condition of success for the national revolution, and it sought to extend its influence into rural areas.

The first Marxist theoretical work, *Mushkelat al-Fellah,* by Sadek Saad, a highly trained engineer, appeared in the spring of 1945. "The problems of food supplies, the rise in prices and the other internal difficulties created by the war have made people aware of the flaws in our social structure and forced them to think about the remedies: not just this or that superficial stopgap step but, rather, basic reforms." The author called for the promulgation of "laws that would prevent individuals and companies from owning in future more than fifty *feddans* of arable land. In this fashion there will be a reserve of land that will be divided equally among the landless peasants and the farm workers, who include two million poor peasants . . . The poor workers have more right than anyone else to the land that they work with their hands"; whence the necessity of confiscating, without compensation, all holdings in excess of fifty *feddans*. At the same time, it would be useful to encourage the creation of agricultural co-operatives, or collective farms, in the rural areas.[30]

In this same period the Workers' Committee of National Liberation, a political and trade union organization of the working class, prepared a program demanding a limitation of 200 *feddans* on landed property if the fifty-*feddan* figure proved unworkable, the abolition of the private *wakf*, the creation of farm co-operatives, and the improvement of the peasants' living and cultural standards. The two labor federations already mentioned—the Congress of Egyptian Trade Unions and the Preparatory Committee for the Congress of Egyptian Trade Unions—presented similar programs in 1945–46.

In order to justify to the Senate the repressions unleashed on July 11, 1946, Ismail Sidky quoted the Egyptian progressive press, which he had just dissolved, and especially this sentence: "The unjust distribution of the national wealth makes a new division of land imperative: it should be allotted to the peasants in the form of small parcels; this measure should be accompanied by the establishment of a co-operative system."[31]

In 1945 Mirrit Butros-Ghali, on behalf of Gamaat al-Nahda al-Kawmiyya (The Association for National Renaissance), proposed a twenty-five-year program of agrarian reform: it

called for a ban on new acquisition of land by the large owners, noninterference with the fragmentation of the large estates through inheritance, establishment of a three-*feddan*
minimum for the division of arable land and, finally, redistribution among the poor fellahin of the holdings of the *wakf*,
through the department of estates and its agencies. What
attracted more attention than the concrete proposals in this
program was its warnings: "Social sickness is gradually
spreading through the countryside . . . If this movement is
neglected at all, it is full of dangers . . . Reform will be accomplished with them [the large proprietors] or against them;
it would be preferable for everyone if it were carried out with
their consent and better still with their co-operation . . . In
a time of revolution," the author continues, "agrarian reform is
concentrated on the compulsory elimination of large estates
and sometimes of their owners; in Egypt in the present circumstances it should be carried out by a wise and provident
government that wishes to profit from a period of relative
calm to accomplish a comprehensive reform . . . Political
opinion is turning resolutely toward the Left: a general desire
for renewal, for social progress, is becoming more and more
strongly manifest . . . but its dominant direction has not yet
clearly appeared."[32]

In 1949 Rashed el-Barawi, who then held the chair of economic history in the Faculty of Business Administration at
Cairo University, completed a project for the modification
of the system of landownership with a view to encouraging
small and medium holdings. This was also the period when
Dr. Ahmed Hussein created Gam'iyyat al-Fellah and made
himself the champion of plans that "might aid in the multiplication of small family holdings, the regularization of relations between landlords and tenants and the establishment
of a minimum wage for farm workers."

In the same year, during the electoral campaign, seventy-
two Independent candidates for the Chamber of Deputies,
grouped around the ideas of Mohammed Khattab, Mirrit
Butros-Ghali, the Peasant Organization and also the powerful Egyptian Federation of Industries, issued a joint program
demanding the limitation of landed property and higher taxes

on large holdings "in order to compel the rich landed proprietors to redirect their investments toward industry."

In the new Chamber of Deputies, which convened in 1950,
the only Socialist deputy, Ibrahim Shukry, called for the limitation of holdings to fifty *feddans,* while Ali el-Shishini and
Mirrit Butros-Ghali went up to 100 *feddans;* the former also
wanted to allow sixty more *feddans* for a wife and thirty more
for each child, the whole to be accompanied by progressive
taxation and the regulation of rentals.

On behalf of Ahmed Hussein's Socialist party, the magazine *al-Ishtirakiyya* launched a campaign against the great
feudalists.

Among the Moslem Brothers themselves Sayed Kotb, the
representative of radicalism, clearly saw the necessity of preventing a revolution by the peasants. Mohammed Khattab, he
wrote, "thinks as a conscious capitalist. In effect, he recognizes
that the structure of landownership has to be modified in
order to prevent the storms that are gathering on the horizon . . ."[33]

The State Department versus Chinese Influence

From overseas, contradictory influences were converging on Egypt.

The socialist countries, above all China, offered the example
of a radical reform in landownership. Now, everyone was
aware how closely the problems that had arisen in Egypt
resembled those which had existed in China, where the national peasant revolution was especially powerful.

Contradictory influences came from the United States. As
early as November 1950, Gordon Gray stated the basic American policy with respect to the Middle East: "It is clear that
the urgent economic problem in the Middle East is the agrarian problem . . . It is essential to extend and improve irrigation, to reclaim the idle land, to modernize agricultural techniques and to take reasonable steps to reform the landownership and insurance systems in the countryside."

In the same year the UN, at the suggestion of the United
States, advised the underdeveloped countries to initiate agrar-

ian reform, implying thus that this was a condition *sine qua non* of any industrialization as well as of any rise in the living standard of the population.

In March 1951 an advisory committee appointed by the President of the United States formulated the following recommendations: "Agrarian reform must be supported in the underdeveloped countries in order to guarantee landownership. In certain countries it would be impossible to combat hunger and socialism except through land reform . . ."

Finally, in February 1952—just after the burning of Cairo, be it noted—the State Department published a brochure entitled *Land Reform, A World Challenge,* in which it called for a change in the systems of landownership and leasing, emphasizing the importance of these measures in the fight against Communism.[34]

Later, in the voluminous work that he devoted to the Agrarian Reform, Sayed Marei, who, as Minister, had long directed its operations, took cognizance of these converging influences: "The broadened acceptance of socialist principles in the world," he wrote, "has led many countries to adopt agrarian reform";[35] naturally he did not directly mention the American influence, but he showed the bond between the landed aristocracy and imperialism, quoting the well-known remark by Allenby: "The English can evacuate Egypt with an easy mind: in effect they have created a class of large landowners on whom Great Britain can rely to assure her policy in Egypt."

A Peasant Communism?

On what did the American experts base their counsels of preventive reform? On clear-cut facts, for once: in the last years of the war, crime in rural areas had skyrocketed as the external manifestation of the peasants' hatred of the owners;[36] between 1949 and 1951, peasant risings on the large estates multiplied, especially at Kufur Negm and Bahut. The peasants attacked the private guards and even the police barracks with modern weaponry, setting fire to offices and demanding the land that they worked. One after another—Badraui Ashur Pasha, Prince Yussef Kamal, Crown Prince Mohammed

Ali, Fuad Serag Eddine Pasha, Abdel Latif Talaat Pasha, the high chamberlain—saw their estates become the battlefields of insurrection in which, occasionally, the peasants resorted to arms. And this occurred even on the royal estates. This was the period when, reflecting on the setbacks of the NCWS in the years 1945–46, the Left—under the influence of Shohdi Attia el-Shafei—had shown its determination to penetrate the rural areas and rally the peasants. And in fact, around the big industrial centers—particularly Mahalla el-Kubra, Shubra el-Kheima, Kafr el-Dawwar, and Shargiya, east of the Suez Canal—the networks grew, finding support among schoolteachers, seasonal laborers, minor office workers. On the one hand, between the ultramodern factories, where trade unions and Communist organizations represented an appreciable force, as well as the cities filled with "united front" committees, and, on the other, the *ezbehs* of the pashas, the *dairas* (large estates) of the princes, and the estates of the king and the land holding companies, there was an increasingly frequent coming and going. The "peasant sectors" of the Marxist organizations of the years 1944–48 were now fully entrenched, endowed with professional staffs, with committees uniting the local student, the nationalist schoolteacher, the fellah, the farm worker and poor peasant to whom land seemed a question of life and death.

Blood Flows at Kafr el-Dawwar

It was altogether natural that the Free Officers' coup d'état and the overthrow of King Faruk should have inflamed hearts and exalted imaginations. In the rural areas there was already talk of agrarian reform. Revolutionary echoes came from the big workers' centers. Political confusion was at its height, and some people went as far as to wish for a *real* popular revolution.[37] At Kafr el-Dawwar, the site of the Anglo-Egyptian factories of the Beyda Dyers Company (most of the capital was English, and all of it was managed by Ahmed Abbud), the union decided to strike. Its leaders, Mustafa Khamis and Mohammed Hassan el-Bakary, addressed the crowd, in which the workers and peasants of the area were fraternizing. They spoke of a new era, of the end of injustice, of oppression. This was August 13. On the same day the army surrounded the factory, dispersed the demonstrators and set up a military tribunal that tried the two labor leaders on the spot and sentenced them to death. They were hanged high the next day.[38]

From the outset the army's action smashed by terror the first attempt at popular revolution that emanated from a popular leadership and was capable, despite the confusion of its objectives and the weakness of its basic staff, of turning into a peasant insurrection of stature.

It was these days of Kafr el-Dawwar that gave rise to the concern with diligent action. The main purpose remained the reorientation of capital toward industry; but that August 13 showed all the magnitude of the danger and established the tactics.

The Agrarian Reform Law

Less than a month after Kafr el-Dawwar, Law No. 178 of September 9, 1952, initiated the land reform. Despite the gaudy rhetoric of Wing Commander Gamal Salem, it was the leftist members of the Revolutionary Command Council and of the Free Officers' organization, notably Major Khaled Mohieddine and Colonel Yussef Saddik, who finally established its various provisos, assisted by a talented young lawyer and personal friend of President Gamal Abdel Nasser, Ahmed Fuad.

Ali Maher, who was still Premier, attempted to oppose the reform. He suggested a ceiling of 500 *feddans*. The large proprietors adduced constitutional and religious reasons for their opposition. The reform, they said, violated the Constitution of 1923, which was still in force, and by attacking the very principle of private property, it violated the precepts of Islam. They suggested that the law be replaced by the establishment of progressive taxation. The RCC rejected this whole line of argument, "because this method does not get to the root of the political vices that are usually the result of the concentration of great areas of land in the hands of a small number of owners.[39] Let us remember this reasoning: *what was primarily at issue here was a political problem, that of the state power exercised by the landed aristocracy, whose privileges the army intended to reduce for the benefit of the industrial wing.* Ali Maher resigned, and General Mohammed Naguib succeeded him.

What was the substance of the Agrarian Reform of 1952?[40]

(a) The ceiling of landownership was fixed at 200 *feddans* per person. In practice the majority of these owners would have 300 *feddans,* since the law allowed a father of two or more children to retain an additional 100 *feddans.*

(b) Exemption from this limitation was granted to companies owning more than 200 *feddans,* on the ground that they were reclaiming fallow or waste land; to individuals in the same category; to industrial companies that needed more than 200 *feddans* of land for their production; to scientific agricultural companies and charitable organizations; and to owners burdened with debts, under special conditions defined by the law.

(c) Every owner affected by the law would be indemnified in negotiable government bonds for the land taken from him; the price per *feddan* was fixed at ten times its rental value, which itself was seven times the land tax; in addition the owner would be compensated for the value of the trees and buildings, whether permanent or other, on his land. The bonds given to these owners would bear an annual interest of 3 percent for thirty years; they could be used for the payment of taxes, the purchase of waste land, etc.

(d) The expropriated land would be distributed by the state to the peasants within five years, although the owners could sell their land directly to the peasants insofar as the tracts did not fall within the law. The ceiling on sales to peasants was set at five *feddans.* Land allotted to the peasant by the state would be paid for by him over thirty years at 3 percent interest per year, plus an additional charge of 15 percent of the total value of the land under the pretext of payment of the costs of seizure and reconveyance. Finally, every beneficiary of the reform must be an Egyptian of legal age who had never been convicted of any offense bearing on matters of honor; he must be a farmer, a tenant or a worker on the land distributed, or a resident of the village in question.

(e) At the same time the law undertook to establish the relations between the owners and tenants of land. The rental value of the *feddan* was seven times the land tax or else half its crop, if the lease was made on the sharecropping system; gardens, flower plots, etc., were exempt from the system. Finally, no one could rent land unless he was going to work it himself, and no lease could have a shorter term than three years.

(f) A committee especially appointed by the minister (three members representing landowners and tenants, three representatives of the farm workers, one high official as president) would be charged with fixing wages for farm workers in the various regions, from year to year.

(g) Agricultural co-operatives would be established for small holders (owning up to five *feddans*). Their function would be to arrange for farm loans, supplies or fertilizer, livestock, seed, farm machinery, silos and means of transport, and to organize the rotation of crops and to market the harvests. These co-operatives would later have to be grouped in general co-operative associations and co-operative unions under the control of the Ministry of Labor and Social Affairs.

(h) Farm workers would be allowed to form unions for the protection of their common interests.

From Internal Contradictions to Stalemate

What were the results?

In 1962 the state claimed to have redistributed some 645,642 *feddans*, out of a total of 5,964,000 under cultivation at that date, to 226,000 families—in other words, 10 percent of the land to 2,000,000 peasants—which justified Pierre Fromont's observation: "Agrarian reform was a political gesture of sympathy; it was deeply appreciated, but it must be admitted that its practical effect was negligible."[41]

The moderate character of this reform was equally to be seen in the matter of the indemnification of the large landowners. In fact, according to the official admission, "there existed [before 1952] a real inflation of the price of the *feddan,* which had reached £E800, whereas its true value was approximately £E280, so that the rental value of land, which should have been £E28, was pushed up to £E60 . . . Thus more than £E500 million had been plowed unproductively into land between 1923 and 1952 . . ."[42] According to Doreen Warriner's calculations, the majority of the large proprietors had thus amortized the price of their land in fourteen years, and their indemnification under these conditions constituted a real gesture of political appeasement of the powerful of the old system by the state and a solemn rejection of the very principle of revolutionary expropriation.[43]

But what of the new small holder? An investigating team from the newspaper *al-Missa,* under the leadership of Ali el-Shalakani, an economist, was able to ascertain after a long series of studies in the field that the peasant was obliged to pay almost £E50 per year for each *feddan* received from the state: £E14.45 to pay the annual installment on the loan, £E12.065 to help pay for irrigation facilities, etc., £E10 for farm supplies, £E10 to pay off earlier loans in most cases, and other minor charges.[44] Variant calculations led the semi-official *al-Gumhuriyya,* investigating in the village of Beltag, to conclude that the various disbursements incurred by a peasant owning three *feddans* amounted to more than £E125 per year, whereas his income was only £E115.[45]

At the same time, and as if to emphasize the continuity of Egyptian history, the state as the owner of what was called "agrarian-reform land"—that is, acreage not yet distributed to the peasants—drew a profit of £E2,754,800 from it in 1955, thus taking the place of the rich proprietors in exploiting the poor peasants and the farm workers.[46] Very swiftly the government invested substantial sums in order to be able to play its part as owner-manager. Whereas the original idea was that of self-financing, the management of the Agrarian Reform demanded, and got, £E100,000 in December 1952; under the terms of Law No. 131 of 1953, the Agrarian Reform Agency (later Ministry) acquired a legal entity and financial autonomy, was entitled to select an expert staff without the red tape of governmental bureaucracy and had available a capital of

£E82,000,000, so that in practice it had been made the biggest landed proprietor in Egypt.[47]

Since the basic idea was to let the peasant get a share, the end result was a considerable increase in the proportion of small holders living on the verge of starvation: the proportion of those who owned fewer than five *feddans* rose from 35.5 percent before the Agrarian Reform to 49.3 percent. And in February 1951 the government *Yearbook* quoted with approval the ideas of the American Department of Agriculture: "A little piece of land and a few favorable circumstances have more influence than great armies on world peace. This is something that grows inside a man's mind . . . . something that it becomes difficult to uproot and destroy."[48] Yet, as we have seen, an ancestral tradition existed that made the commune the unit of property and rural exploitation in Egypt until the time of Mohammed Ali. There was no need to imitate China. It was enough to look back into history, without losing sight of the new experiments of our own time.

It must be added that if the redistribution of land was carried out for the benefit of the small holders and the tenants, the poor peasants and the farm workers got nothing. In addition, the regulation for land rentals remained a dead letter in the majority of cases. The peasant had to stand up against not only the chicaneries of the large landowner, who always found a way of making a profit, but also the bureaucratic mind and the indifference of the administrators of the reform, concerned only with getting ahead in the service and, often, with getting rich. The Agrarian Reform was conceived and carried out from above in order to block any revolutionary effort by the peasants.

Nevertheless, the provisions relating to land rentals did progressively reduce the owners' incomes, since the rich proprietors were no longer, as they had been before, the sole arbiters of the price level. To a certain extent, and prematurely, it was the same limitation on capital growth that was going to strike at the industrial, commercial and banking sector in 1961. Those among the big landowners who clung to the land would thereafter take the trouble to manage it themselves, and little by little to give up absentee ownership. Their social weight in the rural areas no longer crushed the group of medium owners (five to fifty *feddans*)—the Egyptian kulaks—which the government was determined to consolidate and which it was to surround with an ever-larger class of small proprietors.

It may be asked whether the peasant's living standard was improved. It is difficult to say so, before 1961–63, when the more systematic "organization of agriculture" was initiated. In fact, the surplus of farm workers rose from 42 percent in 1947 to 47 percent in 1954, and this must inevitably have cut down their earning power. The large proprietors had fewer estates to exploit, while the new properties born of the Agrarian Reform hardly needed hired hands, the small owners doing all the work themselves and being only too happy that they could be sure of their meager subsistence.

Dr. Mohammed Dowidar offers a more accurate analysis of this phenomenon: "In order to cultivate the land directly instead of leasing it to poor peasant families, the large landowners had to turn to hired workers. Now, it was the family form of the unit of production that made possible the existence of a labor surplus in the productive cell. In proportion to the growth of this change in the social form of the unit of production, the labor surplus is evidenced by workers offering the sale of their services on the market. The result is an increase in the number of hired farm workers. To this extent the question is no longer one of disguised but of unconcealed unemployment." And he draws the pertinent conclusion: "The availability of a relatively cheap labor force on the market paves the way for an agriculture of tenant farmers."[49]

The farm workers' trade unions, though permitted under the law, were virtually nonexistent. In December 1956 the Ministry of Social Affairs bemoaned the low state of union consciousness in the rural areas as a result of the "feudal influence,"[50] while former Minister Sayed Marei hardly mentions it in his book on agrarian reform. Certainly there did exist, until 1958, a Federation of Farm Workers' Unions in Cairo, with some five thousand members; but hardly anything is known of its activity. The dissolution of the industrial unions and their replacement by one single union in 1958–59 finally reduced to nothing the slender hopes aroused in this area by the law of 1952.

First Reorganization of 1958

These serious defects were noted in the press, especially in *al-Missa,* during the years 1956–58. The government took note of them and therefore, in September 1958, it promulgated a law modifying that of 1952, as follows:

(a) The price of land distributed to new owners would henceforth be payable over forty years instead of thirty.

(b) The annual interest rate of 3 percent for thirty years was reduced to 1.5 percent for forty years.

(c) Charges for expropriation and redistribution were reduced from 15 to 10 percent.

On the whole these reductions were estimated to amount to £E5 per *feddan* annually, according to the calculations of Ali el-Shalakani.[51] It will be conceded that this does not amount to much.

In July 1961 the government made a new and important change in the Agrarian Reform Law within the general framework of the so-called "socialist" legislation and with due regard both for the imperative needs of the economy as a whole and for the need of further neutralizing the old class of large landed proprietors, which began stirring again after the collapse of the Syrian-Egyptian union.

By the end of the ten-year economic-development plan, the objective of which was to double the national income between 1960 and 1970, the program set for the agricultural sector envisaged an increase of one third in the acreage under cultivation—that is, rise of 2,000,000 *feddans* (8,000,000 *feddans* in 1970 against 6,000,000 in 1960). The stubborn disaffection of the former large landowners, excluded more and more from public life and anything but eager to play at pioneering, the absolute necessity of integrating the peasant mass into the framework of the military system, and also the concern, while at the same time increasing their number, with organizing the small holders into a general plan of co-operation in the rural areas, accompanied by the general tendency of the gov-

ernment to toughen its fight against the former middle class
(the laws of the summer and autumn of 1961) and to subjugate
the whole of economic life to the state's plan and to the great
public agencies—all these were factors that impelled the government to correct the law, as it did by means of the Order in
Council of July 25, 1961.

These were its major provisions:

(a) The ceiling on private ownership of land was reduced
from 200 to 100 *feddans* (Article 1).

(b) The 100 *feddans* included waste and fallow land and no
longer only land actually under cultivation (Article 1).

(c) Landowners as well as members of their families were
forbidden to manage an area of more than fifty *feddans* under
the guise of lease, tenure in perpetuity, etc.; but this area must
be reduced by that of the land held in ownership; in fact, only
the small holders could rent, and this was the most important
provision (Article 7).

(d) Exchange value for expropriated land would be made
to the previous owners in the form of registered (nonnegoti-
able) fifteen-year treasury bonds bearing interest at 4 percent
(Article 5).[52]

Immediately after the promulgation of this law, the land
area in the hands of the Ministry of Agrarian Reform amounted
to 1,120,648 *feddans,* divided as follows: 478,000 *feddans* from
the excess seized from the large owners; 500,000 *feddans* with-
drawn after the change in the law of September 1958; 104,311
feddans from the *wakf;* 10,058 *feddans* of alluvial land; 13,860
feddans belonging to the Egyptian-American agency; 6,000 *feddans* belonging to corporations; finally, 4,100 *feddans* belonging to the Ministry of Agriculture. At this time the Ministry
of Agrarian Reform proceeded to distribute exactly 430,852
feddans among 162,773 families of small holders.[53] Accused of
corruption, Sayed Marei was removed[54] and replaced by
Major Abdel Mohsen Abul Nur as Minister of Agrarian Reform
and Land Reclamation, on October 19, 1961. With this appointment the military government meant to signal the end of
the civilian predominance that had previously marked the
management of this agency, born directly of the coup d'état
of July 1952. In November 1961 the new minister adopted a

series of measures revising the law and intended to ease substantially the burdens imposed on new landowners, notably by exempting them from the 10 percent charge levied under the law for administrative costs.[55]

What Is Meant by "Co-operation"?

The Agrarian Reform gave considerable impetus to co-operatives in the rural areas of Egypt. It is important to emphasize here the vital part played by the co-operatives on the agrarian-reform land, which served as a proving ground before the movement was broadened to regions in which small holdings predominated.

At the end of 1956 there were 272 co-operatives, newly established after the law of 1952, with a total membership of 82,326 peasants and a capital of £E777,573. A year later there were 400 co-operative societies with 200,000 peasants, who held a total of 500,000 *feddans.* And yet these figures seem to exceed reality. Mahmud Fawzi, director of co-operatives in the Ministry of Agrarian Reform, gave the following figures for September 1958: 272 co-operatives, which provided their members with services valued at £E5 million and sold 308,720 *kantars** of cotton.[56] In 1961–62, the agrarian-reform land was divided into forty-three regions that directed the work of 364 co-operative societies with a capital of £E654,563. These societies provided their members with services worth £E5 million, especially in the matter of cotton sales.[57]

Despite the lack of precision in the figures, it certainly appears that until the disastrous harvest of 1961, the selling price of a *kantar* of cotton was £E2 higher than on the local market as a result of the economies effected by the consolidation of the harvest, which, it was said, gave the growers a surplus of £E300,000. According to the authorities, the average income per grower rose from £E9.8 per year in 1952 to £E32.7 in 1954, once the small holders had been combined in co-operatives. An example that is often cited is that of the model co-operative of Zaafaran: 1,973 members owned 4,948 *feddans;* £E165,544 in services was furnished in 1954, of which

* 1 *kantar*=99 lbs.

£E28,366 was net profit; the average income per *feddan* rose from £E32 in 1953 to £E39.5 in 1954.[58]

The experiment in land reform appears to have borne some fruit. Thus the government planned to distribute reclaimed lands in parcels of ten *feddans*;[59] interest charges would be reduced to 1 percent per year for forty years. The general tendency, as we have seen, was toward the combination of small holdings: these remained the property of their individual small owners, but the whole was combined by regions and a single management determined the rotation of crops, the use of machinery, sales, etc.[60]

It must be very clearly noted, however, that the "co-operation" that is meant here is a co-operation in credit and in the commercialization of agricultural products. There exists no form, no intention, no institution, no policy for a co-operation in the ownership of the land.

The structure and nature of agricultural production remains fundamentally and wholly capitalist.

Neutralizing Autonomous Social Revolution

What is the deeper significance of this land reform? To what extent did it attain its objectives?

The general crisis of Egyptian society after the Second World War, as the sources that we have quoted attest, required a general reconversion. But this must be understood: there was no question of reconversion from capitalism of the colonial type to socialism, but only of a transition from this backward colonial type of capitalism, predominantly agrarian, to a modern, predominantly industrial capitalism, a transition which, as we shall see, must of necessity come to take a state-directed form when it is undertaken by a colonized, and therefore underdeveloped, country.

It is against this background that the Agrarian Reform of 1952 should be viewed. This was a first attempt at functioning as a whole. In order to turn Egyptian society into a modern entity, capable of resolving the terrible problems of underdevelopment and of an increasing population, there was a condition precedent: the compulsion of the landed bourgeoisie, which possessed most of the country's riches, to redirect its investments into the modern, or industrial, sector. Since it was a question of compulsion, it was essential also to undermine the rural social bases of this class, those on which it grounded its political apparatus, and to provide the new form of political organization with a solid social foundation in the rural areas. In the process, the most rigorous vigilance was required lest this reconversion, this transition from the predominance of the agrarian wing to that of the industrial wing, degenerate into a social revolution—that is, in the situation in which Egypt then was, inflamed by the burning of Cairo, into a revolution of the socialist type.

The controlling agencies of big Egyptian industrial and banking capital were hardly disappointed. The National Bank of Egypt greeted the reform in these terms: "Egypt can congratulate herself on the fact that after so many deceptive promises and empty words, the matter has been carried out by a regular government that attacked it within the framework of the law, without leaving the initiative to the masses with the risk of violence and disorder. If the question is viewed from this angle, then any reform whatever, no matter how radical, is preferable to the anarchy of a mass movement."[61] On its own account, in its report for 1952, the EFI congratulated itself on the prospects for the future: "The land reform could be one of the finest pledges of the future for our industry, since the expansion of cultivated areas and the prosperity of the rural economy can accelerate the expansion of industry . . . The land reform should provide a stimulus to a strong movement of capital capable of strengthening the investments in land and industry to the advantage of the landowners, whether old or new."[62] The United States ambassador, Jefferson Caffery, did not conceal his satisfaction.

But wrath ran high within the landed aristocracy, accustomed until then to be in complete control. Sayed Marei spoke of sabotage at several dozen irrigation pumps and of some landowners' refusal to supply their peasants with fertilizer, seed and cash advances for their working expenses; many proprietors appealed to the Council of State to nullify the law as a violation of the Constitution.[63] A son of the prominent

Lamlum family resorted to force in order to prevent the execution of the law, and the government had him arrested, tried with much display and sentenced to hard labor. That was all, at least for the moment.

The Big Landowners Mark Time

But the economic defeat was obvious. In 1955, for instance, of £E45 million taken out of the land, only £E6 million was invested in industry. And the rest? "The mushroom growth of luxury apartment houses could be halted only by legislation (Law No. 344 of 1956). Since 1949, investments in construction have totaled £E15–20 million per year, almost all of them concentrated in Cairo and Alexandria. In 1956, investments in this sector reached 47.3 percent of the total of all investments, and 75.8 percent of all private investments."[64]

What had happened?

Once their first fear was over, the big landed proprietors had understood the profound character of the land reform, especially its desire to avoid a peasant revolution under the Communist slogan "Al-ard li man yafla'huha!" They recognized that the RCC and the state born on July 23 girded them with protection and were solicitous to afford them attractive compensations, following the letter of the law. They saw the Free Officers order the summary execution of Khamis and Bakary three weeks after the expulsion of the king. They attentively observed the very close friendly relations between Jefferson Caffery and the military leaders from 1952 to 1954, and they recognized the true significance of the campaign of arrests and persecutions directed against Communists and progressives from the moment of the seizure of power, the climactic points of which were the years 1954–56 and 1959–64. They understood that there was never any question of permitting any peasant insurrection whatever, or any revolutionary action by the Left. Then, reassured, they came legitimately to suppose that they would be able to pursue their old kind of life in peace and quiet—apartment houses, luxury goods and export of capital—for the golden age of the great estates of yesterday had returned . . .

Identical results were observed in the realm of agricultural production. In fact, the government's distrust with respect to action by the peasant masses and to any popular action was such that it induced the authorities responsible for the enforcement of land reform to practice a policy of fragmenting the land. They allowed the small holdings—of three *feddans,* for the most part—to multiply, though they were barely profitable economically, and this was done under American influence out of concern to do nothing that might resemble, whether to a great or minuscule degree, socialist methods in the rural areas.[65] The result was a temporary decline in agricultural production, a slight drop in the living standard of the poor peasants, and a crisis in land reform. How the government reacted has been shown: it encouraged the co-operatives and then the regrouping of small holdings on the basis of crop rotation and exploitation—that is, a general and growing tendency to focus attention on the collective, social aspects of agriculture while still preserving the private character of landownership.

In reality, the distribution of income among the various social classes of Egyptian rural areas was not basically different in 1958 from what it had been in 1952. Here is the picture of it for 1958, given by Y. Durelle:

I. Income from land of absentee owners and income of the large proprietors working their land (in millions of £E) 75

II. Income of the rural population 325

divided as follows:

	POPULA-TION (thousands)	%	TOTAL INCOME (£E in millions)	PER CAPITA INCOME (£E)
1. *The masses:*				
(a) "landless" peasants	14,000	73	50	3.5
(b) Poor peasants	1,075	6	7	6.1
2. *Medium peasants*	2,850	15	76	26.8
3. *Upper class:*				
(a) "rich" peasants	875	5	76	87.4
(b) rural capitalists	150	1	116	773.3
TOTAL	18,950	100	325	917.1

Durelle analyzes this table as follows:

"(1) The very high density of the rural population . . . 73 percent of the peasants are without land . . .

"(2) The massive extension of the system of direct exploitation,[66] relying on paid labor, and the parallel shrinkage of the traditional system of renting out small parcels . . .

"(3) The steady decline in the intermediate classes . . . which constituted the greatest part of the peasantry a century ago and now represent no more than 15 percent of the rural population . . .

"(4) The continuation of the same techniques of production making use of capital only within very narrow limits . . .

"(5) The polarization of agricultural wealth . . . the old ruling class, which the new government has stripped of its political monopoly, has preserved a privileged economic position in spite of agrarian reform . . ."[67]

On this last point, it should be observed that the law of July 25, 1961, was to make a marked reduction in the margin of economic power of the former landed aristocracy.

Political Elimination of the Landed Aristocracy

In contrast, the dual political objective seems to have been reached, essentially, by 1954.

The landed aristocracy no longer dominated political life: the old political parties were first restricted and then dissolved.

The Moslem Brotherhood alone remained in the field; the Communist organizations were constrained to clandestinity; the Constitution of 1923 was abolished; the former middle class, backed by the Moslem Brotherhood and supported with reservations by the Communists, was defeated in its attempt to concentrate power in the hands of General Mohammed Naguib and to isolate Gamal Abdel Nasser in the spring of 1954.

The tightening of the military dictatorship, followed by the creation of the Republic of Egypt in 1954, the promulgation of the Constitution of 1956 and the election of Gamal Abdel Nasser as President of the Republic, marked the end of the landed aristocracy's power.

As far as the second political objective was concerned—the elimination of the danger of a popular revolution—all that can be said at this stage of our study is that the threat had been temporarily averted. The struggle was to be resumed in unforeseen forms during the two succeeding stages.

In Face of the Rise of Man

The human problems of Egypt in this second half of the twentieth century were growing in acuteness. This was because "from 1915 to 1950 the population had increased by 64 percent, while agricultural production had risen by only 30 percent. In addition, the amount of cultivated land per inhabitant had fallen from .5 acre in 1907 to . . . 0.28 in 1953."[68] It was forecast that after the completion of the Aswan High Dam project, "total agricultural income in 1975 might be slightly more than 50 percent above the level of 1953, while the population would have grown by 61 percent."[69] In short, it was essential to prevent any deterioration in the existing living standard of the peasant, which was inevitable if necessary steps were not taken.

The reclamation of uncultivated land was accelerated; the program, which encompassed 375,000 *feddans* for four years in January 1960, rose in March of that year to 485,000 *feddans* for five years. And the ten-year plan proposed to provide 2,000,000 *feddans* of new land for cultivation. At the same time when, thanks to the massive help of the Soviet Union, the first excavation for the High Dam was under way, German experts were studying the project for the exploitation of the Qattara Depression. Ibrahim Amer suggested revisions in the Agrarian Reform: a ceiling fixed at fifty *feddans*, drastic reductions in the costs to new owners, etc. A classical economist, Gabriel Saab, contended that "the complete mechanization of Egyptian agriculture may become the keystone of the future development of Egypt, for it would open unsuspected perspectives that would make it possible for her to envisage other solutions for her problems than those that would be applicable to China or India." The problem, of course, was to banish the specter of collectivization. But immediately afterward came this: "Mechanization creates a new class in the social scale: the tractor drivers, who, having been well trained and indoctrinated, can become the most effective agents of agricultural progress."[70]

But the fundamental facts of the Egyptian problem could not be got around so easily. The census of October 1960 showed a population of more than 26,000,000. Before 1990 it would be 53,000,000.[71] Land reclamation was still limited by the desert belt that covered nine tenths of the national territory.

So everything had to be concentrated on industrialization.

So the Egypt of yesterday, crippled by her ailments, became "feudal Egypt," *Misr al-ikta'iyya.*

An Erroneous Concept: "Feudal" Egypt

What was there to be said?

For some the question was one of simple semantic confusion resulting from the word *ikta*, which means, literally, a large but clearly defined area and, consequently, a large estate, on the one hand, but also, on the other, feudalism, whence *al-nizam al-ikta'i*, the feudal system; whereas the existence of large landed properties in itself is hardly that, since it can be part of either a barter economy with production relationships of a feudal type or a market economy with capitalist production relationships (especially the paid peasant labor).

Nevertheless, in the period between 1940 and 1952 some sections of the Egyptian political movement had adopted as their own the description of Egypt as a "feudal" country, without taking into account the economic facts.

And this was true above all, of a section of the Left—the Egyptian Movement of National Liberation, which, after the fusion of 1947, became the dominant political force of the Democratic Movement of National Liberation until 1948, a section that developed its beliefs sporadically in the weekly *al-Gamahir* (1947–48). In the minds of some leaders, this thesis served to establish the fact that the Left in the Arab countries was obligated to support the creation of the state of Israel, which was capitalist and middle-class, and therefore one social stage ahead of the Arab nations, the most advanced of which was defined as a "feudal" state. This tendency quickly became the view of a minority. It has entirely disappeared today—as a thesis—not only in the program of the Egyptian Marxist movement but also in the press and in studies emanating from the progressive Left from 1956 to 1958—that is, the three years known as the time of the Bandung policy,* during which the Egyptian Left was able to express itself and to attract a very broad audience for its theses since 1955. The word "feudal" retains a certain emotional value for agitation and is still used currently to that end.

The other and much more important section was the major newspapers, especially the *Akhbar el-Yom* group, the spokesman for the Saadist party and the Independents—in other words, for the industrial faction of big capital. This section was joined by the rest of the press very soon after July 23, 1952 (except for Khaled Mohieddine's *al-Missa*, from October 1956 to March 1959), as well as by the radio and the book publishers (except for the works of Ibrahim Amer and Fawzi Guergues), etc.

The question for the new regime was one of appearing as the creator of modern Egypt, which it did by ignoring the work accomplished by the landed bourgeoisie since Mohammed Ali and especially that of the Wafd, and at the same time concealing its own class character; thus the army movement assumed the guise of an innovator in the absolute, *ex nihilo,* and hence impossible to reduce to a class analysis.

An Egypt was disappearing—a whole past—"feudal" Egypt. Another Egypt was emerging, thanks to the "sacred movement" —"modern" Egypt. Between the one and the other there was no capitalism at all, no capitalist exploitation in the present, for all exploitation was of the past, that "feudal" past so rightly despised by all.[72]

* First gathering, in April 1955, of the Asian and African national movements, initiated by China and India; it created the Afro-Asian Peoples' Solidarity Movement, whose secretariat was installed in Cairo.

2

THE ARMY AND
THE INDUSTRIAL
REVOLUTION

Now THAT THEY were the masters of power, how did the Free Officers propose to move in order to give body to that modern Egypt of which they wished to be the creators?

There is a whole history to be written, the history of the dialogue between the army and the bourgeoisie, a dialogue that was carried on in several stages by the leadership core of the Free Officers, the Revolutionary Command Council (RCC) and the various sections of the Egyptian bourgeoisie from the time of Kafr el-Dawwar to the nationalization of the Bank Misr, from the solicitation of foreign capital to the seizure of foreign holdings after Suez, from the Agrarian Reform to the "socialist" legislation of 1961 and 1963.

Even in an earlier period, as we have seen, the landed wing of the bourgeoisie refused to be reconverted, to invest in industry for its own profit. It reinforced itself in its apartment buildings, its bank accounts, its exports of capital, its *pasha* style of living.

The period that began with the coup d'état of July 23, 1952, was to continue approximately until the Suez crisis of July–October 1956. It was a period of search, of groping. At the heart of everything was the economic problem, even though at that time it still wore a political cloak because the national territory had not yet been evacuated.

All in all, it was a question of encouraging capital, Egyptian and foreign, to knock down the barriers that blocked the road to industrialization, to modernity, to power.

The state governed by the military turned to the counsel of experts of the Egyptian Federation of Industries, in which Hafez Afifi, formerly chairman of the executive committee of the Bank Misr and principal private secretary to the king, had just been succeeded as president on May 22, 1953, by Abdel Rahman Hamada, president of the Misr Spinning & Weaving Company of Mahalla el-Kubra.[1]

Foreign Capital Welcome

Now, the Federation had always and incessantly called for an invitation to foreign capital, thus very accurately reflecting the position of the industrial upper middle class.

The report of the Industry Subcommittee (appointed in 1943 by the EFI) was written by A. J. Dorra. "Favorable circumstances," he said, "will have to be exploited in order, under the best possible conditions, to endow nascent Egyptian industry with the physical equipment, the financial means and the expert personnel that will be the essential bases of its development and its progress . . ." And, immediately afterward: "From certain points of view it will be recognized that Egypt's own means alone, though often sufficient, will not always be proportionate to the possibilities, and in order not to diminish them, there must be no hesitation in asking the great industrial nations for their collaboration."[2]

That was one of the first measures which the new government was going to take. In fact, on the advice of Dr. Abdel Gelil el-Emary, the Minister of Finance, and Dr. Ahmed Hussein, ambassador to Washington, an Order in Council appeared in the *Official Gazette* of July 30, 1952—one week after the coup d'état—in modification of Law No. 138 of 1947 dealing with corporations: the mandatory proportion of Egyptian capital was reduced from 51 to 49 percent. And the ownership of the 49 percent could now include "legal parties," which meant corporations already in existence, a large—if not a majority—part of whose shares was held by foreigners. Only those sectors of the economy bearing on the national interest—especially the security apparatus and the armed forces—might eventually be reserved for companies having a higher percentage of Egyptians.[3]

The EFI hailed the junta's initiative: "This law seems to want to put an end—once and for all, we hope—to that absolutely unjustified fear of foreign capital, a distrust that has haunted our whole financial policy in recent years and contributed to the backwardness of our economic edevolpment."[4] The EFI *Yearbook* for 1953–54 stated the official doctrine in the matter: "We need an extraordinary rise in investments in order to fill the gap from which we have suffered in this area in the past years. Our savings, which, in general, are not adequate to meet the current needs of the country, cannot fulfill the two obligations at the same time. Therefore we called for the encouragement of private investments of foreign origin to the greatest possible extent, and the authorities have finally vindicated us."[5]

Now, quite to the contrary, the facts show that foreign capital, far from setting as its objective the development of the Egyptian national economy, proposed in fact to reap a regular harvest from it, since Egypt, "the cotton plantation of Lancashire," was a fine field for other handsome profits as well. On this point there is a wealth of detailed evidence. Thus, after having pointed out that "the Revolutionary government now in power is exerting great efforts to overcome the persistent hostility to foreign investments," Dr. Riad Ghoneimy's study tells us why: "The main objective of these foreign financial institutions has been to drain off Egyptian deposits in order to invest them abroad rather than in Egypt. Aside from mortgages on land, the major investments of foreign banks have been directed toward sectors that provided high returns, without utilizing the idle resources [of the country], such as the construction of buildings, public services like streetcars and drinking water, and light industry. The greater part of the profits has been exported abroad."[6]

This makes it easier to understand both the highly thankless effort of the government in this field and the reception that it got from foreign governments, led by the United States. The awakening was to be brutal.

"The first months of the military government were marked by an unusual restraint in the field of foreign relations," Tom Little wrote, "and several efforts were made to amend the laws that discouraged foreign companies in Egypt. Thus the corporation law stipulating that 51 percent of the capital of these companies must be Egyptian, was changed in order to allow foreigners to retain control of them . . . The mining law was revised in such a way as to make it acceptable, if not satisfactory, to the oil companies . . ."[7] The government also hoped, through its moderation, to be able to obtain the foreign capital required for its industrialization program—£E500 million, it was said. On the suggestion of Ahmed Fuad, the Permanent Council for the Development of National Production was set up on October 3, 1952, and Dr. Emary persuaded Great Britain to release, grudgingly, meager slices of the blocked "sterling debts." But "from the time of the nationalization of the Suez Canal Company, foreign capital held back. Only oil exploration attracted big capital. It was not a new phenomenon that Western capital did not trust the government of the colonels . . . Foreign enterprises almost always raised two objections to offers to come into Egypt. The first was based on the 1947 labor law, which required foreign companies to employ 90 percent Egyptian workers who would receive 80 percent of the total salaries. The second objection concerned government interference in private companies . . ."[8]

At the same time the RCC went into action on the political level. "We are making every effort to carry out reform, to purge the army and to safeguard the Constitution"—such was the language used by General Mohammed Naguib as commander in chief of the army, in his proclamation of July 24, 1952. But rumors were everywhere: the army was preparing to dissolve the political parties and impose its dictatorship on the country. At once, that very evening, the General Staff addressed the nation: "The General Staff flatly and solemnly promises the people that it will tolerate no obstacle on the road to the establishment of a sound constitutional system. An agreement has been reached with the head of the government [Ali Maher] for the holding of general elections in February, in order that the government have all the time necessary for the purging of its ranks, a step that is essential for any real parliamentary system of government within the framework of the Constitution . . ."[9]

The End of the Parties

We know what ensued: Kafr el-Dawwar, which brought about Ali Maher's resignation.[10] General Naguib became Premier on September 7, 1952. The negotiations between the RCC and the Wafd were only a delaying maneuver; in reality, the Free Officers hardly intended to return even the smallest fraction of their power to the hands of Mustafa el-Nahas, whose public standing remained high and whom *al-Misri* stubbornly defended step by step. The law on the reorganization of parties appeared on September 8, 1952;[11] it was intended to provide a pretext for their dissolution, which could not be delayed. Mustafa el-Nahas agreed to give up the presidency of the Wafd, which he had assumed after the death of Saad Zaghlul; he was to be honorary president. Fifteen parties published their programs and bylaws, as well as the names of their executive committees, as the new law required: the Wafd, the Liberal-Constitutional party, the Kutla party, the Saadist party, the National party, the Socialist party, the Labor party, the Moslem Brotherhood, the Peasant party, the National Feminist party, the Daughters of the Nile, the Socialist Peasant party, the New Democratic party, the New Socialist party, and the Democratic Party of the Nile.[12]

On December 10 the government announced the abrogation of the Constitution.[13] On December 13 the Revolutionary Command Council proclaimed Mohammed Naguib "Leader of the Revolution." Censorship of the press, removed on August 12, had been restored on October 21 in order to prevent any press campaign against the installation of the military dictatorship. On January 16, 1953, the political parties were dissolved, their property was confiscated and their leaders were put under house arrest pending trial. In the same month the purge of the army began: almost 450 officers were struck from the lists; Colonel Rashad Mehanna, a member of the RCC, was relieved of his duties in October and arrested on January 17; on January 20 a military conspiracy was uncovered and its leaders, Lieutenant Colonel Mohammed Hosni el-Damanhuri and his brother, Captain Hassan Rifaat el-Damanhuri, were tried by court-martial; on March 30 Mehanna was sentenced to life imprisonment.[14]

The Liberation Rally

On January 23, 1953, a single political party was founded. It was called the Liberation Rally and on February 6 Gamal Abdel Nasser became its secretary-general. Four days later Mohammed Naguib proclaimed a three-year transition period, during which power would be exercised jointly by the RCC and the Cabinet, which, together, formed the Executive Council, the supreme organ of the state. On January 16 the Liberation Rally had published an eleven-point program:

(1) The complete and unconditional evacuation of foreign [British] troops from the Nile Valley.

(2) Self-determination for the Sudan.

(3) A new constitution, expressing the aspirations of the Egyptian people.

(4) A social system within which all citizens have the right to be protected against the ravages of unemployment, disease and old age—that is, a welfare state.

(5) An economic system designed to assure an equitable distribution of wealth, the total utilization of natural and human resources, and maximum investment of new capital.

(6) A political system within which all citizens are equal before the law and in which freedom of speech, of assembly, of the press and of religion will be guaranteed within the limits of the law.

(7) An educational system designed to develop the feeling of social responsibility by making youth conscious of its obli-

gation as well as its rights, and of the paramount necessity that exists for the country to increase production in order to raise the standard of living.

(8) Friendly relations with all the Arab states.

(9) A regional force planned to reinforce the influence of the Arab League.

(10) The establishment of friendly relations with all friendly states.

(11) Firm adherence to the principles of the United Nations, emphasizing their application to subject peoples."[15]

It is obvious that this is a far cry from the "Arab Nationalism" and "democratic socialism" of the Bandung policy.

On June 16, 1953, four members of the RCC joined Naguib's Cabinet: Gamal Abdel Nasser became Vice-Premier and Minister of the Interior, Abdel Latif el-Boghdadi became Minister of War, Salah Salem became Minister of Culture and National Guidance (i.e., propaganda) and Minister of State for the Sudan, and Abdel Hakim Amer, promoted to lieutenant general, became commander in chief of the armed forces. Two days later, on June 18, the monarchy was formally abolished and the Republic of Egypt was proclaimed.

This dropped the mask that had thus far hidden the real intentions of the army movement, or, rather, of its ruling core united around Gamal Abdel Nasser. The general crisis in Egyptian society, illuminated by the flames of burning Cairo, could end only in a cyclical return of the powerful of yesterday. To speak of a constitution, of elections, was to put the Wafd back in the saddle regardless whether that was what was wanted. Now the forces that were then prepared to pay this price for the end of the military dictatorship—a price that was becoming obvious and more threatening every day—were many, occasionally even anti-Wafdist. The leader was General Naguib himself, bullied by the RCC. The leftist officers, Khaled Mohieddine at their head, and even Colonels Yussef Saddik and Ahmed Shawki, supported by the armored corps and part of the Cairo garrison, were among them. The Wafdist press rallied around *al-Misri* and its editor in chief, Ahmed Abul Fath. The Left had an effective press available—

al-Malayin, the organ of the Democratic Movement of National Liberation (DMNL), which hailed the new government as the triumph of the "national bourgeoisie"; *al-Katib,* the organ of the Peace Movement; *Actualité,* a French-language weekly with a large circulation, and many other, less regular publications—whose influence on university and trade union circles was swiftly accompanied by its growth in the rural areas as a result of the climate created by the land reform.

This, *grosso modo,* was the left wing of the national movement. On the right, the Moslem Brotherhood grew impatient and demanded its share of power. Several military leaders— Abdel Hakim Amer, Kamal Eddine Hussein, Anwar el-Sadate, Hussein el-Shafei and especially Rashad Mehanna and Abdel Moneim Abdel Rauf[16]—had been members of it. It was spared by the decree ordering the dissolution of the parties. From that time on, as the sole organized political force tolerated by the government, the Moslem Brotherhood calculated its chances: while the new Supreme Guide, Judge Hassan el-Hodeiby, showed some inclination to collaborate with the RCC, the intransigent wing—Saleh Ashmawi, Sheik Mohammed el-Ghazali, Hassan Doh, Abdel Hakim Abdin, Colonel Ahmed Abdel Aziz Galal—demanded the right of review over all legislation adopted by the government. The Anglo-Egyptian agreement on the Sudan (February 1953) preceded by General Naguib's mediation among the several Sudanese political parties in order to unify them, and then the opening of conversations between Egypt and Great Britain (January 1954) on the subject of evacuation of British troops gave the Moslem Brotherhood the opportunity to make a show of force.

On January 11, 1954, Hassan Doh, the leader of the MB students, stood side by side with Nawab Safawi, the leader of the Iranian "Fidayan Islam," and addressed a crowd during a large meeting that was being held on the campus of Cairo University at Giza. The MB began to use firearms, knives and bludgeons, and reviled the army and the Communists. Several policemen and students were wounded. On January 14 the Cabinet ordered the dissolution of the powerful fraternity. Immediately its leaders turned to General Naguib, who thus became the pole of all opposition forces.

The Ruined Opportunity of the Spring of 1954

The decisive confrontation took place in February and March of 1954. The United Front, which combined Wafdists, Communists and Mustafa Kamal Sidky's Democratic party, as well as various elements of the army, was carrying on a ceaseless campaign in favor of the restoration of democratic freedoms and a return to a constitutional system. The Moslem Brotherhood called for the end of the military dictatorship and nothing more.

After a number of stormy meetings General Naguib resigned on February 23. When the armored corps led by Khaled Mohieddine intervened, he returned to power.

Gamal Abdel Nasser feinted; then, having neutralized the hostile forces within the army, he incited strikes and mass demonstrations under the auspices of the Liberation Rally on March 25, 26 and 27 in Cairo and Alexandria. On March 28 the RCC announced that the elections for the Constituent Assembly, set earlier for June 1954, would not be held, and it re-formed the government, ousting General Naguib both from the government and from the RCC. On April 15 the RCC announced that all political rights had been stripped from the political leaders of the Wafd, Liberal-Constitutional and Saadist parties who had held ministerial posts between 1942 and 1952. On April 18, 1954, Gamal Abdel Nasser became Premier and merged that post with the presidency of the Revolutionary Command Council.

Between December 1953 and January 1954, the Revolutionary Court, in permanent session, had already sentenced a great number of leaders of the old government to long terms in prison or at hard labor. Beginning in April 1954, it was the press that was brought to heel: on May 4 the government banned *al-Misri,* whose directors had already left Egypt, and thus it got rid of the most powerful Egyptian organ, which was also the spokesman for the whole of democratic sentiment;[17] Ehsan Abdel Koddus, editor in Chief of *Rose el-Yussef,* was brought back into line by a few days in prison.

On October 26 a terrorist belonging to the secret organization of the Moslem Brotherhood fired eight revolver shots at Gamal Abdel Nasser during a rally in Alexandria. At once the police, led by Lieutenant Colonel Zakaria Mohieddine, pounced on the MB: several thousand members—the figure was put later at seven thousand—were arrested by the secret and military police. The military tribunals condemned 867 of them.[18] Broken by torture, their leaders appeared before the People's Court, presided over by Gamal Salem: Abdel Kader Auda, Yussef Talaat, Khamis Hemeida and Hassan el-Hodeiby in particular. Of the seven condemned to death, six were executed on December 8, 1954; only the Supreme Guide was spared. Earlier, stripped of his functions as President of the Republic, General Naguib had been seized and placed under house arrest on November 14.

This period, in which every attempt with a democratic taint was stamped out, marks the unleashing of a second campaign of repression against the Left, the first having followed the events of Kafr el-Dawwar. This new operation was part of the joint plan of Mohammed Naguib and Gamal Abdel Nasser. In fact, Naguib said, "from the very first we had done everything that was necessary in order to eliminate the chief causes of Communism in Egypt, namely, a corrupt monarchy, an unjust system of landownership, the general contempt for the rights of the workers, and the hated foreign occupation." Later, after the break with Nasser, he concluded his memoirs by emphasizing their "common faith in the Egyptian revolution, one goal of which was to eliminate the causes of Communism," and their divergencies of view, which arose, "since neither of us is a philosopher . . . from the 'psychology' of the revolution."[19]

The prosecutions of Communists were multiplied; several dozen were sentenced to hard labor and prison by the military tribunals. The spring of 1954, which marked the defeat of Naguib, was climaxed with the dispatch of 254 leftist militants to concentration camps; sixteen officers of the armored corps were struck from the lists; Khaled Mohieddine was forced to go into exile to Switzerland for more than a year; and the major organs of the Left were suspended.[20]

From now on Gamal Abdel Nasser, president of the all-powerful Revolutionary Command Council, was to be the sole master of political power in Egypt.

While the consolidation of power was thus being completed, the junta increased its activities in foreign affairs, particularly in the direction of the United States and Great Britain. This is an aspect of the matter which, since Suez, has often been overlooked and which the government itself conceals in silence. But it is indeed the external complement to the social and economic policy of the military government during this first phase, even though the efforts made—in conformance with the general spirit of the changes under way—took account, to quite a great degree, of the anti-imperialist basic ideas that dominated Egyptian public opinion.

Dialogue with the Anglo-Americans

From the very start, as we have said, quite clear overtures had been made to foreign capital. The United States ambassador in Cairo, Jefferson Caffery, enjoyed the most cordial relations with the military group; his subordinates, especially the assistant naval attaché, David Evans, and his counselor, Colonel Lakeland, later active in Iraq, were of the same view. On September 3, 1952, Secretary of State Dean Acheson promised Egypt "the active friendship of the United States." Fulbright scholarships multiplied. The various credits rose from $6 million to $40 million between 1952 and 1954. Within the framework of the land reform that the State Department had constantly advocated, a so-called Egyptian-American Rural Improvement Service was set up with Egyptian capital of £E5,450,000 and American capital of £E3,469,000, in order to reclaim and redistribute a model area of 37,000 feddans.[21]

The purpose of the United States was clear: to win from the new government, which hardly concealed its aversion to the Communists, its adherence in one form or another to a military organism of collective defense in the Middle East, an organism directly attached to NATO that would be able to surround the southern approaches to the Soviet Union with a view to those military bases so dear to John Foster Dulles.

He, meanwhile, had succeeded Dean Acheson, and in May 1953 he began to sound out the Egyptian government. On the morning of his arrival, Ahmed Abul Fath, the owner of *al-Misri,* ran an eight-column headline: WE HATE YOU, MISTER DULLES! Later in the article he added: "You thought that you could buy us with your Point Four; it is you who are in need of a moral Point Four!" Under these conditions it was difficult for the RCC to take further steps.

The basic problem, however, was still that of the British occupation. There was certainly no further thought of resuming the guerrilla warfare against the Canal base. Negotiations were opened, at first on the Sudan. General Naguib persuaded the Unionist parties to combine against the Umma party, which was devoted to the English, then he promised the two opposing wings that he would recognize the right of the Sudan to self-determination, for he was convinced that the Sudanese would inevitably join Egypt. On February 12, 1953, the Anglo-Egyptian agreement on the Sudan was signed, with Ismail el-Azhary, leader of the National Unionist party, as Prime Minister. Anticipating the effective date of the agreement and assured of the Umma party's support, Azhary proclaimed his country's independence on January 1, 1956, and it was immediately recognized by Great Britain and Egypt.

Negotiations for the troop evacuation were begun between Nasser and the British ambassador, Sir Ralph Stevenson, in the spring of 1953.[22] After months of patient probing and the break of talks on May 6, the Egyptian negotiator agreed, in principle, to "reactivate" the base in the event of an attack on Turkey. From January to May 1954, a series of guerrilla attacks was made against the base in order to remind Winston Churchill that things could turn worse. In May the attacks stopped. In June, Great Britain released £10 million in blocked sterling debts. In July the British government made new proposals: the base would be evacuated of its troops and only civilian technicians would remain, in order to maintain the base with the help of specialist companies.

On July 27 the major points were initialed by the two delegations. Finally, on October 19, 1954, the Anglo-Egyptian treaty for the evacuation of the Suez Canal base was signed; surrendered by the British troops, the base was to be reactivated only in the event of aggression against Egypt, any other Arab country or Turkey. "The dark page of Anglo-Egyptian relations has been turned. Another page is now being written. Great Britain's prestige and position in the Middle East have been reinforced. And now," Gamal Abdel Nasser concluded, "there remains virtually no reason why Great Britain and Egypt cannot work together in a constructive fashion."[23]

Egyptian Capital Holds Back

This was the look of Egypt at the end of 1954: power belonged to the Revolutionary Command Council, which had crushed or neutralized all political opposition and was turning toward dictatorship. Evacuation had finally been won and relations with the Anglo-Americans had become more healthy. Everything, it seemed, was auspicious for an invitation to the big Western powers, but also to Egyptian capital, to take up the responsibilities for economic development, the key to every problem.

But big Egyptian capital, chiefly in the landed wing, which had just undergone the agrarian reform, refused to invest in industry, as we have seen.

In 1952 new investments amounted to £E8.2 million (including £E2 million in the form of corporations), of which one third was in industry. But in 1953 this figure fell to £E7.9 million (including £E1.9 million in the form of corporations). "In contrast, savings at the end of December 1953 amounted to £E64 million against £E58 million at the same date of the preceding year; bank deposits had risen to £E233 million against £E217 million, and the total of all media of payment was £E426 million." But, the EFI pointed out in a tone of growing alarm, "total investments by banks and the credits they have extended to the economy are not more than £E137 million, against £E138 million [in the previous year]. These figures show the extent to which private capital recoils before the difficulties of a fiscal, social and administrative nature that it always confronts."[24]

It was not the means but the will to use them that was lacking. The picture was hardly to change between 1952 and 1957; indeed, the proportion of loans granted by Egyptian commercial banks as a whole, in relation to the total volume of deposits, went from 71.8 percent to 76.6 percent after having achieved the record total of 81.6 percent in 1954.[25] Industrial production rose slowly, too slowly. On the basis of 1954 as an index of 100, this production, which was 92.9 in 1952, reached 109 in 1955, and 123.3 in 1957.[26] The total of new investment in industry (in new enterprises and in additions to existing ones), which was £E26,208,405 in 1956, abruptly dropped to £E12,907,432 in 1957, after the great panic of the rich at the time of Suez.[27] The Industrial Bank itself, though founded in 1949 to encourage Egyptian industry, evidenced its reservations: at the end of 1957 it had granted only £E4.5 million in loans to industry out of a capital of almost £E9 million—in other words, only 50 percent; it made no effort to exercise its right to increase its capital by the issue of new shares in the amount of £E7.5 million; the majority of the loans (76 percent, to be quite precise) was in amounts of more than £E25,000—that is, they were loans made to large companies—while those of less than £E5,000 represented only 5.6 percent.[28]

What could be said except that individuals were hesitant to form industrial companies and that above all the banks were hesitant to provide the development of the new economy, which was predominantly industrial, with the capital that it vitally needed?

And yet business circles, Egyptian and foreign, could not help recognizing that the accession of the officers to power had made a change in the type of men who assumed economic responsibilities. Under the old system, when the landed aristocracy was dominant, ministers, business executives and politicians were as a rule trained in the law, liberal in tendency, and often French in orientation.

Aside from the Wafd, which he had isolated from the life

of the nation, Gamal Abdel Nasser had clashed with many of these men, notably Abdel-Razzak el-Sanhury, president of the Council of State, who was considered the greatest lawyer in Egypt, and Wahid Ra'fat, an expert in foreign affairs. A perpetual conspirator until then, Nasser now felt that he was in a hostile atmosphere, or at least a reserved one. That was why he turned to a different group of people: they were mainly economists, engineers or administrators, educated in England or America, and most of them holding doctor's degrees. Each was an expert in a specific field rather than a politician or theoretician—perfect for a military government whose leaders intended to retain an exclusive monopoly over thought and political decision.

This evolution of the higher levels of the government deserves to be emphasized. It makes it possible to see that while the general policy of the state, both domestic and foreign, favored economic growth in collaboration with the West, it was also anxious to give the country a more modern administration, familiar with recent developments in science, technology and economics and, consequently, better able to interpret the industrialists' desire for expansion. "The problem of our industry," the Egyptian Federation of Industry pointed out in 1952–53, "rather than restricting itself to the improvement of its means and the organization of factories, consists in creating the legislative and administrative climate in which our activity can develop; in technical training and the manner in which it should be conceived; in savings and the means of stimulating them; in investment and the security that should safeguard it; in credit and its adaptation to our economic conditions; in those broad areas that call for wise remedies through a rational revision of economic, fiscal and social legislation."[29]

From 1952 to 1956 the military government worked in this direction.

In 1953 a law made new industries exempt from taxes for five years; profits that these industries reinvested in expansion would receive a 50 percent tax exemption (Law of June 30).

On February 3, 1954, the government granted an oil-exploration concession for the Western Desert to the Coronado Oil Company. On February 10 the Egyptian Iron & Steel Company was formed with the participation of the Bank Misr, the Industrial Bank and, chiefly, the DEMAG of Hamburg. On March 18, experts from Electricité de France were commissioned to prepare a twenty-year electrification program for the country. But it was the United States to which the military leaders turned: on September 24 Egypt asked the International Bank for Reconstruction and Development for a loan intended to finance the construction of the High Dam. On November 6 an economic agreement was signed between the two countries; it provided for a grant of $40 million to finance certain projects for irrigation and for railroad and highway construction. Once more the law on the investment of foreign capital was amended, on September 21, in order to encourage world capital still further; it provided that "the profit derived from the investment of foreign capital may be transferred abroad in the currency of the country of origin," and that "five years after the date of arrival in Egypt . . . foreign capital may be retransferred abroad at the rate of one-fifth per year" [Article III]. Somewhat earlier a French banking mission, led by the president of the Comptoir National d'Escompte de Paris, had arrived in Cairo (on June 5) to study French participation in the construction of the High Dam; it recognized that this project, in spite of its magnitude, "was not disproportionate to the economic possibilities of Egypt,"[30] and it sent a task force of engineers to the site.

Finally, on November 27, the government turned to Egyptian capital: it issued three internal loans amounting to £E25 million. In 1955–56 the government was to issue new internal loans amounting to £E54.2 and £E25 million.

Why Czech Arms?

The year 1955 was one of lost hopes. From Major Ali Sabry's mission to the Pentagon during the autumn of 1952 to the final negotiations with the American ambassador conducted by Gamal Abdel Nasser himself in September 1955, the RCC spent three years begging the United States, the leading friendly country at that time, for the arms required to make the Egyptian army equal to Israel's. Nothing could be done, it was argued in substance from the American side, as long as Egypt refused her adherence to some mutual defense treaty and this Cairo would not give.

On September 27, 1955, in response to the pressure of public opinion and of the officer corps, which was becoming insistent, Nasser announced the conclusion of a trade agreement under whose terms Czechoslovakia committed herself to supply arms "according to the needs of the Egyptian army, on a purely commercial basis." On November 21 and 22 the first conference of the countries signatory to the Baghdad Pact was held: Turkey, Iraq, Iran, Pakistan, Great Britain, plus the United States as an observer. The cold war was openly brought into the Middle East, and the new group of states found its southern bastion in Israel, while the English and American squadrons guarded the sea. Egypt replied to this with two mutual-aid agreements, one with Syria (October 20) and the other with Saudi Arabia (October 27). But it was obvious that the best retort could be only the creation of a strong modern army. In November an economic mission to the United States under the chairmanship of Dr. A. M. Kayssuni ran up against the conditions set by Eugene Black, president of the IBRD: control of the Egyptian budget by the IBRD, and a ban on any new borrowing; in order to modernize herself Egypt would thus be called upon to return to the days of Anglo-French control under Ismail, the prelude to the occupation of 1882! Certain leaders spoke of accepting . . . In the person of its ambassador, Daniel Solod, the Soviet Union came into the picture.

How the contest ended we know, as we know the fundamental part that the Soviet Union played in the continuing construction of the High Dam. Economic development, of course, was also continuing within the country: the imposition of an import tax of 7 percent except on products required by industry (September 1); an increase in the capital of the Egyptian Iron & Steel Company from £E2,100,000 to £E6,370,000, of which 20 percent belonged to DEMAG (October 27); projects for the construction of a shipyard at Alexandria, of a network of atomic-energy reactors, of a huge chemical-fertilizer plant near the High Dam, of a new high-capacity refinery, etc.

The "Strong Man" and His Allies

Why, after all this, such reservations, such hesitations, indeed the resistance that characterized the years 1952 to 1956?

One thing made the leaders of the industrial wing of the Egyptian bourgeoisie hesitant to commit themselves in spite of all the gains: the fact that the army intended to make its own policies—that is, by retaining the monopoly of power, to control the whole of Egypt, down to and including the bourgeoisie itself, which would be kept under guardianship and in servitude.

The dictatorship was there, the "strong man" for whom the *Akhbar el-Yom* group had been insistently calling in its editorials since 1945, powerfully seconded, moreover, by Fikry Abaza in *al-Mussawar* and even by Ehsan Abdel Koddus at the time of the scandal of the traffic in defective weapons. Safe from any popular interference, the strong authority settled the differences with London, carried out the land reform in an orderly manner and without expropriation of any kind, opened the doors of Egypt to foreign capital, especially American, stimulated industry by all the means that its leaders suggested and that lay within its own power, ousted the king from power with his clique of aristocrats, neutralized and isolated the landed bourgeoisie even while calling on it to assume a new function in industry, destroyed the Moslem Brotherhood, oriented as it was toward the past and guilty of xenophobia and religious fanaticism, decimated the ranks of the Communist organizations that had been aroused by the Chinese example, set up institutions, found the men who would best interpret the needs of industrialization, and reinforced the army and the machinery of the state.

All this counted, undoubtedly, in the calculations of business and industrial groups. But this authority was a lone wolf. It was hardly concerned to surround itself with an elected assembly in which the various sectors of the Egyptian middle class might make themselves heard and directly defend their interests, or even indeed keep an eye on the executive. These same circles had only an exceedingly weak voice in the selection of technocratic ministers, even though these came from their class; they were not its representatives at the seat of power. Once they were in office, their supreme criterion became loyalty to "the revolution"—this was what the RCC called its own action after 1953; until then, one spoke always of the "movement of the army," or the "sacred movement"— and to their chief, the victor over all the factions.

By refusing to admit the anti-Wafdist politicians of the past—such as Ibrahim Abdel-Hadi, Ali Maher, Hafez Afifi— to the power now being formed, the Revolutionary Command Council thought that it would be easier to detach the most capable elements of the industrial bourgeoisie and to incorporate them into the apparatus of authority. But the essence of Egypt's wealth was still in the hands of the landed aristocracy, which, violently opposed to the government, refused by a large majority to assist in the construction of the new Egypt.

Thus it came about that the central group of the Egyptian middle class, at once financial and industrial, the Misr complex, remained the major economic power in the modernist wing. At the same time its leading figures, for the most part, remained aloof from the parties of the old days and consequently were available to assume managerial functions in the new system, which was cut to the measure of their appetite for power.

It would not be possible to date the new direction taken by the military government from the Bandung Conference (April 1955). In fact, talks with the West on the subject of arms continued until October, and on the High Dam until the summer of 1956. In addition, at the very moment when Nasser stepped into his airplane to fly to Indonesia on the night of April 10, 1955, he ordered the arrest of thirty leading leftists, who were immediately interned in the camp at Abu Zaabal. But it is true that the Bandung experience was to weight the scales: Chou En-lai made a deep impression on the Egyptian delegation, and afterward came the armaments agreement with Czechoslovakia and then the

Soviet offers with regard to the High Dam—two events that were to be of major importance.

The Suez Crisis

The second phase of the military government in search of social representation—of its social identity—began in 1956 at the time of the Suez crisis, and it was to continue until the summer of 1961. But within this phase, as we shall see, it is possible to distinguish two stages (summer of 1956 to December 1958, and then January 1959 to July 1961).

Unquestionably the shock dealt to the military leaders by the double refusal of the State Department and the IBRD was profoundly felt on the psychological level. The NATO experts still thought at that time that they could confound Nasser and his apparatus with their little groups of agents, their minor allies who did what they were told. For the West the awakening was brutal. But the military leaders were well aware that neither the Egyptian bourgeoisie, in which the landed aristocracy still remained the major owner of the wealth, nor large foreign capital, dedicated to imperialism, had any desire to aid them in their task, which the geography and history of Egypt had made crushing.

In order to assure the subsistence of a population that was growing constantly at a rate varying between 2 and 2.5 percent per year, in order to stabilize the living standard of the people, and also in order to achieve some slight improvement, capital must be found and invested: £100 million per year, 60 percent of it for industry, Professor Hussein Khallaf estimated in 1955.[31] Now, in 1954 the net creation of capital had been £E65 million, of which 60 percent had been swallowed up by public and private construction,[32] leaving barely £E26 million for industry, agriculture and transport together—in fact, only £E6.9 million for industry . . . One after the other, the Egyptian Land Bank, in its board of directors report for 1955,[33] and then Dr. Zaki Saad, president of the National Bank of Egypt, in 1956,[34] issued official statements of refusal to invest, which set the bourgeoisie in opposition to the desire to industrialize. In spite of encouragements and warnings, the same tendency was shown in 1955: £E28.5 million were invested in construction, against only £E7.7 million in industry.[35]

The army went into action on the economic front.

Having been advised by Dr. Ahmed Hussein, the Egyptian ambassador in Washington, that Cairo still preferred financing by the United States and the IBRD to the Soviet offers,[36] on December 17, 1955, the United States and Great Britain announced their participation: the United States would supply $56 million, Great Britain $14 million. The Egyptian delegation—Dr. Abdel Moneim el-Kayssuni, Colonel Samir Helmy, Dr. Mohammed Ahmed Selim—won over by the West, was exultant.

But on July 19, 1956, John Foster Dulles brutally informed the Egyptian ambassador of the American decision not to take part in the High Dam. On the next day Great Britain did the same.

On July 26, 1956, Gamal Abdel Nasser, who had been President of the Republic of Egypt for a month, announced the nationalization of the Universal Maritime Suez Canal Company during a speech in Alexandria.[37] The purpose of the action was both economic and political. It would be possible to find a source of investment capital in the Canal's receipts (£E16 million per year) while at the same time re-establishing Egyptian sovereignty over a particularly important sector of the economy and the national territory.

On October 29, after three months of military and diplomatic preparation, the Israeli army invaded the Sinai peninsula. On October 31 the Anglo-French expeditionary corps went into action in the Canal Zone. On November 14 President Eisenhower said in Philadelphia: "We cannot and will not forgive armed aggression." Washington exerted substantial pressure on its allies to halt the military action. On November 5 Marshal Bulganin, Premier of the USSR, sent a Soviet ultimatum to Ben-Gurion, Mollet and Eden. On November 6 the three nations' armed forces stopped their military action. On December 22 the evacuation of Port Said was concluded.

The death of illusions brought about the complete extirpation of all the resources of imperialism in Egypt and was to provide the military government with an unexpected source of capital that thus far had been denied to it by everyone.[38]

The Egyptianization of Banks and Insurance

On January 15, 1957, three laws, Nos. 22, 23 and 24, were promulgated in Cairo: thenceforth all commercial banks, insurance companies and foreign commercial agencies would have to become Egyptian corporations owned by Egyptian capital and under Egyptian management.

The English, French and Turkish banks were placed under sequestration and on April 18 they were sold to Egyptian banks, as follows: Barclays Bank to the Bank of Alexandria; the Ottoman Bank and the Ionian Bank to the Bank of the Republic; the Crédit Lyonnais and the Comptoir National d'Escompte de Paris to the Bank of Cairo; the Crédit Agricole et Hypothécaire d'Egypte to the Bank of Financial Liability; the Oriental Credit Bank to the Commercial Union Bank. Two of these banks—the Bank of Alexandria, a subsidiary of the Economic Agency, and the Commercial Union Bank—were created especially to participate in the purchase of the foreign banks. Finally, the Egyptian Land Bank, under French management, was purchased by the Economic Agency in September. Between January 1957 and January 14, 1962, the other foreign banks were bought by Egyptian banks under the provisions of the law.[39]

In the field of insurance there were at that time almost two hundred companies, of which only thirteen were Egyptian; of the latter, one alone was genuinely Egyptian—the Misr Insurance Company—for the others were only subsidiaries of companies whose home offices were in other countries. These thirteen companies collected only 40 percent of all premiums paid. The French companies accounted for 47 percent of all the foreign companies' business. Three large Egyptian companies were set up to purchase the assets of the English and French companies: the United Insurance Company, the Al-Gumhuriyya Insurance Company and the Africa

Insurance Company. The Egyptian Reinsurance Company was established on January 1, 1958, to shore up the Egyptian sector.[40]

These two, as we know, were the key areas of finance, for in the last analysis the foreign trade agencies were subordinated to them. And here too we see what might be called "negative" aspects—dispossession and extirpation.

In order to complete the diptych one must examine the kind of organization that was envisaged by the military government. This organization included two elements whose importance has steadily increased since their creation: the High Committee for National Planning (established by Presidential order on January 13, 1957) and the Economic Agency (created by Law No. 20 of the same date).

Brief History of Planning

The idea of an overall plan for economic and social development was not new in Egypt.

Once again it was the Marxist theoreticians who had been working on this idea, especially after 1945, in the political and economic studies of the period, particularly *Mushkelat al-tamwin* (*The Problem of Food Supply*), by Sadek Saad, and *Ahdafuna al-wataniyya* (*Our National Aspirations*), by Shohdi Attia el-Shafei and Abdel Maabud el-Gibeili, as well as in two weekly newspapers, *al-Fagr al-Gadid* and *al-Gamahir*. During the years 1945–52, planning became one of the motivating ideas of the national movement, side by side with agrarian reform, to be put into action after the evacuation of British troops and the re-establishment of democracy. Immediately after the coup d'état, Ahmed Fuad turned the RCC toward a planned economy. But it was the great Polish economist, Oscar Lange, who was then visiting Cairo on business, to whom the military leaders owed their conversion to economic planning in 1954. The agencies to which it was entrusted underwent frequent changes of name: the Permanent Council for the Development of National Production was backed in 1952 by the High Agency for Planning and Co-ordination; in 1953 a Preparatory Committee for a Joint Congress of Officials of RCC and Ministers was created; it was immediately followed by the Permanent Council of General Services; in March 1955 the National Planning Committee was established; in 1957, without changing its name, it absorbed all the planning agencies already mentioned. This entity was soon to be divided into the High Council for National Planning, under the presidency of the chief of state, and the National Planning Committee, which was its executive arm. On August 17, 1961, a new Ministry of Planning was set up under Ahmed Ali Farag as Minister and Dr. Ibrahim Hilmy Abdel Rahman as Vice-Minister: this ministry embraced all the planning services. It was always subject to the High Council which was an inter-ministerial committee, but it was Abdel Latif el-Boghdadi, Vice-President of the Republic, who was now responsible for production. He became titular Minister of Finance and Planning on October 19, 1961, Ahmed Ali Farag was appointed Minister of State for Planning, and Dr. Abdel Rahman was transferred to the directorship of the Institute of Planning. Meanwhile the Cabinet revision of September 30, 1962, had turned Planning (and the Treasury) over to Dr. Abdel Moneim el-Kayssuni.[41]

Why a plan? Quite simply, the leaders said, because private enterprise had refused to act. "The economic structure of the country before the Revolution had been given over to the service of the colonialist power, the feudalists and their henchmen. Production was essentially agricultural . . . This economic structure based on a corrupt governmental administration, at the mercy of partisan conflicts and the private interests of the ruling circles, was certainly unable to provide a real economic impetus." And, further along: "The necessity to create planning entities was imposed in imperative fashion by the fact that there existed in both regions of the United Arab Republic no agencies competent even to propose and initiate, in quasi-automatic fashion and within a reasonable time, the basics required by an increase in investments and production."[42]

During the first phase of this second stage (from the summer of 1956 to December 1958), the planning agencies were organized and prepared the ground. The first Five-Year Plan dates from 1956-57, but actual work began only during the second phase. It is important to point out here that the intervention of the state in the organization of the economy was the direct result of the failure of the Egyptian middle class to overcome the problems that were created by the transition from a colonial-type capitalism, predominantly agrarian, to an industrial and technocratic capitalism. It was in order to ease this fundamental deficiency that the army had to arrogate the power of direction and decision in economic matters. And here, as we shall see, it renewed its ties with the great monolithic tradition of Egypt.

What Was the Economic Agency?

The second instrument of the state's presence in the economic domain was the Economic Agency. According to the original plan, it was supposed to combine under a single head all the functions assumed by various ministries and departments in the companies of mixed type that existed on January 13, 1957, which amounted to £E17 million.[43] The nationalization of the Anglo-French banks, insurance companies and corporations, and then the general process of Egyptianization, swelled the capital of the EA's companies to £E58,680,000 by the end of 1958. On December 31, 1960, the EA controlled £E80,039,000 in capital, 64 companies (including 5 banks and 6 insurance companies) and 80,000 workers in plants and offices, and had earned profits of some £E3.3 million for the year 1960.[44] As events developed, the task of the EA was no longer limited solely to continuing the work of the large amount of foreign capital invested in Egypt before Suez. It created new enterprises, and by way of its investments, played a more and more important part in the realization of the Plan, as we shall see shortly.

In its dual role of successor and initiator, the EA emerged clearly as the representative of state capitalism in the period under study: instead of the former owners and managers, the agency managed companies, and it created new ones that it held in full ownership, in both instances employing a large force of paid workers under the same conditions as those in private firms.

What at this time (1956–58) was the attitude of the private sector of the economy—that is, the industrial and financial upper bourgeoisie of Egypt? What was the exact nature of the relations that it maintained with the military leadership?

Good Business . . .

On the economic level the private sector did excellent business, as the barometer of the National Bank of Egypt showed.

An early study covering the finances of 148 Egyptian corporations whose combined holdings amounted to 53 percent (£E112.9 million) of the total capital of all Egyptian corporations offered the following results for 1957–58: "The ratio of income to capital invested, which reflects the earning capacity of a business, reached 15.1 percent for all groups together and varied from a maximum of 38.8 percent for the food and beverage industries to a minimum of 4.9 percent for the real-estate sector, while it was 25.5 percent in the textile group."[45]

Prosperity grew still more in the next year: "Total profits recorded by [144] companies during the year under study [1958–9] rose by £E3 million, or 7 percent above the previous year; they reached the total of £E44.2 million, which amounted to 35 percent of the total capital and 23 percent of that held by investors, against 34 percent and 22 percent, respectively, during the year 1957–8 . . . In addition, the net income of stockholders rose from 10 percent in 1957–8 to 11 percent in 1958–9 in all sectors, except those of transportation and the food industries . . . If the building and land-company sectors are omitted (in which profits are lower), the result is an average of 12.5 percent for the other sectors, while that of chemicals alone recorded an 18.8 percent profit rate for 1958–9."[46]

The Misr and Abbud Groups

The Misr complex towered over the private sector. Its tentacles were everywhere.[47] The Bank Misr, the brain of the complex, was still managed by the triumvirate of Mohammed Rushdy, Mohammed el-Attal and Ahmed Fuad, set in office by the RCC in 1952. Its capital, which was £E1 million in 1950, had risen to £E2 million by 1960; its reserves from £E4,225,000 to £E7,614,000; its deposits from £E54,643,000 to £E96,008,000; and its net profits from £E788,000 to £E1,-135,000.[48] In 1958 the textile factories in the Misr complex produced more than one quarter of the whole Egyptian output. The complex held 20 percent of the shares in the new Egyptian Iron & Steel Company of Heluan; it controlled the Co-operative Petroleum Company (with a capital of £E10 million), which had the monopoly for the distribution of petroleum products throughout the country; it held part ownership in several companies in the Abbud complex, especially those making chemical products and fertilizer. In reality, this was a true center of monopoly, which was constantly extending its power and control over the whole Egyptian economy.

The campaign that Talaat Harb had waged for the creation of an Egyptian textile industry under the control of the Bank Misr is a history of its own: diplomatic intrigue, pressure from powerful sources, difficulties in obtaining effective tariff protection, the training of skilled workers, the formation of a proletariat of peasant origin, etc.[49] We have shown, as we traced the outline of the history of the Egyptian middle class, how the Misr complex became little by little the City Hall of all sectors of the bourgeoisie. On several occasions, large foreign firms threatened to set up highly equipped competitive industries in Egypt, and whenever this ghost walked, the Bank Misr had to make up its mind to organize new companies in collaboration with the foreign firms. This was particularly true of the Misr Insurance Company, founded with the aid of Bowring of London and the Assicurazione Generale di Triesta; again with the Misr Spinning & Fine Weaving Company of Kafr el-Dawwar and the Beyda Dyers, both born of an agreement with the Bradford Dyers' Association modeled on the German *Interessengemeinschaften* (pooling agreements);[50] and later with Misr Airways. Internal relations within the complex emphasized its extraordinary concentration: in effect, it was the Bank Misr that guaranteed the basis of financing for the Misr companies, under the provisions of the charters that were the same in all the companies and according to which capital had to be subscribed as a whole, 25 percent being paid down at the time of purchase. In this way the Bank Misr assured itself of control over a small group of financiers as well as exclusive control of the initial operation and later of complete management.

Economists like Dr. Ali el-Gereitly have observed that the degree of concentration reached here is greater even than in the case of the *Grossbanken* (giant banks).[51] In fact, every year the Bank Misr rotated the presidencies of its new companies among the members of its board of directors, so that in 1927 Mahmud Shukry Pasha was president of four of the Misr companies. In addition, until 1955 the bank maintained a financial controller's office in each company, so that all of them became mere "industrial" branches of the Bank Misr.

The twenty-nine industrial companies set up by the Bank Misr between 1922 and 1957 constituted an imposing complex that dominated the whole Egyptian economy,[52] but they constituted as well a veritable nursery of directors and junior management, the accent being put on the efficiency of the organization and on both theoretical and practical training rather than on the individual qualities of the aspiring entrepreneur.[53] Later it was learned that fifty persons held 42 percent of the shares in the Bank Misr and that ten of these fifty owned 20 percent of the stock, while the millionnaire Ahmed Abbud alone held 14 percent of the bank's shares . . .[54]

Side by side with the Misr complex was the Abbud complex. The peaks were of the same height, but the styles differed. Ahmed Abbud, a self-made man, was an "entrepreneur" of the classic type. His "empire," as they say, was the fruit of fifteen years of ceaseless work: the Khedivial Mail Lines, the Egyptian Sugar Mill & Refinery Company, a huge chemical-fertilizer company, several textile mills, and still others in virtually every field. Closely linked to the Palace and to English and American interests, he played an important part, even a preponderant one, in the Bank Misr and the EFI, and he had a voice in the board of directors of the old Suez Canal Company. His complex of companies, in which exploitation of the workers was unrestricted, did not possess the staffs patiently developed by the Misr complex. Here the top man, Ahmed Abbud, was everything. He often violated the existing labor laws, and his repressive commandos never waited for the state's intervention to break strikes and silence malcontents.[55]

This whole world of finance, industry and business prospered as never before in the shadow of a strong authority concerned with order and economic progress. But these complexes had the habit of power. In another time they made and unmade ministries, negotiated with foreign powers, ran the press, the parties, Parliament: they were and they used the power of the state. Now their power was intact, their investments were clearly increasing and their profits were substantial. The hegemony of the landed aristocracy, which had occasionally got in their way, had been swept away. Certainly there had been that Suez affair, which temporarily broke their bridges to the west and forced them into a de facto alliance with the socialist countries. But after all, Egypt had got hold of the former foreign assets, which would now go to the aid of industrialization, even though this capital had been put into the hands of the Economic Agency for the most part instead of finding its way to the private banks and corporations.

The union of the military apparatus and of the big industrial and financial capital was to take place both on the political and on the economic level.

The Alliance between the Army and the Industrial Bourgeoisie

On the political level, four major measures marked that combination during the 1956–58 phase: the Constitution of June 25, 1956, the foundation of the National Union (May 28, 1957), the election of the Council of the Nation (National Assembly) (July 1957), and finally the union of Egypt and Syria into the United Arab Republic on February 1, 1958.

Obviously the experience of Bandung had not been in vain. Gamal Abdel Nasser took cognizance of the break made by the young, newly independent states, and he realized the vital importance of mobilizing the people for defense and development work and, consequently, of adopting a certain form of guided democracy; in the nascence of Afro-Asian solidarity he discovered a support which would be increasingly important for the tasks he intended to carry out in Egypt.

On his return to Cairo, he inaugurated what was thereafter called the Bandung period (1956–58). The Communists, progressives and leftist liberals interned at Abu Zaabal were released in small groups. And it was in this atmosphere that Nasser, who had not yet given up hope of American aid while still fitting out his divisions with Czech arms, evolved limited steps of liberalization in order better to shore up his authority.

On January 16, 1956, he published a draft Constitution of the Republic of Egypt. For the first time in history, Egypt officially declared herself Arab: "Egypt is an independent and sovereign Arab state. She is a democratic republic. The Egyptian people is a part of the Arab nation" (Article 1). Several articles followed which confirmed hopes of a certain democratic renewal: "Social solidarity is at the foundation of Egyptian society" (Article 4); "the state guarantees liberty, security, tranquillity and equality of opportunity to all Egyptians" (Article 6); "no one shall exert physical or psychological duress on an accused person" (Article 37); "freedom of thought and of scientific research is guaranteed" (Article 44); "the creation of trade unions is an established right" (Article 55). On the economic level, planning and state capitalism were recognized (Article 7) while at the same time "private economic activity shall be free" (Article 8). Title III ("Public Rights and Duties") unquestionably recognized all the freedoms, but always "within the framework of the law," whereas the old Constitution of 1923 had reflected the absolute nature of certain freedoms, notably personal freedom.

The legislative power was restricted to one elected National Assembly, called Maglis al-Umma (Title IV, Chapter II, Articles 65–118). But ministers were to be appointed or relieved of their duties by the President of the Republic (Article 146). No political party would be allowed; however, "the citizens constitute a National Union with a view to accomplishing the purposes of the Revolution and co-ordinating their efforts for the construction of a healthy nation from the political, social and economic points of view." There is the key to the whole system, though relegated to Title VI, dealing with "interim and final measures." "The National Union will nominate the candidates for the Council of the Nation (National Assembly)" (Article 192).

On June 23 a double referendum was held: Gamal Abdel Nasser was proclaimed President of the Republic of Egypt with 99.84 percent of the votes cast; the proposed Constitution was adopted by 99.8 percent of the voters. One month later came the attack on Suez.

The National Union

On May 28, 1957, a Presidential decree set up the National Union, of which only the Executive Committee had been appointed in order to screen the candidates for election to the legislature: the Executive Committee was composed of Abdel Latif el-Boghdadi, Zakaria Mohieddine, Abdel Hakim Amer and its chairman, President Nasser. Out of 2,508 candidacies proposed from the 284 electoral districts, all of which had been newly redrawn in order to prevent the Wafd from recapturing its old territories, the Executive Committee approved 1,188.

The result of the election, announced on July 15, clearly proved that the Council of the Nation would provide a forum for the various sections of the Egyptian middle class. The successful candidates included 16 ministers, 3 undersecretaries of state, 46 lawyers, 46 farmers, 40 village *omdehs* (mayors), 33 army officers, 20 physicians, 20 high officials, 4 business owners, 2 radio announcers, 1 sheik, 9 industrialists, 15 landowners, 14 police officers, 12 engineers, 9 professors, 10 merchants, 8 magistrates, 8 journalists, five sheiks *el-balad* (borough mayors), 4 assistant accountants, 4 pharmacists, 2 women, 7 clerical employees and 4 workers.[56] The Council's first meeting was held on July 22 for the purpose of electing its president, who was Abdel Latif el-Boghdadi.

Meanwhile the work of making the National Union effective was being actively pursued. The decree published on November 2 covered its constitution, the objectives assigned to which were "the accomplishment of the purposes of the revolution of July 23, 1952, the creation of a socialist, democratic, co-operativist society free of all political, social and economic exploitation." (Article 1). An elaborate hierarchy of organization, governed by the elective principle, culminated in the upper executive committee, which would be appointed by the President.[57] On November 9 Colonel Anwar el-Sadate became secretary-general of the NU.

Stirrings against Dictatorship

The dialogue that developed in the time between the return of the Council of the Nation during the autumn of 1957 and its dissolution on February 1, 1958, as a result of the merger between Syria and Egypt, did not turn out to be what the military leaders had hoped for. In fact, in spite of all the screening and pressures, in spite of the arbitrary redefinition of electoral districts, the Council had not been an assembly of dupes. It included a large number of prosperous men, and most of the provincial delegates favored the old system with its agrarian dominance. The Left could count on the four worker deputies and two other progressive deputies: these six, however, were to be the only ones kept out of the National Union at the very moment when all their colleagues were admitted to it.[58] The old democratic opposition of the spring of 1954 rallied its forces, at first timorously, and then more and more openly. The deputies intended to make the laws, since they lacked the power to dismiss the Cabinet (Council of Ministers).

What exactly occurred?

Of course, there was the former landed bourgeoisie, part of which had been decimated but large sectors of which were still influential in the rural areas. There was the upper industrial and financial bourgeoisie, which intended to take in hand the whole body of economic and financial legislation. There were also representatives of the professions, as well as technocrats and specialists, who wanted to take part in the construction of the modern society that was supposed to be open to all and particularly to scientists and technicians. There were those who were nostalgic for the Wafd, and those who had not forgotten the destruction of the Moslem Brotherhood. But over all this there hovered, in a cloud of words, the government's desire for liberalization and the democratic spirit always allied to the demand for independence within the Egyptian national movement. In the Egypt of 1956–58, subjugated by the military apparatus, only one force insisted on autonomy and had a philosophy, a doctrine, a program and an organization which were distinct. That force was the Left: that is, the still illegal Communist organizations—the Workers' Vanguard, the Unified Egyptian Communist party, the Egyptian Communist party—and the very broad progressive sector among both the intellectuals and the trade union movement, which, though not organically part of the Communist movement, was to be its ally and, often, its legal means of expression.

To the credit of the Egyptian Marxists it must be recognized that in spite of their dissension, their illegal status, the almost uninterrupted persecutions since 1946 which the military government had carried to a pitch of cruelty never before reached, they had never faltered in their determination to be the political intellect of Egypt. Their opponents admitted the high theoretical level of their leaders, the political maturity of the movement as a whole, and the reception which, ever since the time of the National Committee of Workers and Students, Marxism had always been able to obtain by the general public.

At the Abu Zaabal camp, which the intelligence officers called *makbarat al-ahya* (the cemetery of the living), the leaders of the Egyptian Left were preparing themselves for the unification of the Communist movement, the tactics for a tacit national front with the military and the problems of the political, ideological, social and cultural development of the new Egypt that was foreshadowed by the agreement with Czechoslovakia, the friendship with the socialist countries, state capitalism and the premises of Suez. It was from the Abu-Zaabal camp that, beginning in November 1955, the first resolutions of support came for Nasser, emphasis always being laid nonetheless on the necessity for restoring democratic freedoms and a constitutional system in order to give substance to national unity. The Workers' Vanguard gave the signal; it was to be followed by the Unified Egyptian Communist party and then by the Egyptian Communist party. The central committees outside followed suit.

The ordeal of Suez was to be decisive. At the time of the bombardment of Cairo, the Communist organizations went into the streets, organizing firearms lessons and setting up resistance committees, while writers and journalists of the Left blanketed the country with intense patriotic propaganda that produced a few splendid poems. In the hour of greatest peril it was the Egyptian Left that solidified the home front.

The sympathy and admiration of the common people for the Left were matched by a genuine ground swell in favor of the Soviet Union: "The Soviet government is firmly resolved to resort to the use of force to crush the aggressors and restore peace in the Orient," Marshal Bulganin said on November 5 to the representatives of the three attacking powers. That was well known to everyone, and Nasser had to recognize it.

On October 7, 1956, the President of the Republic founded a new evening newspaper, *al-Missa,* the editorship of which he turned over to Major Khaled Mohieddine. Its objective was to provide the Left, if possible the non-Communist Left, with a legal platform duly confined within the general framework of state policy. From October 7, 1956, to March 12, 1959, *al-Missa* was the ideological workshop of the new Egypt. Communists, progressives and liberal intellectuals collaborated in it. *Al-Missa* renewed the great tradition of opinion journalism that had flourished before the war; it devoted numerous sections (almost four of its eight pages every day) to heavily documented studies in which Egyptian Marxists analyzed Egyptian society in transition and offered their solutions. Every day Nasser followed what appeared in it: "Well, what are your doctors saying today?" The voice on the phone became insistent . . .

It was the staff of *al-Missa* that developed the distinction between the state's Arab nationalism and the democratic idea of a federal union among the Arab nations. It also proposed the modification of land reform, supplied the proposals for cultural renewal that were to be adopted later, in large part, by the responsible minister; it studied the operation of state capitalism, published the best of Egyptian literary output of the period, introduced scientific research into the heart of the economy, and affirmed Egyptian individuality within Arabism.

Several publishing houses were established, notably Dar al-Nadim and Al-Dar al-Misriyya li 'l-Kutub under Lutfallah Soliman, Dar al Fikr under Ibrahim Abdel Halim, Al-Mu-'assassa al-Kammiyya li 'l-Nashr wa 'l-Tawzie, under Hussein Talaat and Raymond Duek, Dar al-Dimokratiyya al-Gadida, and still more. Novelists, essayists, poets and philosophers published works that set the general tone of the intellectual life of the country. In spite of their expulsion from the university in 1954, the Marxist intellectuals supplied the best of what appeared in newly created magazines, some of them official. They were active in the theater and in broadcasting, which was indebted to them in particular for its "Second Program," the cultural program.

It is understandable that this independent force, which had regrouped and was broadening its audience among the people from day to day, should have occasioned considerable thought among the masters of Egypt. In the Council of the Nation (National Assembly) the deputy from Giza, Abul Fadl el-Gizawi, questioned the all-powerful Minister of the Interior on the concentration camps, the treatment of prisoners, and the legal basis for administrative internment. The session became stormy.

A few days earlier—on December 10, to be exact—Kamal Eddine Hussein, Minister of Education and Instruction, who was predisposed to a purge of the student movement, had had to hear an overwhelming majority of the Council of the Nation order him to open the doors of the university to every secondary-school graduate who requested admission. This was part of a campaign in which the newspapers took part, all of them standing with the deputies against the regimentation of the university. Confronted with a wave of public anger, Kamal Eddine Hussein resigned. But on the President's order he rescinded his resignation, and the Council of the Nation was dissolved.

What was at stake in the climate created by Bandung, by

the Soviet ultimatum and by the successes of the Left was the very principle of military dictatorship. Everything was propitious for Nasser to go further, to encourage this powerful tide of the popular forces and to liberalize the government in order to provide better guarantees for its future. The President of the Republic enjoyed an overwhelming popularity at the time, but his associates, and above all his military apparatus, were denounced and despised by all. If he wished, he could govern the country with the support of new forces—the industrial middle class, the small and medium landowners, the liberal professions, the leftist intellectuals, the trade unions—always on condition that he recognize their independent existence: that is, their right to exist as political parties. No one challenged his power. But the majority of his partisans thought in terms of a return to democracy. A new spring of 1954 was in preparation, but this time it was more formidable because it was to come after Bandung and Suez.

Effects of the Syrian-Egyptian Merger

Now, it was just at this time of exceptionally intense and complex political cogitation that the Syrian affair arose.

For the moment everything was prettified, duly rationalized: the Arab nation was resolving itself and it was wholly natural that Egypt and Syria, linked since the days of the Pharaohs by innumerable common experiences, should be in the vanguard. After the collapse of the merger and following the astonishingly frank self-criticism by the head of the UAR on October 16, 1961, Mohammed Hassanein Heykal, the President's adviser and spokesman and editor in chief of *al-Ahram*, was to disclose the other side of the merger.[59] His account was to repeat many of the facts alleged by Khaled Bakdash and elaborated from week to week by *al-Akhbar* and *al-Nida* of Beirut: disunity among the leaders of the traditional Syrian middle-class parties; fear of the Baath* Socialists of Akram el-

* The Baath Socialist party had been formed in the 1940's by a merger of Hurani's Socialist party and the larger Baath (Resurgence) party led by Michel Aflak and Salah Bitar. It had followers in Lebanon, Syria, Jordan and Iraq, but not in Egypt.

Hurani and Michel Aflak in the light of the prospect of a Communist gain in the legislative elections of July 1958; military weakness in the face of Israeli threats; the prestige of the Egyptian Revolution. Thus entreated to unify by Damascus, Gamal Abdel Nasser hesitated, alleging the lack of common frontiers, the differences in political and economic experience, the threats of the West, etc. But business circles in Cairo—notably the Misr group, the Bank of Cairo (founded in 1952 by the Serag Eddine, Badrawi, Doss and Alluba families and then enlarged in 1957 by the EA, which handed over the French banks to it), but also the Economic Agency—pressed the President to agree to this union, which could only benefit the growth of the Egyptian economy. The young officers, the technocratic groups and the high officials connected with the military apparatus exerted pressure in the same direction. In the end the fear of Communism provided the decisive impetus: a leftist government in Damascus could only precipitate a crisis in Cairo and provide backing for the National Front, which had been reborn after Suez.

On February 1, 1958, Presidents Gamal Abdel Nasser and Shukri el-Quwatli proclaimed the United Arab Republic. On February 5 both Parliaments ratified the merger. On February 21 it was confirmed by referendum in both countries and Nasser was elected to the presidency by an overwhelming majority. At once both Parliaments were dissolved. On March 5 a new provisional Constitution of the United Arab Republic was promulgated. On March 8 an agreement between the UAR and Yemen was reached for the creation of the Union of Arab States. The danger had been averted, amid general rejoicing, though the man in the street in Egypt showed some surprise at the Arab turn that his destiny was taking.

The military group and the industrial and financial upper bourgeoisie thus found a new ground for alliance. Not only would the creation of the United Arab Republic make it possible for them to block the Left; it would also be the signal for a surge of investment and export, opening new outlets for the graduates of the Egyptian universities and, in fact, making Syria a province of Egypt.

The years 1957–58, moreover, were marked by a substantial rise in foreign dealings, especially in exports, as well as by a geographical redistribution of Egypt's customers.

On January 21, 1958 the new Minister of Industry, Dr. Aziz Sidky, won approval for his five-year industrialization plan. On June 1 the Plan was published: £E250 million was to be invested in five years, of which £E164.5 million would go into industry, £E21.5 million into mineral resources and £E35 million into petroleum. At the end of the five years, it was reckoned, the national income would have risen by £E86.5 million, the national resources by £E225 million, the number of workers by 50 percent and their wages by £E55 million.[60]

On December 5 President Nasser announced the decision to accomplish the Plan in three years: "The national income will then have risen by £E130 million. The Plan will create jobs for half a million workers. Industry's share in the national income will be 22 percent . . . We have to work twice as fast: once for the hundred years of backwardness that have passed, once to provide work for the 350,000 persons who are born to us each year." Soviet aid, under the provisions of the agreement of January 29, 1958, was truly gigantic: 700 million rubles against a twelve-year loan bearing an annual interest of 2.5 percent, the first repayment to be made after five years. The very structure of Egypt's foreign trade was radically altered: in 1957, three fifths of the cotton export was shipped to the socialist countries. A whole series of economic agreements with the People's Democracies in Europe and with the People's Republic of China was to be matched by negotiations and agreements with several other countries, notably West Germany, which was soon to outdistance all her Western competitors and compete directly with the Soviet Union; Japan, Italy and Spain were to play important parts. On March 27, 1958, Dr. Emary, then head of the National Bank of Egypt, uttered a note of dissent as the voice of the financial interests: Egypt's economic policy, he said in substance, was leading to a crisis because it was oriented toward the USSR, for Egypt could not get along without the West, her traditional partner.

In other words, the industrial and financial upper bourgeoi-

sie hardly appreciated the orientation that the events of
Suez had forced on the military government. New outlets
had indeed been found, but vigilance was essential in order
that nothing be done that might expose Egypt to Communism,
both domestic and international. Therefore, this same middle
class was vastly relieved by the unification with Syria. The
Misr complex and the Bank of Cairo established experts and
subsidiaries in Syria a few weeks after the merger. This movement was to be accelerated in 1959, 1960 and 1961.

Meanwhile, not all was happening for the best on the home
front between the two great allies. The government promulgated a series of laws dealing with industry: one of them
(No. 21 of 1958) concerned "the organization and stimulation of industry in the Egyptian region," which was thereafter to operate in accord with the objectives of the Plan;
on May 29 a decree covering the creation of the General
Agency for the Consolidation of Industry tightened the grip
taken by the state apparatus on the industrial sector, because
this agency was to include five members appointed by the
Minister of Industry, five representatives of the EFI and five
members chosen by reason of their duties—that is, high
officials: on the same date and again on June 9, there were
two decrees that provided for the "creation of Chambers of
Industry," twenty chambers in all, "to be considered as public
institutions." Finally, the omnipotent Egyptian Federation
of Industry had been reorganized on May 29; the Minister of
Industry appointed not only the chairman of its board of
directors but also one third of the members.[61] Dr. Mohammed
Ahmed Selim, a great engineer who had been won over to
American influence, became its president on April 25, 1960[62]

Why the Repression of 1959?

Three events were landmarks in 1958, a year in
which the military apparatus, powerfully backed by the
USSR after Suez, began to throw off the consequences of the
ordeal, especially the boycott by the Western powers.

We have seen how effective the action of the Left was, in
spite of the dissention among the Communists, at the time of

the inauguration of the Council of the Nation. Now, the three Communist organizations had created a Committee of Co-ordination in the spring of 1957, and in the autumn it was developed into a Committee of Unity. In November the Egyptian Communist party and the Unified Egyptian Communist party merged to form the United Egyptian Communist party, while the Workers' Vanguard changed its name to the Egyptian Communist party of Workers and Peasants. Finally, these two organizations merged on January 8, 1958, and founded the Egyptian Communist party. This date was three weeks before the proclamation of the UAR. It was the period of mergers. For the Egyptian Communists this represented the culmination of the extremely arduous efforts maintained since 1945 in a climate of persistent persecutions and at the height of the upheavals in Egyptian society. The military apparatus made no mistaken appraisal of this: what had been irritating was becoming, or might become, dangerous.[63]

The second major event that precipitated the crisis was the Afro-Asian Peoples' Solidarity Conference, which was held in Cairo from December 26, 1957, to January 1, 1958.[64] In the press, on the radio, in the universities and the trade unions, the Left organized a spontaneous demonstration of anti-imperialist resolve and emphasized the function of civil liberties in popular action. The conference officials, bound in any case to the official policy still based on the principles of Bandung, were left behind and compelled to let matters take their course. But the secretariat was established in Cairo, and a former aristocrat and cavalry colonel, the author of several dozen newspaper serials, Yussef el-Seba'i, was placed at its head in an effort to curb its revolutionary growth more effectively.

The Iraqi revolution of July 14, 1958, was the third decisive event. In its first weeks, indeed, there was an amazing burgeoning of democracy in Iraq. The Communist party was by far the most powerful, and it exerted a widespread and effective influence in propaganda and organization. It set up a National Front in which the Iraqi Communist party, the National Democratic party of Kamel el-Jaderzhi, and other groups of lesser importance collaborated. General Abdel Karim Kassem did not interfere, because he wanted to have a counterweight to the Baathist partisans of unification with the UAR. He allowed credence to be given to the idea that the Iraq of 1958 represented a different prospect for all the Arab nationalists: the democratic and liberal alternative of Arab nationalism, of which President Nasser was supposed to represent the dictatorial side. This time there was a direct threat to the very existence of the UAR, in which the Left and the liberal nationalists at last saw rising over the horizon a positive solution, an end to the nightmare in which Arab unity had to be paid for with the destruction of all freedom.

As early as the autumn of 1958, the machinery of repression and propaganda went into action, progressively increasing its pressure on the Left, which, at home and abroad, was guilty of disruption. Trade union leaders were rearrested barely a year after they had been released from Abu Zaabal. The military tribunals resumed jurisdiction over Communist defendants.

In September, Anwar el-Sadate sent for a leader of the Egyptian Communist party, a prominent figure in the literary world, and for seven consecutive hours endeavored to persuade him to bring his party into the National Union; otherwise, he said, the Communists had to understand that they would undergo the fate of the Moslem Brotherhood, which meant destruction by way of torture. The secretary-general of the National Union was answered with a courteous but definitive refusal. An extremely violent press and radio campaign was launched against Iraq, the enemy of Arab nationalism. On October 12 John Foster Dulles, who had already asserted on April 6 that "the United States has a perfect understanding with President Nasser," announced the resumption of American aid to Egypt, with a first installment of $13 million.

Gamal Abdel Nasser chose Port Said and the date of December 23, 1958, the anniversary of the victory against the aggressors, for the launching of his offensive against the Left and, more particularly, against the Communist party.

These, he said, were "new enemies, enemies who felt that the victory of Arab nationalism meant the doom of their aims." These new enemies "are striving to deceive the people and to spread rumors in order to open the door to imperialism and to the agents of imperialism and Zionism." In fact, "they reject the union of this nation in the struggle against the enemies of Arab nationalism and Arab unity. They go even as far as to raise objections to Arab nationalism and Arab unity. Certain members even declared in the past week that they favored separation and that there should be neither Arab unity nor nationalism. That amounts to a call to Zionism to infiltrate itself into Arab nationalism, a call to the reactionary elements to return and exploit our country . . ."[65]

On January 1, 1959, in the very early morning, while New Year celebrations were still going on, 280 leaders and functionaries of the Egyptian Communist party were arrested. A few hours earlier, several dozen writers had just sent a long letter to the President, defending the honor of the Left and reminding him that it supported the neutralist and anti-imperialist policy of the UAR, a policy compromised by the slanders of Port Said. The staff of *al-Missa*, partly decimated by this first wave of repression, let the President know that it would continue to support the general policy of the UAR but without associating itself with the offensive unleashed in the entire press against the Arab Communists, Iraq and the Soviet Union. The authorities decided to spare *al-Missa* in the hope of being able to make use of it again.

Almost at the same time Colonel Abdul Wahab el-Shawwaf launched the uprising of Mosul in northern Iraq (March 1959), immediately drowned in blood by the Iraqi air force and the Communist militia. In Egypt and Syria the reaction showed that the time of temporization was at an end. This time it was a matter of destroying the machinery of the Communist parties and also of reducing the progressives to silence, particularly the intellectuals and the trade unionists. On March 12 Khaled Mohieddine, the editor in chief, was dismissed from *al-Missa;* the next day the surviving staff was thrown out. Huge demonstrations, directed by the National

Union, howled hatred and death around the symbolic cata-
falques of the Mosul victims in Cairo and Alexandria. On
March 20 the second wave of arrests swept up many hundreds,
even thousands of people in Egypt and Syria.[66]

The "Bandung period" vanished in terrorism.

And yet, thirteen months after the launching of the campaign against the Left, two laws (Nos. 39 and 40 of February
11, 1960) were promulgated for the nationalization of the
Bank Misr and the National Bank of Egypt. Then, in July
1961, came the series of "socialist" laws.

What had happened at the top?

Toward a Statist Economy

The fundamental factor, during this second phase
(January 1959–June 1961), was the considerable and continued increase of the state's part in economic life, to the
detriment of the private sector. It took many roads: expansion
of the Economic Agency's function and of the state's economic undertakings; a tighter network of laws ensuring the
state's control of industry and corporations; and, finally, the
Five-Year Plan for 1960–65.*

Two among the state's direct enterprises held the attention
of the military leaders: the Suez Canal and the Economic
Agency. When Dr. Hilmy Baghat Badawy died, Colonel
Mahmud Yunes was put at the head of the Suez Canal
Authority. The thorny negotiations between the Egyptian
government and the IBRD were finally concluded on December 21, 1959: the EA received a loan of $56.5 million from the

* Here is a capsule rundown of the various development plans: the
first Five-Year Plan went into effect on January 1, 1958, but on December
5 the same year, it was changed to a Three-Year Plan. On August 2,
1960, a Ten-Year Plan was promulgated, with the ultimate objective of
doubling the national income within that period, but within this overall
plan, there were two specific Five-Year Plans. Hence, any further
mention of, for example, "the First Five-Year Plan," refers to the Plan
for 1960–65. Cf. Patrick O'Brien, *The Revolution in Egypt's Economic
System* (Oxford U. Press, London, 1966), pp. 104–300.

IBRD, plus $5 million more from a group of American banks, the whole bearing interest of 6 percent for a term of fifteen years, in order to carry out work required for the improvement of navigation in the Suez Canal.[67] The Egyptian management, under the supervision of army engineers, had proved to be more dynamic and effective than the old international company: in 1955 receipts amounted to £E36 million; in the 1960–61 period they reached £E51.5 million; 14,666 ships totaling 115,000,000 tons had transited the Canal in 1955; in 1960 these figures rose 60 percent, to 18,734 ships totaling 185,000,000 tons; the number of pilots, all holding ocean-going masters' papers, rose from 206 to 226, of whom 141 were Egyptians; finally, the new agency devoted 25 percent of its income to improvement work on the Canal, instead of the 4 percent thus employed before nationalization.[68] The RCC concluded that military experts offered more efficient management for huge projects than did their civilian colleagues, especially those in private industry.

Within the Economic Agency, where the ineffectual Hassan Ibrahim had been replaced by Dr. Kayssuni, who was surrounded by a general staff that combined civilian technicians and high-ranking officers, the volume of business rose without interruption. First the Misr complex and then the Abbud complex merged at least in part with the EA. In the Misr complex the first move was made by the Misr Foreign Trade Company, the most important in its field in Egypt; then came Misr's Beyda Dyers, by far the largest firm in textile processing; Misr's insurance company; Misr Airways (the only airline in the country); and finally the Misr Maritime Navigation Company; they all combined and merged partially with the EA in 1958–59. At the same time Ahmed Abbud's Khedivial Mail Lines and his fertilizer and chemical-products factories also joined the EA. These were highly prosperous companies which made this move into the EA under government pressure; in fact, "the total of net dividends distributed during the year 1960 reached £E16 million, against £E13.5 million in 1959—in other words, a rise of 18.5 percent."[69] Such a combination lent itself better to organization, which was indispensable if the plan was to be carried to fruition.

"To Double the National Income . . ."

In reality, the first Five-Year Plan, which later became a Three-Year Plan, gave the impetus to the process of industrialization, but it did so at the cost of an unbalanced budget, which the experts at once pointed out and for which they held Dr. Aziz Sidky responsible. In turn, then, Hassan Abbas Zaki, later Minister of the Treasury in the Council of the Nation, Dr. Koestner, at this time director of the research department of the National Bank of Egypt, and others, underlined the importance of maintaining a healthy fiscal policy and making sure of the necessary markets.[70] In fact, this plan was only a proving ground. But the new team, headed by Dr. Kayssuni and Dr. Ibrahim Hilmy Abdel Rahman, went to work. On November 27, 1958, President Nasser had made an important speech to the Co-operative Conference. He elaborated on the idea of planning in detail and spoke of outside sources of capital: £E62 million from the USSR, £E44 million from West Germany, £E30 million from Japan and £E7.5 million from East Germany.[71]

"With a view to doubling the national income in ten years . . ."—that was the introduction to Decree Number 1327 of August 2, 1960, which set the objectives of planning and stated "the general objectives of the Plan for the first five years (1960–65)."

In ten years, Dr. Ibrahim Hilmy Abdel Rahman estimated, the national income should rise from £E1.3 billion to £E2.6 billion in 1969–70; consumption expenditures then would reach £E2 billion, against £E1.1 billion in 1959–60, and the national savings would reach £E600 million, whereas they amounted to only £E200 million in 1959–60.[72] The first Five-Year Plan (1960–65) proposed to increase the national income by 40 percent, with a growth rate of 81.8 percent in the sectors of industry, electricity and construction. To this end, local production would have to be increased by 42.6 percent, the rate for the abovementioned sectors being 60.1 percent. In order to do this, it would be necessary to invest a total sum of £E1.697 billion, including £E439 million for industry,

£E237 million for transportation and £E140 million for electric power. The rate of increase for unskilled labor would be 17 percent, while that in "industry, electricity and construction" would be 25.4 percent; wages would rise by 34 percent; labor output would be raised by an average of 21.8 percent, but by 29.4 percent in the unskilled sector. The percentage of domestic savings in relation to the national income would be raised from 11 percent to 21 percent, thus ensuring the financing of at least 65 percent of the investment plan. Consumption would rise by only 24 percent.[73]

The reasoning adduced in justification of the Plan was this: first and foremost, the incapacity of private industry to improve the national income in the proportions and the time made imperative by the growth of the population; second, the necessity "for a balanced development of the national economy"; finally, an argument of a political character: "If the national economy were not subjected to planning, the gap [in wealth and income between the two extremes of society] would continue to widen and would entail the division of our society into two distinct classes: a minority class, which would steadily diminish, owning the income from production, and another class whose numbers would constantly rise, the class that would enjoy only an infinitesimal share of the income from production. It would be superfluous to emphasize the serious repercussions that such a situation would produce in the social structure."[74] Indeed. Here again the military leaders demonstrated greater foresight than did big capital.

This big capital, moreover, was summoned and besought, often in pressing fashion, to show some evidence of initiative under the umbrella of the state. The representatives of the two leader groups met in the government, whose strength was a subject of boasts, but nevertheless those of the military faction—officers and experts—were more and more often the victors.

Why this appeal to private capital? Dr. Aziz Sidky explained it with an artlessness which, in the circumstances, was revealing: "Since it was necessary for us to carry out economic development in its broadest sense and as quickly as possible," he said in December 1959, "we found it necessary to offer private

capital, endowed as it is with all its potentials, the opportunity to take part in industrial projects either alone or in
co-operation with capital from the public sector."[75] A technocratic theoretician, Gamal el-Oteifi, showed clearly that if
"the government prefers the theory of a mixed economy to
that of nationalization," it was because the government preferred that "private capital participate [in development
projects] side by side with the public sector, instead of bearing
the whole burden of financing and exploiting projects itself."[76]
In other words, if, in spite of the undeniable success of the
public sector, the military leaders called on private initiative, it
was because they intended to draw the utmost advantage from
all its still unused resources and potentialities, in some way to
make it contribute right to the end, since at the moment the
state did not yet have available all the financial means or
necessary organization to ensure an upturn.

The Bourgeoisie Weighs Its Chances

What bases for judgment did big Egyptian capital
have at this time as guides for its decisions?

In the sphere of internal politics, the Council of the Nation
had ceased, after the proclamation of Syrian-Egyptian unity,
to be that Assembly in which, in spite of everything, industrialists, businessmen, and financial and professional groups
could make themselves heard and obtain the passage of certain measures, or even, in truth, block others (often in an indirect manner) which they considered too precipitate. But the
loss of this body, which in the end was no more than a forum
for ventilation of opinions, had since been compensated by
two major gains: the mutilation of the Left in Egypt herself
and the opening of the Syrian market to the aspirations of
Egyptian monopolies.

Prisons converted into concentration camps—Maharik, in the
El Kharga oasis, and the military prisons in the Citadel,
the Dams and above all Abu Zaabal—could not hold back the
fragmented news of ill treatment, daily bullying and torture.
So there came word of the deaths under torture of Mohammed
Osman, a government employee (April 2, 1959) at Tanta; of

Mustafa Shawki, a student of commerce (June 1, 1959), at Tanta; of Dr. Farid Haddad, a respected Cairo physician (November 28, 1959), in the military prison of Alexandria; of Saad el-Turki, a municipal employee in Beni Suef (December 31, 1959), in the same prison, where, in addition, the victims included Ali Metwalli el-Dib, one of the leaders of the textile union at Shubra el-Kheima (January 3, 1960); Shohdi Attia el-Shafei, former English-language supervisor in the Ministry of Public Education and also a writer and former president of Dar al-Abhath al-Ilmiyya and of the weekly *al-Gamahir* (June 15, 1960); Mohammed Rushdy Khalil, engineer and organizer of popular resistance at Shubrah (July 25, 1960); and Sayed Amine, leader of the Cairo textile union (October 1960).[77]

On December 11, 1960, the Beirut weekly, *al-Akhbar*, published the text of an anguishing document on torture in Egypt, signed by Abu Seif Yussef, Ismail el-Mahdawi and Ahmed Salem. On December 23, all three were arrested, as well as a group of two hundred militants.[78] This agony of the Egyptian Left, enveloped in silence and the climate of a holy war against Marxism, must have allayed the fears of big capital, which itself had never dared to go so far, except perhaps in 1930–35 under the iron rule of Ismail Sidky.

Furthermore, at the same time that it was thus smashing the Left, the military government laid Syria wide open to the penetration of Egyptian capital. The Misr complex and the Bank of Cairo were unquestionably in the front rank; they were soon followed by all the major banks, the big industrial and commercial corporations and the Economic Agency. While Egyptian imports from Syria rose between 1957 and 1961 from £E3.5 million to £E7.4 million, Egyptian exports to Syria rose from £E1.4 million to £E6.2 million. The Egyptian monopolies had simply supplanted Syria's traditional trading partners —notably Iraq, Lebanon and France—by means of ever-more restrictive regulations that channeled banking, foreign trade and foreign credits. As a final step, the projected unification of the two countries' currencies in a single Arab dinar was supposed to complete the subjugation of the Syrian economy.

In October 1959, there were two big trials of Communists

in the State Security Tribunal, sitting in Alexandria. A first group of sixty-four leaders of the Egyptian Communist party was soon followed by a second group consisting of forty-eight members of the fraction who had broken away from the party and demanded that the Left join the National Union, a move that would in fact have amounted to an abdication to the military authority. Very harsh sentences of hard labor were imposed, but they were not made public until much later. But there were also a few acquittals, particularly those of Mahmud Amin el-Alem, a leading Marxist philosopher and literary critic, and Dr. Abdel Azim Anis, physicist and editor of foreign affairs on *al-Missa;* but they were kept in prison nonetheless.

Regimentation of the trade union movement was at its peak. In 1956, in the euphoria entirely due to Bandung, several laws had broadened the possibilities for the creation of new unions. There were then 1,249 unions with 459,029 members, among whom Communist influence was anything but negligible and who merged their efforts within the General Federation of Trade Unions under the presidency of Anwar Salama, the pro-Nasser leader of the petroleum workers' union. Law No. 91 of April 5, 1959, then created a new labor code, which tightened government control of the unions (Articles 157 and 174).[79] A short time later, unions were suspended throughout the territory of the UAR. Arrests and expulsions mounted rapidly. The RCC installed its own agents and sympathizers. On May 5, 1960, a new law (No. 132) authorized sixty-four unions in the form of a single union for each occupation—a kind of guild system.[80]

In short, and seen from the point of view of the great Egyptian financial and industrial interests, the domestic situation was "encouraging."

Could the same be said of foreign affairs?

Here things were more complex.

Problems of Equilibrium

In spite of the repression unleashed against the Egyptian Communist party and the whole Left, and in spite of the violent tone in the conflict between Nikita Khrushchev and President Nasser, and in the shortwave warfare that pitted Cairo against Peking and Sofia in particular, the Egyptian government had to take into consideration both the sympathy of public opinion toward the Soviet Union and popular admiration for the People's Republic of China, which in addition was closely bound to the UAR within the Afro-Asian solidarity movement.

It also had to take into account the fact that through the West's own fault and as a result of Suez, the Egyptian economy as a whole (investments from abroad and foreign trade) was deeply enmeshed with that of the socialist bloc. In 1960 the socialist countries bought 43.3 percent of Egyptian exports (the USSR alone was responsible for 43 percent of all the purchases made by the socialist countries) and supplied 24.8 percent of Egypt's imports. Commercial exchanges with China, which had shown a profit for Egypt of £E3.5 million an 1959, reached the figure of £E8.7 in favor of Egyptian exporters in 1960. In contrast, there remained a large deficit with the United States, for it amounted to £E30 million, whereas that with Great Britain was £E9 million.[81]

The tendency will stand out more sharply if the years 1952 and 1961 are compared: the West European nations and America, which in 1952 represented 66 percent of Egypt's imports and 57 percent of her exports, accounted in 1961 for only 52 percent and 22 percent respectively, while the shares of the Arab and socialist countries were constantly increasing.[82] The hard-times friends were also the best customers. Nevertheless there was a strong effort on both sides to restore the balance.

Even in the days of John Foster Dulles, United States participation was high, but especially after the election of President Kennedy, when its contribution to the 1960 Five-Year Plan amounted to $162 million, against $173 million from the USSR. Diplomatic exchanges and correspondence between the two Presidents increased. Certain circles in America encouraged the inclination of Nahum Goldmann, president of the World Zionist Organization, to arrive at a *modus vivendi* with the Arab countries: this was at the bottom of the Lavon case, which was stifled in a conspiracy of silence in order to stack the cards for the benefit of world opinion, which was encouraged to regard David Ben-Gurion as a pioneer emeritus of democracy assigned to duty at the outposts of the Orient. Great Britain, which had patiently been negotiating to this end since 1957, renewed diplomatic relations with Egypt.

Sir Harold Beeley, Her Majesty's ambassador in Cairo, announced that there no longer existed any differences between the two countries, and he launched a whole series of moves on the economic, commercial and cultural levels in order to regain for Great Britain, as far as this was possible, the best of the advantages that had once been hers on the banks of the Nile.[83] Japan took part in the Five-Year Plan projects, contributing 33 percent of all foreign aid. Under the impetus of the new policy called for by Enrico Mattei, head of E.N.I.T. (later "killed" in a plane crash), and Premier Amintore Fanfani, Italy announced that she was giving Egypt priority in her investments abroad. France was still one of the largest buyers of cotton. But it was West Germany that proved the most active, relying basically on the sympathy for national socialism that had been strong within the Egyptian officers' corps ever since the time of El Alamein: five thousand students were sent to Germany, which proposed to provide 48.4 percent of the foreign participation in the first Five-Year Plan; joint Egyptian-German companies were formed, and economic, administrative, police and similar experts were sent from West Germany.

As was to have been expected, this renewal with the West was matched by a reconciliation drive in the direction of Egypt's Arab rivals. The fratricidal Egyptian-Iraq campaign was replaced by quite close co-operation within the Arab League as soon as Iraq launched her drive to smash the Iraqi Communist party in 1960. And let us not forget that it was on General Kassem's urgings that Tunisian Premier Habib Bourguiba resumed his place in the League. President Nasser visited the Sudan and Pakistan, where he was cordially received by the authorities. And a voluminous exchange of letters between the President of the UAR and King Hussein of Jordan paved the way for a reconciliation.[84]

In fact, it appeared as if Anglo-American influence, after

Kennedy's accession to the presidency and on the counsel of one of his advisers, Henry Alfred Kissinger, the theoretician of "containment," were being exerted in the firm intention of setting up an Arab protective belt, predominantly Egyptian, on the southwest borders of the socialist bloc. This operation was well under way, the experts thought, and the representatives of big Egyptian capital agreed; but the contradictions remained sharp among the various Arab countries and between the "realists" in power and public opinion, to say nothing of the problem of Israel, which had become much more acute since the aggression of 1956.

Decidedly, in spite of the dark spots in the picture, it was possible for big Egyptian capital to answer "yes."

For after 1959 it had the assurance that it would be able to go on doing a golden business, as it had never stopped doing in the previous five years.[85] The growth of investments was therefore to gain speed in 1959 and 1960: "Thirty-six corporations were formed during 1960," the National Bank of Egypt tells us, "against 19 in 1959; they included 26 industrial companies, 7 commercial companies, 1 mining company, 1 construction company (in public works) and 3 transportation companies . . . The nominal capital of these companies was £E30.7 million, a rise of £E25.2 million, or 460 percent, over the previous year."[86]

And yet at the source, which meant financing, and at the terminal point, which meant dividends, the big-capital group noticed several anomalies. Thus Law No. 163 of 1957 was drawn in such a way as to limit the hold of the banks on the industrial sector: no bank might own more than 25 percent of the stock of any corporation whatever. In other words, the RCC wanted at all costs to avoid the creation of a new complex of the Misr type, which was much too influential in the country as a whole to suit the military. Economists close to business circles and steeped in German and French traditions rose against this law, especially Dr. Kamal Eddine Sidky and Dr. Ali Abdel Rassul, who reiterated the theses of Dr. Gereitly.[87] Decoded, this meant that private enterprise was no longer assured of banking support as substantial as what the Bank Misr had provided for its companies. On January 11,

1959, the corporation law prohibited distribution of a dividend of more than 10 percent of the year's income to stockholders, while at the same time requiring the companies to precede such distribution with the allocation of 5 percent of their profits to the purchase of government bonds. The first clause provoked an indignant outcry, and three days later the government raised the dividend ceiling to 20 percent.[88] But these were danger signals that would not be forgotten.

Nor had the industrialists overlooked another anomaly, this one dealing with the Industrial Bank, which in practice was a public agency: while the total credit advanced by all banks to industry was £E64 million at the end of 1958, the Industrial Bank itself had put up only an infinitesimal part of this sum— £E5.3 million. What is more, this ridiculous amount was most strangely allocated: fifty-five loans of more than £E10,000 made up 90 percent of the total, while 77 percent of the loans were for a term of only one year . . .[89] A curious way for the state to assist private enterprise, the industrial circles thought.

The Nationalization of the Banks

But the nationalization of the two major organs of financial power in Egypt, the National Bank of Egypt and the Bank Misr, on February 11, 1960, indisputably marked the turning point in the development of the alliance between the industrial and financial upper middle class and the military apparatus. Under the nationalization laws, the shares of the two banks were converted into government bonds redeemable after twelve years at their stock exchange closing prices of February 10 and bearing interest at 5 percent. Both boards of directors were retained in office, as were the two presidents, Dr. Emary of the NBE and Mohammed Rushdy of the Misr.

The government's line of reasoning in the case of the NBE raised hardly any difficulties: this bank, whose origins we have mentioned, had been the central bank of the state since 1957. It was therefore natural that, as such, it should be under the management of the state. Furthermore, the confusion between its functions as a bank of issue and those of a commercial bank—a confusion that had dogged its history since its foundation—had inflicted losses of some £E30 million on the state, rising out of blocked holdings; but more than anything else, the NBE's consistent practice of investing its assets in the English market had caused a loss of £E150 million to the Egyptian treasury as a result of the sterling devaluation of 1949.[90]

What justification, however, was to be found for the nationalization of the Bank Misr when industrialization was at a high pitch? From the first, the state put the problem on the political and social plane, subordinating economic and financial reasons.[91]

In his address to Ain Shams University, Dr. Kayssuni pleaded the state's case: the Bank Misr, he said in substance, owned much more than 25 percent of the stock of its companies and thus had violated the law of 1957; it was difficult to compel it to sell the surplus in its portfolio without bringing on a panic on the Stock Exchange; the Bank Misr, whose deposits exceeded £E100 million, had in actuality become the apex of a real holding company like those that had been forbidden by the Anti-Trust Law in the United States; moreover, "this enormous power of the bank was derived from the mass of demand deposits, large and small, that were the property of hundreds of thousands of people"; and finally, "in order to reach the objectives of the [1960] Five-Year Plan within the time limit, we need to have available executory organs that are capable, well trained and able to assume the responsibilities that will be given to them; in sum, "the Bank Misr and its companies constitute a major complex, powerful and well organized on the economic level, which we could either break up into small fractions, in accordance with the banking and insurance law, or preserve, but by transferring the right of direction and management to the state instead of allowing it to remain in the hands of individuals." At the same time the staff of the Ministry of Economics was making public "the complete facts on the relations between the government and the Bank Misr since 1939"[92]: the public was reminded that it was through direct government help (Law No. 40 of 1941) that the bank had been able to acquire new money to the extent of £E2,757,443, the amount of its deficit resulting

from its policy of excessively liberal loans to companies within
the complex, and that until 1960 the management of the bank
had evaded all the compromises proposed by the Finance
Administrative Court for the reimbursement of the state, while
the debt had meanwhile increased substantially through the
accumulation of interest obligations.

Certainly this statement contained a number of arguments of
merit, skillfully developed with all the ability of the talented
professor who delivered it. The fact remained that financial
differences were matters for the courts, whereas nationalization was a political action.

The government, furthermore, explained its position quite
clearly in the press, which it controlled. "There is no doubt,"
al-Ahram said, "that by means of its corporations the Bank
Misr had reached a stage of concentrated monopoly that could
also impose its dominance on the government. While it is true
that the Bank Misr has never attempted to act as a monopoly,
it is proper to point out that the interests of the monopoly
and the threat of dominance existed independently of the fact
whether they were utilized. And though the Bank Misr, as it
was before, had not intended to adopt a monopolistic position
because of the personal convictions of its directors, or because of the firmness of the present government, which makes
such action impossible, the fact remains that the question
should not be dependent on personal determination or the
degree of the government's power, but that it should be resolved by a rule and founded on a doctrine that clarifies its
limitations and its separations . . ."

A potential danger, then? Indeed. Presently the official
exegete cited one example among many. "The banks," he
said, "merely sell money at a profit. But if they maintain
relations with corporations or factories, then there can be no
doubt that such a situation influences the policy of these
banks insofar as the sale of money is concerned. Hence, if one
of these banks, for instance, has an interest in a textile company, it is obvious that this fact will determine its attitude
in the event that it is asked to finance the establishment of a
textile mill, etc."

Thus, then, *the heart of the matter was the power of decision in the economic and social sphere.* It was hardly the principle of private property that was at issue here, but rather the question of knowing which of the two groups, in fact and in the last resort, would have the power to select the means of accomplishing its vision of things to be, within the Egyptian structure.

In addition, and as if to confirm this interpretation of the crisis in the nick of time, the nationalization law affected only Misr's bank, while all its corporations retained their prior position. Accordingly rechristened the Misr Agency in April 1961, the complex absorbed the Belgian & International Bank in Egypt, which had been nationalized immediately after the rupture with Belgium (March 8, 1961) and now became the Bank of Africa.

On March 19 two other and more important companies, the El-Nasr Import-Export Company and the Oriental Cotton Company, were absorbed in the new agency. The bank's managing trio kept their jobs, but they were now subordinated to the board of directors of the Misr Agency, headed at first by a minister, Hassan Abbas Zaki, and after June 21, 1961, put under the chairmanship of Dr. Helmy el-Said, director of the economic office of the President of the Republic. He was assisted by the bank's triumvirs and several technocrats from the military staff: Samir Helmy, Magdi Ali Yunes, Hassan Marei, el-Sayed Eweiss, Ahmed Tewfik el-Bakry and Mohammed Ali Hassan.[93] Meanwhile the bank's branches in Syria, as well as those of the Bank of Cairo and certain Egyptian insurance companies in Syria, were incorporated into the Economic Agency, which thus replaced the Egyptian financier groups in the exploitation of the "northern province."[94]

How did big capital react? The economists allied with economic liberalism protested, even though they admitted the need for the Five-Year Plan: Dr. Emary, one of the greatest Egyptian experts, resigned as head of the NBE on March 25; he was immediately replaced by Dr. Abdel Hakim el-Rifai, a former professor more or less in retirement. On November 20 Rifai was made president of the Central Bank of Egypt and Dr. Mohammed Abu Shadi became president of the NBE, now a commercial bank only.

To be accurate, not too much is known of the reactions. Alarmist rumors circulated in business circles. The government strove to drown them in a multiplicity of spectacular gestures, with a view to making Egypt the factory of the Arab world, the greatest industrial base in Africa and the major economic power of the Middle East. Business and industrial groups were called upon to take part in the policy of expansion, the themes of which were developed theoretically at the time under the guise of "Arab nationalism." The emphasis, quite naturally, was laid on the export of consumer goods, in view of the disparity between the growth of production of the new factories and the negligible rise in purchasing power. "It is important to co-ordinate the action of the Misr Agency and the companies it comprises, particularly in the African countries, in order to exploit the abundant opportunities that exist there, and to study the newest developments in promotion in order to be able to give our products the proper exposure," Hassan Abbas Zaki, Executive Minister of Economics, said on April 27, 1961.[96] Several officials in the lower echelons made it their business to reassure capital. "The public sector," Dr. Mohammed Fuad Ibrahim explained, "has always kept control of the private sector in all the countries on their way to economic development; nevertheless, once such a state has made progress along this line and the average income of every citizen has increased, it will be seen that a great number of companies will return to the hands of the private sector, whereas the public sector will go back to its previous function";[97] and Dr. Abdel Rahman el-Banna, Undersecretary of State in the Central Ministry of Economics, asserted that "the objective of government intervention is to avoid losses . . . ; once a project has become successful, the government will sell the share that it owns."[98]

The installation of the powerful state sector, charged with expansion at home as well as abroad, was carried forward at an accelerated pace. The National Bank of Egypt bought the Banca Italo-Egiziana (£E5 million in deposits) on March 19 and the Greek-owned N. Tepeghiozi Bank of Commerce the next day; before 1961 had ended, its projects included an increase in the number of branches from 36 to 45, and from

11 to 23 cotton and grain warehouses around the country. On April 15, 1961, a High Council for Public Agencies was created and put under the presidency of Abdel Hakim Amer, who had been promoted to the rank of marshal on the occasion of the Syrian-Egyptian merger. Its members included the Economic Agency, the Misr Agency, the El-Nasr Agency (especially charged with the execution of the industrial projects of the 1960 Five-Year Plan), the Co-operative Production Agency, the Economic Consumption Agency and the Co-operative Agricultural Agency.[99] This was to make it possible immediately to launch "important researches carried out by the banks in order to create an independent corporation that would be dedicated to the realization of banking projects in various countries of Africa and Asia in co-operation with certain capitalists in those countries."[100]

Arab Oil and Underdevelopment

It was the Arab front, of course, that the government envisaged as the first theater of action for big capital, which was increasingly under the control of the public sector in the hands of the officers and their experts. The UAR delegations to economic sessions of the Arab League carried on a sustained campaign for the creation of an Arab Common Market and the achievement of Arab economic unity within ten years; in spite of Lebanon's reservations and Tunisia's boycott, the Arab Economic Council was formed on March 13, 1960. Several measures were adopted: the elimination of restrictions of nationality for corporations in Arab countries; a customs union; the creation of an Arab entity in the IBRD which was later headed by Dr. Emary, who became vice-president of the bank in 1962; a plan to establish an Arab Development Agency was initiated in spite of the misgivings of several countries. As many official Egyptian reports attest, this would permit Egypt, by far the most advanced of the Arab countries from an economic point of view and also the only one having a strong and relatively effective state power, to enjoy complete freedom of action throughout the Arab world, "from the Atlantic to the Arabian Gulf," formerly the private preserve of the imperialist monopolies. Lebanon, Iraq and Turkey, however, raised obstacles to this expansion, and the project for the ADA became a dead issue (April–May 1961).

In reality the heart of the problem on the Arab level, as on the purely Egyptian level, was the financing of the development process, which was inevitably long and difficult. It was not, at least basically, as a market to absorb manufactured products that the Arab world interested the two groups joined in power in Egypt, but rather as a tremendous source of wealth in oil and potential financial resources. It was the peripheral Arab oil resources—in Iraq, Kuwait, Bahrein, Qatar, Saudi Arabia—that Egypt meant to bring back within the inter-Arab circuit, which was predominantly Egyptian, for it was this oil alone whose resources were sufficient to finance and fuel Egypt's vast endeavor as the factory of the Arab world.

On May 19, 1961, Mohammed Hassanein Heykal, in a ringing editorial in *al-Ahram*, set forth President Nasser's ideas. Starting from a report of the First National City Bank of New York on Arab oil, dated April 1959, Heykal advanced the following argument: Egypt, the vanguard of "Arab nationalism" and, as such, responsible for the whole movement, had launched a bitter battle against Western imperialism; later she had had to accept the sacrifices required for the creation of an initial source for economic development "without even a glance at the tremendous riches going to waste beneath the desert sands," alone at grips with her destiny; every year $1.25 billion in oil income was allocated by the aforesaid Arab countries to every kind of purpose except "the strengthening of intrinsic Arab power"; it was henceforth no longer possible to imagine that the Arab potentates might still have some unfulfilled desire—in wealth, in pleasures, in luxury, even in extravagance—after those decades of irresponsibility; the time had at last arrived "for anarchy to be taken in hand," for a spiritual rebirth, for the dedication of oil income to the development of the producing countries "in order to construct an intrinsic Arab power with the United Arab Republic."[101]

The Primacy of the Military Apparatus

The new balance of the forces controlling the country's economic life was reflected even at the heart of political power. Undoubtedly the years 1959–61, in question here, were those in which the military group gave the greatest part of its effort to the integration of Syria into the structure of the military government. But the combination of the two situations—the reorganization of Egyptian economic leadership and Syrian-Egyptian unification—made readjustments even more painful.

This was observed particularly in the composition and functioning of the new Council of the Nation of the UAR, and in the domain of decentralization as well, whether of local administration or of the executive power in the two "regions" of the UAR.

By virtue of Article 13 of the Provisional Constitution of the UAR, proclaimed on March 5, 1958, President Gamal Abdel Nasser himself appointed the 600 members of the new National Assembly—400 for Egypt and 200 for Syria.[102]—on July 18, 1960. Three days later the President delivered the opening address, in which he hailed "the emergence of a great state in this Orient, a state that is neither an intruder nor an oppressor"; Anwar el-Sadate was elected president of the Assembly, but a violent incident erupted with a Syrian deputy, Mohammed el-Kassar, regarding the elections to the vice-presidencies, which were won by Mohammed Fuad Galal and Rateb el-Hussami.[103]

In actuality the state's activities were extending beyond the reach of the Council of the Nation. Thus the two most important measures affecting internal policy in 1960 were promulgated even before the deputies met. These were the joint budget and the budgets of the two regions for the fiscal year 1960–61, promulgated by an Order in Council on July 14, 1960, and also the memorable decree of May 24, 1960, on "the organization of the press." The ownership of the newspaper publishing companies Al-Ahram, Akhbar el-Yom, Rose el-Yussef and Dar al-Hilal—that is, the entire Egyptian press except the Al-Tahrir company, which also published the semi-official papers, *al-Gumhuriyya* and *al-Missa*—as well as the foreign-language newspapers that formerly belonged to the Oriental Advertising Company, was "vested in the National Union," whose members alone would be allowed to practice journalism in the future. What was sought, the explanatory note said, was "to prevent the domination of capital in the political and social media."[104]

Why was the government vexed with the press, which had been so tractable since the mutilation of *al-Missa* in March 1959? The answer was given to the journalists by President Nasser in person during a round-table conference on May 29: "You have dealt with problems of our society. But you have never explained the concept of the society in which you would like to live. You have turned backward many years, many decades . . . But no one has attempted to confront the problems that are ours and to propose solutions and thorough-going studies." In addition, he criticized the superficial aspect of the newspapers, their competitive sensationalism, in fact their pornography, as well as a complete lack of contact with reality, with everyday life of the people. [105]

What the government reproached in the journalists was their disaffection toward itself, their lack of trust in the proclamations that accompanied the ever-harsher measures of restriction. Now, it was possible to tolerate such a state of affairs in normal times, but things could not remain the same at a time when the problems posed by unification were growing more pronounced and when, as well, the sessions of the Council of the Nation were about to begin, though it was composed of hand-picked men. There must be no repetition of the unrest in 1957–8, when the opposition within the National Assembly could find arguments in the program of *al-Missa* and the articles of its young Marxist "doctors." And as if to prove that it was not the old behavior that irritated the government, the National Union itself decided to appoint the heads of the four newspaper publishers: *al-Ahram–al-Hilal* would be run by Fikri Abaza, a sworn enemy of the Wafd under the old system, one of the spokesmen of the minority parties of the right, a specialist in political double-talk, a member of the powerful Abaza family and closely linked to the Misr complex; *Akhbar el-Yom* was entrusted to Mohammed el-Tabei, a veteran of the Egyptian press known for his fascist sympathies; Ehsan Abdel Koddus, having been found politically safe, remained in charge of *Rose el-Yusef*; and Salah Salem retained his post with the government's newspaper publishing company, Dar al-Tahrir. But what was far more important was that Mohammed Hassanein Heykal, President Nasser's closest adviser and formerly one of the editors of *Akhbar el-Yom*, became editor in chief of *al-Ahram*, the most important daily newspaper in Egypt and the Arab world.

From the autumn of 1960 to July 1961, thus reduced to its proper proportions, the Council of the Nation was to busy itself with the arrangements required for the economic-development program, duly ratifying the various reports and speeches of the officials, even though once more the Syrian deputies were to raise discordant voices. From January to April 1961, it would painfully bring into being a committee of ninety members charged with evolving a draft Constitution. Its personnel included 27 lawyers, 5 former ministers, 2 former high officials, 8 former officers, 7 physicians, 1 pharmacist, 3 journalists, 5 clergymen, 1 businessman, 7 farmers, 4 engineers, 9 professors, 6 economists, 2 certified accountants, 3 workers and 3 women.[106]

There was also much talk of decentralization and local government. The law of March 26, however, provided that the President of the Republic should appoint and remove the provincial governors, who were responsible directly to him (Article 5), and it was the Chief Executive that was to select from the National Union the members of the provincial councils and the new city councils, as well as the chief executives of the cities and the village councils (Titles II, III and IV).[107] On August 30, 1961, this law was to be amended again, with the intention of increasing the powers of the governors, bound still more closely to the person of the chief of state, since the termination of his tenure would automatically conclude theirs.[108]

There was less and less room for the elected representatives of any groups other than the National Union, which had become the military leadership's mass political voice. But it will be observed that, with the exception of the governors, the middle and lower officials were all men of the old government recruited after the removal of General Naguib: the same *omdehs,* the same sheiks *el-balad,* the same sheiks *el-hara,** the same rural landowners. In the large cities, however, some-what more emphasis was put on the categories that were involved with the new economy (engineers, economists, mer-chants), in preference to the lawyers and intellectuals of the old days.[109]

Finally, at the level of executive authority—the central government of the UAR and the Executive Council of the two regions—it may be observed, without going into details, that the elimination of the Baath party and the representatives of Syrian political tendencies was accompanied by the installation of a whole network of officers, notably Syrians, as well as the strengthening of the powers held by the managers of the ap-paratus, especially Abdel Latif el-Boghdadi, Abdel Hakim Amer and Kamal Eddine Hussein. The two revisions of October 7, 1958, and September 20, 1960, as well as the un-ending wave of resignations, shifts and promotions, also operated toward this end.[110]

Here too the balance was overthrown in favor of the military apparatus; the upper bourgeoisie, which continued to share in authority, no longer enjoyed the political influence that it had had during the years 1955–58.

* Local district official in cities, assumed to represent the people in minor municipal affairs.

CHAPTER 3

DISMANTLING
OF THE OLD
BOURGEOISIE

THE SUMMER OF 1961 began in an atmosphere
of deadlock. In the name of "Arab nationalism" and in order
to satisfy the Egyptian financial circles' hunger for new outlets,
the military government had answered Syria's appeal and
agreed to assume that organic unity to which not only history
and geography but also economics opposed detailed arguments, whose validity it would inevitably be necessary to
acknowledge later. All the timetables had to be revised, and
effort was diffused throughout this new state joined by no
common territory. The dissensions that were shaking Syria
compelled the leaders to compromise, to postpone target dates,
to try to incorporate Syrian political circles, rebellious at any
continuity.

But in Egypt the formidable problems of development remained, in the face of a phenomenal growth in population.[1]
In spite of the intense organizational work undertaken during
the second period (1955–61), in spite of Egyptianization, the
1958 Five-Year Plan, the nationalizations, in spite of the very
considerable foreign aid that placed Egypt in the second rank
of Afro-Asian powers (behind India) in this respect, the
country's wealth was still being employed only in part, while
its capital was getting very little use, and that in a rather in-
coherent fashion. Above all, the great industrial and financial

bourgeoisie was keeping aloof. Endowed with theoreticians (in economics), with top- and middle-level executives and administrators, with tremendous capital, with connections that reached into political circles, notably in the Council of the Nation, with its own newspapers and its own publising houses, with its hold on education, it remained an independent force. The increasing difficulties with Syria gave the military leaders reason to fear that their economic projects would be impeded and even that an insidious subversion might be able to exploit the discontent of several important sectors, notably the disaffection of the intellectuals toward the government; it was possible that the general public might be asked to consider some less autocratic means of building a modern Egypt.

Once more, after the spring of 1954 and the beginning of the Bandung period, the RCC could choose between a certain liberalization and the strengthening of the military authority. This time, however, after Suez, the power group was not alone; it had gradually installed a network of leaders newly recruited to public life—soldiers and technocrats—who held a solid grip not only on the state apparatus but also on the management of economic and financial policy by way of the public sector. The margin of choice was thus considerably narrowed. In fact, the basic options, taken, as we have seen, under the duress of events, were developing in accordance with what appeared more and more to be the exigency of an internal necessity, of their own logic.

The Nationalizations of July 1961

Once again Gamal Adbel Nasser took the initiative, for he was still a master of timing. In June, and particularly in July, while the National Assembly was in recess, a number of Orders in Council and Presidential decrees appeared that were to alter profoundly the balance of the existing social forces. The National Bank of Egypt emphasized three groups of laws: those dealing with redistribution of the national income; those assuring the pre-eminence of the public sector as against private enterprise and the monopoly groups; and revision of the Agrarian Reform, which we have already discussed.[2] This, however, was an analysis of a formalist kind, since the essential purpose of all three categories was to diminish the resources, the (economic) potential and the (political) influence of big Egyptian capital to the advantage of the military group, by now the master of the public sector. But it must be added that these measures as a whole were intended also to inject all available resources into the bloodstream of economic development and to make possible a considerable increase at the same time in savings and in demand in the home market.

A first series of laws affected the commercial sector, and more especially that of cotton: all merchant enterprises and commercial agencies were to be owned only by citizens of the UAR (Law No. 47 of June 6, 1961); the Alexandria Commodity Exchange was suspended, the monopoly on cotton purchases for 1961–62 was given to the Egyptian Cotton Authority, and, above all, cotton-exporting firms were compelled to become Egyptian corporations with a minimum capital of £E200,000, of which 50 percent must mandatorily be held by the public sector (Laws Nos. 69, 70, 71 and 120 of June 22 to July 20). The Egyptian Cotton Authority was given public-agency status; it was attached to the Ministry of Economics and invested with an autonomous entity (Decree No. 972 of June 30); the Central Bank of Egypt was authorized to apply the public deposits of agencies in the public sector to the funds for the financing of projects under the Five-Year Plan (Law No. 102 of July 5).

A second series of laws was directed against inequalities in income: limited or joint-stock companies were required, after the mandatory allocation of 5 percent of their profits for the purchase of government bonds, to allot 25 percent to employees and workers, paying 10 percent in cash, 5 percent toward their housing and 10 percent for social security (Law No. 111 of July 19);[3] a ceiling was established on compensation payable to company and agency officers at £E5,000 per year (Law No. 113 of July 19); boards of directors were limited to seven members, including one representative of office employees and one of labor (Law No. 114 of July 19); above all, the rate of progressive taxation was raised to a maximum of 90 percent on incomes of more than £E10,000 per year (Law No. 115 of July 19); all persons were forbidden to hold more than one position, whether in government administration, in public agencies, in corporations or in other enterprises (Law No. 125 of July 21); finally, the graduated tax on buildings was substantially increased, especially for luxury apartment houses (Law No. 129 of July 25).

But it was in the key area of ownership and management of productive enterprises that the government struck its most spectacular blows, which decisively transformed its ally to its subordinate in the exercise of power.

Two laws, first of all, had foreshadowed the offensive of July 20. In addition to the measure that entailed the merger of Abbud's Khedivial Mail Line with the General Steamship Company (thereafter to be the property of the Public Transportation and Communications Agency under Law No. 109 of July 9), a second law (No. 110 of July 9, amended later by Law No. 121 of July 20) transferred ownership in the four chief cotton-baling companies to a new public agency and converted their shares into 4 percent government bonds.

On July 20 three laws (Nos. 117, 118 and 119) struck decisive blows. The first provided for the pure and simple nationalization of all banks and insurance companies, plus fifty other corporations, shipping companies and other firms operating in the area of heavy and basic industries. Their shares were to be converted into fifteen-year, 4 percent government bonds. The second law, covering eighty-three companies in the fields of light processing and public works, provided that at least 50 percent of their capital must be held by a public agency. The third law, which affected 147 medium industrial companies (notably in textiles) belonging to groups or families, established state participation through state ownership of all shares held by each stockholder in excess of £E10,000.[4]

Several supplementary laws soon followed in order to close any loopholes: the Cairo and Alexandria stock exchanges were suspended for two months (Law No. 116 of July 19); the concessions granted to the Lebon Gas Company in Alexandria and the Cairo Streetcar Company were revoked and the companies' assets were transferred to two public agencies (Laws Nos. 122 and 123 of July 20); public works amounting to more than £ E30,000—which meant the majority of undertakings of this kind—could no longer be carried out by private enterprise; only public corporations, of which half was owned by public agencies, could acquire such contracts (Decree No. 1203 of July 20); the workweek was fixed at forty-two hours and all overtime was prohibited (Law No. 133 of July 27); no ministry, public agency or private company was permitted to take any steps toward obtaining foreign credit without prior authorization by the Ministries of Economics and of the Treasury (Decree No. 1495 of September 24).[5]

What happened to the Misr complex in all this upheaval? Only one Misr company, the foreign trade enterprise, was totally nationalized, because of its monopolistic nature. Another, the cotton-ginning company, became part of the second group, in which the state held 50 percent of the stock. But the great majority of the companies—ten in all—fell into the third, relatively protected group.

The government stated its case, opening the records of its disagreements with its capitalist ally. Ali Sabry, Minister for the Presidency of the Republic, laid the emphasis on the economic justifications. "It was necessary," he said, "to mobilize the nation's savings in a deliberate fashion in order to accomplish the national objective: development . . . Similarly, this economic mobilization must be carried out in conformance with our basic principles: it must respect the individual's right to existence, his right to creation and growth, and his right to property within the framework of the law . . . It was on the foundation of these positions that the word 'nationalization' was coined; 'nationalization' is ownership by the nation in the true literal sense of the word . . . For us the public sector is not a method chosen for the liquidation of property but rather one that should lead to the broadening of its base . . ."[6]

All this remained theoretical. It was M. H. Heykal—returning to the themes developed by the President in his speeches of July 23 and 26, 1961, for the ninth anniversary of the coup d'état—who provided the keys to the matter. The first steps in nationalization after Suez, he explained in substance, made the public sector—in other words, the state—the major entrepreneur, the essential moving force in the field of economic development. At the same time the Egyptianization measures brought private enterprise back into the hands of Egyptian capitalists, who had occasionally served as fronts for foreigners who used to pull the strings. During the past five years— from 1956 to 1961—the number of trade representatives' offices established abroad by large Egyptian companies had quintupled, and several thousand people waiting for the chance to grow rich had finally found the means to do so under the banner of nationalism and revolution, thanks to the combination of nationalization and Egyptianization. In this way "public socialist disbursements were contributing to an increase in the number of millionnaires."

This was when the real danger arose, the danger that had made the power of decision the issue: financiers, promoters, merchants and industrialists had united in order to determine the profit rate that it was proper to derive from their major customer—the state; several major projects that were part of the Five-Year Plan had broken down, since no private enterprise wanted to assume its burdens, which were occasionally less profitable than their traditional operations; a strange lack of genuine competition had been observed in the matter of prices, as if a tacit agreement had suddenly been reached to leave such and such a deal to such and such a company at whatever price it chose to set; and nepotism was widespread —in fact, it might even be said to have become an institution. By way of economics the Egyptian upper bourgeoisie intended in this way to regain the right of control of which the military had deprived it within the Council of the Nation.

The matter became more complicated at the end of 1959. It was at that time, in fact, that on the one hand the law restricting corporate profits and on the other hand the broad outlines of the 1960 Five-Year Plan made it plain to big capital that it was going to be compelled to provide a very important contribution to the goal of increasing the national income by approximately 10 percent per year for ten years and that this would require substantial investments—according to the experts' reckoning, 25 percent of the national income. "It was then that exploiting capital sought to flee before the wind of revolution that was beginning to sweep across the nation's horizon and also to protect itself against the Revolutionary laws, which it had to evade in order to accomplish its own ends." Since corporation profits were limited to the ceiling of 1958, plus an increase of 10 percent per year, big capital set up its own "sales offices," to which the boards of directors entrusted the distribution of their products, operating outside the requirements of the law from the very start. In this way it was the small stockholders who paid, since, in their search for maximum profits, the companies often sold their output at a loss to "buying agencies," thus increasing the profits in the pockets of the big capitalists. There was also another, more classic method: disproportionate increases in reserve funds and depreciation allowances on new equipment, often amortized in four or five years and thus reducing their value to a purely nominal figure while the machines were still almost new. The difference, of course, stuck to the hands of the large stockholders, beyond the reach not only of the tax collector but also of investment.[7] An "economic Suez" was becoming inevitable[8] if there was to be a neutralization of the increasing influence exerted on the economic level by this industrial and financial upper bourgeoisie which was determined to use its weight in the orientation of general policies and thus to participate in power even if the specifically political trappings of power were not permitted to it. Such was the basic content of President Nasser's two speeches delivered on July 23 and 26, 1961, to mark the ninth anniversary of the coup d'état.[9]

What must be clearly noted is the fact that the state under a military government, which had supplanted the capitalists in the ownership and management of a substantial sector of economic activity, regarded that substitution as a reform measure taken within the limits of the principle of respect for the right of private ownership not only of consumer goods but equally of the means of production.

It was thus that the three laws of July 20 provided, employing different methods in each instance, for the indemnification of stockholders, which meant the owners of the corporations affected by these laws, with registered government bonds bearing interest of 4 percent for fifteen years on a face value established by closing stock exchange prices on the day preceding the promulgation of the laws. As in the case of land reform, it was a question of upholding the sacred principle of private property, on which, however, the state imposed a ceiling made imperative by the requirements of financing the development plan.

The principal blow was struck on the sociopolitical level: it consisted in the reduction of the social influence, in the broadest meaning of the term, of the bourgeoisie, whether that be the old landed aristocracy or the industrial and financial sector allied with the military group during the first two stages and, consequently, with that group's power of decision and political action.

The End of Syrian-Egyptian Union

Panic reigned in the big-capital circles of Cairo and Alexandria, but also and mainly among the merchants and the influential circles of Damascus and Aleppo. For them, and above all for the men of the "Five" Association,[10] much less well structured than the Egyptian middle class, the only prospect ahead was their elimination for the benefit of the Egyptian nation's leaders. On August 16, three weeks after the July laws, the executive branch of the UAR was revised: hereafter there would no longer be two regional Executive Councils under the Central Cabinet, but a single entity, the Central Cabinet of the UAR, directly under President Nasser, who would be assisted by seven Vice-Presidents of the Republic (including two Syrians, Nur Eddine Kahala, in charge of production problems, and Colonel Abdel Hamid Seraj, in charge of internal affairs).[11]

Early in the morning of September 28, 1961, Syrian units garrisoned at Katana, near Damascus, began to move on the capital. Marshal Abdel Hakim Amer was arrested after rejecting an ultimatum presented by the Syrian officers. A battle broke out between the officers of Aleppo, adherents of unity with Egypt, and the coalition of political parties and officers in Damascus who intended to re-establish Syrian independence. The outcome is history: once it was clear that Syria wanted to leave the UAR, President Nasser avoided the hornet's nest of military intervention, accepted the accomplished fact and decided to cut his losses.[12] That was the first phase.

The problem now confronting the military government was the general direction of Egyptian policy. Discussion began in whispers throughout the country, and even within the army itself: should Egypt sacrifice her time, her resources and her prestige on the altar of nationalism or of Arab expansion?

To the general public, the unification with Syria, in spite of all the extensive propaganda a posteriori, did not mesh with the deepest traditions of the national movement nor, indeed, with Egyptian sentiment and perspective in these matters. The merger had been made without any great enthusiasm, and no Egyptian had grown up in the spirit of sacrifice for Arab unity. This was the background against which the severance of Syria was silhouetted. The fact remained, however, that for the man in the street, to say nothing of the dispossessed bourgoisie that was champing at the bit, it was the first major defeat for President Nasser and, perhaps, the weakening of his power. It was from this point of view, then, and not from national grief that public feeling in Egypt was to be understood. Reactions abroad varied: the Communist bloc, including Yugoslavia, and several Afro-Asian countries emphasized the points scored by the imperialist powers and the relative loss to the prestige of one of the leaders of neutralism in the world; but the Communist parties, while recognizing this fact, also emphasized the setback to the antidemocratic dictatorship set up by the military government.[13] In the West, rejoicing was at a peak, and, it was thought, the tyrant's days were numbered. The primacy thus given to emotionalism and the lust for vengeance blocked out the essential issue: the relation between the military government and the basic forces of the Egyptian people.

That was instinctively understood by Gamal Abdel Nasser. His resounding self-criticism of October 16 was designed to present him to the Egyptian people as a victim of good-hearted

Egypt, which, in spite of ups and downs, had rushed to the aid of a Syria in the clutches of anarchy. On October 16 Nasser endeavored to identify himself with Egyptian resentment. He wondered, for the first time in public, what causes had brought about the defeat that he had suffered. "We," he said, "have been the victims of a dangerous illusion to which we were led by an exaggerated trust in ourselves and in others. We have always rejected any reconciliation with imperialism. But we have committed the sin of a reconciliation with reaction . . . which demonstrated its readiness to ally itself with imperialism itself in order to regain its privileged positions. Imperialism has changed its tactic of penetration of our country, while we have made no change in our way of standing up to it." The illusion "of imagining that it might be possible for us to reconcile ourselves to the reactionary trend on national grounds" had represented a danger aggravated by "the inadequacy of popular organization." What of the National Union? "Our fault lay in having opened the National Union to reactionary forces, which, having established themselves within it, paralyzed its revolutionary effectiveness." A third reason: "We have not made the necessary effort to make the masses aware of their rights, to let them know that they could and should defend those rights." Two further reasons dealt with the state apparatus itself: "We have not succeeded in effecting the development of the governmental machinery to the level of revolutionary action"; the result was "the subjugation of the masses to the state apparatus, with all the faults that this entails," and at the same time—the fifth reason for the defeat—"the opportunity for numerous factors in our society to open breaches for opportunism."[14]

The Offensive Against the Upper Bourgeoisie

Above and beyond the adroitness of this, it must be noted that the general line of the self-criticism was in reality directed against the ally of 1952 to 1961, against that bourgeoisie which refused to be indentured, but also against everything that in the state apparatus was still tainted by the habits of the old order: inefficiency, nepotism, pyramided despotism, outmoded bureaucracy, all of them factors which furthered the cause of the "ally"—in other words, which blocked that of the military hegemony. It was not only the governmental apparatus but also the government's single party which had proved to be a veritable breeding-ground for those who were nostalgic for old times.

If the laws of July 1961 were intended to neutralize the upper bourgeoisie, the speech of October 16 showed clearly that what was ahead for it was dismantling.

This time it was not the Communists who would be accused of collusion with the imperialists, as at the time of the unification.

From October 1961 to February 1962 the offensive against the old bourgeoisie was developed on the two levels of economics and politics. In order to lead it, the military government, within which all the old members of the Revolutionary Command Council maintained solidarity around their chief, reorganized the Cabinet. On October 18 the new Cabinet was formed: 25 ministers, of whom 5 were Vice-Presidents of the Republic, and 3 vice-ministers; of this total of 28 men, 13 belonged to the officer corps, since the President of the Republic and the five Vice-Presidents were all military men.[15] On October 22 Zakaria Mohieddine, Vice-President of the Republic and Minister of the Interior, announced the arrest of 40 prominent men, most of them Wafdists, and the sequestration of the property of 167 "reactionary capitalists"—in fact, all the great families of the traditional Egypt.[16] This second measure was quickly expanded: it spread out to 600 people by mid-November, their properties being managed by several dozen administrators placed under the authority of Abdel Latif Ezzat; 80 banks, insurance companies and other corporations were put under the authority of Hafez Abdel Hamid el-Kashef on the ground of "emergency sequestration."[17]

Why the arrests? According to some versions,[18] a group that included thirty higher officers devoted to the interests of the old bourgeoisie had presented to Marshal Amer, their commander in chief, a document demanding the end of the dictatorship and the restoration of democratic liberties and the parliamentary system. These officers were supposed to have made contact primarily with the Wafdist leaders, whence the step of preventive arrests in order to check the opposition movement, which could not help finding a favorable field and an incitement in the Syrian secession. At any rate, this was the thesis elaborated by Zakaria Mohieddine, who, however, did not mention the matter of the officers.

Once the alarm had passed without sequel, all the men arrested were released on February 13 and 14, 1962.[19] Several orders for sequestration were also rescinded, and 348 orders of "isolation" were also revoked, although the millionnaire Ahmed Abbud, whose face, frozen in bitterness, was displayed in all the papers, was haled before the State Security Tribunal on a charge of embezzlement;[20] and it was learned that the total of the holdings of which he was divested by the state, for the most part in government bonds, came to £E33 million. Examples were made of other millionnaires: the Sultan family, whose fortune went back to the grandfather's betrayal of Arabi's revolution in 1882, which at the time brought him 33,000 *feddans* of good land as a gift from the occupant. And François Tagher, it was said, had suddenly become rich by the war after beginning as a stockholder in a small textile mill with a total capital of £E10,000 in 1942 and then skillfully maneuvering the rights to a large part of the cotton stockpile held by the government; he had a fortune of more than £E3 million at the end of the war. Now a big industrialist, he was accused of having systematically transferred £E10 million every year to London while he kept £E6 million in Egypt as bank deposits for himself and his family.

"Was it possible to persuade the millionnaires to divest themselves willingly of part of their private fortunes in order to create a public fortune that would be invested in development?" Heykal wondered before he turned his guns on the Council of the Nation. That body, he said, "as a result of circumstances and because of its own composition, represented an interval in the political revolution, as well as the temporization that was imposed by the circumstances of the unification with Syria." He cited one example among many: "The Council of the Nation—and this is said without any ill will—rejected the law to increase land taxes . . . The government exerted itself to win it over by various means—in the interest of the peasant himself—to agree to fixing this tax to be paid by the peasant at the old rate, but the Council insisted on keeping the tax at a rate seven times higher [the rate fixed by the old Agrarian Reform Law] . . . This was the major reason why the socialist laws of July were not submitted to the Council of the Nation, which would not have approved them in spite of their vital urgency for the beginning of the social revolution."[21]

The work of the agencies assigned to the demolition was to lay bare the inner mechanisms of Egyptian society and to provide a rich harvest for the sociologists. The results, verified by the Central Bank, were published exclusively by *al-Ahram* during the period between October 20 and November 1, 1961. There is the stuff of a thesis in them. For the moment, remembering the limits of this study, here is a rapid analysis of them:

(1) The first document dealt with the wealth owned by the members of the third group, which was the target of Law No. 119 of July 20. This was the law providing for the state's acquisition of all shares in 147 companies in excess of £E10,000 worth per person. It dealt, as we have said, with light industry; the holdings of these same men in banks, insurance companies and heavy and basic industries barely appear in this list. It mentions 595 men (and a small number of companies) that fit into this category, notably of the following families: Cozzika, Meligi, Matossian, Deif, Kahil, Salama, Catzeflis, Habashi, Tagher, Shishini, Serag Eddine, Badraui, Doss, Muro, Abdel Maksud Ahmed, Kabbani, Farghali, Tahri, Agguri, Barhamsha, Abdel Hadi, Farkuh, Takla, Cassab, Ovadia Salem, Mishriki, Abdel Wahab, Jebara, Diab, Debbané, Goganian, Hamaui, Shehata, Abdel Dayem, Nokrashy, Tawil, Khuri, Sursock, Geraya, Zanati, Mallawani, Ghindi, Yussef, Hakim, Stravitch, Selim, Saad, Sebahi, Ghali, Habib, Sueidan, Mehseb, Giannoti, et al. There were a few important names of business and finance; but this first list, somehow, gives hardly more than the small holdings, since the major part was invested in the banks and corporations nationalized either totally or by 50 percent.

(2) The second list, which contains 558 names, deals with

the same category. This time the prominent families affected include such names as Ashur, Sabry, Badaui, Kavalgian, Sinaglia, Papadopulo, Silaides, Abul Naga, Homsy, Eweiss, Dosh, Hussein, Talaat Harb, Negeim, Wahba, Suaya, Lozi, Kholi, Sednaui, Ismail, El-Abd, Off, Mamduh Mursi, Emad, Ammar, Abaza, Kallini, Sallum, Samakiyya, Mehelmy, Barakat, Grassi, Attal, Shawarby, Kahla, Hamada, Miskawi, Boyadzhev, Shami, Mohammed Hassan, Kettana, Yercel, etc.

(3) The third list was that of the stockholders of one of the largest land corporations in Egypt, the Abukir Real Estate Company, which was totally nationalized and which, before July, owned enormous areas running from Abukir, east of Alexandria, and passing through the city, to the Western Desert. The list mentions the number of shares held by several hundred owners, without, however, stating their total wealth. A high proportion of foreign names will be observed, and the Greek, Italian and Levantine names with their Mediterranean connotations are like a backdrop to Lawrence Durrell's *Quartet* . . .[22]

(4) The same curiously cosmopolitan physiognomy appears again in the fourth list, which, this time, deals with the stockholders of the Wadi Kom-Ombo Corporation, with a capital of £E1,755,000. The largest real estate corporation in Egypt, owning the best areas of Said and also the monopoly on sugar-cane plantations, it too was largely in the hands of foreign capitalists.

(5) A fifth list identifies the chief stockholders of the complex of the four largest cotton-ginning companies in Egypt: the El-Gharbiya Cotton-Ginning Company, the Alexandria Commercial Company, the Misr Cotton Company of Kafr el-Zayyat and the National Cotton-Ginning Company. Other, less important companies are also analyzed here: Costi Yakimoglu & Company, H. Cooper & Company and the Egyptian Cotton Export Company. The proportion of foreign stockholders is again very high.

(6) The sixth list furnishes an analysis of a group of big companies belonging to various sectors: the Egyptian Research & Operations Company, the National Metallurgical Industries Company, the Delta Trading Company, the Spinning, Weaving

& Knitting Company, Delta Steel Mills, the Egyptian Public Works Company, the Bassili Pasha Wood Company, the Egyptian Wood & Materials Company (SIM), the Egyptian Preserved Food Company (KAHA).

(7) The seventh list identifies the stockholders of the New Egyptian Company, which embraced, we are told, operations in land reclamation, mining in various areas, a large real estate sector, irrigation and drainage work. There is no indication of the number of shares held by the thousands of persons listed, so that it is impossible to tell whether they are small shareholders or millionnaires. But the selection of this company is especially difficult to understand when others, much more powerful and duly named in the official lists, are left in obscurity.

(8) The eighth list names a group of companies belonging to all sectors. Here, we are told, is the portrait of ownership "divided between two groups: one foreign in name and spirit, the other composed of a privileged minority . . . ; then, outside both these groups, there are men who succeeded by their own work and effort and who have the right to own all the things that they have succeeded in acquiring." The companies are these: Sudanese Import-Export, Egyptian Import-Export Bank, Egyptian Import, Trading & Exchange Company, Mediterranean General Trading, Commercial Exchange Company for the Middle East, UNITAS Commercial & Financial Company, Commercial Insurance, World Commerce & Industry, Zilkha Banking, African Insurance, Cairo Banking, Egyptian Banking Company for Capital Growth, Suarès Banking, Egyptian Commercial Banking, Egyptian Import-Export Banking, Bank of Commerce, El-Nil Insurance, Popular Savings Society, Savings Bank, Egyptian National Insurance, Yussef Nessim Mosseri Banking, Egyptian Insurance, Alexandria Insurance, Bank of Port Said.

(9) The ninth list, again, offers a sampling of large Egyptian companies belonging to various sectors, with a detailed statement of the capital invested by the major stockholders: Cotton & Financial Business Company, Upper Egypt Cotton Ginning, Berg Tatalian & Company, Great United Dyeing, Public Industrial & Works Engineering, El-Nil Arab Trading, El-

Nil Trading, El-Nil Reinforced Concrete Construction Company (SPECO), El-Nil Highway Construction Company, El-Nil Mechanical Foundations (FIBRO), El-Nil Highway Company, El-Nil Engineering Construction, Trade & Road Company, Al-Shams Automobile Company, Al-Ahram Ironworks, Gattegno Department Store Company, Sheffield & Company, Daud Rouffeh Company, Hannaux Department Stores of Alexandria, the Commercial Company, United Nile Engineering & Trade (UNIL), Northeast Africa Company.

(10) The tenth and final group is also composed of a selection from various sectors: Alexandria Cotton Trading, the Cotton Trading Company, Egyptian Cotton Ginning & Export, El-Nil Said Bus Company, El-Nil Beheira Bus Company, El-Nil Minufiya Bus Company, El-Nil Canal & Southern Delta Bus Company, Alexandria Industrial Milling, Gharbiya Land Company, El-Nil Gharbiya & Kafr el-Sheik Bus Company, El-Nil Freight Company of Cairo, Castro Bros. & Co., Egyptian Spinning Factories, Nellos Warehouses, Alexandria Pure-Silk & Rayon Weaving Factory, Egyptian Blanket Company.[23]

The nationalization program continued in successive waves: 137 shipping and stevedoring firms were consolidated into a single entity, in which the state held 50 percent of the assets (September 25, 1962); a law was promulgated that forbade any foreigner except Palestinians to own farmland (January 17, 1963); 55 cotton-ginning companies with 101 factories were incorporated into the Egyptian Public Agency (EPA) for Cotton (April 7, 1963); 13 cotton-exporting companies were incorporated into the same agency (April 3, 1963); 19 pharmaceutical producers were nationalized and 50 laboratories were closed (June 16, 1963); 8 ocean and river transport companies were nationalized and 16 trucking companies were merged into 7 public-sector companies (June 18, 1963); 5 glass factories in Alexandria were requisitioned (July 25, 1963); Dar al-Ma'aref, the largest Egyptian book-publishing company, was put under sequestration and merged with *al-Ahram* (August 19, 1963); 177 companies, of whose assets the state already owned 50 percent, were fully nationalized (November 11, 1963); the agencies of 40 foreign insurance companies were closed after the expiration of the liquidation period stipulated in 1957 (November 12, 1963); 6 farming companies owning 13,000 *feddans* were nationalized (November 17, 1963); all commercial banks were merged into 5 large banks joined to the EPA for Banking (October 10, 1963); wholesaling was eliminated and the companies that had engaged in it were replaced by co-operatives, while at the same time retailers were consolidated into "economic units" (November 10, 1963).

CHAPTER 4

ANATOMY OF THE
NEW CLASS

WHAT COULD, what should replace those political and financial managerial staffs of the Council of the
Nation and of the boards of directors of the banks, insurance
companies, industry and business?

The choice that was made institutionalized and confirmed
the social character of the military regime during and
after this third stage of its development. And whatever the
methods and means that could be counted upon to multiply
and change in great and small degree during the stages to
come, it would never again be possible to go backward, to
dismantle the public sector for example, to restore the monopolies to the hands that had formerly held them or to reestablish the hegemony of the old bourgeoisie, the ally of
imperialism.

What Was the Public Sector?

Let us look first of all at the economic and social
infrastructure as it was affected by the evolutionary course
initiated at the time of Suez but principally by the measures
taken during the summer and autumn of 1961.

The laws of July 1961, as we have seen, gave pre-eminence
to the public sector, which now owned the banks, insurance

companies, heavy and basic industries, transportation and foreign trade in fee simple; it participated to the extent of 50 percent in the ownership of the greater number of light industries and medium-sized corporations, and owned variable shares of all that was left, depending on the number of holdings in excess of £E10,000 belonging to the large stockholders. The whole was oriented in the direction that was determined by the Five-Year Plan, and the power of decision of the representatives of private capital in the second and third categories of companies was materially diminished.

And it was now that this situation, which weighed heavily in favor of the public sector, was reinforced by the so-called security sequestrations of October and November 1961—that is, the destitution of the remaining groups of capitalists, large and medium, of their legitimate prerogatives of decision, however limited, and of management, without any impairment of their share in ownership. What was the state going to do with this economy in the height of transformation to which it considered itself the heir? How was it to organize this swarm of entities of varying types and conditions?

On December 16 a Presidential decree disclosed the decision that had been taken: all existing companies, amounting in all to 367, would be redistributed among 38 public agencies headed by the High Council for Public Agencies, the president of which would be the chief of state.

Here is the original plan for this organization, which would unquestionably have to undergo many subsequent modifications:

I. *Ministry of Industry:*

1. Egyptian Public Agency for Mines (12 companies); 2. EPA for Food Industries (35 companies); 3. for Textiles (38 companies); 4. for Chemical Industries (31 companies); 5. for Construction Materials and Brick (9 companies); 6. for Metallurgical Industries (8 companies); 7. for Engineering Industries (24 companies); 8. for Oil (8 companies); 9. for Co-operative Production and Small Industries.

II. *Ministry of War:*

10. EPA for Military Production (2 companies).

III. *Ministry of Agriculture:*

11. EPA for Farm Co-operatives (10 companies).

IV. *Ministry of Communications:*

12. EPA for Internal Transport (18 companies); 13. for Ocean Transport (1 company).

V. *Ministry of Housing and Public Services:*

14. EPA for Co-operative Housing; 15. for Contracts and Construction (16 companies); 16. for Public Buildings; 17. for Housing and Reconstruction (5 companies).

VI. *Ministry of Agrarian Reform and Land Reclamation:*

18. EPA for Desert Reclamation; 19. for Land Development (2 companies); 20. for Land Reclamation (5 companies).

VII. *Ministry of Labor:*

21. EPA for Workmen's Compensation Insurance.

VIII. *Ministry of State:*

22. EPA for Radio and Television (1 company); 23. for Tourism and Hotels (5 companies); 24. for Information, Advertising, Distribution and Printing.

IX. *Ministry of Food Supply:*

25. EPA for Consumption (31 companies); 26. Egyptian Public Co-operative Agency for Consumption; 27. EPA for Silos and Warehouses (3 companies); 28. for Fisheries (2 companies).

X. *Ministry of Health:*

29. EPA for Pharmaceutical and Chemical Products and Medical Equipment (7 companies).

XI. *Ministry of Economics:*

30. EPA for Commerce (37 companies); 31 for Cotton Trading (19 companies); 32. for Banking (27 banks); 33. for Insurance (16 companies); 34. for Savings (2 companies).

XII. *Ministry of Culture and National Guidance:*

35. EPA for the Support of the Film Industry (1 company); 36. for the Theater and Music (1 company); 37. for Composition, Translation, Printing and Publishing (1 company).

XIII. *Ministry of Public Works:*

38. EPA for Electricity.[1]

The decree referred to "all existing companies," which meant those belonging to the public sector as well as those that were still in the hands of capitalists of the private sector. Relations between the two sectors were not clearly defined. What was more, the Preparatory Committee for the National Congress of Popular Forces (NCPF), which met during this period, put both sectors under the same label, which was "national capitalism." Nevertheless, it was obvious that the private sector was composed only of those few companies among the 367 affected by this regulation which were still in the hands of private capital; in fact, in the cities—as in the rural areas—there was a multitude of small and medium-sized enterprises—workshops, artisans, small stores, small factories, etc.—that had hardly altered its sociological structure. Unquestionably the July laws "had made the public sector the major power, giving it total control of the greater part of economic activity," as the National Bank of Egypt conceded, but "the nature of the relations between each public agency and the companies affiliated with it, on the one hand, and the relation between these agencies and the ministries on the other, have not been set forth in detail."[2]

These were questions that the representatives of "national capitalism," especially those of private enterprise, were insistently asking of themselves and of the public authorities, particularly during the discussions in February and March 1962 which accompanied the election of that group's delegates to the National Congress of Popular Forces.

The seminar on the subject held by *al-Ahram* afforded some guideposts. "The Salt & Soda Company," said Zaki Mohammed Lashin, a grocer in the Rod el-Farag section of Cairo, "produces soap and similar products; it sells seventy percent of its output to the public sector, and the rest to grocery wholesalers and retailers. What is more, not only the Salt & Soda Company but indeed all the big companies do the same thing." Another retail merchant, Mohammed Amin Nafe', said, "The private sector's position is surrounded by many contradictions, and the discrimination that is practiced between the two sectors is so bewildering in its application that it makes us feel uneasy." Kamal Ramadan stated that it "is not possible to find any trace of exploitation today, when a merchant who hides his goods is taken into court, and when co-operatives are springing up everywhere, so that it becomes impossible for commercial enterprises to raise their prices." And he added: "Let's speak frankly. At a time when the possibilities available to the public sector in the fields of imports and financial assistance are plentiful, we see the private sector virtually impotent to move and make progress because it is barred from any possibility of doing its job." Abdel Mohsen Shita deplored the fact that "the biggest part of the private sector's profits now winds up in the government because of the tax laws and the ceilings on income." Two representatives of the public sector—Gamal el-Borolossi and Mohammed Shedid—emphasized that it was "unthinkable" that the private sector should act in competition with the public sector, which had the chief power, and they talked about "complementariness." Many suggestions were offered, but they ended in a deadlock. And we are told that the day after the seminar, Zaki Lashin made it a point to send a circular letter to a thousand small merchants, asking them to state in detail exactly what they wanted.[3]

Once the majority of those responsible felt that everyday economic life was marked by confusion and uncertainty as to intentions, it was inevitable that both sides should begin to think again about their conceptualizations. And the question that arose, occasionally in the open in spite of the noisy professions of trust in the government, was this: State capitalism or socialism?

Without leaving the domain of the economic and social infrastructure, let us see what evidence is at hand for judgment on this phase of the evolution.

There was first of all the existence of the public sector, which wielded the vital part of the country's economic power under the various formulas stipulated by the three laws of July 20: total ownership (in the case of the banks, insurance companies, heavy industries, basic branches of the economy, transportation and foreign trade), and in addition total ownership of the new companies set up by the agencies of the public sector;[4] half ownership (corporations operating in industry and business but of lesser importance); variable degrees of ownership (light industries and family-owned companies, either limited or joint-stock).

The state was extending its control over the whole economic activity, both by means of the Five-Year Plan and by the transfer of the 367 most important companies to the 38 public agencies (under supervision of various ministries) which we have listed.

But even before we attempt to analyze the private sector, one specific phenomenon must be pointed out within this general framework of statist nationalization. This bears in a more precise way on the nature of the system of ownership of enterprises in the public sector. In fact, the capital of the banks, insurance companies and industrial and commercial enterprises—whether they were joint-stock or limited companies—was divided into two sections: one part became the direct property of the state (this was the case in the first group of firms nationalized by Law No. 117; but it was true also of the 50 percent ownership of companies in the second group that was transferred to the public sector under the terms of Law No. 118; and it applied equally to the variable proportion represented by the excess-above-£E10,000 ceiling per stockholder in the third group of companies, covered by Law No. 119); the balance remained in the hands of private owners (50 percent of the capital of the companies in the second group, as well as all holdings up to £E10,000 per shareholder in the third group of companies).

Registered government bonds, which were thus made non-negotiable on the stock exchange, constituted financial compensation in installments for the loss of legal ownership imposed on the stockholders to the benefit of the state. And the state permitted the holders of these bonds a maximum of £E5,000 to sell up to £E1,000 of them to the banks in order to cushion their losses and acquire a certain liquidity. The state also provided that shares of stock held by individuals were to be broken up into units of £E1 in order to increase the opportunities for small savers to become stockholders.[5]

But the state was most assuredly the sole and total owner

of the companies in the first category, which were added to the key sectors already nationalized prior to July 1961; it was also half owner of the companies in the second group, and owner of varying shares (from 10 to 50 percent, occasionally even a good deal more) of the third-category companies. In each of these cases, the state-as-owner offered an installment compensation, which was in reality a kind of temporary annuity, to the former owners who had had to turn over their stock to it: this took the form of the fifteen-year government bonds at 4 percent interest—in effect, the equivalent of what had been given to the landowners affected by the Agrarian Reform of 1952. There was a single exception: companies entirely created—that is, financed—by agencies in the public sector, to which, of course, they belonged *in toto;* here no compensation had to be paid to anyone.

The transfer of the essential ownership of production facilities to the state was accompanied, quite naturally, by the complete disruption of the traditional method of various managing companies.

Under the provisions of Law No. 114 of July 19, 1961, a board of directors would henceforth consist of a maximum of seven members, of whom one would be a representative of the office employees and another of labor, each of these being elected by his fellow workers. In August a new law, No. 137, changed these provisions and still further diminished the authority of the owners: the two employee delegates were to be elected jointly by office staff and labor, and the board of directors must include one to three directors or department heads of the company.[6]

What was the aspect of the private sector after these severe measures of nationalization?

The detailed schedule of the real forces of which it was composed was not small, at least from the point of view of quantity. Among the companies affected by the July laws, there were first of all the stockholders of the 83 medium-sized firms in the second group, half of whose shares were split into units of £E1 each, the other half having been paid for in government bonds; there were also the stockholders of the 145 firms in the third group, who would retain holdings up to £E10,000, the excess being converted into government bonds. From March on, the shares of these third-category companies were listed on the stock exchange, and Dr. Kayssuni announced that the £E10,000 ceiling applied only to the date of the promulgation of the law, July 20, 1961; thereafter any individual could buy as many shares as he wished,[7] in order to stimulate "national capitalism." But the 367 companies divided among the 38 public agencies after December 1961 did not constitute the whole Egyptian economy. In fact, there still existed several thousand enterprises—workshops, artisans, stores, small factories, small banks, etc.—occasionally even in the form of individually owned firms; in short, what was generally referred to as the average middle class, in fact the urban lower middle class.[8] At the time no accurate figures were available which would make it possible to evaluate accurately the shares of these two groups constituting the private sector. But there can be no doubt that this sector in a way provided a source of contribution to the public sector and that it was hardly possible, even theoretically, to talk of equality.

The New Technocracy

Another factor was the make-up of the new management staffs in the economy. The upper levels—ministers, presidents and members of public agencies, presidents of companies—were all appointed by the President of the Republic; as for the trustees in sequestrations, they were appointed by ministerial decree.

From where were they recruited? As early as 1951, but especially with the first Nasser Cabinet in 1954, as we have seen, the choice of the Revolutionary Command Council fell by preference to technicians, economists and engineers with Anglo-Saxon training—graduates of the London School of Economics and Political Science, Harvard, the Massachusetts Institute of Technology—for the RCC had decisively turned its back on the old tradition of ministers and managing directors trained in law schools and deeply impregnated with French influences. It was these same men—notably Dr. Abdel

Moneim el-Kayssuni, Dr. Aziz Sidky, Dr. Kamal Ramzi Stino, Ahmed Abdu el-Shorabassi, Dr. Mustafa Khalil, Mussa Arafa, Ahmed Ali Farag, Dr. Mohammed Naguib Hasshad, Dr. Mohammed el-Nabaui el-Mohandes, Abdel Wahab el-Bishri—who made up the civilian ministerial group of 1961, the test of events having proved or disproved qualifications and brought out several new figures.

There was the same tendency in the Economic Agency, the one agency whose governing body has been the subject of analysis: among the company directors who were part of it at the end of December 1961—that is, before the effective date of the new general reorganization into 38 public agencies, which was to put an end to the EA's existence—there were 42 engineers, 38 graduates in business administration, 26 lawyers, 43 graduates in other disciplines, and 21 men without university degree.[9] Now, it must be remembered that courses in engineering and business administration, just as in those of sciences and medicine, were conducted partly in English, but above all in accordance with the traditions of the British universities and with the same reference works, or very nearly, and this was the case until 1960. Before the nationalization measures took effect, such executives worked in the private sector's plants and offices; others tried to go into business or professional practice on their own; a minority resigned itself to the meager emoluments offered by public employment. But the greater part of those who worked in private companies occupied middle-management positions; until 1961 the top posts—board directors and officers—were, in the main, reserved either to the large stockholders themselves or to their favorites.

The nationalization laws turned these men into top management, since for the most part the old privileged groups had been removed. But they were not alone: Several hundred state functionaries, energetic and long highly envious of the privileges and the possibilities of advancement enjoyed by their colleagues in the private sector, were shifted into the economic agencies, to which they contributed both their tradition of bureaucracy and their desire to make a showing. The government made great inroads on the universities, both for graduates and for teachers,[10] in order to ensure the scientific quality of the work that would have to be done by the new staffs. A discussion began among professors, experts and managers to ascertain how best to train the new executives, a discussion that very soon turned into a coalition of economists, scientists and engineers against "the others," who, essentially, were their colleagues educated in law and the humanities.[11]

Little by little the names of the new managers of the economy selected by the government were published in the press. Here, for instance, is the distribution of managerial personnel among 37 (of the 38) public agencies in April and May 1962: of 301 board members (directors, let us make it clear, of the agencies, not of the companies of which they were composed), there were 57 engineers and scientists, 57 holders of doctor's degrees, and 187 high state officials, army officers, company officials, most of them graduates in law or business administration, or even occasionally in both literature and engineering.[12] In April, nominations were opened for the boards of 238 corporations, which belonged to fourteen public agencies and constituted the high-production sectors; they were soon joined by the elected representatives of office employees and labor. These boards showed almost the same proportions as observed in the agency boards: one-third engineers and scientists, of whom one fourth held doctorates, the rest being high officials and graduates in business administration, law and literature; an explanatory note showed that many councilors and higher-court judges, both in retirement and even still in service, several Undersecretaries of State, managing directors, heads of government departments, many lawyers, former members of the Council of the Nation, many university professors and a very large number of former capitalists, particularly in public-works companies, were still where they had always been, but now as board chairmen.[13] All in all, there were few military men. At the same time, there was a real drive for intellectual improvement among the young officers appointed to posts on the managerial levels of the economy: Those who expressed the desire, and they were numerous, were detached to take courses at the universities, especially in the faculties of law, economics, political science and business administration; a great many cadets and cadet candidates enrolled in the new Military Technical Faculty set up on September 10, 1961, whose seven-year curriculum was designed to train managerial staffs both of career officers and of civilian engineers.[14] "Doctors" mushroomed among the officers, even at the ministerial level: wearing the uniform was no longer enough to grant access as of right to economic management.

At the middle-management level the effort was considerable: 30,000 students were admitted to trade schools in 1960, 16,000 of them in high schools; in 1961 the total figure was 37,000, including 11,315 in high schools and 1,250 in technical institutes. In 1965, according to Ali Sho'eib, Undersecretary of State for Technical Education, this figure would reach 220,000, against only 18,000 before 1952; vocational training alone accounted for 34.5 percent of the total educational budget during the 1960 Five-Year Plan.[15] Official estimates forecast an increase of 1,037,000 in the number of skilled workers by 1964-65.[16]

The purpose was indeed to create a new social category, *tabakat al-mudirin* (the managerial class), beginning with the many scattered and inadequately co-ordinated components that were available. One of the most talented of them, Abdel Moneim el-Tanamly, president of the Egyptian Land Bank, alluded to James Burnham but admitted at once that the overpowering presence of the state imposed limits on the new group.[17]

This became apparent in the case of a new law regulating associations for professional people. The original plan forbade members of these groups to take part in politics and gave the government the right to set aside decisions by the associations; the President of the Republic could go even as far as to order their dissolution. Lawyers and physicians rose up against this provision; engineers demanded recognition for levels of qualification and seniority—in other words, they rejected any regimentation that would treat them like trade unions; and pharmacists insisted on being recognized as members of a commercial profession.[18]

Intellectuals and Officers

In 1954 Ahmed Baha 'Eddine had asserted: "The greatest hope we have for progress at this time is that represented by the third force, the intellectual class."[19] Such was not the thinking of the government, which expressed itself coarsely in the voice of Heykal at the time of the "crisis of the intellectuals." "Where," he demanded, "were the intellectuals in those days [before 1952]? Where was their mission as the vanguard in the leadership of the masses? In reality, with the exception of a few individuals, the intellectuals were far from the battle. Some had joined forces with those opposed to the interests of the masses by reason of their class connections. Others, driven by the desire to survive, were satisfied to keep aloof, following their own interests without taking part in the course of events, for that might have led to dangerous consequences . . . Thus the intellectuals were unable to see the picture clearly and distinctly. A few, however, began to have qualms of conscience. A Revolutionary leadership arose out of the ranks of the young avant-garde who created a movement in the ranks of the army; their direct contact with the masses, their success in the formulation of their demands constituted a continuous and permanent reminder to the intellectuals of their own impotence to fulfill their function as an avant-garde . . ."[20] The intellectuals' hopes, it was clear, were far from harmonizing with the Free Officers' view of the value and possible function of the Egyptian intelligentsia.

The fact was that the officers denied to every other social class, to any national group other than the army, the right and duty to lead the rebirth of Egypt. They alone possessed the tool of power essential to a country still under the military subjugation of imperialism. And yet, Anwar el-Sadate confides to us, "the nice people imagined that the army was a simple instrument of domination, a kind of whip in the king's hands with which he could keep the poor at his mercy and which was always there, within reach, to give them a lashing if they dared to stir at all . . . They thought that the army was

Faruk's praetorian guard and not the nation's safeguard . . .
A whole hierarchy of fears was rooted in the minds of the ignorant multitudes . . . That was why, as long as it was not
certain of the army's sentiments toward it, the masses never
thought of freeing themselves through insurrection, lest they
find their action crushed in fire and blood . . ."[21]

Among the 327 signers of the National party's manifesto
in 1879, however, there were 93 officers. It was this tradition
that the Free Officers intended to revive. "The army," an
anonymous manifesto asserted, "is not a barracks separated
from the people by high walls, but rather, for all classes of the
people, a university in the true sense, which teaches them,
strengthens their bodies and elevates their spirit . . . We declare to our soldiers that no army could ever win a victory
without the help of scientists at their microscopes . . . and
of each individual member of our nation."[22]

Those who issued these statements—the members of the
organization of Free Officers—also became the leaders of
the army after 1952, the highest government officials, and then,
after the nationalizations of 1957, those of the economy, especially in the public sector, which grew incessantly larger.
"The military élite and its mass organizations," in the words
of M. Berger,[23] ruled alone at first and then very quickly
arrived at the alliance of 1952–61 with the industrial middle
class; during that period a junction was effected between the
military and technocratic élites; the thinkers were left to examine their consciences. This was the new tandem in power in
Egypt after the summer of 1961. But where were the social
forces of the country when the old coalition of the rich and
their imperialist masters was thrown off?

President Nasser's self-criticism of October 16, 1961,
made it clear that the government had taken cognizance of
the danger represented by the political vacuum. Could the
army govern alone, on behalf of the nation?

Nasser's reply was negative. Certainly the army was still
at the heart of everything, at the center of the apparatus, at
the summit of power. But there was a dual problem: first of

all the problem of structure, and then of the leader groups and managerial teams capable of assuming the responsibility for setting the new economic and social direction into motion. The power of decision, in spite of slogans and phrases full of promises, remained the sole domain of the ruling nucleus presided over by Nasser.

Toward the National Congress of Popular Forces

First of all the problem of structures—in other words, of the institutional framework into which future leaders would have to be integrated. And it was here that, once again, the authoritarianism of the military group demonstrated its resolve to make the first move, to supplant any political initiative coming from the various classes in the nation.

On November 4, 1961, President Nasser announced three measures:

(1) The creation of a body called the Preparatory Committee for the National Congress of Popular Forces, which was to study the methods of selecting the representatives from the various sectors of the people who would constitute the NCPF;

(2) The election of the National Congress of Popular Forces; the President of the Republic would submit to it a draft Charter of National Action, which was both the result of the experience gained since 1952 and the definition of the goals of the revolution; this document would be offered for debate within the NCPF and its various committees; the whole body would then draw up the Charter.

(3) On the basis of this Charter, elections would be held for the local committees of the National Union under the procedures to be defined by the NCPF. These elected committees would constitute the base of the General Congress of the National Union, which would be the paramount popular power and, as such, would be assigned to formulate the Constitution.[24]

On November 18, 250 members of the Preparatory Committee for the NCPF were appointed by Presidential decree, as follows: 24 representatives of the peasants (18 co-operativist peasants, 4 agricultural engineers, 2 farmers); 29 workers (13 presidents of trade unions, 15 workers, 1 representative of the workers' department of the National Union); 37 representatives of the professions, including university professors (7 presidents of professional associations, 5 engineers, 2 pharmacists, 7 journalists and writers, 11 lawyers, 3 physicians, 3 teachers); 21 representatives of business (15 directors of agencies and companies, 7 representatives of co-operatives); 23 members of the old Council of the Nation; 10 women; 59 Administration officials (5 Vice-Presidents of the Republic, 20 ministers, 3 vice-ministers, 24 governors, 4 Undersecretaries of State);[25] and 57 unclassified members.

The purpose was to make a fresh start, to provide well defined social foundations—in other words, to institutionalize its social representativeness—for this military regime, which had been hindered by the exigencies of growth, both in the area of progress and by outside influences, to follow a line of evolution that it had hardly conceived of taking in 1952.

On November 25 President Nasser spoke for four hours to the members of the Preparatory Committee: he retraced the history of the relations between the army and the bourgeoisie, "the cowardly bourgeoisie," as he called it, and also of those between the Egyptian state and imperialism. He showed how the government had been led to review its action, to evolve a doctrine as it went along, to accept the necessity for socialism. In the next few days Nasser established a dialogue with the members of the Preparatory Committee.

On the fourth day, November 29, the real debate began; it was continued on December 3. One man took it upon himself to call for the restoration of civil liberties for all and for a return to democracy. Then he pleaded the case of the Left, persecuted and tortured at the very time when the government was calling itself "Socialist." Khaled Mohammed Khaled could be seen and heard on television in every home and café in Egypt. He was one of the best known of the postwar essayists, the author of a dozen works in which Islamic reformism was paced by a continuous demand for freedom, both under the old order and after 1952. "Let us speak frankly," the President answered him. "Did we arrest the Moslem Brotherhood's members and try them without cause, or was there indeed a secret army ready to descend on the people?" But it was chiefly the Marxists who were at issue: "On the subject of the imprisoned Communists," President Nasser continued, "we are not against Marxism any more than we are against the Left in any way whatever; what we are against is only the act of taking instructions from a foreign power . . . The members of the Egyptian Communist party of whom I am speaking received their instructions from Sofia, where their leadership is, as before that they received their instructions from Rome, and, before that, from France, or even, during the war, from England. I know many of them . . . But, good Lord, if there are Marxists who do not get their orders from abroad, it stands to reason that we would not take measures against them. Our socialism is not Communism. And yet we allow plenty of Communists in the country, plenty of fellow travelers, plenty of Marxists, all of whom voice their opinions with impunity as long as they do not take their orders from abroad, from a foreign power . . ." It required three speches by President Nasser to circumvent the arguments of Khaled Mohammed Khaled, who was preaching the end of the dictatorship: "The enemies of Mohammed's message," Khaled cried, "those who did not believe in the new religion, were accepted by the Prophet as members of the new society, which guaranteed their rights . . . Believe me, gentlemen, it is not in anyone's interest—I repeat, not in anyone's interest—to arm the people with slogans of violence in this period of transition. On the contrary, everyone must recognize his own character, his nature composed of goodness, of vigilance, of thankfulness, and of love. Let our people be strong in its own character. It is a strong and intelligent people that cannot be conquered . . . Your adversaries, Mr. President, and we ourselves have only one single argument: Where is Parliament? Where is the Constitution? Where is the opposition? I think we should answer these points before we do anything else so that we may go forward under your banner to political maturity . . ."[26]

Stupefied, the members of the committee could not evade the problem; already on the first day, Khaled Mohammed Khaled had said: "Now that ten years have elapsed since God raised the flag of the Revolution, it is our duty to give back to the nation all its freedoms, immediately and without delay!"[27] But the matter was drowned in procedural bickerings. On December 6 the president of the Bar Association himself, Mustafa el-Baradei, demanded "the creation of an opposition party on condition that the parties work in the interests of the country and the nation," and he added: "This, moreover, is the meaning of liberty as every Arab knows it."[28]

But it was in the workings of Subcommittee No. 1, specifically charged with completing the arrangements for the election of the NCPF, which was the chief purpose of the Preparatory Committee's discussions,[29] that the actual policy of the government in the matter of political composition could be followed.[30] Eight categories of citizens were to be taken under consideration; the issue was "the fundamental forces of the people which were joined in organizations appropriate to each."

Detailed study of these forces and of the representation that was granted to them affords useful clues to the military authority's concept of the managerial class with which it intended to endow the country.

Each category was studied under several headings, of which the two most important were "the number of members enrolled in organizations" and "the contribution to the national income made by those enrolled in organizations"; the relation established between these two factors was then examined in the light of vital statistics, thus making it possible to arrive at the equitable proportioning—subject to correction according to political criteria—of the delegates to the forthcoming Congress.

These were the factors in the calculations, and their results:

(1) *Peasants*: 3,200,000, including 1,154,332 enrolled in organizations; the ratio between these two figures produced a "demographic weight" of 44.3 percent; £E173 million in contribution to the national income (estimated at a total of £E650 million); the ratio between these two factors gave this category 35.4 percent of the total social value (set at 100). This proportion was reduced to 25 percent and the number of

delegates was fixed at 375: 80 members of Agrarian Reform co-operatives, 265 members of agricultural co-operatives, 7 members of farm trade unions, 15 farm workers in the governmental sector, 8 members of the fishermen's associations;

(2) *Workers:* 1,600,000, of whom 466,328 were organized (17.9 percent); £E200 million (30.8 percent) in contribution to income; the actual ratio, which was 24.4 percent, was adjusted to 20 percent. The workers would be entitled to 300 delegates, as follows: 120 representatives of the industrial sector (518,000 workers), 26 from the commercial sector (125,000 salaried employees), 64 from the services sector (325,000 salaried employees), 90 from the governmental workers (329,000 workers);

(3) *National Capitalism:* 600,000 persons, of whom 276,824 were organized (10.6 percent); £E56.2 million (8.7 percent) contributed to the national income; the real ratio of 9.7 percent was rounded off to 10 percent. This sector would be entitled to 150 delegates, as follows: 75 representatives of industry, and 75 of commerce.

(4) *Members of professional associations:* 172,957, all organized (6.6 percent); £E143.2 million (22 percent) contributed to income; the real ratio, 14.3 percent, was rounded off to 15 percent; the professions would be entitled to 225 delegates, the allocation of whom was not prescribed;

(5) *Nonunionized functionaries:* 700,000, including 194,000 organized in trade unions (7.5 percent); £E71.3 million (10.9 percent) contributed to income; the real ratio of 9.2 percent was adjusted to 9 percent. The functionaries would be entitled to 135 delegates, 100 of whom would represent the nonunionized;

(6) *University teaching staffs:* 7,500, all organized (.4 percent); £E6.3 million (1 percent) contributed to income; the real ratio of .7 percent, was multiplied ten times to 7 percent. The university professors would be entitled to 105 delegates: 11 representing research agencies (including four from the National Center for Scientific Research), 4 from Al Azhar, 27 from Cairo University, 18 from Ain Shams University, 17 from Alexandria University, 6 from the University of Assiut, and 22 from the Higher Institutes;

(7) *Students:* 305,000, all organized in students' unions (11.7 percent); no contribution to the national income. Their weight in the body of society, estimated at 7 percent, would entitle them to 105 delegates: 4 representatives from Al Azhar, 20 from Cairo, fifteen from Ain Shams, 14 from Alexandria, 4 from Assiut and 13 from the Higher Institutes;

(8) *Women:* 6,500,000, of whom 25,457 were organized (1 percent); no figures on their contribution to the national income, since working women were included in the various other sectors (peasants, workers. etc.); their weight, estimated at 7 percent, would entitle them to 105 delegates: 63 representatives from the professions (including 34 for teaching), 5 artists, 10 workers, 21 representatives of the feminist movement and the co-operatives, 6 from the women's associations.[32]

But there was a more serious matter: what was known as "isolation." This penalty was defined as "the deprivation of the exercise of the political rights recognized for the people as a whole, and removal from all participation in any political organization whatever, whether in the rank and file or at the top of the political organization or the socialist organizations connected with it, such as trade unions, co-operative societies, professional unions and meetings." The subcommittee distinguished between two categories here: "Isolation as applied to the enemies of the socialist revolution of the people; and the removal of any person whose interests are in opposition to those of the people during the present stage of socialist construction." Specific objects of "isolation" were the landowners affected by the Agrarian Reform of 1952 and 1961; persons affected by the nationalization measures of 1960 and 1961; persons hostile to the Revolution and subjected to sequestration or arrest at the end of 1961; any person guilty of having attempted to influence public opinion in favor of political corruption; any person guilty of having taken advantage of his position in a public or private agency with a view to realizing personal profit or destroying the principles on which these agencies were erected.[33]

In vain Khaled Mohammed Khaled strove to emphasize the margin for arbitrary decision that was thereafter to strike many innocent persons: he could not win even the inclusion of an amendment to the official text stipulating that these measures be strictly and exclusively limited to the elections for the NCPF.[34]

And so, on May 21, 1962, before the 1,750 members of the National Congress of Popular Forces, assembled in the grand auditorium of Cairo University, President Gamal Abdel Nasser devoted six hours to the reading aloud of the Charter of National Action.

part three

In Search of a
National Ideology

The vocation of one class for domination means that it is possible, on the basis of its class interests, on the basis of its class consciousness, to organize the whole of society in conformance with these interests. And the question that in the last analysis determines any class struggle is this: What class has this capability and this class consciousness at the given moment?

. . . With capitalism, with the disappearance of the structure of states, and with the constitution of a society with *purely economic* divisions, class consciousness has reached the stage *at which it can become conscious.* Now the social conflict is reflected in an ideological conflict for consciousness, for the disclosure or concealment of the class character of society. But the possibility of this conflict already foreshadows the dialectical contradictions, the internal dissolution of the pure class society.

—GEORGE LUKACS, *History and Class Consciousness*

CHAPTER ٥

THE CRISIS OF THE INTELLECTUALS

"To say that the intellectuals collaborated with the revolutionary driving force after July 23 is not to define the goal that was to be reached. What was at work here was a kind of political loyality. The natural and obligatory function of the intellectuals was not merely to 'collaborate' with the Revolution but to enter into 'relations of interaction' with it, to 'sponsor' its cause, to 'assume' it, to 'give' it, through their thinking, its 'revolutionary theory,' to forge its revolutionary faith from the very depths of their consciences and their knowledge—that is, to point out its road to basic and radical change in Egyptian society.

"Collaboration in the state's projects undoubtedly constitutes an important and fundamental part of the function of the intellectuals in the service of national evolution. But revolutionary effort during the present stage of the people's struggle, the work of preparing the Revolution and putting the Revolution into motion, consists in rebuilding the social structure, in taking part in it with knowledge and experience, as well as with the conscience that is their product . . ."

The Great Debate of March–July 1961

Such were the terms of the dilemma before which the government intended to set the Egyptian intelligentsia through the voice of Heykal,[1] nine years after the coup d'état. This dilemma was also a balance sheet of failure: nine years after the fall of the monarchy and the Agrarian Reform, three years after Suez and the reconquest of independence, the essential tasks were still to be performed. The intellectuals, the chief force of renewal and national motivation since 1882, worked in government posts, wrote books that had indeed to be published, even held high office in public agencies. What they refused to give the government was their hearts and, as a result, their ideas. Now, without this intelligentsia, which had not been afraid to make every sacrifice and had not hesitated to fuel every effort, without this battered intelligentsia, cut off from its most fertile source, penned in the camps, subjected to brutality and humiliation, without this wealth of which Egypt had a greater abundance and a higher proportion than any other Arab and Eastern country, nothing was possible. None of this could justify the military government or even serve it as a pretext in its great task of construction whose slogan was: "Double the national income in ten years."

Therefore it must shatter this apathy so strongly impregnated with a political character, this refusal of ideological obedience, this insistence on aloofness that characterized the élite of knowledge that refused to play the game set by *The Philosophy of the Revolution*. That was to be the preoccupation of the team of young theoreticians of *al-Ahram* gathered around its mentor, Mohammed Hassanein Heykal, from March 12 to July 14, 1961, during what was certainly the greatest controversy launched by the government since 1952.[2]

The affair began with a series of five articles by Lutfi el-Kholy. After having stated an erroneous definition of intellectuals,[3] he deplored "the false tendency that works toward the imprisonment of Arab culture under the turban of the law of Islam," traced the work of the forerunners after the French expedition had compelled Omar Makram* and his companions of Al Azhar to "go to the people," reviewed the divisions of the

* *Naqib al-ashraf*, i.e., dean of the notables during Bonaparte's occupation of Egypt (1798–1801), and later on, under Mohammed Ali, led the national movement with vision and courage. He was ousted around 1810 by Mohammed Ali, who feared Makram's populist views.

intelligentsia into various tendencies during the interval between the two wars; he recalled "the contradictory and conflicting analyses of the Revolution and its character," a revolution, he said, that had established "the rule of a political power independent of the interests of social forces and classes," and thus he arrived at a definition of the crisis as a crisis of "creativity," which cannot exist without the right to make mistakes and to criticize freely; a crisis of "depth"—in other words, of intensive exploration of the national heritage and reality, and a crisis of "method," the elements of which he defined as follows: "Unity of our Arab people in its national struggle; planning of the course to be followed in erecting our national economy on a socialist base; profound examination of democracy from the dual point of view of form and content, with due consideration given to our own conditions and circumstances; liberation of the potential of intellectual and artistic creation in order to enrich our own national patrimony and that of humanity." Asked why the Egyptian intelligentsia, always the spearhead on the political and ideological planes until 1952, and then again from 1956 to 1958, was now holding aloof and creating this crisis that so alarmed the government, the author, a crafty, progressive lawyer until his internment in 1959 and then a convert to the government and editor of the theoretical page of *al-Ahram*, and later of *al-Tali'a* (1965), did not reply.

There were others who were to do so, in various guises, which often were not lacking in subtlety, and were never devoid of shadings. Dr. Abdel Razek Hassan[4] pointed out the dissensions among the intelligentsia after the economic and social changes brought about by the two world wars, more particularly by the second; some of the intellectuals returned to the newly rich middle class, while others, reduced to bare livelihoods, rebelled; but a third group remained at loose ends, undecided: "The crisis that the Arab intellectuals are going through is a crisis of faith, faith in themselves, faith in the society in which they live." Why? Still no reply. Dr. Abdel Malek Auda[5] thrust further: "The number of intellectuals in the underdeveloped countries is limited, whereas public jobs are numerous, with assured incomes and prominent social standing"; this condition creates "a dominant climate, a mixture of fear and adventurism, of fighting spirit and indifference, of feelings of responsibility and opportunism; this climate which combines opposites, and which is the essence of despair and flight, is expressed in the proverb of our people, *mafish fayda* [nothing can be done about it]." The three factors that he identified in the crisis—"isolation," "withdrawal into self," and "diffusion"—increased after 1945; it was then that "deviations toward the extreme right and the extreme left were intensified; the emergence of these deviationist and separatist sectors on the levels of thought, faith and organization made it possible for them to become dominant then in the educated youth that was growing up." At that period the division of the Allies into two blocs on a world scale, the collapse of imperialism in Asia, which was accompanied by the growth of the national-liberation movement throughout the world, and finally the Palestine war and the brutal disclosure of the corruption of the reactionary Arab structure were also factors that accelerated the process of crisis.

Several cultural "notables" interjected themselves at this point, but the theoretical question that they posed proved already obsolete: Abbas el-Akkad, the dean of the thinkers of the classic and Islamic conservative wing, accused "the modern intellectual of always thinking of what he calls his rights, of what he believes them to be, and very seldom of his obligations";[6] the evolutionist philosopher, Ismail Mazhar, bemoaned the fact that the intelligentsia "had wandered away from spiritual values"; the pro-American logical positivist, Zaki Naguib Mahmud, expressed anger at "the call that had been sounded too soon, before arrival at maturity, which could bring only disappointment instead of exaltation"; only Hussein Fawzi briefly put his finger on the heart of the problem, which was the idea of culture: "Until now it has been only the physical forms of civilization that have been dominant, far outdistancing, by many long stages, the mental and emotional level of the Nile Valley regions . . . We are powerless to make the effort required in order to derive a broad benefit from that civilization, while the reactionaries are quite incapable of depriving themselves of the physical instruments and components of that same civilization."

Were they all going to lose themselves in the mazes of philosophy—that is, in areas where the government could easily be thrust into a situation of inferiority? To tell the truth, the "crisis of the intellectuals" struck at the heart of the government's political endeavor. That was why Heykal intervened on June 2 to focus the problem in what was to become the first of a series of six long editorials, later collected in book form.

There were in actuality, he said, three crises: "the first arose at the time when the demand was made that the army go back to its barracks after the Revolution of July 23 . . . ; the second at the time when the demand was made for the restoration of the parliamentary system and the return of the political parties . . . ; the third during what was called at that time the choice between 'men who could be trusted' and 'experts,' at the time when officers were made officials of a certain number of corporations, agencies and institutions, and appointed to posts that seemed to be of an essentially technical nature and therefore reserved for specialists." The three crises were therefore indeed three faces of a single crisis: the ouster of the managers—economic, political and cultural—from the various sections of the bourgeoisie and the Egyptian Left in order to bring things under a control directly issuing from the military apparatus or closely bound to it. Then, through the analysis of the isolation of the intellectuals that we have already mentioned, he defined their "crisis" as the behavior of frustration.

This was not the opinion of the intellectuals—far from it.

A first discussion was held beginning on June 8. It opened with an analysis of the key concept at issue, that of "the intellectual," an analysis that was oriented in the direction of the creative sectors of the culture: those, in fact, that were abstaining. To Dr. Louis Awad,[7] "the intellectuals constitute a category of cultivated men who have played a leadership part through the editing of newspapers and teaching at the universities . . . But it should be broadened to all those among their readers, students or ordinary citizens, who provide the echo [to their leadership]; in short, to any person with serious interests." And he added, putting his finger on the state of the intellectuals in the underdeveloped countries: "A great number of us who play a part in the cultural development of others could not pretend to have any great creative capacity in the present period. As far as I am concerned, I feel in a state of receptivity face to face with such men as Sartre and Russell . . ." One after the other, Clovis Maksud,[8] Abdel Razek Hassan and Abdel Malek Auda spoke. It was Dr. Magdi Wahba[9] who was the most accurate. "The intellectual," he said, "is primarily the learned man; second, he is the man who uses his culture as a tool in his work and his social relations; third, he is the man who is aware of the culture of others in a conscious way." The discussion went on, always on the philosophical plane. Clovis Maksud dealt subtly with the various levels of "cultural duality," between "the Islamic tendency, the effort to bring back to life the Islamic idea as a component factor in personality, and the process of selectivity beginning with Western civilizations," between "the various stages of selectivity, either between Fabian* socialist thinking and Marxism or focused on a romantic orientation, the national existence as such being conceived as the source of all things, all thinking and all direction."

Louis Awad elaborated in another speech on the idea of culture; the crisis of the intellectuals was in reality composed of two crises: one was a long-term crisis of "the notion of civilization," of what the Egyptian man of the twentieth century is, what he is in terms of his past, certainly, but also in terms of the goals for the future that he sets himself; then there was the immediate crisis "of the interaction that exists or does not exist between the intellectuals and the Revolution"; for him it was the first that was the important one, for it embodied "the real problem that every intellectual in our country must confront." It can easily be imagined that Lutfi el-Kholy, mindful of Heykal's orders, tried to get around these ideas by opposing them with the arguments of the speed of evolution and a mechanistic conditioning of thought through the social context, both of which were intended to settle this dangerous business as rapidly as possible.[10]

Magdi Wahba discussed the crisis of confidence in six steps:

* The Fabian Society was founded in England in 1884 by Sidney and Beatrice Webb, H. G. Wells, George Bernard Shaw, and others. It favored the spread of socialism by peaceful means.

the nonparticipation of the intellectuals in the army's action of July 23, 1952; the feeling of frustration; withdrawal into self —in other words, "the intellectuals' return to their cultural barracks"; the uniqueness of the Egyptian phenomenon by reason of Egypt's development relative to that of the other newly independent countries, a fact that created dissension between the different sectors of Egyptian society and therefore among the different intellectual groups, whereas in Black Africa, for example, the intellectuals constituted "the vanguard of the new apparatus of the state"; the economic poverty of the Egyptian intellectuals, lower-middle-class in origin, a fact that "compels them to appear as propagandists for the government's rule instead of being its critics"; finally, "the overabundance of civilization" that was a result of the imitation of foreign models to such a point that the Wafdists, the Moslem Brotherhood or the Communists alike could not provide "a revolutionary theory or philosophy of society." And he concluded with this argument in favor of freedom of thought: "The intellectual feels that Gamal Abdel Nasser is basically right. But at the same time he feels the need to formulate a certain amount of criticism by the very fact of his nature. This internal contradiction in the very heart of the Arab intellectual's personality tears him apart inside and makes him an unproductive being."

On June 12 and 13 there was a confrontation between the theses that denied any effort on the part of the intellectuals before 1961 to examine the problems of Egypt's society and her future, the line taken in particular by Mohammed el-Khafif, and the defense of what had been done until that date, a defense undertaken by Abdel Razek Hassan and Louis Awad. Awad very properly observed: "This revolution existed in its entirety before 1952; otherwise it would have been impossible for it to occur"; but this, as is obvious, struck down the myth of its creation *ex nihilo*.

On June 24 there was another discussion. In the interval, the voice of the government was clearly heard on two occasions. It was on June 16, in fact, that Heykal issued his call to order, part of which forms the introduction to this chapter, and that the intelligentsia was put on notice that its task was to provide the military rulers with the ideology that they needed. Major Salah Dessuki, a leading rightist, governor° of Cairo and chairman of the National Educational Committee, had entered the lists on June 12 to declare that "there is no crisis of the intellectuals." With remarkable violence he denounced "the intellectuals of those classes [the feudalists, the reactionaries, the political parties] that had shown themselves the most stubborn in their opposition and the most violent in the attacks that they have made against contrary opinions," and he submitted three propositions, to replace completely what had been said thus far: "The intellectuals constitute neither a class nor a social category, since their attitudes have always conformed to those of the groups and classes to which they belong; the army Revolution of July 23 was a revolution of intellectuals in its very essence; the intellectuals who, with their class, joined the ranks of the Revolution are more numerous and more powerful than the rabble who stood at the head of their enemies; the crisis that has arisen between the power of the revolutionary impulse and the intelligentsia is in reality a crisis with a group of culture professionals divided into those who are professionals because of their work and those who want to bring about a change based on principles imported from abroad . . ."

Having thus established that the officers were the intellectuals—how could there be any talk of a crisis after that? —the governor of Cairo lashed out against the Communists in his second article, on June 24: "While the Moslem Brotherhood movement," he said, "was the outgrowth of a struggle by a few fanatics, the Communist movement was that of a few agents . . . since the first Communist propagandists in Cairo were Zionist Jews . . . Later the Communists joined the ranks of the Revolution, all the while dreaming of the day when they could take it over in a moment of inattention. Events could not fail to unmask them, however, whenever it came to the point of having to choose between the desires of the people and the instructions sent from afar. Every time, the Com-

° There are twenty-four local administrative units called governorates. Five are urban: Cairo, Alexandria, Suez, Port Said and Ismailia. There are eight provincial governorates each in Upper and Lower Egypt, and three frontier governorates for the border areas.

munists formed ranks behind the writings of Moscow . . ." No facts. No instances. No evidence.

In truth, at the time of the second discussion, the atmosphere was so strained that it needed only a trifle to touch off reactions envenomed by rancor. The speeches of such "pure" university professors as Hussein Khallaf, Ahmed Zaki Saleh and Rushdy Said contributed nothing new. After Magdi Wahba's measured plea on behalf of freedom, Abdel Razek Hassan demanded that "no one take advantage of the tendencies that exist in certain groups in order resolutely to exclude them from any participation in public affairs, for this could later be damaging to all." Mohammed el-Khafif took the occasion to restore to those who were of his class the credit for their studies, at least in part, and then demanded "the institution of a system that will allow any man to say what he thinks, so that whoever wishes to express his views does not have to keep silent lest something happen to him, and thus be reduced to huddling in passivity." Finally, so that he would not be left out, Lutfi el-Kholy suggested that "the problem of freedom of speech remains on the agenda of society, since it has not thus far been resolved in a realistic fashion for the benefit of our development."

In actual fact, the most pressing, as well as long-term, problem that was posed in the search for a concept of civilization adaptable to the contemporary Egyptian—the basic, immediate problem—was that of civil liberties, of democracy. That was what emerged from the timorous but repeated forays of the intellectuals whom we have quoted, most of them prominent members of the old Left—Communist, Marxist or Marxist-oriented—of the years from 1945 to 1959. That the relations between the military rulers and the Marxists were at the heart of the debate, that the Marxists' contributions, even in the opinion of their enemies, had been singularly fruitful, that, in other words, no recruiting of the intelligentsia to the government was possible without a prior solution to the problem of relations between the Revolutionary Command Council and the Left, at the time subjected to the harshest ordeals in the concentration camps—all this was made clear both in Salah Dessuki's two articles and in Heykal's series, which was written, let us repeat, by the President's direct spokesman and confidant.

What did Heykal say? "At this moment the action of the forces of the revolutionary drive was twofold: a positive movement, a search for a road of revolutionary development, and a negative movement, an attempt to rid itself of the vacillating elements that sought to divert it from that road. This latter movement was made the more difficult because of the concomitant action of certain elements that did demand a change but refused to conceive it outside a predetermined pattern. Among these elements, for instance, were the Communists!"[11]

What was this all about? Essentially, the aim was to deny to the Marxist Left the right and power to formulate quite independently, or even in agreement with the government (as in the days of *al-Missa* in 1956–58), an alternative to the one offered to Egyptians by the military rulers as an unavoidable necessity—an alternative for the creation of a modern Egypt, in independence, certainly in vigilance, but also in openness to the world, in fruitful collaboration with the positive currents of contemporary culture, in democracy, which alone was capable of providing a foundation for socialism.

And yet it was precisely at the time when the military rulers were crying out their need for an ideology and for leading cadres that this Left, broken on the rack, was called on to come back to life, on condition that it abdicate all independent existence, all autonomous personality, every wisp of being itself.

What was striking, during these crucial years 1955 to 1958, was the fact that the need for an ideology emerged to top priority among popular and official concerns.

It was not that the Egypt of the years before 1952 had lived outside the reach of that will to provide itself with a structure of ideas which at the same time would take into account not only the living element that the past could offer to the essence of everyday minds and lives, but also the present, which was the vessel of inheritance and the projection into the future of the evolution that was to be undertaken voluntarily, consciously—ideally, so to speak. But it is important to note that only at the moment when the Egyptian bourgeoisie, after removing the obstacle of the landed aristocracy, had seized power—in coalition with the Free Officers, it is true, during the first two phases; only at the moment when it revealed, through political action but also through legislative reorganization, its totally capitalist aspect, which was oriented toward advanced technical skill and state capitalism; only at this exact moment, and not before, did the government voice its desire to equip itself with a national ideology. It was the desire of the government, for the influence of the Left had earlier established ideology in the forefront of Egyptian reality. But this time it was the state and the dominant forces in economy and politics that turned toward thought and myths.

The Free Officers held sway from 1952 to 1954. What was their ideology? Officially none, except the triptych of "Unity, Order, Work." "The principles of the Revolution," Ehsan Abdel Koddus wrote in March 1954, "can all be reduced to a single word, an abstract idea: reform, *isla'h* . . . The leaders of the Revolution may have ideas or an ideology, but all it amounts to is one single idea: 'the army for the people.' No other ideals at all. No other ideology at all."[12] Virtually at the same time Fathi Raduan, the first Minister of Culture and National Guidance, could write these words: "What is Egypt's policy? That is a question which cannot yet be answered . . ."[13] These two statements, among so many dozens of others, clearly show the lack of any philosophy, of even any desire to acquire an ideology, before the establishment of an alliance between the military apparatus in power and the modernist upper bourgeoisie in 1954.

From that time on, the signs became numerous: the publication of *The Philosophy of the Revolution* in April 1954, under the signature of Gamal Abdel Nasser; the creation of the Islamic Congress (which convened in Mecca in 1955 and was headed by Anwar el-Sadate), in order to acquire control of the co-ordinates of pan-Islamism formerly in the hands of the Moslem Brotherhood; participation in the Bandung Conference and the proclamation of positive neutralism (1955);

the theory of Arab nationalism (1956–58); economic planning and co-operativist democratic socialism (1956–60); the attempt to resolve the crisis of the intellectuals, and the establishment of a virtual state monopoly in the domain of culture (1961–62).

This, let us repeat, was all on the side of the state, for the private sector of the intelligentsia that survived proved prolific before it was blacked out by the cloak of cultural planning and control.

Introduction to Contemporary Egyptian Thought

But the ideology that evolved after 1956 was far from being a creation *ex nihilo,* as the theoreticians of the government like to believe. It may even be said that the military government's ideology constituted the culmination of one of the fundamental tendencies of contemporary Egyptian thought, deeply marked not only by the economic and geographical necessities that we have discussed, but also by the world struggle between socialism and capitalism in the hour of imperialism's decline.

What were the component elements of an Egyptian ideology (of any possible Egyptian military ideology) at the time of the seizure of power in 1952?

For the purposes of analysis it is advisable to divide them under two headings: autochthonous elements and foreign influences.

In the Egyptian area, the cultural renewal that marked the second half of the nineteenth century—under the influence of the renascence stimulated by Bonaparte's expedition, but also beginning with the effort at modernization initiated by Rifaa Rafe' el-Tahtawi* (1801–73)[14]—was to make of Egypt (which enjoyed a relative independence within the Ottoman Empire, thanks to Mohammed Ali and the campaigns of Ibrahim, and also because of the importance of her economic and demographic potential and her long historic tradition) culturally

---

* The initiator and leading figure of Egypt's renaissance, in the fields of the press as well as the theory of the national movement, and the first socialist-leaning thinker. More than anyone else, he can be recognized as the founding father and inspirer of modern Egyptian culture and social thought.

the most advanced country in the Arab Orient and at the same time a haven of refuge for Arab thinkers, journalists and writers, especially Syrians and Lebanese, Christians and Moslem liberals, persecuted for their convictions in the more vulnerable *wilayets* (provinces) of the Levant. Throughout the nineteenth century, in spite of the British occupation and the obscurantist policy of Cromer and Dunlop,* French influences fertilized the cultural renewal of Egypt. Students trained at French universities provided the country with generations of intellectuals who, in their turn, endowed Egypt with her autonomous cultural substructure outside the traditional education and orthodoxy of Al Azhar. There was an abundance of great names, some of them relatively well known abroad, notably Ali Mubarak Pasha, founder of the public-school system. But mention should also be made of Mohammed Kadri Pasha, the leading jurist of his time; Dr. Mohammed el-Bakly Pasha, an eminent physician; Abdalla Abul Saud, who founded *Wadi el-Nil,* the first Egyptian newspaper, in 1866 (the Takla brothers' *al-Ahram* dates from 1875).

Beginning in the 1880s, however, and forcefully influenced by Gamal Eddine el-Afghani (1838–97), who brought contemporary political Islam to life, a movement was to develop that would reach its peak under the military government. Afghani's chosen disciple, who worked with him in their Parisian exile (1884) on the publication of *al-Orwa al-Wothka,* the organ of pan-Islamic nationalism, was none other than Sheik Mohammed Abdu (1849–1905). In him the Islamic tendency of the national movement and the Egyptian and Arab cultural revival found its theoretician. What must be emphasized in this thinking is its insistence on the adaptation of medieval Islam to modern civilization. In order to do this it is necessary to go back to the source, which is the Koran, to purge contemporary Islam of all the encrustations of tradition that unsettle and irritate the modern mind. Once this primary requirement has been fulfilled, basic Islam must be restored to its rank at the center of the social and political life, the culture and the

---

*Douglas Dunlop headed Egyptian educational policy for a generation (until 1918), and is widely accused of having deliberately ruined any attempt at creating a real educated élite.

thought of the contemporary Arab and Islamic states; absolutely no separation between religion and the state is possible; the prevailing culture, European in its inspiration, must be restricted according to the criteria of modernized Islam. This is the thesis of Islamic fundamentalism—the return to the sources and an autonomous ideology. On the philosophic level, Islam is the law, but only because common sense corroborates it; it is possible to envisage some ventilation of ideas, a certain margin for discussion, but the advocates of reason must respect the reserved area in which religion alone teaches and legislates in full sovereignty, and which often affects the problems of society. In the field of politics, Mohammed Abdu deplored the divisive factors that weakened Islam; he took part in Arabi's revolution of 1882 with great reluctance but proved to be primarily concerned with arriving at a compromise with Lord Cromer, who backed him against Khedive Abbas II, then linked to the nationalists: in order to assure the progress of a nation one must rely on the élite. What must be utterly rejected, on the plane of both thought and action, is the possibility of explosion represented by the centrifugal action of discordant forces. Religion governs the whole and gives it strength and coherence.[15]

This was the beginning of the divergence between the two wings of the Egyptian renascence. Mohammed Abdu's ideas impregnated the National party of Mustafa Kamel and Mohammed Farid; they were at the root of the renovation of Al Azhar under its rectors Sheik Mustafa Abdel Razzek and Sheik Maraghi; and above all they provided the lower-middle-class shopkeepers, the artisans and the traditionalist intellectuals of city and country alike—by way of the fundamentalism of Rashid Rida, the Syrian disciple and biographer of Sheik Abdu who in Cairo founded a journal, *al-Manar*, which was, until the thirties, the main organ of the militant trend in right-wing political Islam—with the foundations of what was to constitute the ideology of the Moslem Brotherhood from 1927 on. The acceptance of Islam's primacy as a general doctrine in matters of theology, philosophy and culture; renewal conceived as a return to the sources of orthodoxy; the central position of religion within society; the rejection of any ideological and cultural autonomy; the battle against the factors of division and internal conflict in the *umma;* the subordination of reason and critical activity to the ancestral faith; the accent put on internal renewal through the restoration of the power of Islam, the struggles for national liberation and political democracy being regarded as substitutes, indeed as dangerous games of foreign inspiration; the expansion of the concept of the nation to include the entire Islamic world—all these theses are to be found not only among the partisans of Hassan el-Banna but also in the Islamic organizations and movements that proliferated in Egypt between the two world wars and above all in the resurgence of the Arab idea in Egypt at about the same period. More than anything else, Mohammed Abdu's teaching supplied a confirmation and a pledge to that part of Egyptian society— long kept out of the process of European-style modernization begun by Mohammed Ali's missions and become the private preserve of the prosperous circles in the two capitals— which was trying to find itself, trying to get a foothold for a new start from genuine and autochthonous sources, which could create a rebirth erupting, so to speak, from the depths of Egypt's essential being, to which the struggle against Europe seemed to give an exclusively Islamic dimension.

Nevertheless, while Islamic, reformist and nationalist fundamentalism was taking root, sociologically, in the most backward and nondynamic sectors of the economy and Egyptian society between 1882 and 1952 (the lower middle class of shopkeepers and artisans, especially in the provinces; clergymen and religious schools; certain groups of the landed aristocracy), the main forces of the rising middle class enlisted, in various ways, in the second great tendency of Egyptian thought, the trend of modernist and, generally speaking, rationalist and liberal-democratic inspiration.

Beginning with considerations of Egyptian history, of Aristotelianism, of the destiny of the national movement during the early years of British occupation, marked especially by the brilliant personality of Abdallah el-Nadim, the leading men, who were the landed aristocracy, found in Ahmed Lutfi el-Sayed—"the master of the age," as he was to be called later— the theoretician at the same time of Egyptianness confronted with cosmopolitan Islamism, of moderate liberalism confronted with nationalist agitation tainted with pan-Islamism, of realism and rationality, whose presence was made necessary by the exercise of power, however limited it might have been at that period. The group of thinkers of *al-Garida* (an influential weekly founded by Sayed) was also to be one of secular and modernist reformists, such as Kassem Amine, the champion of feminism; Ahmed Fathi Zaghlul, the master translator, and above all Saad Zaghlul, the founder of the Wafd in 1919 and the creator of independent Egypt.

The predominance of the landed middle class, the urban traders and the intelligentsia, whose electoral voice the Wafd in a way constituted, was to become visible in a remarkable cultural flowering: Taha Hussein introduced the historical method into the fields of religion and literature; Ali Abdel Razzek preached the separation of religion and state; the evolutionism of Dr. Shibli Shemeil, the birth of the novel with Farah Antun, the influence of the Fabian Society made Salama Mussa the spokesman of socialist thought; the novel took wing with Mohammed Hussein Heykal, in another field the theoretician of the return to the Egypt of the Pharaohs; Abbas el-Akkad, who became the thinker of the Nietzschean Right; Tewfik el-Hakim, the creator of the modern Egyptian theater; Saad Zaghlul, Mustafa el-Nahas, Makram Ebeid, Sabri Abu Alam, Aziz Fahmy and Mohammed Mandur—the last two under the influence of the Marxist Left—supplied a liberal and democratic political doctrine in the name of the Wafd; the law school, under French inspiration, laid the foundation for Egyptian legislation after the end of the Capitulations,* thanks to Abdel Razzak el-Sanhury, Ali Badawi and Wahid Ra'fat, among so many others; the university had its day of glory through the impetus of Taha Hussein, Ali Ibrahim, Ali Mustafa Musharrafa, Abdel Wahab Muro; the plastic arts were graced with the great name of Mahmud Mukhtar and by

---

* A system of extraterritorial privileges under the Ottoman Empire, which gave European (Christian) residents immunity from Ottoman laws. In Egypt this meant that Europeans could not be sued or tried other than in their own Consular Courts, until Ismail created the Mixed Courts in 1867. The system was gradually abolished in the late nineteenth and twentieth centuries; in Egypt, in 1937 (Montreux Treaty).

Mahmud Said of Alexandria; music by Sayed Darwish; the humanities, the large newspapers, the rise of radio broadcasting, the multiplication of universities side by side with the growth of universal free and compulsory public schooling—all were done in the name of liberalism, of modern culture and of democracy.

Finally, in the 1940s, the Marxist school began its rise, and after 1945–46, it became the motive force in the cultural evolution at the precise moment when the Wafd was withdrawing into the self-satisfaction and prestige of power. Through its action and under its influence, the liberal and rationalist trend turned in the direction of socialism. It is to this school, quite naturally, that we are indebted for the creation of a realist literature and esthetic adorned by such names as Mahmud Amin el-Alem, Abdel Rahman el-Sharkawi, Abdel Rahman el-Khamissi, Yussef Idriss, Mohammed Sidky and Kamal Abdel Halim; a new philosophical school extended and accentuated the Egyptian and liberal character of Egyptian thought with Abu Seif Yussef, Mahmud el-Alem and Ismail el-Mahdawy in particular; historians, economists and political theoreticians published important works, many of which have previously been quoted in this book, but also those of Abdel Razek Hassan, Fuad Mursi, Ismail Sabri Abdallah, etc. The influence of this fertile and controversial new contribution made itself felt especially in the Egyptian school of painting and sculpture (Gamal el-Seginy, A. H. Gazzar, H. Abdallah, Mohammed Eweiss, Gazbiyya Sidky, Gamal Kamel, etc.); in the novels of Naguib Mahfuz and Mohammed el-Bedewi particularly; in the architecture of Hassan Fathi; while Hussein Fawzi developed his general theory of the Egyptian personality, thus establishing the idea of civilization at the heart of everything, and Mohammed Kamel Hussein, Abdel Rahman Badawi, Yussef Murad and Mustafa Sueif, among others, contributed an important body of philosophical work representing the whole range of contemporary tendencies.

The rise of the industrial wing of the Egyptian bourgeoisie in the 1930s, in alliance both with the landed aristocracy and with British finance but yet starting from profoundly Egyptian sources, was mainifested in basic works, notably that of Sobhi

Wahida, the theoretician of Egyptian history, and above all in the proliferation of ideas that revealed the impatience of these new forces in the face of the indifference and dead weight of the rich landowners. It is here that the source must be sought for the emergence of heroic themes directly inspired by Nietzsche in Abdel Rahman Badawi, which were to wind up in national socialism with Ahmed Hussein, Fathi Raduan and the *Akhbar el-Yom* group (led by Mustafa Amine and Mohammed Hassanein Heykal)—that is, the lay preachers of "strong rule," many of whom were to join forces with Hassan el-Banna, Abdel Kader Auda and Sayed Kotb, the leaders and ideologists of the Moslem Brotherhood.[16]

The Ideological Formation of Gamal Abdel Nasser . . .

These were the basic facts of the problem of ideology in Egypt as they entered the consciousness of the young cadet Gamal Abdel Nasser Hussein, a first-year student at the Military Academy of Abbassia (Cairo), to which he had been admitted on March 17, 1937, through the direct intercession of Ibrahim Khairy Pasha, Undersecretary of State for War. He had been rejected by the entrance committee a year earlier for taking part in the nationalist demonstrations of 1935, though the real reason was his birth into a family of minor functionaries; for the officers' corps, directly connected to the Palace and placed under the domination of the British military mission, was at that time reserved for the sons of prominent families.

During this period the young student belonged to those middle-class circles for which the Wafd would provide the opportunity to become part of the state machinery, especially the army, higher education and diplomacy. The treaty of 1936 and, later, the abolition of the Capitulations in 1937 opened the doors of the Military Academy for the first time to young men born into the middle and lower classes of the population. As a matter of course they were all intensely patriotic, most of them devoted in the Wafd and its great Minister of War, General Hamdi Seif el-Nasr Pasha; all of them were burning with the desire to set their country free of the military occupation forces and to restore its greatness and dignity. To be certain of this, one has only to reread the letter, so often quoted since, that the young Gamal, chairman of the Executive Committee of High School Students, wrote to his friend Hassan el-Nasshar, on September 2, 1935, little more than two months before its author, at the head of his young comrades of the Al Nahda School in Faggalah (Cairo), demonstrated under fire from the Lee-Enfield rifles and under the clubs of the police, and three months before December 12, 1935, when King Fuad found himself constrained to reinstate the Constitution of 1932, thus opening the way for the return of the Wafd:

". . . It seems to me that the country is in agony. Despair is everywhere. Who can banish it? The government of Egypt is founded on corruption and favoritism. Who can change it? The Constitution has been suspended. The Protectorate is going to be proclaimed. Who can tell imperialism: 'Stop there'? . . .

"Where is the burning nationalism of 1919? Where are there men ready to sacrifice themselves for the sacred soil of the fatherland? . . . Where is the man who can re-create the country so that feeble, humiliated Egypt can rise again, can live free and independent? Where is dignity? Where is nationalism? Where is that thing called the activism of youth? . . .

"Mustafa Kamel said: 'To live in despair is no life.' Today we are in the depths of despair . . .

"It is said that the Egyptian is cowardly, that he is scared of the slightest noise. We need a leader who will take him into battle for his country. And then that Egyptian will become a thunder that will make the structures of persecution shudder.

"Mustafa Kamel said: 'Though my heart shift from left to right, though the Pyramids move, though the Nile change its course, I for one will not change my principles.' Everything that has happened thus far is a long overture to greater and more important work . . ."[17]

In senior high school Gamal read the biography of Mustafa Kamel and *The Defenders of Islam*, to which Kamel had contributed the Preface, as well as the books of Abdel Rahman el-Kawakibi, the chief critic of autocracy in the name of democratic principles; the works of Ahmed Amin on Afghani and

Abdu, the collected articles from the newspapers of the National party, *al-Lewa* and *al-Akhbar;* the lives of Voltaire and Rousseau (Gamal Abdel Nasser's first article for his school publication was called "Voltaire, Man of Freedom"), the Arabic translations of *Les Misérables* and Dickens' *A Tale of Two Cities,* the poems of the "prince of poets," Ahmed Shawki, and those of Hafez Ibrahim, a book by Ali el-Ghayati on Islamic nationalism, and above all Tewfik el-Hakim's *Awdat al-ro'h* (*The Soul Regained*). And he appropriated to himself the conclusions of his French teacher, M. Fouquet: "Yes, what this people lacks is the man who will be the embodiment of its soul and hopes, and who will be the symbol of its ideal. Let that man arise and then there will be no cause for astonishment if this intricately bound people, this people united in suffering and ready for sacrifice, accomplishes another miracle besides that of the Pyramids . . ."

What did the young cadet read during the eighteen months that he spent in the Military Academy while he waited for his second-lieutenant star, which he received on July 1, 1938? One group of books, the greatest part, dealt with the biographies of famous men: Bonaparte (four books), Mustafa Kemal Atatürk, Alexander, Bismarck, Foch, Garibaldi, Hindenburg, Lawrence, Marlborough, Winston Churchill, Gordon (two books), and others; the second group dealt with Egyptian and Arab history and politics (twelve books, including the first three of Abdel Rahman el-Rafei's history of the national movement); many military treatises; the periodicals included The (London) *Times Weekly Edition,* the *National Geographic Magazine,* and five others in English. Napoleon was indeed the major object of Gamal Abdel Nasser's interest, along with the history of Germany, the chief rival to the British occupying power, for three works on Germany can be found on this list; there were also three books by Liddell Hart and three by Winston Churchill.

In 1943 Gamal Abdel Nasser, a captain and graduate of the Staff College, returned to the Military Academy as an instructor. He read profusely. This time it was Egypt in the frame of reference of the Mediterranean that held first place (twenty-five books); the Japanese miracle (three books) and

Hitler's Germany (two books) attracted him; he became acquainted with the work of Clausewitz, he reread Tewfik el-Hakim and provided himself with a very solid theoretical military training (Clausewitz, Fuller, Liddell Hart, Lindsell and the major official British publications); for the first time Nasser schooled himself in economic facts (Bonné's work on the Middle East), became interested in the Boer War, and read the works of André Siegfried, Charles-Roux and Arnold Wilson on Suez and Panama.[18] And there can be no doubt that the experience gained during the battle of El Alamein enriched all this reading and gave the lectures of Major Nasser, professor of history at the Staff College in 1943, a highly individual appeal to the young officers, among whom he now began to recruit those who would later constitute the organization of the Free Officers.

. . . and of His Associates

Only one of the military rulers, Colonel Anwar el-Sadate, published a collection of autobiographical documents (in 1957) which, according to Nasser himself, constitutes "the quintessence of the secret drives and psychological motivations of our peaceful revolution."[19] The nationalism of the man who until 1952 was one of the two major leaders of the Free Officers, later responsible for the "civilian branch" which provided the military regime with its first experts and trained staffs to supplement the military core stemming from the "military branch" directed by Nasser, proved to be unmistakably oriented toward German national socialism.

Aside from these three largely autobiographical works (*The Philosophy of the Revolution* and the two volumes written by Anwar el-Sadate, to which it is useful to add General Naguib's *Egypt's Destiny* (1955) as a further reminder—it portrays him in the guise of a moderate reformist influenced by Wafdist liberalism and Islamic reformism), there is hardly any of the personal interpretation that one would have the right to expect from the other leaders of the army movement. At the very most there are a few articles by Salah Salem scattered through *al-Tahrir* and *al-Shaab,* a hurried study by Colonel Sarwat

Okasha,[20] and also the important collection of Khaled Mohieddine's articles for *al-Missa*, which he managed from September
1956 to March 1959. The essence remains hidden, and so do
the chief protagonists, about whom the participants and the
eyewitnesses of what happened seemed not yet ready to talk
in the present circumstances.

It was a young Indiana professor, P. J. Vatikiotis, who tried
to tabulate the cultural factors that helped to mold twenty
officers, all members of the leadership nucleus of the Free
Officers. Here are his major findings on the subject of ideological shaping, the theme of this chapter:

1. Gamal Abdel Nasser, infantry lieutenant colonel on the
General Staff; five months in the law faculty; instructor at
the Infantry School, the Administrative School, the Staff College; connected with the Wafd, then with the Moslem Brotherhood, and finally with Marxist organizations.

2. Abdel Hakim Amer, staff major at the General Headquarters of the Infantry; member of the Moslem Brotherhood.

3. Abdel Latif el-Boghdadi, staff lieutenant colonel, air
force; graduate of the two first-level military academies (infantry and air force); mission in Yemen (1948); connected
with Misr Airways in 1947–48 (thus later gaining the confidence of the Misr complex), and then in charge of the airport west of Cairo (1948); before that, engaged in sabotage
operations against the British (1940–42).

4. Kamal Eddine Hussein, staff major, artillery; instructor at
the Staff College; member of the Moslem Brotherhood, supervising the training of *fida'yyin* in 1947–48.

5. Hassan Ibrahim, air force major; member of the *Misr
al-Fatat* party; missions abroad after 1945.

6. Khaled Mohieddine, staff major, armored forces; graduate
of Cairo University (1951) in economics and business administration; member of Marxist organizations.

7. Zakaria Mohieddine, staff lieutenant colonel, infantry.

8. Mohammed Naguib, staff major general; graduate of
Cairo University (1927) in law; commander in chief of infantry (1950–51); Free Officers' candidate for the presidency
of the Officers' Club.

9. Anwar el-Sadate, infantry colonel; member of the *Misr*

al-Fatat party and then of the Moslem Brotherhood; organized anti-British sabotage in 1941–42.

10. Gamal Salem, lieutenant colonel, air force; member of the Egyptian Socialist (formerly Misr al-Fatat) party.

11. Salah Salem, staff major, General Headquarters; tactics instructor at the Staff College.

12. Hussein el-Shafei, staff lieutenant colonel, armored forces, former member of the MB.

13. Sarwat Okasha, staff lieutenant colonel; graduate of the Institute of Journalism at Cairo University (1944), later doctor in literature (Sorbonne, 1964); military attaché.

14. Kamal Rifaat, lieutenant colonel, infantry; member of Marxist organizations (1947–51); anti-British activities (1951–1952).

15. Tewfik Abdel Fattah, staff lieutenant colonel, infantry.

16. Mohammed Mahmud Nasser, major general, medical corps; graduate of the School of Medicine at Cairo University (1936).

17. Abbas Radwan, staff lieutenant colonel, infantry; instructor at the Infantry School.

18. Fathi Rizk, major general, transportation corps.

19. Hussein Zulfikar Sabry, lieutenant colonel, air force; graduate of the two military academies (infantry and air force); anti-British action in conjunction with Marshal Rommel in 1941.[21]

Four additional biographies should be appended, notably those of Colonel Yussef Saddik—formerly a member of the Communist organization, DMNL—and Colonel Rashad Mehanna, linked to the Moslem Brotherhood; Lieutenant Colonel Ali Sabry of the air force; and Major Abdel Kader Hatem. The Sabry brothers and Sarwat Okasha came from the old ruling class. But the analysis of the middle military-leader staffs remains to be undertaken, in terms both of their social origins and of their ideology at the time of the coup d'état. It would then become clear that a large number had belonged in one way or another to the Wafdist groups or public until February 4, 1942, when King Faruk, his palace encircled with armor and troops, had to comply with British demands; had not Gamal Abdel Nasser himself, in 1935, been chairman of the Executive Committee of High School Students, which was striving to prepare the return of the Wafd and the constitutional system?

Of these twenty-three leading officers, only three—Ali Sabry, Hussein Zulkifar Sabry and Sarwat Okasha—had been exposed to European influences, both through their social origins and through their secondary or higher schooling.

All the others—twenty of the twenty-three—belonged to the urban and rural lower middle class, the same class whose ties to pan-Islamic nationalism or the groups of profascist activists we have already described. Thus, especially after February 4, the overwhelming majority of the leadership of the Free Officers must be viewed in the perspective of the junction between the two groups opposed to rationalist and democratic liberalism, which in 1952 was represented by the Wafdists and Marxists—in other words, the organizations of the National Front. And it is permissible to assume that the same proportion recurred in the ranks of the progressively descending levels of the military hierarchy at the time of the coup d'état, at least after the successive purges that followed the seizure of power and, above all, the ouster of General Naguib.

The Reorientation of Cultural Policy

Now that the roots of the problem have been set in their historical perspective, it becomes possible to ascertain the general aspect of the military government's ideology in a rational manner.

Like any entity that is resolved to insist on its own autonomous and transcendent existence, the military government set itself up in opposition. Throughout the first decade, on every level and in a systematic fashion, it opposed the two major wings, the two successive manifestations of the rationalist, liberal and democratic trend of Egyptian thought. Certainly the modes of that opposition varied as much as its intensity. This was a question not only of principles but of tactics. However, the opposition remained, defining the system and localizing its ideology.

It rejected all of Western culture and values, which it de-nounced for their imperialism. The entire contribution of France and England—the essence of the relations between Europe and Egypt since Bonaparte and Mohammed Ali—was under accusation, which began with the Suez crisis. In fact, the three-power attack provided the military rulers with the opportunity to settle their score with the intelligentsia of Anglo-French inspiration whence had come, until 1956 and even until 1958, the major portion of Egypt's teachers, journalists, writers, thinkers, artists, lawyers and diplomats. The aggression did not stop at the military and political levels; in Egypt the government officials had clearly understood that the monopoly of arms faced another monopoly, far more dangerous in the long run: the monopoly of culture. The celebration of Cairo University's golden jubilee on December 21, 1958, provided Gamal Abdel Nasser with the opportunity to define his philosophy of culture: "Our Arab people has been lacking in two of the most important developments that have affected the destiny of mankind—I mean steam and electricity. At the time when the world was entering the steam-engine age, we were still living under the domination of medieval phantasms; and when the age of electricity started, we had barely begun to move away from those illusions . . . In order to make room for the atomic age and the space age, it is not enough to concentrate on scientific research; we must prepare ourselves for it mentally, spiritually and psychologically . . . While it used to be possible to drive the camel at the same time as the automobile, this is no longer possible in the rocket age . . . Knowledge constitutes the motive force in the time ahead; it is, in fact, true freedom. You know that from the political point of view, we are opposed to the so-called monopoly of knowledge . . . Another thing about which I should like to speak frankly: thus far we have lived on the ideas and inventions of others, with very rare exceptions. It is now no longer possible, in this age of enlightenment, to live on the glory of having been the first to raise high the torch of civilization, later carried by Alexandria to Athens. It is no longer possible for us as Arabs to praise ourselves for having preserved science and civilizations while Europe was foundering in the darkness of the Middle Ages, so that we could turn over this inheritance to her at the dawn of the Renaissance and then sink into a profound slumber . . . We should turn our efforts toward the most creative avenues. We should prepare ourselves to go far, for science and thought never stop advancing and no boundaries can be set for them . . ."[22]

And on June 26, 1959, speaking to the professors of Alexandria University, he emphasized his tenet: "The struggle in today's world is no longer a conflict of arms but rather a conflict of knowledge. That is why knowledge has been transformed into secrets, forbidden and exclusive. If we wish to build our country, we have to unearth knowledge with our hands, and ideas with our brains. Today it is possible for us to turn to other nations within the limits of their resources; but we should by our own efforts unearth whatever is held back from us . . ."[23]

These two appeals, especially the one in 1958 at the height of the euphoria of the Bandung period, came, however, barely four years after the massive purge that destroyed the careers of almost seventy professors, lecturers and instructors in Egypt's universities. All those who were affected—and some of them were outstanding—belonged to the liberal wing, whether they were Wafdists, Marxists or merely freethinkers, even advocates of constitutionalism, and not one was later restored to his post. The 1956 operation was accompanied by the appointment of a new Minister of Education and Instruction, Major Kamal Eddine Hussein, better known for his docility than for his learning,[24] with the definite purpose of regaining control of the universities, purging the dangerously critical student movement, and changing the structure and personnel of education at every level. The executive staffs of liberal background were removed—titular and assistant Undersecretaries of State, directors general, directors, inspectors general, inspectors—and the apparatus was then taken in hand by Mohammed Said el-Eryan, one of the most virulent apostles of pan-Islamism and a resolute enemy of Western culture, who took his revenge on the staffs trained and appointed by Ahmed Lutfi el-Sayed, Taha Hussein and Naguib el-Hilaly.

What the government intended to incorporate into the cultural foundation of the future Arab Egypt was the science and technology of Europe and America; the President of the Republic emphasized these objectives whenever he made any move in the cultural area. Thus the remarkable range of foreign missions after Suez; it is true that several thousand students were sent to the Soviet Union, Czechoslovakia and several other socialist countries, but it was West Germany that broke all records with a figure of some five thousand students, closely followed by the United States. France and Great Britain were for the moment thrust aside, and the missions were redirected toward relatively neutral countries—Austria, Belgium and Switzerland in particular—from 1956 to 1958.

It was logical that the rejection of traditional Western culture during the 1956–58 period—for Egypt, be it understood—at no time reached the point of the veritable crusade of hate that was launched against Marxism, especially in 1959–60. That was because this time the issue was no longer simply what might be called the militant branch of Western culture, but also an internationalist and atheist ideology with which Arab nationalism could not make any accommodation. We shall come back to this. For the moment it is sufficient to observe the differences in the reactions of the military toward the two branches of European culture.

What was left standing after this double negation?

First of all, Islam—Islam as revised by Mohammed Abdu and his school, whose ideas reached a large part of the Free Officers by way of the Moslem Brotherhood.

Next—and this was the contribution of the trend allied with the industrial upper middle class (the Misr complex, *Akhbar el-Yom*, etc.)—there were the elements of fascist or protofascist ideology, German rather than Italian in inspiration. There was Ahmed Hussein's party with the multiple names, and also Fathi Raduan's New National party, both of which assumed the task of mediation between ideology and an important sector of the military apparatus.

These two trends were interjected against a background that controlled the whole: radical nationalism, or, rather, nationalitarianism, the determination to restore life and power to a humiliated Egypt. Islam and national socialism, and nothing more, would be the means of attaining the end, at least in the eyes of Gamal Abdel Nasser during the years of search.

In the trenches of the Palestine war, in Erak el-Manshia, where he conducted himself as a leader and a hero, Gamal Abdel Nasser gave serious thought to his activities. "We were fighting then in Palestine," he wrote six years later in his *Philosophy of the Revolution*, "but all our dreams were in Egypt . . ." And he recalled the remark of Colonel Ahmed Abdel Aziz, killed in action, when the General Staff and the king's advisers were disgracing themselves in the dealings in defective weapons: "The main battlefield is in Egypt . . ."

In Egypt, where the battle for the minds and the hearts must now be launched.

With what forces?

New Staffs for Ideological Guidance

The problem became acute in 1959—that is, at the time of the great crusade against the Egyptian Marxists. The European-liberal-trained intelligentsia had already, after the Naguib affair, indicated a movement of withdrawal. The sequels to Suez made it a suspect of prime importance. Finally, the internment of its fellow travelers, progressives and Communists, incited panic.

Hence 1959 was the beginning of a period of ideological reconstruction. True, the administrative machinery was provided by the Ministry of Culture and National Guidance, in which Sarwat Okasha had succeeded Salah Salem and Fathi Raduan. But thought had to be given to ideology on the theoretical level, the component elements of a new doctrine had to be evolved. This was a matter for thinkers. Therefore it was necessary to bring together those who showed a readiness to act, to fill the places of the élites eliminated by force.

During the autumn of 1958, President Nasser gave much thought to his proposed Leadership School, which he intended to entrust to Khaled Mohieddine. A few months later the repressions began; the project was postponed.

In 1960–61 came the creation of an Arab Socialist Association, presided over by Kamal Rifaat, and including Mahdi Ben Barka of Morocco, Clovis Maksud and Gubran el-Majdalani of Lebanon, Fuad el-Rikabi of Jordan and Mohammed Auda, Ahmed Baha'Eddine, Kamel Zeheiry and Lutfi el-Kholy of Egypt, among others.

The Minister of State responsible for press and broadcasting affairs, Abdel Kader Hatem, headed the board of directors of the Egyptian Political Science Association, which included the names of Dr. Yehia Eweiss, Colonel Mohammed Kamal Eddine Abdel Rahman, Sayed Ibrahim, Mohammed Sadek Akl, Saad Galal, Abdel Salam Abul Saud, Kamal Abdel Aziz and Sayed el-Badawi.[25]

Major Amin Shaker, former principal private secretary to the President, founded the Association of National Consciousness in 1959. He was assisted by several professors—Mahmud el-Gowhari, Mohammed Metwalli, then governor of Minufiya, and Professor Rashad Rushdi—as well as Ahmed Mahmud Abdel Nabi. The membership roster included the names of Adly Andraos, Mohammed Shaker, Abu Karam, Mohammed Ezzat Abdel Wahab, Salah Amer, Dr. Ahmed Abu Zikri, Dr. Mohammed el-Nabawi, Mahmud el-Mohandess (then Minister of Hygiene) and Mohsen Idris.[26]

A group of professors and specialists, headed by Professor Mahmud Yussef el-Shawarby, founded the Association for Research and National Orientation, whose board of directors was composed of Mahmud Hassaballa, Mohammed Abdel Moneim Labib, Ismail Sirry, Professor Osman Amine, Professor Ibrahim Anis, Abdel Fattah Naguib, Mahmud Hassanein, Abdel Hay Hegazi, Ahmud Hosni Mahmud, Dia'Eddine el-Rayess, Abbas el-Itriby and Major General Naguib Afifi.[27]

In 1959 an organization that seemed to have special responsibilities was created under the name of the National Education Committee. Headed by Major Salah Ghaleb, later governor of Cairo, it had fifteen members: Murad Ghaleb, ambassador to Moscow; Dr. Ibrahim Hilmy Abdel Rahman, Undersecretary of State for the 1960 Five-Year Plan; Dr. Abdalla el-Eryan, professor of public international law at Cairo University; Kamal Rifaat; Dr. Rifaat el-Mahgub, professor of political economy at Cairo University; Samir Fahmy, an engineer; Ahmed Mukhtar Kotb, former public prosecutor in charge of press (i.e., political) affairs; Dr. Said el-Naggar; Ahmed Abdu el-Shorabassi; Mohammed Said el-Eryan; Dr. Nazmy Luca; Dr. Mustafa Kamel Helmy; Hassan el-Saati, a sociologist; Mahmud Kamel: Dr. Hassan Abdel Fattah; and Dr. Abdalla el-Arabi. Its objects were the training of youth leaders and the formulation of a national doctrine. Among the prominent members of the committee, Kamal Rifaat must be singled out: he was a Minister of State who was to emerge more and more openly as the theoretician of the ministerial team.

That group was also to establish, in April and May 1960, an association whose specific purpose was to study—on a theoretical plane—contemporary socialism. Its members included Murad Ghaleb, Salah Dessuki, Ibrahim Hilmy Abdel Rahman and Ahmed Mukhtar Kotb, and also such journalists as Ahmed Baha'Eddine and university professors, economists and businessmen.[28]

The High Council for Arts, Letters and Social Sciences, headed by the inept Colonel Yussef el-Seba'i from 1956 to 1961, when he yielded his post to the Minister of Culture and National Guidance, Sarwat Okasha, created a Center for Arab, African and Asian Political Studies under the auspices of its juridical and political committee.[29] This was a committee of experts that brought together several professors of the new School of Economic and Political Sciences established in 1961 at Cairo University, where the teaching was in the hands of a galaxy of young professors, notably Dean Mohammed Zaki Shafei, Butros Butros-Ghali, Abdel Malek Auda, Helmy Murad, Said el-Naggar, Wahib Messiha, Mohammed el-Badry, Sueilem el-Emary, and several others who were listed on the staff of the bimonthly magazine *al-Ahram al-Iktissadi*, skillfully edited by Professor Butros Butros-Ghali.[30]

Finally the press groups were once more reorganized, in

April 1962. Dar al-Tahrir's board of directors was now headed by Kamal el-Hennawi and included Mustafa Bahgat Badawi (managing director), Kamel el-Shennawi, Mustafa el-Mestekawy, Helmy Sallam, Nasser Eddine el-Nashashiby, Mussa Sabry, Amin Abul Enein, a representative of the office staff and another of the workers. The Akhbar el-Yom group, headed by Mustafa Amine, had Sayed Abul Naga as managing director; the board of directors included Ahmed Baha'Eddine, Hussein Fahmy, Kassem Farahat and the two employee representatives. Dar al-Hilal, headed by Ali Amine with Abdel Rauf Nafe' as managing director, had a board composed of Amina el-Said, Saleh Gawdat, Anis Malki, Fikry Abaza (general counsel to the editors) and the two employee members. The Rose el-Yussef group was headed by Ehsan Abdel Koddus (who also served as managing director), and he was assisted by Yussef el-Seba'i, (a second managing director), Abdel Ghani Abdel Fattah and the two employee representatives. Al-Ahram had been reorganized earlier, under Mohammed Hassanein Heykal, with Na'um Bahari as managing director and a board composed of Tewfik el-Hakim, Bishara Takla, Mohammed Fuad Ibrahim, Gamal el-Oteifi and the two employee members.[31]

This was the "modernist" side.

But the Islamic tendency, which, as we have shown, was active and fundamental, a constituent part of the Free Officers' ideology, was endowed with new means of action.

At its center was the thousand-year-old Al Azhar University. On June 22, 1961, the Council of the Nation approved a law for the reorganization of the famous institution. It embodied the essence of the reform proposals developed by Sheik Mohammed Abdu at the start of the century; Al Azhar was to become a genuine Islamic university, in which those who completed the undergraduate and graduate courses available there would have access to four new faculties: Islamic Law, Foundations of Religion, Arab Studies, and General Relations and Administration, under the authority of the rector, Dr. Mohammed el-Bahey.[32] Thus religious authority was separated from pedagogical functions and entrusted to the Sheik of Al Azhar, Mahmud Shaltut. The whole was headed by two ministers, Kamal Eddine Hussein and Kamal Rifaat; Dr. Bahey became a titular minister in September 1962.

A second key post was the Ministry of *Wakfs* (religious holdings). It was entrusted to the former secretary-general of the Liberation Rally, Major Ahmed Abdalla Toeima, on August 16, 1961. But on October 19 the High Council for Islamic Affairs became the body charged with the theoretical and practical, though not the administrative, tasks of the ministry; seven specialized committees were headed by Sheik Mohammed Abu Zahra, Dr. Hussein Aref, Commissioner Ali Ali Mansur, Abdel Halim el-Ghindi, Abdel Aziz el-Aliy el-Motawwah, Professor Osman Khalil and El-Sayed Ali el-Sayed.[33] Professor Abdalla el-Arabi ran the Institute of Islamic Studies, which trained experts in African and Asian problems.[34] A Council of Moral Orientation was created by a merger of the Wakf and Al Azhar ministries.[35] There was also the question of an Islamic Front Against Atheism and Corruption in the High Council for Islamic Affairs,[36] as well as the problem of a Supreme Council for Islamic Affairs in the Ministry of Wakfs.[37] The project for the Institute of Islamic Studies seemed more serious: it was proposed as an Egyptian center for study and research in matters of Islam, endowed with rich resources and a staff of qualified professors, and charged with taking the initiative in the area of Islamology and Orientalism;[38] it seemed to be following in the path of the Central Institute of Islamic Research set up in 1955 under the direction of Professor Yehia el-Khashab.

Much earlier, in September 1954, Colonel Anwar el-Sadate had taken over the direction of the Islamic Congress, of which he had previously been secretary-general. Among the objectives of the Congress, which clearly intended to fill the vacuum created by the destruction of the Moslem Brotherhood organization which was then under way, and to serve as a bridge between Cairo and the whole Islamic world of Asia, Africa and the other continents, these must be pointed out: "(1) To spread Islamic culture without any restriction and to prepare the Moslem peoples, which adhere strictly to the teachings of Islam and its moral principles, to raise the level of their education and their social systems; (2) to bring into harmony the economic policies of the Moslem states in order to enable them to work together in the exploitation of the Moslem countries' economic resources; (3) to co-operate in providing every Moslem nation with the best administrative and financial system . . ." It was understood that "the [Islamic] Congress and the Arab League will collaborate in the achievement of these ends." Each of the three committees—cultural, economic, and administrative and financial—would be made up of "Moslem experts."[39] The Congress engaged in intense efforts of exploration and communication with Islamic peoples, notably in Black Africa. Kamal Eddine Hussein, already president of the executive (Prime Minister) of what at that time was "the Egyptian region," and chiefly responsible for the National Union, became president of the Congress in place of Sadate on January 26, 1961. He was assisted in this position by Major Ibrahim el-Ta'haui as secretary-general and Mohammed Said el-Eryan as assistant secretary-general.[40]

The two arms of the ideological apparatus were now in position.

CHAPTER 6

THE STAGES
OF NEUTRALISM

FATHI RADUAN and Ehsan Abdel Koddus were
inventing nothing when they uderscored the lack of a general
policy and an ideology on the part of the military leadership
until 1954. Let us look at *The Philosophy of the Revolution*,
which bears the date of the same year: there is no mention of
positive neutralism or even of neutrality; there is no definition
of principle with respect to relations with the forces that were
in conflict for the world.[1]

Yet, beginning in 1955–56, "positive neutralism" was taking
root in Egyptian soil. Being chronologically the first of the
three major elements of which the military government's
ideology was composed, and whose background was nationalitarianism, it owed its priority to the very nature of Egyptian
needs. No Egyptian government could give first rank among its
national concerns to the quest for a political and social philosophy as long as the greatest problem, the evacuation of the
British forces, remained unresolved. The political and diplomatic effort that the government exerted in order to resolve
this question, especially after the crisis in the spring of 1954,
was to bring up the whole question of its relations with the
Western powers, both directly (on the level of what was
called the "defense" of the Middle East, and hence the plane
of direct relations between Egypt and the United States)
and indirectly (the nature of the Israeli menace before Suez).

It was only later, after Egypt had totally and entirely re-

gained her independence, that it became possible and necessary to set to work on the development of an ideology.

Let us briefly recall the political elements that influenced
this orientation toward neutralism.[2] They were of two kinds:
negative elements, arising out of Western policy with regard
to the military government, and positive elements—that is, the
ideological and political influences of foreign countries.

The West Forces Egypt's Hand

It was primarily the negative elements that compelled Nasser to abandon Egypt's traditional orientation toward Europe. In the midst of the Anglo-Egyptian negotiations
he injected this remark: "It is useless to talk of neutralism,
since the term has no meaning, especially in time of war,
unless the country [adhering to that policy] is strong enough
to protect its neutrality."[3] His Minister of Culture and National
Guidance, Salah Salem, said: "You can call our new policy
'neutrality' or anything else that suits you. Some people will
have a different idea of neutrality; what we mean is that we
adopt a hostile attitude and refuse to co-operate in any way
with anyone who takes a position against our dignity and our
freedom, while we support and collaborate with whoever
helps and supports us."[4] In short, these positions were close to
those held by the former Wafd Minister of Foreign Affairs,
Dr. Mohammed Salah Eddine, in 1950–51.

Several clues clearly show that the first large commercial
transactions with the socialist countries were intended, in the
minds of the Egyptian rulers, to force the hand of the West
and no more. The Anglo-Egyptian treaty of 1954 gave Nasser
the opportunity to deploy his forces with obvious satisfaction.
Economic co-operation with the United States under the Point
Four program was slow in expanding. On November 6, 1954,
the Washington government allocated $40 million in eco-
nomic assistance, while in Cairo a German, General
Fahrmbacher, headed the German mission charged with
creating the new army.

These were peripheral maneuvers. The West very quickly
put its new machinery of action into place: on February 24,

1955, the Iraqi-Turkish treaty was signed in Baghdad; a month later Great Britain joined the pact, which thus emerged as the instrument designed to replace the British base at Suez and to perpetuate British influence in the Middle East. On February 26, exactly six days after David Ben-Gurion took over the Israeli Ministry of Defense, the Israeli army made an attack in force on the Egyptian positions in the Gaza area; thirty-eight men were killed, and thirty-one were wounded.[5]

Nasser could no longer evade the inevitable. He reacted at first on the political level, for he succeeded, in March 1955, in establishing a three-nation Arab command (Egypt, Syria and Yemen) which flanked the Baghdad powers on the south. But it was essential to equip the army with the weapons that were required to make it an effective force in the face of the threats that had so clearly shown themselves. Now, it was just on this point that the NATO powers had strangled Egypt: Ali Sabry's mission to the United States had ended in failure after several months of talks (autumn of 1952), but the United States had sent Egypt some police equipment; the American government exerted pressure on Spain and persuaded her to cancel a $3 million arms order intended for Egypt; Great Britain, after insisting on being paid in advance, resorted to delaying tactics and set delivery dates running to several years in the future; Nasser informed Washington and London that further refusal by the West would force him to turn toward the USSR; in July 1955 Great Britain sold two destroyers to Egypt after doing the same for Israel; in 1953–54 France supplied small quantities of arms; on June 30 the United States had announced that it would sell Egypt $27 million's worth of arms, but the talks dragged on until September 27.[6]

Why this attempt to back out? "Abdel Nasser wanted military assistance devoid of conditions, while we had our own terms," Ambassador Jefferson Caffery testified before congressional committees. Admiral Arthur W. Radford, chairman of the Joint Chiefs of Staff, added: "What the Egyptians wanted to buy, if I remember correctly, was the kind of weapons that we did not want to see them get . . ."[7]

On September 2, 1955, Nasser announced the conclusion

of an arms agreement with Czechoslovakia; this time, according to the experts, the accord was for material of the first quality (heavy artillery, the latest-model tanks, etc.) to a value of $80 million, to be paid for in cotton.

There was the same policy in the domain of economic development. Secretary of State John Foster Dulles wanted to sell participation in the financing of the Aswan High Dam project at the price of Egyptian allegiance to the West; having failed, he brutally refused to help Egypt and thus, as we know, brought on the Suez crisis, which was to end with the nationalization not only of the Suez Canal Company but also of the British and French banks and big corporations—the basic forces of foreign penetration in Egypt.

This process of suffocation was to be matched by the search for a compensation. Where were the ideas and strength to be found?

The Influence of Asia

First of all, there were the Arab states; ideological evolution and political action within this "primary sphere" were to provide the essence of Arab nationalism. There were the socialist countries, which were not well known in Egypt and which the ruling classes distrusted; thus far the dialogue had been held only with Western Europe, and Egypt was little by little going to discover, almost over her (official) dead body, that "second Europe" unsullied by imperialism. The new Africa in gestation could provide support and allies; but it could no more be a source of strength than of ideology. There remained the basic body of the former colonial world, vast and powerful Asia, of which, except for India, Egyptian polity knew little. It was in this world that the majority of Moslems lived, the Arab world in a way furnishing Asia's central core and brain. This is where, after the Second World War, the great revolutions of national liberation had culminated in the creation of relatively strong nations which had undertaken to set out on the conquest of a better life and their deep personal identity, by various roads: Communism in the People's Republic of China; capitalism mixed with planned economies and state intervention in India and Indonesia; Burma, Vietnam and Afghanistan offered a whole range of neutralist openings.

In October 1952 the Egyptian government began to examine a Pakistani suggestion dealing with the establishment of an Afro-Asian Third World bloc.[8] A month later one of the greatest labor experts of the Ministry of Social Affairs, Abdel Moghni Said, published a book in which he called for the formation of a neutralist bloc with India and other unwarlike nations.[9] On December 23, 1952, on the invitation of the Egyptian government, the first meeting of the representatives of twelve African and Asian nations was held; resolutions pledged support of the Arab position on Palestine, on payment of reparations by Germany to Israel, and on French policy in North Africa.[10] On two occasions during 1952–53 Jawaharlal Nehru visited the Egyptian leaders in search of guidance. At the end of the second visit an Egyptian spokesman indicated that "it is possible that Egypt may ally herself with the neutralist bloc of Asian nations in order to try to put an end to the imperialist occupation of the Suez Canal Zone by Great Britain."[11] A third trip to Cairo by the Indian Prime Minister resulted in an official statement, dated February 16, 1955, and revealing "the existence of an identity of viewpoints on the great international questions" between the two countries. On April 6 a friendship treaty between India and Egypt was signed in Cairo, and the five principles of Pancha Sila enjoyed full rights in Egypt thereafter: respect for the territorial integrity and sovereignty of states, nonaggression, reciprocal nonintervention in internal affairs, equality and mutual benefit, and peaceful coexistence. From April 17 to 24, 1955, a conference of thirty countries of Asia and Africa was held in Bandung on the suggestion of the Asian members of the "Colombo group," i.e., India, Pakistan and Ceylon, thus leaving other members outside (Australia, New Zealand and Great Britain). President Nasser, who headed the Egyptian delegation, appraised the forces that he observed in action; elected chairman of the committee charged with selecting and formulating the resolutions of the conference, he was impressed with the consummate skill of the Chinese diplomats, who deliberately restricted themselves to a subordinate position; he was angered by the servility of the small group of pro-Western countries (the Philippines, Pakistan and Thailand, among others); and he relied on the centralist majority group. On his homeward journey he stopped in Karachi, New Delhi and Kabul. "My visit to India," he was to say later, "was the turning point in my political understanding. I learned and recognized that the only wise policy for us consisted in adopting positive neutralism and nonalignment. On my return home, the reception that greeted this policy convinced me that it was the sole possible policy that could attract the broadest support of the Arab people."[12] The five principles adopted by Nehru and Chou En-lai in April 1954 began to be known in Egypt, where they won the virtually unanimous acceptance by the general public.

This "Asian" contribution was to receive from "the other Europe" a transfusion that assumed a Yugoslav color. Several Yugoslav missions followed one another to Cairo, particularly the military mission in September and October 1954. But it was not until September 5, 1955, that Marshal Josip Broz Tito and President Nasser first met, on board the *Galeb* in the roadstead of Suez. The Yugoslav chief of state made his first official visit to Cairo from December 28, 1955, to January 6, 1956; friendship was established on the basis of the principles of Bandung, and the two leaders declared their identity of views on the major international problems, as well as their determination to pursue a positive, active and constructive policy, the only means of bringing about a reconciliation between the two blocs. Egyptian-Yugoslav understanding was affirmed during the Brioni meeting (July 1956); it made it possible to define the new orientation of official policy, which, guided by "the principles of love of peace and active coexistence and nonalignment with blocs," should permit "the easing of tension in the world, thanks to the general and growing efforts to broaden international co-operation and strengthen confidence among peoples through the ever more successful application of the method of negotiation to the resolution of problems in dispute." The two countries inaugurated an increasingly close co-operation in all areas that is still growing today. Joined by Nehru, the Egyptian and Yugoslav leaders formulated the major theses of positive neutralism: "The present division of the world into powerful blocs tends to keep fears alive. Efforts must be made to achieve peace not through division but through collective security on a world-wide basis, through the broadening of the domain of freedom and through the disappearance of domination of one country by another. It is essential to enter on the road to disarmament in order to reduce the fears of a conflict . . . The furtherance of efforts to accelerate the growth of the underdeveloped countries constitutes one of the chief tasks in the establishment of a permanent and stable peace among nations . . ."[13]

From 1955 to 1958, positive neutralism carried its banner through the Arab world under Egyptian impetus. From the Western side the imperialist attitude was stated without equivocation in the famous "Fechteler report," actually based on a well-known article, "The Sea of Decision," published in 1951 by Commander Talerico in *U.S. Naval Institute Proceedings*: "In the light of a constantly threatening international situation, a stable confederation of the Arab states would exert great weight in all decisions bearing on the choice of the theater of operations for an offensive action against a Eurasian aggressor . . . The strength of the United States will be based on its clear predominance in Mediterranean affairs by means of its military and economic assistance and through political mediation . . . By way of the Mediterranean, and with the help of the Arab peoples and of advance bases in the Arab states, the Eurasian aggressor and his ideologies will be vanquished in a decisive manner . . ."[14] The deterioration of the situation in the Arab countries, and especially in Egypt, was confirmed by the defeat of the offensive against Egypt in 1956 and by the accentuation of the active aspect of her positive neutralism. Some people wished to see in this no more than the theoretical manifestation of bargaining between the two blocs. Others, however, notably John Marlowe, clearly recognized the social basis of this ideology: "The great majority of cultivated Arabs was emotionally neutral in the cold war between East and West. For one thing, the whole nationalist tradition of the previous twenty-five years was unremittingly opposed to the idea of a new alliance with the West . . . For another, this same neutralist tradition allowed itself no illusions on the status of a Soviet satellite and it had no wish to exchange one imperialist master for another . . . Pro-Russian sentiments in the Middle East were hardly limited to the politicians of the Left."[15]

Nasser devoted himself to giving shape and expression to these almost unanimous forces. The tone of the earlier statements, before Bandung, had clearly been conciliatory, insisting on the peaceful and spiritual aspect of neutralism. The offensive of the West precipitated the turn toward the bloc of socialist countries, in which Egypt would find all the tools that were needed to vanquish underdevelopment and attain to modernity and power: unmatched terms for loans to finance the projects of the 1958 Five-Year Plan; financing and complete supervision of the High Dam; supplies of arms and military equipment of the latest type and in abundant quantities, as well as construction of Egyptian arms factories; outlets for the cotton crop; the training of technicians and specialists; support in the international area, notably in a broad fashion in the UN, in the Israeli affair and in the Algerian conflict.

The Three Sectors of Egyptian Neutralism

In reality, Egyptian neutralism in the years 1955–58 had three sectors: a right—the industrial and financial upper bourgeoisie, traditionally anti-Communist but aware that it was compelled to defend itself against the West and resolved to make a profit through bargaining tactics; a left, which got its doctrine from the *al-Missa* group and made the anti-imperialist struggle the crux of the battle for peace and coexistence, seen from the point of view of countries that had been or were still colonies;[16] in the center, the military apparatus sought to balance these centrifugal tendencies. In this first period, as at Bandung, President Nasser felt constrained to opt for a coalition between the center and the left. Anti-imperialist activity was growing on the African continent: Islamic propaganda was being intensified by means of Anwar el-Sadate's Islamic Congress; several thousand African students were being educated in Egyptian schools and universities; teaching missions were sent out,[17] and in the summer of 1957 special radio programs called the *Voice of Free Africa* were devised, which were broadcast in seven languages in 1960– 1961;[18] Cairo was made the seat of the offices of popular anti-imperialist movements (notably under Salah Ben Yussef from Tunisia and Félix Moumié from Cameroon, both assassinated in 1961, but also Somali, Kenyan, Congolese and later Angolan and other movements). The press made no secret of the fact that Egypt, the major African power, was discovering her own continent.

An unsigned pamphlet published by the Information Service made a retrospective catalogue of the basic characteristics of positive neutralism:

"(1) First of all, and to the finish, to safeguard national independence against imperialist aggression in an international situation in which national government and a refusal to barter away independence have been brought within the realm of the possible. In other words, this is a practical battle against imperialism in order to eliminate it from all parts of the world, to free national economies from any foreign influence, rejecting foreign alliances, denouncing imperialism at home and abroad, and supporting national movements in countries which have not won independence or in which independence is threatened.

"(2) . . . Solidarity . . . It is inevitable that the states professing positive neutralism should seek allies in order to bring about the collapse of imperialist plans for aggression from without and conspiracies within, to establish economic blockades and to gain assistance in the industrialization of their countries and in their economic development in order to consolidate their national independence. These allies are represented by the other countries in Asia and Africa that profess positive neutralism and are ready to assist one another in confronting imperialism and its crimes. But they are represented also by the socialist countries as the parties most interested in the preservation of peace, an essential condition for the consolidation and development of their economies. This fusion of the common interests of the socialist countries and of the nationalist countries in Asia and Africa creates the possibilities for economic assistance to be furnished by the former to the latter without political conditions . . .

"(3) . . . an independent attitude on international problems . . . , not necessarily a third position, which in no way means passivity . . . ; our attitude is dictated by the national interests of our country and by the interests of peace.

"(4) Once the positive idea has been accepted, it becomes obvious that for us there can be no question of neutrality in the struggle under way between imperialism and the peoples striving to preserve their independence, in the world struggle for world peace . . .

"(5) Positive neutralism does not confuse friend with foe, nor does it put them on equal footing in its evaluation of them and dealings with them . . ."

Why Nonalignment?

The year 1958 was the year of transition from positive neutralism to nonalignment. Why 1958?

There were two series of events.

First of all there was the Afro-Asian Peoples' Solidarity Conference (December 26, 1957–January 1, 1958), which had been recommended by the Asian leftist parties, particularly the Indian Communist party, accepted by President Nasser after protracted hesitation in order to prove that "Dulles cannot isolate Egypt," and regarded by the military rulers as a means of creating in Cairo, through its permanent general secretariat, an agency that would enable them to broaden their influence in nationalist political movements on the African continent. This time, impressive delegations arrived from forty-six African and Asian countries (with the notable exceptions of Iran, the Philippines, Pakistan, Turkey, Saudi Arabia and Liberia), who placed their emphasis on the struggle against underdevelopment and against all forms of neoimperialism on the political, economic and cultural planes. In spite of the censorship and the very composition of the Egyptian delegation, the Left succeeded in setting the tone, powerfully assisted by the revolutionary groups within the various delegations. The government was frightened, and said as much through Anwar el-Sadate; he managed to get Colonel Yussef el-Seba'i elected to the key post of permanent secretary-general and to put Mursy Saad Eddine, a trained anti-Communist, at the head of the secretariat's machinery. The goal was the neutralization of growing Communist influence, especially by the People's Republic of China, and the prevention of any eruption of the nationalist and Marxist Left in certain African countries.

This first front, on which positive neutralism began to seem too explosive for its initiators, was extended by a second set of factors, which we have already described as the determinants in the offensive against the Left from January to March 1959: the unification of the Communist movement, the differences with the Syrian Communist party on the formula for Arab unity, and the swing to the left by the Iraqi revolution.

A third event arose to add its influence, in unexpected fashion, to the government's political thinking. This was the visit of the President of the UAR to the Soviet Union from April 29 to May 16, 1958. Throughout his stay there, President Nasser stated in very clear terms his doctrinal and political independence, and also his desire to receive aid without conditions; he acknowledged that "there has never been interference of any kind whatsoever," and that the Soviet Union, "apart from the fact that it stood by us in time of aggression, has always made available to us all possible aid to help us to break the blockade that had been imposed on us by imperialism, and also to industrialize our country"; every address that he made echoed Egyptian gratitude to the Soviet Union and reiterated that Egyptian policy was based on the principles of Bandung.[19] But the display of Soviet military power, especially at the Leningrad naval base, was not designed to reassure Nasser. The President confided his apprehensions to his intimates; it was advisable to keep one's distance and not drop one's guard with this ally, who was inordinately powerful and who, furthermore, did not haggle over massive aid on all levels. For if she did otherwise, she would only prove Tito's contentions and stand revealed to the Africans and Asians as an imperialist power.

Distance was kept as soon as Nasser was back in Cairo. "Before I made this journey," he told the throng that had come to greet him, "I had been informed that the United States had adopted a new policy with regard to the UAR, that hereafter it would respect our neutrality and our independence . . . In your name I replied that we wanted friendship, and I expressed the hope that these intentions were genuine."[20] At the beginning of the summer the press censors were instructed to prohibit any direct attack on Secretary Dulles and American policy as a whole. But in the opinion of the Egyptian leaders, the civil war in Lebanon supplied proof that "American policy is still geared toward inflicting a devastating blow at Arab nationalism."[21] In spite of everything the readjustment was carried further, and the anti-Communist speech of December 23 at Port Said, the prelude to the offensive against the Left, was to inaugurate the second stage in the field of neutralism, that of "nonalignment."

Several essayists assumed the task of theoretical formulation—journalists, professors, politicians, among whom one must single out the name of Professor Butros Butros-Ghali.

"Positive neutralism," he wrote, "rests on two policies, one negative and the other positive. The negative aspect springs directly from juridical neutralism; it is that of nonparticipation in the cold war now in progress between the Soviet bloc and the Western bloc; this presupposes, on the part of the country that elects this course, abstention from all participation in the military alliances that the two competing blocs are trying to create."

Then the course was changed abruptly toward a balance between the two blocs, which was at the very heart of the concept of nonalignment; positive neutralism operated against imperialist duress (occupations, colonial wars, nuclear bases, military treaties, etc.): "These countries should treat each of the two blocs on an equal footing in economic, cultural and social matters. This means that they should treat each of the two blocs on an equal footing in the matter of international obligations, giving neither any privileges in relation to the other, any more than rights or duties. In sum, the positive-neutralism states work toward the goal of arriving at an equilibrium . . . that will guarantee their security and prevent any aggression by either of the two blocs against that security: this is the result sought by positive neutralism."

The basis for this nondiscriminatory policy lay in the UN Charter.[22] In the event of a world war, "the nonaligned state is in a position to evaluate the situation in terms of its own personal interest." "Why have we elected to concentrate our interest and our propaganda on positive neutralism even more than on peaceful coexistence?" the author asked himself. It was because "the states adopting the doctrine of positive neutralism are not concerned with the doctrinal, economic and political conflict between the two opposing blocs, in contrast to those who call for peaceful coexistence . . . It is possible that these latter states have secret objectives that they intend to accomplish through and beyond this call for peaceful co-existence . . . The positive-neutralism states do not have modern [nuclear] weapons. While peaceful coexistence concentrates on regulating the relations between two [nuclear] armed camps, positive neutralism is concerned with regulating the relations between a group of [nuclear] armed states and another, unarmed group . . . While the peaceful-coexistence states call on one another to renounce the nuclear arms that each of them possesses, the positive-neutralism states strive to win the general disarmament of all states. The philosophy implicit in peaceful coexistence is the reciprocal fear of weapons of massive destruction, or even a return to the policy of the balance of power . . . whereas the philosophy implicit in positive neutralism is an idealism based on moral values. While the peaceful-coexistence nations represent industrialized countries, rich and highly developed, the positive-neutralism nations are advanced agricultural countries."[23]

In other words, the time had passed for the great alliance between the countries of the socialist bloc on the one hand, and on the other, the new independent states and the national-liberation movements in the colonial countries, under the cloak of positive neutralism. This central thesis of Lenin's, which was to be impressively corroborated by the Bandung period, might still, objectively, be based on fact, as it was after 1945, but, the military leaders thought, nothing must be done to justify or demonstrate it subjectively. Objectively, this would be adding grist to the Soviet mill, whereas what mattered was to get the most grain out of it.

Neutralism and Anti-Communism

The readjustment interjected a number of question marks: Did domestic anti-Communism mean the reversal of the alliances? In this area Nasser moved with extreme caution in spite of the American overtures, which became pressing. Alone at the helm, he well knew the depth of the feelings of friendship and gratitude entertained by the people of Egypt toward the socialist countries, and most especially toward the Soviet Union since Suez. He knew what the help of the socialist bloc meant in the construction of the new economy. He told a group of American journalists that whereas "the United States was putting pressure on us to follow a policy that suited it, even if it hardly suited us . . . the Soviet Union, on the other hand, was extending its total support to us."[24] How, then, was this highly elusive neutralism to be defined? "Our call for neutralism is one thing and our right to self-defense against any aggression is another. That is a sacred right. It is the West that directs its propaganda against us, as well as its political, economic and cold-war campaigns; . . . while doing this, the West recruits its agents against us in the area."[25]

In 1959, then, the United Arab Republic wanted to be non-aligned. The new course in the militant neutralism of the Bandung period was to undergo a severe test.

On May 7, in fact, Khrushchev publicly criticized the UAR's new anti-Communist turn. For three months, controversy raged on the Egyptian side while the diplomats strove to keep the relations between the two countries unchanged.[26] Between September and December 1959, relations with Peking deteri-

orated, for China found Egyptian anti-Communism irrecon-
cilable with shoulder-to-shoulder work in the Afro-Asian
general secretariat. Violent discussions in the press and on the
radio broke out between Egypt and Bulgaria at the beginning
of 1960, the more intense because Khaled Bakdash, the secretary-general of the Syrian Communist party, was living in
Sofia. In the summer of 1960 there were signs of easing. In
Damietta, where he dedicated the model textile mill built by
the USSR, President Nasser paid tribute to the great ally of
1956, "to the unselfishness that the Moscow government has
demonstrated toward us." On June 21, speaking in Bucharest,
Khrushchev set things straight: "It was thanks to the Soviet
Union that Egypt was not crushed in 1956." And the Egyptian
press gave prominent display to the Soviet Premier's analysis.
Then an Egyptian parliamentary delegation, headed by Anwar
el-Sadate, spent two weeks in the USSR (April and May 1961).
This was to be the occasion of a friendly dispute that was
brought to the attention of the Egyptian public much later.
But immediately afterward the news of the death of the
Lebanese Communist party leader, Farajallah el-Helu under
torture in Mazza Prison in Damascus, aroused the anger of the
socialist countries and indeed of world opinion. This time the
propaganda was turned directly on the Soviet Union. Kamal
Eddine Hussein spoke of "a new aggression in 1959, when they
[the Russians] tried to interfere in our affairs and defend
parties that were foreign agents."[27] Fikry Abaza, torchbearer
to the "man of destiny" slogan under Faruk, denounced sub-
mission to the Soviet Union in *al-Mussawar*: the Arabs had
paid heavily for the help received in 1956 and should now
throw off any "complex" toward their benefactors. *Al-Ahram*
referred to the Titoist experience, "which has been maturely
examined by Arab public opinion; it has understood all this
experience represents as a break out of [Soviet] domination
and enfiefment."[28] The Egyptian government was going to
concentrate on isloating, as far as possible, the representatives
of the Soviet Republics of Asia within the Afro-Asian entities
(permanent general secretariat, Economic Conference, Third
Congress of Arab Writers, etc.), on the pretext that they were
part and parcel of a fully aligned great power.

From Bandung to Belgrade

Now work was directed toward a new formula of nonaligned neutralism. Here Marshal Tito, with President Nasser, played a leading part, while Nehru held back. In point of fact, as the Egyptian leaders saw it, Bandung no longer existed. The symbol had followed the policy, too far advanced and vulnerable to exploitation by the Communists on the strategic scale: "Bandung," Heykal explained, "represented a stage, a collection of memories, of fond moments that we experienced . . ." The page was turned. And Nasser's adviser explained the evolution of neutralist ideology in three steps: "nonengagement" before 1955, when the Third World nations felt that they were too weak and too crippled to act; "positive neutralism" after Bandung and Suez, at the time when the imperialist counteroffensive compelled the new independent states to make a pact with the devil; finally, "nonalignment" in the present period of nuclear balance between the two blocs.[29] These were the themes which President Nasser repeated in his important speech of September 1, 1961, in Belgrade and which were to be found more fully developed in the resolutions of the "twenty-five" nonaligned nations at the conference.[30]

Between Bandung and Belgrade a sharp divergence had come to light within the Afro-Asian world. Rising out of Asia in the wake of the Second World War, neutralism now found its major avenue in Africa and turned toward Latin America. It was to Egypt that the Dark Continent owed this contact with Bandung. Other countries, Ghana and Guinea in particular, incited a realignment of the African anti-imperialist countries: the UAR, Ghana, Guinea, Mali, Morocco (five of the "six" at the Casablanca Conference in January 1961). Within the black world, Presidents Sékou Touré of Guinea, Kwame Nkrumah of Ghana, and Modibo Keita of Mali devoted themselves to finding a neutralist alternative for Eurafrica. The connection with Latin America was made by way of Cuba; and it was noted at the Belgrade Conference that observers were in attendance from Brazil, Bolivia and Ecuador. The Belgrade-Cairo axis polarized this restructuration of the new nations and foreshadowed their desire to make contact with a certain form of socialist reality.

Let us note, by the way, that the members of the "nonaligned" Belgrade Conference refused to invite Cuba and to adopt a motion in favor of German reunification.

Once the ordeal of 1956 was over, the military government had succeeded therefore in disengaging itself, in not allowing the alliance of the dark days to become institutionalized within the framework of a general strategy. Once the massive commitment of the socialist bloc had been assured, the military leaders meant to keep it to the tactical level, without, however, turning the Belgrade combination into that vast Afro-Asian wall of the "uncommitted" which certain "new look" American experts would have liked to have as a barrier to contain the Communist thrust to the south.

The Congo Experience

Nothing illustrates the "nonaligned" face of Egyptian neutralism better than its African policy during the years 1961–62[31]

The Congo affair was the preoccupation of the second half of 1960. From the moment when the first UN "Blue Helmets" were sent in, it became obvious that Patrice Lumumba's government, established in accord with the Belgian-Congolese constitutional agreement and recognized by the UN and a large number of nations, could rely only on the single battalion of Egyptian parachute commandos under Colonel Saad Eddine el-Shazly. General Kittany, who commanded the Moroccan detachment, and the Ethiopian brigade temporized and refused to commit themselves. Cairo very quickly recognized that the Congo had become the major stake of the cold war in Africa at that time. Certainly it was still theoretically possible to support Premier Lumumba substantially, to give him the means of unifying the Congo according to the precise terms of the agreements that had put him at the head of the first independent Congolese government; but this meant taking a risk, the risk of having to back the Soviet position against the United States, which was then determined to put

Joseph Kasavubu and Cyrille Adoula in office, temporarily isolating Moise Tshombe of Katanga. Instead of moving against the UN's occupation of the Leopoldville airport and radio transmitter, Cairo ordered its troops to disengage, denounced the imperialist conspiracy and then decided, on September 12, to withdraw the battalion. Left alone to face the mercenaries and the plots, Lumumba was arrested on December 3 and then assassinated on Tshombe's orders.[32] Tactical caution? But also a desire not to turn again to "positive" action, and thus risk not putting the two blocs on an equal footing . . .

The major effort was devoted to the unification of the continent's active forces both toward a consistent struggle against imperialism and neoimperialism and toward the refusal of any commitment with respect to the two blocs. The step that Nasser thus took should make it possible for him to speak on behalf of Africa and to find within the Dark Continent the elements of a political alliance made more and more necessary by Israeli penetration of Africa.[33]

The second All-African Peoples' Conference (in Tunis, January 1960) brought together twenty-nine countries and dedicated its efforts to building a broad platform for national-liberation movements. The Afro-Asian Economic Conference in Cairo in (April and May of 1960) recruited only thirty-three countries as active members, since this character was denied to the USSR and the eight Moslem Soviet republics; the conference marked time and brought forth vague recommendations. On the African level, the Positive Action Conference in Accra (April 1960) and especially the second Afro-Asian Peoples' Solidarity Conference in Conakry in the same month consolidated Egypt's neutralist tendency. It was during this latter meeting that Israel was condemned for the first time by the Third World on the ground that "she is carrying out an expansionist and imperialist policy and taking part in the achievement of a new imperialism through the economic infiltration of independent countries." The Afro-Asian Peoples' Solidarity Conference in Stalinabad (October 1960) paved the way for the Beirut meeting (in November) of the twenty-seven members belonging to the Afro-Asian Executive

Committee, which "adopted the decisions of the Conakry Conference on the subject of the state of Israel." The denunciation of Israel continued at the African Labor Conference in Lagos (December 1960).[34] The heads of five states, as well as one revolutionary government, the Provisional Government of the Republic of Algeria (PGRA), took part in the Casablanca Conference (January 1961). The Palestinian problem was second only to Algeria on its agenda: The participants condemned "the collusion between France and Israel in the nuclear domain," and noted with anger that Israel had always stood shoulder to shoulder with the imperialists whenever an important decision had to be made on matters vital to the conferring countries, especially Algeria, the Congo and nuclear testing. That was why the conference denounced Israel "as a tool in the service of imperialism and neocolonialism, not only in the Middle East but also in Africa and Asia."[35] These themes were repeated and elaborated on during the meeting of the Economic Conference for Africa in Addis Ababa (February 1961).[36] In March the All-African Peoples' Conference in Cairo brought together the "six" of Casablanca.

In August, Presidents Tito and Nasser issued their call for a conference embracing "all the uncommitted chiefs of state of Europe, Africa, Asia and America." This was the Belgrade Conference (August 5–31, 1961). On the first day there emerged a theoretical definition of the new neutralism, which it was possible to describe as a "nonaligned neutralism." The term was to be applicable to nations that met the following conditions:

"(1) The pursuit of an independent policy based on the principle of peaceful coexistence and the adoption of a policy of nonalignment, or one tending toward that objective;

"(2) Support in all circumstances for popular liberation movements;

"(3) Abstention from any military pact that might implicate the country in current East-West differences;

"(4) Abstention from any bilateral or mutual-defense treaty that might lead to the same result;

"(5) Refusal to permit military bases of either bloc on the national territory."

A number of additional African meetings and conferences took place during 1961: the Pan-African Trade Union Federation (Casablanca, May); the African High Command (Cairo, July); the African Cultural Committee (Tangier, August); the Political Committee of the Casablanca Group (Cairo, August).

In 1962 the movement gained new scope under the revolutionary colors of independent Algeria.

The Organization of African Unity meeting in Addis Ababa (May 1963) made it possible for the President of the UAR to form new friendships, notably among the anti-French states, by emphasizing the problem of Israel; it was Premier Ahmed Ben Bella of Algeria who took up the torch of militant anti-imperialism and established the Arab liberation movement in the heart of Africa.

Balance Sheet of the Equilibrium Policy

On the whole, the balance sheet of these years of oscillation between "positivity" and nonalignment is impressive.

With regard to the socialist countries, Egypt held third place, immediately after Indonesia and India, in the field of economic assistance. The main projects in heavy and basic industries, as well as the whole of the High Dam, were being carried out thanks in particular to the Soviet Union, Czechoslovakia, East Germany and Hungary. The socialist bloc represented one third of Egypt's foreign trade (rising from £E48 million in 1952 to £E153.3 million in 1958, and dropping to £E130 million in 1961); except in the case of China, trade was growing every year, and the balance of trade was in Egypt's favor. Long-term economic and trade agreements granted Egypt £E230 million in credit facilities. Three large loans amounted to a total of £E186 million.[37] Distant maturity dates, low rates of interest (2 or 2.5 percent for fifteen years), loans allocated to the basic projects in the 1960 Five-Year Plan, payment in cotton, training and education of Egyptian engineers and technicians under the best conditions, early delivery dates—everything combined to make the socialist countries' assistance the greatest ally of the military rulers in the accomplishment of the national objective, in spite of the repression of the Communist party and the Left. And Marshal Abdel Hakim Amer paid tribute to "the Soviet decision to supply us with arms, a decision that broke the armaments monopoly established by imperialism in order to strengthen its position in the Middle East."[38]

What was happening on the Western side? From the United States, on which, according to the *Times* of London, she was "largely dependent,"[39] Egypt had received, over the seven years 1955–61, loans and aid amounting to $500 million, consisting for the most part in farm surpluses.[40] Kayssuni's mission to the United States (April and May 1962) marked the large-scale resumption with the Western powers under the influence of the Kennedy Administration. Two agreements were reached, first of all with the IBRD and the American government, in spite of King Ibn Saud's obstructionism: Egypt received a $42 million advance from the IBRD, Westinghouse agreed to take part in the construction of a central power station for Cairo ($32 million for thirty years at 2 percent interest), and General Motors contracted to supply Diesel locomotives ($10 million). A proposal for a second agreement was initiated; it called for the United States to furnish $450 million in foodstuffs over three years, and $27.5 million for the railway system. The United States, Japan, Great Britian, West Germany and Italy negotiated a joint participation in the projects of the Five-Year Plan.[41]

In spite of German military deliveries to Israel in reparations, which were much more substantial than the volume of trade with Egypt,[42] West Germany's economic and cultural penetration of Egypt had made her the leading Western power on the banks of the Nile. The economic agreement of June 26, 1961 (£E105 million in loans) was and remains the largest from any of the NATO powers, since it was entirely devoted to economic construction: DM 500 million for the Euphrates dam in Syria, DM 150 million for the infrastructure, DM 400 million for industry.[43] Italy, under the impetus of the Fanfani-Mattei combination, came immediately after,[44] followed by Japan. The resumption with Great Britain was obvious, though less spectacular; English policy in Syria, Lebanon and notably Jordan during the spring of 1962 aroused bitter reaction in Cairo.[45] And the Evian agreements,* followed by the release of the French diplomats arrested in Cairo in 1962 on charges of "espionage," announced the renewal of Franco-Egyptian collaboration and indeed friendship, which dated back more than one and a half centuries.[46]

By analyzing the figures more closely, one gains a better idea of what was acquired in the economic area: £E500 million in loans and aid was received by Egypt up to July 1962, and only £E27 million had been used by the end of 1961. The distribution of foreign trade shows us that the socialist states were the largest customers, while the Western powers headed the list of Egypt's suppliers. Generally the trade balance was favorable to Egypt in the first category and unfavorable in the second.

Neutralism and National Personality

At the end of this short analysis it is possible to see that the essential basis of Egyptian neutralism remained the same throughout its two phases. It was a matter of setting in motion the most effective means of obtaining, from the two major forces that shared the world, a contribution to the national battle against underdevelopment. In order to arrive at this, Egypt—in an early period—undid the bonds of allegiance to the Western bloc imposed on her by imperialist domination; whence the emphasis that was placed then on "positivity," on the controversial, militant aspect—that is, directed against the masters of the past. The search for equilibrium between the two blocs became possible only during the second phase, at the time when the independent national state, solidly entrenched on its ground after Suez, could renew its ties to the West without risk, having meanwhile received

* The cease-fire agreement between France and the Provisional Government of Algeria meant the end of the Algerian conflict, and a general revival of traditionally good French-Arab relations, particularly cultural. This had a direct bearing on Egypt.

the massive aid of the socialist bloc that we have discussed. The tone was no longer one of militant action but, rather, of a kind of "equilibrism." The new Kennedy policy, moreover, lent itself admirably to this new Egyptian tactic: if it could not reconquer the ground lost militarily by the West, the United States intended to erect a kind of world-wide buffer, predominantly economic, against the temptations of Communism. In its view President Nasser was the most effective anti-Communist in the Arab world and the Middle East; he alone, among the leaders in that area, proposed a solution, both nationalitarian and social, that made it possible to minimize revolutionary measures, a solution that was backed by an extremely tough apparatus in command of technical experts in large numbers and of acceptable quality.[47]

Egyptian neutralism was conceived primarily on the scale of relations between Egypt and the West, then progressively broadened to include all of the Afro-Asian world, formalized within the African continent, then deployed on a world scale in the direction of America, under Yugoslav guidance, as an alternative to the cold war between the two great rival nuclear blocs. This neutralism, born in Asia, constituted the general structure of the military rulers' ideology, in which it was also a major component part.

Chronologically the first element, which immediately became obvious to the rest of the world, signified something other than a mere bargaining device. And Nasser had defined it thus on January 27, 1958: "Our national pride and our faith in ourselves."

The rejection of political alienation had led to the restoration of the nation's autonomous personality on the world stage.*

The extent to which, however, this convergence with the new American policy, and the increasingly confident co-operation with those Western states not tainted with "old imperialism" (the United States and West Germany in par-

---

* Cf. my attempt at exploring the philosophic implications of this policy in "Introduction à la pensée arabe contemporaine," in *Anthologie de la littérature contemporaine, II: les Essais* (Paris, 1965), pp. 9–33.

ticular), might prove capable of affecting or indeed trammeling Egyptian neutralism—that was the question arising after the spectacular reconciliation of 1961-62. The fact remained that world opinion on the one hand, and the pressure of Egyptian public opinion on the other, could not fail to counterbalance the pro-Western aims personified in the emergence of Ali Sabry as the second man in the government just ten years after the coup d'état.

CHAPTER 7

EGYPTIAN PROBLEMS OF ARAB NATIONALISM

WE COME NOW to the shifting sands of prejudice. It is interesting to observe, in fact, the extent to which the Arab countries' desire to conceive their national renascence in a structure of unification is still little known and approached with bias in the West. Shadows of the imperialist era and the Europe-centered habits of many centuries distort the inadequate information available to those who are interested. And the fury of the controversies that rage around Arab nationalism in the Near East is not calculated to encourage scientific investigation.

The Egypt that we are examining, however, the nation that is being made and that lives its life before our eyes, considers itself Arab, and not simply a part of the Arab world, and Gamal Abdel Nasser has given Arab nationalism a working reality of which theoreticians had incessantly dreamed for more than a century.[1]

For the purposes of analysis it is possible to examine the specifically Egyptian problems of Arab nationalism—theoretical conception, modes of application—as a component factor in the ideology of the military government in three phases: from 1952 to 1958; from 1958 to 1961 (corresponding to Syrian-Egyptian unification into the United Arab Republic);

and after the Syrian schism. This question was developed in an often strained dispute between the military and nationalist wing of the government and the Marxist wing of the national movement. It was a tightly knit dialectic that could not help but illuminate the origin of "co-operativist democratic socialism," the third component of the ideology under study.

Two Stages of National Existence

Often, when he later recalled the origins of Arab nationalism, Gamal Abdel Nasser mentioned the year 1953 as the point of departure. This was the year when he wrote *The Philosophy of the Revolution.** What it said is well known. But the sequence must be retraced.

"As far as I am concerned," Nasser wrote, "I remember that the premises of Arab consciousness began to infiltrate my thinking at the time when, as a high school student, I went on strike with my companions on December 2 of every year as a sign of protest against the Balfour Declaration made by Great Britain to the Jews,† under which she conferred on them a national right in Palestine after unjustly stealing it from its rightful owners." To the question "Why this protest?" Nasser had hardly any reply aside from emotionalism. It was only later, when he entered the Staff College, that he examined "the Palestine campaign and the problems of the Mediterranean in detail"; the Palestine war of 1948 seemed to him then "a duty made imperative by the necessity of self-defense." Throughout the war Captain Nasser, then a staff officer of the Sixth Infantry Battalion, cogitated on the reasons for the disintegration of the Arab armed forces: imperialist conspiracies with the dynasties in power and military weakness, but principally dissension. "When the blockade ended and the Palestine battles were over, when I returned to my country, the entire area seemed in my mind to be only

---

* In fact, this pamphlet was drafted by Mohammed Hassanein Heykal.
† The 1917 Balfour Declaration, of course, was made to the Zionists. —Translator.

a single whole . . . a single region with identical conditions, the same factors, even down to the forces that were conspiring against it. Among these forces the most obvious was imperialism." The reflections of 1948–49 led to the questions of 1953: "The time has passed when the barbed wire of borders marked the boundaries of states that they divided and isolated . . . From now on, no state can continue refusing to look about it in quest of its position and its conditions in space, in order to ascertain what it is possible for it to do and what constitutes its living space, its field of action and the positive part that it can play in this troubled world . . . Is it possible for us not to know that there exists around us an Arab circle and that this circle is part of us as we are part of it, our historical backgrounds blended, our interests bound together, in truth and in fact and not merely in words? . . . Is it possible for us to ignore the fact that a Moslem world exists to which we are bound by ties that not only are those of religion but are attested to by history?" A little later he says again that the two factors that make "the Arab circle, without any possibility of doubt, the most important of all and the closest to us" are of a historical and religious character. Though Nasser says nothing of the reading which shaped his mind in those days and which we have mentioned, he recalls Pirandello's *Six Characters in Search of an Author:* "I do not know why I always imagine that in this region where we live there exists a wandering character in quest of the hero who will bring him to life. I do not know why I imagine that this character, exhausted from his wanderings through all the vast area that stretches everywhere around us, finally collapsed, at the end of his strength, on the borders of our country, enjoining us to make a move, to fill the part and put on the costume, since no one but we could do it so well. I hasten to add that this part is not a leadership function. Rather, it is a task of interaction and experimentation with all these factors, in order to make possible the release of the colossal strength potentially stored in each of these tendencies that surround it, a mission that will succeed in making the experiment of the creation of a powerful force in this area, a force that will work to improve its condition and to play a positive part in the building of mankind's future."

What is striking in these excerpts is the fact that the author establishes himself, in a way, inside the Egyptian view of the outside world, of the Arab circle, which, historically and emotionally, is the closest to and most involved with Egypt, with which, however, it does not become fused. It is important to bear in mind this same position of the problem of Arab nationalism before the phrase was coined; it will make it possible to understand the development after the Syrian schism.

We are far from the urgency of unity, the Fichtean vocation to national fusion which had rung for a century through Syria, the center of gravity of the Arab nucleus. Gamal Eddine el-Afghani's pan-Islamic nationalism, reformism (modernist with Tahtawi or religious with Mohammed Abdu), the development of the ideology of the Egyptian national movement (depending on whether it flew the colors of Islam with Nadim, even those of Turkey with Mustafa Kamel and Mohammed Farid, or claimed the Egyptian uniqueness of Egypt under Ahmed Lutfi el-Sayed and his disciples, notably Saad Zaghlul), and the accentuation of this uniqueness between the two wars through the voice of the Wafd and the thinkers of liberal tendencies (Taha Hussein, Dr. Mohammed Hussein Heykal and Salama Mussa in particular)—all were steps that kept Egyptian national consciousness out of the next-door currents of Arabism, the problems of which, however, no Egyptian government could ignore after Zaghlul's death.[2]

That was because in the interval the Islamic nationalist tide had gained strength in Egypt, notably among the Moslem Brotherhood and the group around Rashid Rida's *al-Manar*, while the liberal wing of the bourgeoisie was waiting to reckon its chances of influence and support in the Arab world. It was then that Makram Ebeid declared: "The Egyptians are Arabs."[3] This was in 1939, a date that was a turning point. Several measures marked the first stage, which was thus approaching its end, of Arabism between the two wars: the settlement of the dispute between Iraq and Saudi Arabia and the treaty of friendship (April 17, 1931); the treaty of friendship between Iraq and Yemen (May 11, 1931); the treaty between Saudi Arabia and Yemen (May 20, 1934); the Iraqi-Saudi treaty of alliance and Arab brotherhood (April 1936), which was also signed by Yemen (April 29, 1937); the treaty between Egypt and Saudi Arabia liquidating their old quarrel (May 1936); intergovernmental talks on Palestine (1937 and 1938). A second stage formed the prelude to the Arab consolidation of 1945: the participation of Egypt, Iraq, Trans-Jordan, Saudi Arabia and Yemen in the Round Table Conference on Palestine at the invitation of the British government (London, 1939); the embryo of economic unification in the Middle East Supply Center (1941); and the creation of the Arab Union in Cairo (May 25, 1942). The pro-Axis revolt by Rashid Ali el-Kilany in Iraq was met at once by the declaration in which Eden stated that "I find it natural and fitting that the cultural and economic ties between the Arab nations, and also the political ties, should be strengthened" (May 29, 1941). In Cairo, Mustafa el-Nahas decided to take the initiative: on March 30, 1943, he told Parliament that he was going to explore the possibilities bearing on Arab unity at the governmental level; from July 1943 to February 1944, the head of the Egyptian government held bilateral talks with the six other Arab states; on October 7, 1944, the Preparatory Committee for the Pan-Arab Conference published the "protocol of Alexandria"; it appointed a subcommittee that drafted a first proposal for a treaty on March 3, 1945; on March 22 the Preparatory Committee approved the final text of the pact, revised in the direction of greater decentralization, particularly in matters of foreign policy (striking out, notably, the paragraph that began: "In no case shall it be permissible to adopt a foreign policy that might be prejudicial to that of the League or of any of its member states . . ."), and the League of Arab States was created.[4] The defeat in Palestine led to the signing of the Collective Security Pact by the Arab states (June 1950).[5]

This progressive consolidation, which thus took the form of strengthened co-ordination among states, rather than that of a process of unification, was paced by two trends in the realm of political philosophy.

In Egypt—from the Wafd of 1939–45 to *The Philosophy of the Revolution*—the Arab movement was seen as a historic and cultural necessity, as an instrument of political and economic realism, in sum, as the complement to the individual growth of Egypt. Such, at least, was the point of view of the state. "In reality," wrote Abdel Rahman Azzam Pasha, the League's first secretary-general, "we are in urgent need of all the Arab countries. As an Egyptian, I say that our future is tied to our need of the Arab countries more than to their need of Egypt. Every year we have 400,000 new births, which means that in ten years Egypt's birth rate equals the population of a country like Syria or Iraq, while we live in a narrow valley. Believe me, everything you hear about the conquest of the deserts will prove in the course of time to be a pure product of imagination. Our future life will be successful if we become an industrial people. It will be almost impossible for Egypt to exist as a military state, a state that guarantees its own military defense first of all and assures its inhabitants of subsistence, without carrying out a thorough industrial revolution. That evolution in itself obliges us to have living space. This living space consists in our brothers, who understand us and who offer us an advantage in relation to the others. On the economic level we need the Arab states, which, as has been demonstrated, possess the richest resources in the raw materials essential to our future industry and which at the same time constitute the only market open to our future life. We cannot leave Syria to do whatever she pleases on her own, for she represents our basic strategy. Syria should live in our living space . . . " Similarly Talaat Harb, the founder and president of the Misr complex, had turned toward the Arab countries and discovered the Orient as early as 1925, as his reports show; in diametrical opposition to the course set by Saad Zaghlul, he sketched the first outline of what would later be Arab nationalism: "We Egyptians will continue to fulfill our obligation in the service of common Arabism. Perhaps then we shall see the efforts of the other [Arab] countries tending toward organization for the purpose of carrying further what we do, so that out of this meeting there will grow a body of knowledge and bases for exploration that will sustain the spirit of the Orient . . ."[6]

Such was also the desire of the national movement, focused on the slogans of "evacuation" and "unity of the Nile Valley" which the Wafd had adopted. The Marxist Left, in direct conflict with the ideology and machinery of the Moslem Brotherhood in the universities and in the trade unions, busied itself with formulating Arab problems in its program and theoretical analyses; it later stressed the unity of the Arab peoples' fight against imperialism and domestic reaction, and underscored the imperative necessity of separating politics from religion.[7]

It was in terms of the objectives and needs of the Arab movement of national liberation, furthermore, that Gamal Abdel Nasser arrived at the idea of Arab unity in 1953. From 1952 to 1958 the military government strengthened the substructure of the Arab unity movement and heightened the Arab aspect of its propaganda: the Egyptian-Saudi Joint Defense Agreement (October 27, 1955), which was later joined by Yemen (April 1956); the Collective Solidarity Treaty between Egypt, Syria, Jordan and Saudi Arabia (January 19, 1957); the third and fourth Arab Cultural congresses (1957 and 1959); the first resolutions of the subcommittee of the Arab League's political committee on the subject of economic union (August 1956); the Syrian-Jordanian agreement for economic union (August 5, 1956); the evolution of the plan for Arab economic union, under Egyptian influence, after the merger of Syria and Egypt.[8]

At the other end of the ideological spectrum were the numerous Syrian parties, with the exception of the Communist party, plus certain Lebanese Arab parties, while the Iraqi parties adopted positions similar to Egypt's. In Damascus the Arab Resurgence (Baath) party, under Michel Aflak and Akram el-Hurani, drew up the theses that Nasser progressively adopted after 1956 and then, in 1958, in a decisive fashion: "The Arab fatherland is an indissoluble political and economic unit; no Arab territory could meet the very conditions of its existence if it remained isolated from the other territories. The Arab Nation, the *umma*, constitutes a spiritual and cultural unit;

all existing differences among its members are superficial and false and will entirely disappear when the Arab consciousness reawakens ... The Arab fatherland is composed of the territory inhabited by the Arab Nation, a territory that is bounded by the Taurus and Pusht-i-Kuh mountains, the Gulf of Basra (the Arabic-Persian Gulf), the Arabian Sea, the mountains of Abyssinia, the great Sahara, the Atlantic Ocean and the Mediterranean Sea. Every man is an Arab whose language is Arabic, who lives or desires to live on Arab soil, and who believes in his adherence to the Arab nation."[9]

The Constitution of the Republic of Egypt of January 16, 1956, echoed these propositions: "Egypt is an independent and sovereign Arab state. She is a democratic republic. The Egyptian people is a part of the Arab Nation" (Article 1); "Islam is the religion of the state and the Arabic language is its official language" (Article 3)—but it was clear that Egypt's existence was neither necessarily nor wholly dependent on the Arab *umma;* rather, she allied herself with it on the basis of the community of their universe of culture, religion, language and historical connections. The Egyptian people wanted to be Arab, but for all that it was not going to renounce its seventy-century-old individuality.

The Decisive Shift of 1958

How, then, is the ideological shift of 1958 to be explained? Three sets of facts make it possible to do so.

First of all, there was the demonstration of solidarity by the general public in the Arab countries toward Egypt at the time of the Suez attack: general strikes in Iraq, Pakistan, Syria, Jordan, Lebanon, the Sudan, Libya, Tunisia, Morocco, Bahrein, Qatar, Kuwait and Aden; student and worker demonstrations; the enlistment of volunteers for the defense of the Canal; effective sabotage of the pipeline on the Syrian-Iraqi border and Homs as a token of reprisal. The wave of solidarity that spread from Tangier to the Arabian Gulf brought to light a new leadership whose action proved more effective than that of the traditional politicians: the Arab labor unions, particularly in the oil industry. It was the action launched at the time of Suez from which the two powerful Arab labor federations were born: the International Federation of Arab Trade Unions (IFATU) and the Arab Federation of Oil and Chemical Industry Workers (AFOCIW). The first, established in Damascus in March 1956 by six national federations (of Egypt, Syria, Lebanon, Northern Lebanon, Jordan and Libya), took shape at the second congress (Cairo, April 27, 1959): Mohammed Assad Rageh, who belonged to the Egyptian Federation of Oil and Chemical Industry Workers—like Anwar Salama, later Minister of Labor—was named to the key post of secretary-general, while Mansur Abdel Moneim, actually the alter ego of the Libyan president, Selim Shita, became administrative controller. Three new federations were formed—Iraq's, Aden's and the Sudanese Federation of Trade Unions, whose president, El-Shafei Ahmed el-Sheik, was imprisoned with the majority of the leadership by Ibrahim Abbud's government in 1959—but there was one defection, by Jordan. The Moroccan Labor Federation let it be known that it would maintain good relations with the IFATU, while the General Union of Tunisian Workers remained aloof; the Algerian labor movement was undoubtedly obliged to await the establishment of an independent Algerian state before it could adopt a policy. The history of the creation of the AFOCIW is highly instructive: the former CIO in the United States had launched the idea of the International Federation of Petroleum Workers (IFPW), whose organizing congress was held in Paris in 1954; Anwar Salama was a member of its governing council before his election as second vice-president at the second congress (in Rome, July 1957). But when the IFPW decided to open a Middle East office in Cairo, the Arab unions immediately pulled back and founded their own federation, the AFOCIW, in Cairo on December 27, 1958.[10] There was talk of a third federation at the time of Egyptian and American differences regarding the right of passage through the Canal in 1957–58; this was the Federation of Arab Longshoremen's Unions.

The point of departure was still the national struggle against imperialism; it was centered on Egypt, against which the West concentrated its efforts. Very soon, however, and in spite of governmental directives, the labor federations were collaborating with the WFTU much more than with the International Federation of Free Trade Unions (IFFTU), especially on the Algerian problem.[11] The movement showed such strength that King Hussein of Jordan was compelled to place his British-trained Arab Legion under a unified Arab command headed by an exceptionally able Egyptian, Major General Mohammed Hafez Ismail, replacing Glubb Pasha, who once more embarked on the writing of his memoirs. Thanks to Suez, the West thus put a substantial and, what is more, efficient force at President Nasser's disposal, to act on behalf of Arab solidarity. Instead of destroying the Egyptian military government, the Suez affair confirmed it as the unchallenged leader of the Arab national movement.[12]

Two other series of events were to accelerate the process.

We have already discussed the modes and motivations of the unification of Syria and Egypt into the United Arab Republic. The moving force on the Syrian side was indeed the Arab Resurgence (Baath) party; in response to increasingly forceful pleas, President Nasser could not avoid accepting its tenets, at least in essence. For him and also for Egyptian opinion this represented a new stiffening of Arabism, which, having begun as a general background, became essential, and defined the character and the tasks of both the government and society in general.

A third series of influences was those arising out of the progressive reinforcement of the two great sectors that shared economic power and collaborated at the seat of Egyptian political power after Suez: state capitalism under the direction of the military, and the industrial and financial upper bourgeoisie, particularly the Misr complex. The difficulties that faced the short-term expansion of the domestic market without drastic measures compelled this coalition to look for foreign markets. The "nearest circle," the Arab Orient, it seemed, should offer the desired outlet.

The proclamation of the United Arab Republic on February 1, 1958, by Presidents Gamal Abdel Nasser and Shukri el-

Quwatli from the balcony of the old Abdin Palace opened the second phase in the evolution of the doctrine and practice of Arab nationalism.

After Suez, but particularly after the Syrian-Egyptian union, Arab nationalism seemed in the military leaders' view to be the surest means of effecting a junction of the three "circles"— the Arab, the African and the Islamic. It was on the basis of the example of the most powerful Arab state, which was unified to boot, that Nasser was able to shine throughout the Islamic world and to obtain a hearing in the new states of Black Africa, to say nothing of the rest of the Arab world.

To tell the truth, at the peak of his power and popularity Nasser was keenly aware that the Egyptian general public was hesitant to throw itself body and soul into this new course. It was certainly aware of Egypt's weight in the Arab circle, and it looked on its neighbors with a genuine sympathy that at the same time was accompanied by a rather formidable ignorance of individual problems and by a certain remoteness, itself a consequence of the age-old history of the Egyptian nation as a distinct unit.[13]

Wherever he looked, Nasser found very few deep roots of Arabism in the national sentiment of that Egypt which objectively, however—by reason of geography, culture and politicoeconomic weight—was indeed the center of the Arab world. Certainly it was possible to draw on the texts of Syrian, Lebanese and Palestinian theoreticians of Arab nationalism. So a young group of talented Egyptian writers—the staffs of *Rose el-Yussef* and *Sabah el-Kheir*, notably, inspired by Ehsan Abdel Koddus, Ahmed Baha'Eddine, Fathi Ghanem, Salah Abdel Sabbur, and Raga' el-Nakkash, but also the more diffuse group of *al-Gumhuriyya*, Mohammed Auda and Amid el-Imam —began a study of Arab writings hitherto little known in Egypt. Sate' el-Hossari, dean of the Institute of Higher Arab Studies in Cairo, began to reach large sectors of the intelligentsia. Others, less well known, dedicated themselves to specialized studies: this was the case for Raif Khury, Nicolas Ziyadeh, Shakib Arslan, Yussef Heykal, Nabih Fares, Abdalla el-Alayly, Abdel Rahman Shabandar, Hazem Nuseibeh, Costi Zureik; of the Beirut magazine *al-Adab*, and particularly of

Saadun Hammadi, Farid Abu Atiyya and Abdalla Abdel Daem;[14] analyses were made of the Great Powers' policies, especially Britain's, in Arab matters, and of Faisal's first Arab revolution in conjunction with the action undertaken by Colonel T. E. Lawrence during the First World War. In addition, the genesis and history of the League, the experiences of the North African Arab states, Egyptian relations with the world since Afghani and Abdu, and the attempts made by various movements in the direction of Arabism were among the problems that most concerned the young nationalist theoreticians of Cairo, while their Marxist colleagues devoted themselves primarily to the effects of positive neutralism on the transformation of Egyptian society. In 1956 the nationalist theoreticians established their connection with the Syrian Baath group; the ideas of the philosopher Michel Aflak and of Clovis Maksud made a profound impression in these circles by virtue both of their cogency and of their equipment in polemic philosophy.[15]

The basic thesis was provided by the inter-Arab cultural agreements of 1957–58:

"The creation of an aware and enlightened Arab generation having faith in God, dedicated to the Arab fatherland, conscious of its national and humanitarian mission, having faith in itself and its Nation, setting itself the highest ideals in the domain of personal and social conduct, inspired by the resolve of a joint struggle and possessed of the means for positive action, armed with knowledge and character, in order to reinforce the prestige of the glorious Arab Nation and to assure its right to freedom, security and a worthy life."[16]

Meanwhile, in the very heart of the official camp, subtle differences between Egyptian and Syrian nationalists were appearing because the Egyptians, even if they had been wildly enthusiastic (doctrinally or tactically), could not overlook seven thousand years of their own independent national history. For them it was to be a task of integrating this huge and ironic body into the Arab circle, side by side with the virulent forces of the centripetal Syrian-Palestinian nationalists and a very rich range of local distinctions of a historical character. For the militant Syrian group, on the other hand, Arab nationalism had always been the very means of survival as an autonomous national entity; the feebleness of internal cohesion, the shadow of imperialism, the multiplication of ethnic and religious minority groups had constantly undermined the foundations of any nationalitarian existence in that "Greater Syria" which Iraq regarded as a Fertile Crescent.[17]

Throughout 1958 President Nasser labored unceasingly at the negotiation of mediations between Egypt and the Arab circle; he had to convince the Egyptian general public quite aside from any mystique:

"The forces of imperialism have spared no effort in their active attempts to alienate the heart of the Arabs, to divide them artificially into countries, states, clans and parties, and to sow the seed of discord and hatred among them. These forces have likewise sought to destroy Arab nationalism at the very heart of the Arab Nation, in Palestine, and to establish Zionist nationalism in its place . . ." (March 9, 1958).

"It is said that this is an artificial movement. That is not true. No one could create such a movement within the Arab world. It is in reality a movement deeply rooted in our hearts, in every man's heart, as it is in our very lives. Every man among us is steeped in it. That is why, when the revolution occurred in Iraq, Arab nationalism triumphed in Iraq and rejoiced in it . . . Our strength arises out of the solidarity that manifests itself in Arab nationalism; that is the powerful weapon of which we were so long deprived and whose power we are now using . . ." (September 3).

"The Arab nationalism that we championed in 1952 consists, for the Arab Nation, in freeing itself from the fetters and the rack of occupation, of its humiliation by imperialism. It is crystallized in the Arab Nation's struggle to progress, to raise the standard of its society, to work in this way toward that real rebirth of which it has been deprived and which has been the privilege of so many countries for so long a time . . . By Arab nationalism we mean that we should be independent and that that independence is born of our conscience. We should no longer be in servitude to any other country or to imperialism, any more than we should be a part of any sphere of influence. That is what Arab nationalism is: Arab nationalism is union, unity, solidarity, which should be erected on the rights, the interests of the Arabs and not on those of imperialism or spheres of influence . . . That is why, from the very first day of this Revolution, we were led to declare that Arab nationalism constituted the only possible security for an Arab country. We said that the defense of the Arab Nation should arise out of its own inner being and not from pacts dominated by the Great Powers . . ." (November 13).

"The year 1957 has truly been a decisive year in respect to Arab nationalism . . . 'Arab nationalism' is not a phrase to be repeated; it is not a slogan but, rather, a great objective and an ideal. Today, when we savor our freedom, our dignity and our independence, we know that all this is equally savored by our Arab brothers in every Arab country. Today we feel that we have the right to live in that vast Nation, where there is hardly any more room for imperialism, humiliation, domination or occupation. You, my brothers of Port Said, have set the highest example in the defense of freedom and independence against the Great Powers and their fleets—and you have been victorious. We are born to be free, or to die, if need be, for the cause of freedom. We are born to be free men in this land that is ours, for what would life be without freedom or dignity? Such, my brothers, are the principles for which we have done battle—genuine independence, genuine freedom, genuine strength—all born of our consciousness of ourselves and serving our own interests. All this constitutes the context of Arab nationalism, Arab solidarity and Arab unity . . ." (December 21).

"We cannot isolate ourselves from any crisis in our area. We cannot abstain from supporting, in every way possible, the movements whose goals are the breaking of chains. But at the same time we sincerely desire that the situation be resolved and that matters return to normal so that we may be able to face the urgent problems of political consolidation, economic stability and domestic productivity. This is precisely what the Western powers constantly strive to prevent, for their permanent purpose is to divide us and destroy our area . . ." (Declaration of September 28 to R. K. Karanjia).[18]

In 1958 the organic unity of Syria and Egypt was consolidated. The same themes recurred in 1959, but the emphasis was placed on economic and social evolution parallel to the changes of the infrastructure. President Nasser made the point in his speech to the UN's General Assembly on September 27, 1960. "Our country, the United Arab Republic," he said, "is undergoing three simultaneous revolutions at the present time. One is a political revolution that expresses itself in resistance to imperialism in all its phases . . . One is a social revolution that expresses itself in resistance to feudalism and monopolies, as well as in a highly self-denying effort to increase production in order to raise the living standard and guarantee equal opportunities to our citizens in the quest for social justice . . . Finally, an Arab revolution expresses itself in resistance to the artificial division and the moral and material barriers erected by those who seek to govern our country through the Machiavellian method of 'divide and rule.' We proclaim our faith in a single Arab Nation. The Arab Nation has always had unity of language, which is that of thought. The Arab Nation has always known historic unity, which means unity of consciousness. There is hardly any national basis more coherent and more stable than these. Hence it is no mere random chance that all the Arab states which have won their independence have stipulated, in the constitutions framed after their independence, that their peoples constituted part of the Arab Nation. Similarly, it is not out of mere emotion that the Arab peoples sincerely believe that any aggression against any one of them constitutes an aggression against all of them . . . At the same time we declare to you also that conscious evolution, based on the call for peace and the example set by concrete creative effort, constitutes our road toward that unity which we have have chosen . . ."[19]

While Arabism was taken for granted in the northern region of the UAR (Syria), it is revealing to observe the efforts exerted by the government to rally Egyptian minds to the credo of Arab nationalism. In the last analysis it was a matter of convincing the Egyptian public opinion of the basic, indeed ancestral Arab character of Egypt. Previously, in 1956, Ahmed Baha'Eddine had discovered, in the work of the Egyptologist Moharram Kamal, then curator of the Egyptian Museum in

Cairo, on *The Influences of the Civilization of the Pharaohs on Today's Egypt,* a disturbing volume that threatened to provide a scientific platform for those who opposed the dissolution of the Egyptian personality in the bosom of Arabism.[20] The name itself, "Egypt," vanished from the postage stamps on February 23, 1960. The High Council for the Universities decided to introduce a new compulsory course, "Arab Society," into all branches, effective February 27;[21] the Ministry of Culture launched a project for a very interesting program to republish or make better known the major works of Arab literature and thought over the centuries; Mustafa el-Seherti, author of the first Egyptian book on the new Arab ideology,[22] was named its director (1961). Professors multiplied their activities: group treatises, manifestos and research works flowered on "Arab nationalism" and "Arab society," some of which were not lacking in interest, particularly in the historical, religious and literary fields.[23] While the political and cultural bodies undertook to rehabilitate the great names of the national movement—Omar Makram at grips with Bonaparte and Mohammed Ali, Tahtawi, Colonel Arabi and his comrades, Mohammed Abdu, Nadim, Mustafa Kamel and Mohammed Farid in particular—the new programs in the elementary and secondary schools, through the inspiration of Mohammed Said el-Eryan and his experts, performed a similar task for pre-Islamic Egypt, completely ignoring six centuries of Coptic history* and dealing allusively with the Egypt of the Pharaohs.[24] In the same way the 1919–52 period, which marked the predominance of the liberal and humanistic tendency with the Wafd, was virtually erased from existence.[25] The Congress of Arab Emigrants Abroad, particularly concerning those in Latin America, which was held in Cairo in July 1960, was the prelude to the creation of a special Arab citizenship designed for them.[26]

The stream of Egyptian Arab nationalism very quickly joined

---

* Known in the West as "the Roman period." Founded on the teachings of St. Mark, Coptic Christianism ("Copt" is a word derivated from the Greek *Aigýptios*, i.e., Egyptian) was headed by the Patriarch (now Pope) of Alexandria, who extended his jurisdiction to the sources of the Nile and Ethiopia. The Coptic Church was intensely national throughout history. It refused successively both Rome's and Byzantium's sovereignty, and opened Egypt for the Arab army of Amr ibn-al-As in 641. There are now between 4 and 5 million Copts out of 30 million Egyptians.

the Islamic current. In actuality the nationalitarianly inclined historical-political efforts aroused little response among the intelligentsia,[27] while the mass of the people was still preoccupied with its permanent problems, which were only just beginning to be attacked. In contrast, the cultural factor, and more especially the religious, was still lively in Egypt and, consequently, capable of providing a theoretical and emotional foundation for Arab nationalism. Besides, as we have said, the Islamic or even pan-Islamic trend was solidly institutionalized in the country in spite of the elimination of the Moslem Brotherhood.

"If we say that the Arabs are the best nation offered to mankind," explained Sheik Hassan el-Bakuri, a former MB leader and then Minister of *Wakfs*, "it is because that is a truth revealed by the Koran and a reality expressed in its verses . . ."[28] In 1958–59 the Moslem Brotherhood discreetly came back into being. Its apparatus dismantled, its staffs and leaders assassinated or tortured, the remainder of its members, acting individually, joined the National Union. But a number of theoreticians came together in the publishing firm of Dar al-Uruba, which issued the works of Sayed Kotb and Mohammed el-Ghazali, and even Abdel Kader Auda's *Islamic Criminal Law*—the author, one of the strongest figures in the MB, had been hanged in 1954. There was a wealth of output, notably in the fields of philosophy, history, theology, politics and literature, celebrating the themes of Islamic renewal, interpreted in the militant sense of an Afghani, not to say a Hassan el-Banna: Mohammed el-Bahey and Ahmed Hassan el-Zayat at Al Azhar University; Ismail Adham, Mustafa el-Sebai (an MB deputy from Damascus), Mohammed Yussef Mussa and the Algerian philosopher Malek Bennabi in the fields of philosophy and law; numerous theses, a downpour of brochures, and many books were inspired by the ideology of modernist political Islam; Abbas el-Akkad divided his time between the branch of the American Franklin Publications and Islamic circles. A close check of the announcements published every morning in the newspapers gives an approximate estimate of more than a third of the total Egyptian book publishing of recent years for Islamic works.

Several valuable works, however, must be pointed out for their function in promoting a renascence of Arab culture—literary, mathematical and scientific—and of living religious tradition, beginning with the Mu'tazilites.* We have cited the preponderant part played by the various agencies of the Ministry of Culture. A substantial contribution was made by Abdel Rahman Badawi, the philosopher. And every publishing house now devoted a considerable part of its activities to the furtherance of this renascence.

Nevertheless, the basic trend did not fail to stimulate a disquieting resurgence of discrimination against the Copts, especially with regard to appointments to public offices and even entry into private companies. Public schools, once almost secularized under the Wafd, acquired a profoundly religious aspect. The infection was widespread, and in 1958 the appearance of *Watani*, an independent weekly edited by the great names of the Coptic middle class and the intelligentsia, proved to be hardly the remedy for which many had hoped.

On several occasions the government made known its determination not be trapped into an Islamic fanaticism whose sinister rise the Wafd had been able to stem during the period between the two world wars. This was the gist of the Lahore speech: "Our unification protects Islam through action, through science, through liberation, through co-operation far removed from obscurantism and fanaticism."[29] The journalist Fathi Ghanem attacked imperialist propaganda which contended that "the most important factor in Arab solidarity is religion" in order, he said, "to isolate Christian Arabs and non-Moslem Arab communities in a general way from the rest of the Moslem Arabs [and] to distract the Arabs from envisaging the elevation of their living standard through socialism, the enemy of feudalism and of monopoly capitalism . . . We cannot emphasize the religious aspects of Arab solidarity and neglect its economic and social aspects." The poet Salah Abdel Sabbur underscored this way of looking at things: "All the previous Arab revolutions were only concerned with the national aspect and nothing more—independence, unity, ouster

---

* The first critical-rational trend in Islamic philosophy, with far-reaching effects on contemporary Arabic and Egyptian thought.

of imperialism, elimination of traitors—but they ignored the Arab economy, Arab riches, the prosperity of the Arabs. That was one of the principal reasons for their failure." We are far, very far from the Baath mystique or even the measured analyses of a Clovis Maksud: "An Arab is anyone who is bound, as his destiny, to the great Arab fatherland, either in fact or by an act of will."[30]

The forces in motion, traditional but also economic forces (as a result of the decline in employment in the face of a galloping rise in population), were such, and such too was the ideological indoctrination of the majority in the ranks of the officers with its frenetic double rejection of Western liberalism and, above all, of Marxism, that there was no choice but to fall back on the Islamic religious roots of the Arab nationalism of which Gamal Abdel Nasser was the herald. Such, in a way, was the Egyptian coloration of Arab nationalism: Cairo, the seat of the central government of the UAR, was also the seat of Al Azhar University, the Islamic Congress and the League of Arab States.

The Marxist Conception of Arab Unity

From 1956 to 1958, at the height of the Bandung period, Nasser was not alone in making himself heard. In the fields of theory, propaganda and action, Egyptian Marxism was asserting itself; the general curve of Egyptian evolution led it to perfect a synthesis between the traditional Marxist interpretation that it had embraced since 1939–45 and the new ideas of Arab nationalism.

The operation took place in two stages, though the lag was more pronounced than within the military group.

From 1952 to 1956, Marxist thinking on Arab subjects had a small voice, repressed as it was under the yoke of illegality and also because of the extreme complexity of the internal political situation. Three important books cast some light on this subject. A collection of critical essays, at once esthetic, literary and cultural, by Mahmud Amin el-Alem and Dr. Abdel Azim Anis, *Fi'l-thakafa al-Misriyya* (*On Egyptian Culture*, Beirut, 1955), stated the major theses in the field of the theory of Egyptian culture, in close alliance with the tasks of the national and progressive movement. The Lebanese author of the Preface, Hussein Muruwwa, made no secret of his disappointment at the specifically Egyptian character of the book; he himself and many readers would have preferred it to be "Arab." Ibrahim Amer's *Thawrat Misr al-kawmiyya* (*Egyptian National Revolution*, Cairo, 1957) was silent on the Arab world. Shohdi Attia el-Shafei, in his often quoted work on *The Evolution of the Egyptian National Movement 1882–1956,* gave two pages to the "Arab front": "The policy of the Arab front," he said, "is an inseparable part of Egyptian policy today, which is a policy of peace and national independence." After mentioning the historic links between Egypt and the Arabs since the earliest times, he emphasized that "there has been no movement of popular struggle in Egypt that has not had its repercussions in the Sudan, in Syria, in Palestine, in Lebanon, in Iraq"; he cited the Arab League and the Palestine war, and he paid tribute to the decisive part played by Nasser.[31] All the documents of this period insist on the anti-imperialist content of Arab solidarity on the foreign level and its democratic and progressive content on the internal level; the distinction is always drawn between two types of solidarity of struggle, for, side by side with what was envisaged and applied by the Marxist Left, there was another whose heroes in that day were Nuri el-Said, the Hashemite family and the reactionary Arab groups in power who were concerned with crushing the Left under the cloak of "unity."

The theoretical development was carried out on two levels: that of the progressives, the legal Egyptian Marxists, in *al-Missa* and the books of 1956–58 on the one hand, and then on the formal level of the Egyptian Communist party, particularly after the 1958 unification.

The principal theoretician of Arab nationalism on the staff of *al-Missa* was the head of the foreign affairs department, Abdel Azim Anis—a learned mathematician, once a lecturer at the Imperial College of Science (London) and then in the science faculty in Alexandria, and a former director of Dar Al-Abhath al-Ilmiyya in Alexandria. In 1957–58 he contributed a number of studies in which the anti-imperialist content of this doctrine was presented as the Arab face of Marxism in the field of foreign policy. A group of collaborators developed this point of view around him.[32] Others were to place the emphasis rather on the popular aspect of Arab nationalism, whose concepts on the effacement of Egyptian individuality they were tacitly to reject.

The Dar al-Fikr publishing firm instituted a series on the "problems of Arab nationalism" in 1957. And the cultural magazine *al-Ghad,* which appeared sporadically from 1956 to 1958, published by the same group under Hassan Fuad, followed the direction of the official interpretation.[33]

The confrontation between the official ideologists of Arab nationalism and its Marxist interpreters took place at the third and fourth congresses of Arab Writers. The First Congress (in Damascus, September 9 to 11, 1954) did not even raise the problem of Arab nationalism.[34] The Second Congress (in Bludan, Syria, September 20 to 27, 1956) issued an appeal to the world's writers for their support against the imperialist threat; among its resolutions, the first "reaffirmed the national task of the Arab writer in the stimulation of the Arab spirit, the protection of the Arab heritage, the creation of a conscious society that would achieve an authentic existence for the Arab and make him capable of every sacrifice with a view to assuring the unity of his nation, his freedom, his pride and his dignity."[35] In sum, these were the quasi-Marxist theses of Arab cultural unity that had unanimous support up to that time.

The situation was to change visibly during the Third Congress (in Cairo, December 9 to 16, 1957), which was held when Arab nationalism was soaring. The general theme of the congress, moreover, was "literature and Arab nationalism." All the delegations had a strong governmental tinge, especially the Egyptian, where for the first time Mohammed Said el-Eryan appeared, while Mahmud Amin el-Alem was excluded. Shunted off from official relations, the Marxist writers increased their activities and acquired an enthusiastic public. The resolutions —notably the first five of six parts—restated the theses that were the prelude to the Syrian-Egyptian unification, announced a few weeks later, particularly: "Arab nationalism is a verity born out of the depths of Arab being, out of the thinking of every Arab and his emotions, wherever he lives; it expresses the personality of the Arab nation in its hopes, its needs, its interests, the bonds that exist among all sons of Arabism in the domains of history, of territory, of cultural heritage, of a single language and of a common destiny; it also expresses the determination to struggle for the freedom of the Arab Nation and its unity, so that it can furnish an effective contribution to the construction of a world set free of the evil deeds of imperialism, of the crimes of aggression, of the temptations of domination, as well as to the protection of human civilization and to its development."[36]

The rupture occurred during the Fourth Congress (in Kuwait, January 1959): the UAR delegation, once the leftwing intellectuals had been mowed down by the repression that was launched at the same time, waged a real offensive against the Iraqi delegation, headed by the great poet Mahdi el-Gawahri; the reason was that the Iraqis, who represented a national front of Communists, democrats, liberals, etc., which truly reflected the image of Iraq during the first phase following the overthrow of Nuri el-Said,* had no intention of ratifying the proposals of what they regarded as an annexationist Arab nationalism.[37] After that, the Arab writers held no more congresses.

As for the Egyptian Communist party's position, most fortunately there is in existence a collection of documents of the 1957-58 period—the time of unification—that make it possible to complete the picture from the official party side.

First of all there was the interview given by the Co-ordinating Committee of the three Communist organizations to the correspondent of *L'Unità* on May 14, 1957. The Italian text mentions the "broad outlines of the future party's program" in five points, the second of which provides for "the creation of a federal union among the Arab countries that have succeeded in freeing themselves from imperialist domination"; the French text, however, which was published somewhat later,

---

* Leading pro-British strong man of Iraq under the old regime. Several times Premier. Executed after the July 14, 1958, revolution in Baghdad.

gives this version: ". . . reinforcement of the unity of Arab countries emancipated from imperialist domination."[38]

Immediately after the unification, the Egyptian Communist party published a pamphlet entitled *Mafhum al-kawmiyya al-arabiyya (The Concept of Arab Nationalism)* and signed "Abbas" and "Khaled," both secretaries of the Central Committee. Did a single Arab Nation exist? The two authors examined Arab reality on the basis of the classic Stalinist definition of the Nation: "(1) Arab nationalism is the fruit of the common history of a group of people who have lived together, intermingled, struggled together for hundreds of years . . . (2) Arab nationalism possesses unity of language, the bearer of its heritage and of the quintessence of its historic experience . . . (3) Arab nationalism shares in a single portion of territory, whatever the differences and the diversity of its geographical characteristics . . . (4) Arab nationalism does not share in a unity of economic life . . . But it is clear that this observation is closely linked to the fact that various imperialist countries continue to dominate the potentialities, the resources and the riches of many parts of the Arab fatherland, which thus are bound to the imperialist economy itself. In one form or another the Arab common market existed in the past, before the Western occupation. Imperialism consciously labored to destroy that market and to annihilate the complementary aspects of production in the Arab fatherland; nevertheless the bases of complementary production are still there, although they are dispersed behind artificial frontiers . . . (5) community of psychic shaping (or national character) of the Arab Nation."

On the basis of these elements, "Arab nationalism is not a tactical, political slogan any more than it is a religious fanaticism. Arab nationalism does not represent the expansion of a social class growing out toward new markets with the purpose of setting up a new empire that will serve its expansionist ends. Arab nationalism does represent a phenomenon of growth of a single nation, having all the basic characteristics of the united nation in which all the national popular classes are struggling in order to reunite its dispersed elements, to restore the complementary aspect of its mutilated economy and to make it develop, to create a common market and to regain possession

of its riches and territories stolen by imperialism, to destroy all
the reactionary and imperialist forces that block the road to its
development, to raise the living standard of its sons, to enable
its life to improve, to promote its culture and to collaborate
with all peoples, and the national and socialist states as well,
in order to put an end to all wars and assure world peace."
Whence the equivalence between what the Marxists desired
in the matter of solidarity and joint Arab struggle, and what
Arab nationalism was between Suez and the creation of the
UAR: "Arab nationalism, in its essence, is a popular movement
of combat, the enemy of imperialism. It is imperialism that has
erected the frontiers and the barriers against this nationalism,
whose unity it has thus destroyed while seeking to eradicate
its characteristics and restrict its development. That is why
the struggle for unification is essentially a struggle against
imperialism. Arab nationalism is necessarily a progressive
movement from the social point of view. While waging the
struggle against imperialism, it is also combating its agents
and allies, the feudalists and the monopolists, liberating the
riches of its own soil and the potentialities of its peoples from
exploitation and servitude, assuring the complementary character of its ravaged economy, building and developing its
national economy and furthering the growth of its national
popular culture, thus assuring its sons of a higher living
standard and endowing them with growing democratic freedoms . . ."[39]

The Communists hailed the unification of Syria and Egypt
with enthusiasm. In February 1958, shortly before the proclamation of the UAR, an Egyptian Communist party manifesto on the unification recalled the difficulties and the
reservations of various influential sectors of Egyptian opinion:
"The forces of imperialism and reaction are not satisfied to
divide the Arab Communists from the rest of the Arab patriots; they are beginning to inject anxiety into the national
bourgeoisie in Egypt and Syria. In Egypt they are spreading
the rumor that the unification will ruin the small and middle-
sized merchants and that the Egyptian merchants will be
under the thumb of their Syrian colleagues. These forces are
also propagating rumors according to which the Egyptian

bourgeoisie—which is a stronger capitalism—will pour into
Syria in order to colonize the country and suck the blood of
the Arab people in Syria; they say that it is paving the way
for the abolition of democratic freedoms and that it will increase the repression against the Syrian Communist party
in collaboration with the Syrian reactionaries." There was a
second, more serious objection that went to the heart of the
aspirations of the Left: "Does our opposition to the dissolution of parties mean that the future of democracy is dark in
the UAR? No. The problem of the future of democracy must
not be viewed from the aspect of the existence of parties as
such, but rather under the two following aspects: (1) Popular
national forces will meet in a single state, combine and fight
in an effective manner to broaden and strengthen democratic
freedoms. (2) The independent national policy in force in
the UAR is aimed at the weakening of the imperialist influence and its liquidation. This creates conditions propitious
for the growth of democracy at the same time that the progressive policy tends to liquidate feudalism, to industrialize
the country and to bring progress to agriculture . . . We
should be careful not to deviate on the subject of the problem
of unification and its strengthening, and to set the problem
of the parties in the framework of events. The principal task
consists in the defense of the union that has just been born,
in its protection, in giving it the consciousness of its paramount importance, in emphasizing the watchwords that can
make it grow in the interests of the people . . ."[40]

On February 10, in an internal document, the mass action
office of the Egyptian Communist party's Central Committee
replied to the many members accusing the leadership of a
"rightist tendency," and it recalled the passivity of a large
number of the members: "The most important problem is
to assure the success of the Syrian-Egyptian union and to
create a force for peace in the Middle East."

Instead of criticizing the dissolution of the parties, it would
be better "to take advantage of the revolutionary tide that
has risen with unification . . . to bring the largest possible
masses into action with a view to protecting the union and
assuring its success . . . Every move must be denounced that

seeks to make the Communists appear the enemies of the union, whether in Egypt or in Syria."[41] More important than anything else, the "isolation of the party from the popular masses" must be prevented.

On February 27 the Egyptian Communist party's Political Bureau issued a manifesto to the people on the subject of the unification of Syria and Egypt, hailing it in the warmest terms because it was "the expression of the will of millions of men in all our Arab countries, the fruit of their struggle, the reinforcement of their victories and of the gains they have made, as well as a point of departure toward the complete liberation and the complete unity of our Arab nationalism . . ." At the end of this very long document there was an appeal: "The Political Bureau of the Egyptian Communist party calls upon all of you to devote to the Egyptian-Syrian union all the labor and effort that it deserves. This union constitutes the essence of your struggle against imperialism, of your struggle to raise your living standard and protect world peace."[42]

A second manifesto, distributed on March 13, 1958, was even more enthusiastic: "The birthday of the United Arab Republic is at the same time a birthday for all progressive mankind and one of the fruits of its struggle. It is the birthday of the peoples struggling against imperialism and against the warmongers. A strong and independent state has been born in the Middle East, in Asia and Africa, to reinforce the peoples' struggle against imperialism, to unite the Arab Nation and to inspire it in its struggle for peace, independence and Arab unity . . . Our United Arab Republic was born to unite national and democratic forces, to organize human and economic resources in Egypt and Syria, to build a society in which the Arab working class will achieve prosperity and democracy, a society whose purpose is the creation of socialism . . ."[43]

The first issue of the party's central organ drew up the balance sheet of the objectives obtained by Egyptian-Syrian unification: "(1) It unifies the efforts of two peoples liberated from imperialism against threatening dangers. (2) It defeats the American plan to crumble the Arabs' ranks, to isolate each state in order better to achieve American ends. (3) It

creates a strong state to confront Zionist expansionism . . .
(4) The UAR will be a powerful nucleus for all the national
forces that are fighting for independence, neutralism and
Arab unity . . . (5) The struggle of the Egyptian and Syrian
governments to emancipate the national economy in each
of the two countries from foreign influence and to industrialize
it, the successes scored by Egypt and Syria in the area of the
industrialization agreements with the Soviet Union, the concentration of the two countries' potentials—all these are facts
that will speed the achievement of economic independence,
an essential precondition for the protection of political independence . . ."[44]

Pressure from the majority of the rank and file and the
party cadres very soon made itself felt within the Central
Committee, which was standing helplessly by as Syrian democracy was being destroyed. The Egyptian Communist party
was to start calling attention to certain deplorable aspects,
notably the removal of Khaled el-Azm from the Central Cabinet and the Syrian Executive Council;[45] it criticized the regulation governing labor candidacies for the National Union at
a time "when we can observe a steady decline in the living
standard of the popular classes and masses while profits are
increasing for capitalist agencies and corporations."[46] On
July 20, 1958, Khaled Bakdash attacked the strangulation
of Syria and offered the Syrian Communist party's thirteen-
point program. On September 3 the Iraqi Communist party's
Central Committee issued its call for a federal union.[47] During the summer and autumn of 1958 a number of Communists
were arrested in Egypt, and the soundings taken by Anwar el-
Sadate hardly gave rise to any hope for the enlargement of
democratic freedoms.

It was then, on September 15, that the Egyptian Communist party issued a new pamphlet under the signature of
the Political Bureau. After drawing attention to the fact that
"aggression is capable of infiltrating through a crack in the
domestic front," the Political Bureau revised its earlier position in the direction of a stronger demand concerning the
very content of the union: "Within a nationalism such as
Arab nationalism, which extends over widely distributed lands

where divergent regional, economic, political and social conditions obtain, it becomes necessary to take into consideration two fundamental truths: regional charateristics on the one hand, and economic differences on the other . . . Any unity that might be imposed without taking historical and objective facts into account could never be successful."[48]

September 1958 was the time of Sadate's ultimatum and the revision of the Central Committee's political line. A minority group, small in numbers but versed in activism, which was centered on the Dar al-Fikr publishing firm and had originated in the DMNL, called for merger within the single party, the National Union, in order to avert internal division and prevent repression; the refusal by the overwhelming majority of the party, from the general membership to the leaders, brought on a schism that had been thought impossible, after a unity won at the end of twenty years of fratricidal dissension.[49]

On January 1, 1959, the crisis erupted.

Official Concepts after the Syrian-Egyptian Crisis

The collapse of the Syrian-Egyptian union on September 28, 1961, compelled the military government to revise its conception of Arab nationalism. Theses and method alike warrant our consideration.

Already in August 1961, during an interview on North German television (Hamburg), President Nasser had discussed the problem of Arab unity with a new flexibility. "Arab unity," he said, "as it is understood by the Arab masses, covers a wide range that goes from Arab solidarity to constitutional union . . . Out of this idea, this content, the concept of Arab unity can evolve from solidarity to alliance, to union, to total constitutional unity."[50] Ten days after the military coup in Syria, Heykal undertook an initial analysis of the causes that had led to it: "I have often had occasion to sense the danger that surrounded the experiment of unification in 1958, because of the fact that, essentially, it was based on the person of the 'hero' "; he acknowledged that the only "immovable, solid basis" for unity was that it "be founded on the movement of the masses in the direction of their political, social and economic aspirations." This was tantamount to saying that the union with Syria had literally been imposed on Egypt and that it did not correspond to the objective situation.[51] On October 13 Heykal began a detailed, critical analysis which he carried on until December 1. He struck the knife into the very heart of the undertaking: the insufficiency of historical conditions for the creation of an organic union in March 1958; the vulnerability of Arab nationalism, which turned overnight from a guerrilla campaign against imperialism to a war of position, the UAR being the preferred target; the fact that "the Arab people in Egypt had not yet reached the stage of total preparation for Arab unity"; the disparity between Egypt and Syria in economic and social development; the inadequate communication of information by Damascus to Cairo; the geographical division into two separate areas connected only by the sea; the Egyptian leaders' excessive concern not to impose a strong rule on the Syrians; "a single leader, a single flag, a single national anthem; but otherwise, everything was different between the two provinces . . ." The former ally and counselor, the Baath party, seemed to be concerned exclusively with making certain of its own place, of shunting aside its rivals, going even as far as to practice passive resistance as soon as it became aware that the military rulers did not intend to make it an equal partner. Arab reaction, exemplified by King Ibn Saud and King Hussein, and General Kassem's jealousy were seen as contributing factors in precipitating the crisis, though they were not the cause of it. Finally, the despotism of Colonel Abdel Hamid Seraj and the dilatory tactics of the Communists, notably General Afif el-Bizry, Chief of the General Staff at the time of unification, were brought up.[52]

Immediately after the coup d'état in Damascus, President Nasser posed as the victim of Syrian partisans of union at any price: "To be exact, I told them on January 15, 1958, that it would be advisable to wait five years, to try first for an economic, military and cultural union and then go on later to constitutional union." He said that he had yielded to their entreaties "to save Syria." But afterward, "during these three and a half years, we encountered great difficulties, enormous obstacles, difficulties that had neither a beginning nor an end; almost three quarters of my time was given over to resolving them." Face to face with the Egyptian people watching him and listening to him, Nasser admitted that events in Syrian had aroused "a deep feeling of bitterness"; he called on the nation "not to let considerations of pride govern." "This nation must survive its wounds and its feeling of pain . . . This Republic, your Republic, should stand always as the prop of Arab freedom, to strengthen Arab growth in the direction of fulfillment and justice."[53]

Nothing could be better attuned than these words to the core of the deep national sentiment of the Egyptian people. For, carried by surprise, almost by the acceleration of national unanimity inspired by Suez, into an organic Arab union that even went as far as to proscribe the seven-thousand-year-old name of Egypt, the people now could breathe a sigh of relief. But the end of the Arab adventure also provoked rancor and bitterness toward those who had launched it— the military rulers. In order to recapture Egyptian public opinion, in which the sharpness of sarcasm barely masked the joy of seeing the military autocrats at last humiliated, a clean and decisive break was required.

This was provided by the famous speech of October 16, 1961, often referred to since. The self-criticism that is so well remembered actually came at the end of a long exposition on the new phase in Egypt, called the "social revolution." It was here that the real fight for power was waged. It was here that the shape of the future was begun. It was a retreat not unlike the retreat from Sinai in 1956 in the face of the crushing superiority of the three powers; it was a question of saving and then consolidating what was essential: Egypt, the strong point and the port of embarkation.

This new orientation of Arab policy was to become progressively tougher and clearer. The fifth anniversary of the battle of Port Said provided Nasser with the opportunity to launch a biting, "populist" attack against the Arab sovereigns.[54] Once more it was Heykal who was charged with developing the official point of view. From now on, the social change under way in Egypt would afford the pretext for rejecting any further Arab adventure. "The revolutionary phase that the Arab nation is now undergoing," he said, "was born of a real and solid revolution that makes alliance difficult among the various Arab states, particularly among contradictory interests . . . The real danger does not lie in the gulf between Nasser and Ibn Saud. The real danger lies, rather, in a reconciliation between them, for then the social revolution would be neither real nor solid. It is therefore licit for us to say and believe that what characterizes this revolutionary phase is struggle . . . The new social forces will be able to preserve themselves and attain their objectives with dignity only if they take an active part in the great battle against those who exploit and monopolize the people's wealth and take advantage of every circumstance that is favorable to themselves . . . The unity of the Arab nation is real and solid . . . that is why I say that we must not be frightened by the differences and divergences that divide certain Arab capitals. These divergences are normal within a single nation. Attempts of this kind can seriously impair our historic evolution . . . I say that we have absolutely no need of solidarity. Only division, in the present circumstances, can bring forth a radiant future that will emerge from the shadows of our divisions."[55] That was why Cairo showed such reserve about sounding out pro-Nasser circles in the Syrian army: had "the spring offensive that succeeded in the fall," as Heykal said, served as a lesson?[56]

To the military rulers, Syria seemed to have been a trap. They placed the emphasis, in military terms, on the dangers of the maneuver, the lack of preparation of forces, the virulence of the enemies, the inequality and disproportion between the two elements of the union. The Egyptian people bore the brunt of its lack of preparation, as it was called, but also of its "nonengagement" in that perpetual quest of self-identity which was the core of Syrian Arab nationalism. But at no time did President Nasser and the ruling group acknowledge the underlying cause that doomed the union in the eyes of the Syrian masses who had sought it: the dictatorial character of the government, its hatred for all democracy, its destruction of civil liberties, the dissolution of political parties, the predominance of the political-military apparatus and its police forces.

Did this mean that Cairo had given up its plans for Arab expansion? An official document, "in answer to all those who call for unity with Damascus," shows clearly that though the time might have called for tactical caution, the goal remained the same. These were the conditions posed by the military rulers as preliminaries to any new unity, a unity "whose image will inevitably be different from that of the old one":

"It is essential that national entities remain clearly defined within the structure of unity. Each national entity will have to have its own local government, answerable to the local elected officials. The unity will have to be total in matters of defense, of foreign policy, of a social-action method based on socialism and democracy, of public-education and cultural programs. The unified state will have to be endowed with a single central parliament within which the national entities will have to have equitable representation and to which the central government of the unified state will be responsible. The realization of socialism and democracy, as well as the action undertaken with a view to dissolving class differences in the new Arab society, will gradually contribute, through the will of the peoples, to the growth of a single consciousness and at the same time it will resolve the problems of minorities and communities in certain parts of the Arab world in a free manner and with equality."[57]

In actuality, all that was new was the recognition, which was purely formal, of the existence of "national entities"; the exigency of centralism and subordination of regionalisms to a single political, social and ideological leadership was very clearly reaffirmed, although the document as a whole manifested a greater desire for realism and flexibility.

A few days later it was the turn of Akram Hurani's Baath party to assume its position. It did so in the form of self-criticism: "(1) Our party's concept of unity was marked by an extreme of sentimentality . . . we had no theory concerning the execution of unity . . . (2) The party unhesitatingly agreed to a rapid transition from federal union, which was suggested at the time, to the unity desired by Nasser without recognizing its consequences . . . (3) The party forgot one important truth: that unity is a revolutionary process and that there can be no revolution without a revolutionary movement . . . (4) In this matter the party did not follow democratic procedure; it did not offer this project for discussion in the responsible bodies [sections and branches] . . ." After having thus whitewashed itself of any responsibility for the operation of March 1958, in which, however, as is well known, it had played the decisive part of the inciter, the Baathists went back to the criticisms long since elaborated by the Syrian Communist party and General Bizry.[58] The result was the division of the party into two wings: the Beirut section, which continued the unity policy under the leadership of Michel Aflak and Salah Bitar, and the Damascus section, directed by Akram Hurani before the takeover by the army.[59]

The controversy that raged thereafter between the Syrian Left and Cairo concerned Palestine. Nasser was accused of having made a secret bargain with the State Department for a de facto settlement of the 1948 dispute, closed his eyes to the Johnson project for utilizing the waters of the River Jordan, and thus accepted the existence and the consolidation of the state of Israel. Akram Hurani published the proceedings of the meetings of the UAR's Central Cabinet, in which Nasser seemed to have taken care to do nothing on the military level as long as he was not certain of his ability to crush the enemy. The anniversary of May 15, 1948, gave Heykal the occasion for a statement on the military rulers' intentions: the essential purpose consisted in "reinforcing the indispensable fundamental basis for opening the way to the return [of the Palestine Arab refugees]: namely, subjective Arab strength on the political, economic and social levels"; meanwhile, a first test of strength might be attempted in 1963–64—that is, at the period when Israel, in order to complete the Jordan project, would find herself compelled to enter the demilitarized zone and consequently to come into conflict with the UN's formal decisions; the moral advantage that would then accrue to the Arab countries would add substantial reinforcement to their military and socioeconomic potential, which would be in full growth.[60] On June 26, in his speech to the members of the Legislative Council of the Gaza Strip, Nasser returned to these ideas and elaborated on them.[61]

Finally, Nasser explained his position to Anglo-Saxon opinion for the third time: "No one can buy a man's home, his soul or his basic human rights. One day the whole account will have to be really settled. In order to do this, I believe that we should build the Arab world's economy and raise the people's living standard until such time as we shall have reached a stage of evolution that will permit us to exert such pressure on the Israelis as to make them understand the complete justice of our position."[62] Decoded, this meant no military reprisals for the time being; a strategy of self-strengthening that would compel the enemy of 1948 and 1956 to render justice to the Arab people of Palestine and to keep to its own place. Obviously this is a long way from the annihilation of the state of Israel . . . At the Arab summit conference in Shtaura, Lebanon, the UAR was denounced by the Syrian delegation on charges of expansionism and collusion with American Zionism. On August 28, 1962, the withdrawal of the UAR precipitated the weakening of the Arab League.[63]

In complete contrast, it was the democratic content of Arab nationalism on which the Egyptian Communists insisted unremittingly, especially after the instigation of repression.

Out of the concentration camps, and notably the all-too-notorious Abu Zaabal, came motions and resolutions, all of which emphasized the government's obligation to restore democracy at home, the basic condition of validity for an independent and neutralist foreign policy and for progress toward socialist growth.

After the Syrian coup d'état Communist circles published their own interpretation of it. "The Egyptian Communists," they said, "have frequently emphasized, particularly after December 23, 1958, that every infringement of democracy must necessarily, in the final analysis, lead to the restoration of reaction, and that this must in turn open the way to imperialism for the reconquest of its lost positions in our country." That was what had happened: "the coup d'état . . . was the first victory won by the reactionary forces and, through their intermediation, by the imperialist structures in the Arab Orient since the fall of Jordan in April 1957." After pointing out that Nassar had "pursued a policy aimed at containing the influence of the socialist countries with respect to the national movement in the Arab Orient and the entire world, and at playing on the conflicts between East and West, a policy which reached its climactic point with the recent conferences of the uncommitted countries and the influx of loans and imperialist capital," this document sketched the picture of the factors that had caused the break: "fusion instead of federal unity; antidemocracy based on contempt of Egypt's and Syria's regional characteristics and traditions of struggle; a dictatorial rule which was to persecute patriots, democrats, trade unionists and Communists indiscriminately and which sought to stifle political activity and unseat the National Front in Syria for the benefit of the National Union, a single-party system based on the dominant Egyptian bourgeoisie class which the Syrian middle class was to invade without meeting any resistance; the Egyptian bourgeoisie's grip on the destinies of the Syrian economy to the detriment of the less advanced Syrian middle class, the economic and social measures promulgated in July 1961, which, while they struck at the reaction represented by the feudalists, the monopolists and the large capitalists, at the same time damaged a certain number of national capitalists." This initial defeat had caused "a temporary retreat in the national-liberation movement throughout the Arab world, the reinforcement of Arab reactionary forces . . . the encouragement of imperialism." Henceforth "the cause of nationalism is more than ever the cause of the Arab working class"; "it has been irrefutably established that if Arab unity can be achieved only among countries liberated from the imperialist yoke, so too it can be achieved only on democratic foundations."[64]

The government was not to be altogether unmarked by the attack, as we have seen: the discussions within the Preparatory

Committee of the National Congress of Popular Forces were held against a new background: the vicissitudes of democracy, which the Syrian failure so rudely exemplified.

President Nasser and his men chose a new line—the social revolution, whose ideology would be "co-operativist democratic socialism."

Confrontation with the Baath Party

The Baghdad coup d'état of February 8, 1963, was a brutal reverse to projects for Arab unity. A new Iraqi Cabinet, composed of Baath party ministers headed by Ali Saleh el-Sadi, pro-Nasser nationalists, and officers with Moslem Brotherhood leanings, assumed power through the support of certain units loyal to Colonel Abdel Salam Mohammed Aref; General Kassem was immediately executed, as well as his chief lieutenants, while the Baath's "Green Armbands" hunted down the Communists in Iraqi cities and villages: many were shot point-blank like animals, and ten thousand militants and sympathizers were thrown into concentration camps.

A month later, on March 8–9, an army coup d'état put a civilian and military Baath group in power in Damascus, neutralizing pro-Nasser groups and the Communists, but it restricted itself to a moderate repression, for the bloody events in Iraq had aroused a wave of indignant protests throughout the world, including those of the President of the UAR and the Cairo press.

The opponents of unification having been turned back in Syria as well as in Iraq, the Baath's international leadership, headed by Michel Aflak, decided to take the offensive. The goal was to achieve unity between the UAR, Syria and Iraq. The frenetic activity during the second week in March was aimed at forming a united Iraqi-Syrian Baathist front to stand up to the Egyptian leaders.

The tripartite talks began in Cairo on March 14, 1963. Three sessions—March 14–16, March 19–30 and April 6–14 —were devoted to liquidating the enmities born of the collapse of the Syrian-Egyptian merger and to initiating a plan for trilateral unification. Actually the first two sessions—the only ones in which Aflak took part—bogged down in Syrian-Egyptian quarrels. But on March 22 it was decided that each government should prepare a unification plan and all would then be debated in the third session. On March 31 Mohammed Hassanein Heykal began publishing a series of articles, "Inni attahem!" (I Accuse!) in *al-Ahram*, portraying the Baath party as intent on discrediting Nasser, delaying unification, conducting a campaign of provocation against the UAR and placing all responsibility for the 1961 setback on the Cairo government. Riots broke out between Baathists and pro-Nasser factions in Damascus, leading to the imposition of a curfew.

It was in this tempestuous climate that the Egyptian delegation requested, and obtained, during the third session, the gradual dissolution of the three countries' political parties, in favor of the Arab Socialist Union. Finally, on April 17, 1963, the official announcement of the agreements on the federal union was made public. It emphasized that "unity of purposes and identity of principles require that the unionist forces in the three countries constitute a political front of democratic socialist action . . . within a single political organization that will be bound by the Charter [of National Action] and by the decisions of the unified political front" taken by a federal leadership; but the immediate dissolution of political organizations was not stipulated, for emphasis was placed on preparations for the united political organization:

The President of the Republic, (i.e., the new unified state) to be elected for a four-year term by at least a two-thirds majority of the Federal Assembly, would appoint ministers and higher officials; he would be the commander in chief of the armed forces. The Presidential Council would comprise an equal number of representatives for the three regions; it would choose the Vice-Presidents of the Republic, the Presidents of the three regions and the Council of Defense; its main function would be to develop general policy and to supervise the governmental machinery. The Cabinet would be responsible to the National Assembly; this would consist of a Chamber of Deputies elected by universal suffrage, and a

Federal Council composed of an equal representation for each region; 50 percent of elected representatives must be workers and peasants. Finally, each region would have its own elected Assembly, a Cabinet and a Premier.

"The people will control all production facilities and will dispose of the goods according to a definite plan"; private property and the right to inherit were preserved in principle; side by side with the public sector, a private sector would participate in the development of the economy without exploiting the workers. The federal Constitution was to be submitted to a referendum in the three countries before September 15, 1963.

Meanwhile the conflict between pro-Nasser elements and Baathists was growing sharper: there were riots and demonstrations in Syrian cities; in Cairo, *in extenso* publication of transcripts of the three conference sessions on unification was preparing the public for the rupture with the Baath. In the face of Iraqi-Syrian solidarity, the Egyptian government declared that it was obliged to suspend the three-nation projects. Iraq was torn by the Kurdish insurrection, which the predominantly Baathist central government was putting down with a savagery never before equaled, even in the days of Nuri el-Said. Finally the situation was reversed by the dissension within the Iraqi Baath and the intervention of the Iraqi army: during the week of November 12–19 Marshal Aref seized and consolidated power, while the pro-Syrian faction of the Baath was completely ousted. The UAR government immediately announced its total political and military support of the new government, while Syria found herself deprived of her powerful ally.

So then the quietus came before the end of 1963 to the efforts to establish a cohesive center of political power that would be able to challenge Nasser's Egypt for the Arab leadership with the simultaneous backing of a political organization sharing an autonomous ideology (the Baath) and of Iraq's oil resources. Once again the attempt to outstrip the Egyptian government, this time by countering it on its own ground, had come to nothing. Even more than in October 1961, Nasser could rely on the deep-rooted and outspoken resentment of

Egyptian public opinion against the Baath's tactics—and against the butchers of Baghdad; in fact, against all the governments that had held power there since the assassination of Kassem.

From Yemen to the Arab Summit Meeting

On September 27, 1962, Colonel Abdallah el-Sallal seized power in Yemen through a military coup d'état and drove Imam* Seif el-Islam Mohammed Badr out of the capital. This opened a new battle front for Egypt's Arab policy. On October 3 a mutual-defense and co-operation treaty was concluded between the two countries. The next day a first contingent of Egyptian shock troops arrived at the seaport of Hodeida on the Red Sea. One and a half years later these troops were estimated at forty thousand men, equipped with the most modern weapons, supported by planes and backed by warships and efficient maritime supply lines.

Why this massive commitment in Yemen? The question should be put, rather, in these terms: How was it possible to avoid commitment in Yemen when the leader of that national revolution, himself a soldier to boot, called on the Cairo government to come to his aid against the reigning dynasty in order to emerge from the rigid cast of semislave rule? How could commitment be refused when Great Britain, concerned about Aden and the southeastern Arab principalities, allied herself with Saudi Arabia against Yemen's republican government? This was the undertone of the news dispatches and editorials of the Egyptian press and radio confronted with the increasing unrest of public opinion because of the difficulties to furnish supplies and the casualties in Yemen.

The Cairo government was not ignoring the hostility of public opinion. Various surveys paved the way for Ralph Bunche's mission, as U Thant's representative, to Yemen in March 1963, which was the prelude to the five-point withdrawal (but not cease-fire) plan submitted on March 13 by the UN Secretary-General to the governments of the

---

* *Imam*, literally "the one who leads people into prayer"; hence the title given to reigning monarchs in Yemen.

UAR, Saudi Arabia and Yemen. Agreement was reached under the aegis of the American diplomat Ellsworth Bunker, and General Carl van Horn installed the fifty UN observers charged with supervising the execution of the agreement.

Actually, the United States seemed to be in no hurry to exert pressure on Great Britain and Saudi Arabia to put an end to the fighting. It seemed, rather, as if the evolution of the Egyptian government was provoking American diplomacy to let the abscess of Yemen get worse as a means of pressure against the UAR.

Nevertheless, there had to be an end to the actual fighting.

This was one of the aims of the Conference of Arab Chiefs of State in Cairo on January 13–16, 1964, called on the suggestion of President Nasser. The main decisions dealt with the Palestinian problem: the creation of a unified Arab command under the Egyptian general Ali Ali Amer; the establishment of a special agency, composed of representatives of the chiefs of state but also including Ahmad el-Shukeiry, representing Palestine, to supervise the execution of the summit decisions; concerted efforts to bring the "Palestinian entity" into being; study of possible uses for the waters of the River Jordan; the launching of a general concerted political offensive. But all observers tended to agree that there was also discussion of an Egyptian-Saudi implementation of the agreement with respect to Yemen. Nevertheless, the fighting continued sporadically, and by autumn of 1964 the republican leaders were the virtual masters of the country.

The Economic Resources of the Arab Nation

The reason for this Egyptian determination to explore ways and means to Arab unity with all the Arab states, whatever their forms of government, must be sought elsewhere—in the context of economics and population.

Indeed, there was no attempt by official sources to conceal the facts. The thirteen Arab states' delegations, on the very first day of the summit meeting of January 1964, had been given copies of *Al-mawared al-iktissadiyya li'l-umma al-Arabiyya* (*The Economic Resources of the Arab Nation*), a group study prepared by four young doctors of political economy, Sobhi Abdel Hakim, Yussef Khalil Yussef, Halim Ibrahim Girgis, and Galal Seba'i. The goal was defined as prosperity, not socialism, and this was dependent on three prerequisites: a developing market; potentially exploitable resources; and funds for financing large projects.

What were the premises set up by our young technocrats? Ninety million Arabs launched on development were living in an area of 4.25 million square miles. Consider cereal-grain production: 17 million tons per year, or 420 pounds per person; 7 million tons of wheat, or 35 percent of the world output; yet the Maghreb (Algeria, Tunisia and Morocco) exported more wheat than was imported by Egypt, Libya and Jordan, because its exports were not aimed at Arab territory . . . In addition, the Arab countries produced 9 percent of the world's citrus crop, 8.5 percent of the dates, 8 percent of the grapes. Livestock? 56 million sheep, 27 million goats, 17 million cattle and 3.5 million camels. The Maghreb alone exported 12 percent of the world trade in iron ore. The Arab countries exported phosphate, manganese, lead. They produced 7 percent of the world's cotton; Egypt produced 85 percent of the long-fiber cotton and manufactured a billion yards of textiles—in other words, barely enough to meet local textile demand and absorb only 20 percent of the cotton crop. The Tindouf mines in Algeria had a capacity of 5 million tons a year, a fantastic figure. The Arab states controlled 90 percent of the world's oil reserves and could go on supplying oil for a hundred years at the current annual rate. The return in 1960 on the nine tenths of the oil that was exported turned out to be $1.5 billion.

Yet only 10 percent of Egypt's exports went to the other Arab countries, which in turn supplied 5 percent of her imports. For Iraq these figures were 29 and 3.5 percent, respectively. There were no rail, maritime or regular air connections between the Arab countries. There were no preferential tariffs. There was nothing resembling even the embryo of an Arab Common Market.

Yet the concerted employment of these substantial resources, vulnerable now to pillage and waste, could give the

Arab collective the economic foundations that alone could sustain its will to unity and enable it to conquer underdevelopment.

Thereafter the road to unity was pursued step by step, without haste. Such was the sense of the agreement for "political co-ordination" which was concluded between the UAR and Iraq on May 26, 1964, soon to be followed by a similar agreement with Yemen. The negotiations under way with Algeria have made substantial progress, notably on the level of the definition of the principles and objectives of the National Liberation Front and the Arab Socialist Union—communiqué of June 26, 1964, the central thesis of which was: "Since socialism means essentially the end of man's exploitation of man, the people's ownership of all the means of production, the equitable distribution of the natural wealth, and the free development of the individual, the two delegations declare that there is only one socialism, whereas its methods of application are peculiar to each society."

CHAPTER 8

WHAT IS "CO-OPERATIVIST DEMOCRATIC SOCIALISM"?

"ARAB SOCIALISM," "co-operativist democratic socialism"—these were the names of the social doctrine that the government intended to oppose to Marxism during the peak years 1956–58, a doctrine which was the basis for the economic reforms of July–December 1961, and which served as the rallying cry of state ideology after the secession of Syria.

Step by Step . . .

But no official documents offered it as a state doctrine. The January 1956 Constitution of the Republic of Egypt defined the Egyptian state as a "democratic republic" (Article 1), declaring that "social solidarity is at the basis of Egyptian society" (Article 4), that "the national economy is organized according to plans that follow the principles of social justice," that "although private economic activity is free, it should nevertheless not be prejudicial to the interests of society," and that "capital should be employed in the service of the national economy" (Articles 7, 8 and 9). The Provisional Constitution of the UAR (March 5, 1958) reiterated the same ideas and almost in identical terms (Articles 1 to 6).

Chronologically it was the National Union that was first called upon to set up a socialist front: "The National Union has as its purposes the realization of the aims of the revolution of July 23, 1952, the creation of a co-operative democratic socialist society, free of any political, social or economic exploitation." During the summer of 1960, the National Union held its sessions: regional congresses for Egypt and Syria in June, and then, from July 9 to 16, a General Congress for the UAR as a whole. Its decisions on questions of principle and its final resolutions, numbering 275, amounted to a veritable charter of governmental action. It defined the new doctrine in official terms from a point of view visibly different from that adopted by Nasser in his inaugural address.

At that time the President of the UAR emphasized the economic aspect, notably the necessity of doubling the national income in ten years. The ideal was defined as "social justice." Socialism emerged as "the liberation of every individual from exploitation," and its complement, democracy, as "the participation of each individual in its orientation." There could be no democracy "if feudalism continued to oppress and capital to dominate, if every man's condition was always determined by the status that he had inherited"; there could be no socialism "if the minority that had inherited the opportunities governed and if the majority was barred from decisions, from the development of policy, from the preparation of plans."[1]

Out of these commonplaces of the welfare state the Congress was to shape the embryo of a doctrine. "The democracy in which the Arab people believes and which serves it as a means in politics, as a system in economics, as a bond among the members of society, is the democracy born of our principles, of our ideals, of our traditions, of the needs of our society, the democracy that sets as its objective the guarantee of the freedom of the individual without either despotism or paternalism, the achievement of economic and political freedom for the community from all exploitation or domination, the democracy which guarantees the right of the people to participate in power and to impose its sovereignty, which lifts the brotherhood of the people above the level of creed and partisan spirit in all their guises, and which works toward strengthening the bonds among all members of society so that all will work together in unison of heart, hand in hand, to assure a better future for the entire country.

"Our socialism finds its root in the conscience of our nation and the evolution of its social thought, which has spared it from the class struggle. Thus this socialism has become the practical application of the content of social solidarity; its structure has been founded on the gift, the creation of property, justice in its distribution, recognizing the right of every individual to share in the fruits of the national income and achieving social justice among all individuals.

"Co-operation consists in combining all efforts in a single whole with a view to action, to building and doubling production for the benefit of the individual and society; in uniting diminished potentialities in order to make them a powerful force and a productive energy; co-operation is the road on which all individuals can bring to fruition the economic complementariness that exists among them, and it is the symbol of brotherhood within every united people. In all these areas, co-operation constitutes one of the forms of our democracy and one of its instruments with a view to raising the living standard of the people, to accomplishing its objectives and to arming it against monopoly and exploitation."[2]

The offensive against Marxism, after the 1959–62 repression that reduced the followers of that ideology to silence and also the public controversy with the Soviet Union and the socialist countries, made it possible to discern the contours of the new doctrine. The repeated contacts between the military rulers and certain Communist capitals, notably Moscow, Peking and Sofia, during the years 1959–61 were substantially hampered due to the close collaboration among nations, especially in matters of economic development and, to a lesser degree, on the level of general relations between the neutralist countries and the socialist bloc. Tom Little, who for ten years, until 1956, managed the Egyptian office of the Arab News Agency, succinctly voiced the thinking of the military rulers: "Soviet

policy had nothing to lose and everything to gain; any loss to
the West was its gain, and if the West resisted Arab nationalism, the situation became doubly favorable. . . . Soviet pragmatism did not change the *intention* of Egyptian policy, which
was still to resist both foreign domination and the international, godless ideology of Communism, but its emphasis was
changed by reduced dependence on Western economic associations and increasing dependence on Russia. . . . the Eisenhower Doctrine . . . was misconceived because the Soviet
government was now more concerned to promote its influence
with Arab governments, bourgeois or not, than to promote the
fortunes of the Communist parties. The Arab governments
were themselves repressing their indigenous Communists . . ."[3]

Not only was the summer of 1961 the period of economic
and social legislation, of the Syrian-Egyptian crisis, of the
poorest cotton crop in decades,[4] of the temporary respite in
the program of torture and misery inflicted on Communists
and progressives in Egyptian prisons; the summer of 1961 was
the time of a confrontation that both parties, both states (the
USSR and the UAR) hoped would be free of hatred, if not
of acrimony.

In the beginning of May a delegation of the Council of
the Nation, headed by Anwar el-Sadate, visited the Soviet
Union. On May 3, during a reception in the Kremlin,
Khrushchev had a few words with his guests: "We are Communists. You say you are Arab nationalists but you like
Communism. For various reasons, you and we look at the
world in different ways. But this should not create a barrier
between us. If our people, under a Communist system, live
better than yours, how can you say that you are against Communism? Communism consists in ideas that you cannot shut
up in prisons. You say you want socialism, but you do not
understand the true socialism that leads to Communism. In
the present stage of your development you are still at the
letter A. In all good faith I warn you, I tell you that Communism is sacred . . ." And the editor in chief of *al-Ahram*,
who reported these remarks, added: "It behooves us to leave
the door open to Moscow lest we commit ourselves to the
prospect of a future co-operation with the Arab world that

would be carried out by way of groups which have put themselves outside the ranks of national unanimity and which the
Arab people in every country has already condemned as
renegades and deviationists . . ."[5] The propaganda services in
Damascus and Cairo recruited professors and journalists to
write anti-Communist material of an especially virulent nature,
notably *Hakikat al-shuyu'iyya* (The Truth of Communism)
and *Hazihi hia al-shuyu'iyya* (This Is Communism). Ismail
Mazhar, one of the major evolutionist thinkers during the interval between the two world wars, published two theoretical
works, the last just before his death—*Al-Islam, la al-shuyu'iyya*
(Islam, Not Communism) and *Al-tadamun al-ishtiraki, la al-
shuyu'iyya* (Socialist Solidarity, Not Communism).

We and Communism

An important work by Heykal, *We and Communism,*
drew a seven-point parallel that most certainly reflected Nasser's thinking. These were its essentials:

(1) First of all, there is the manner in which the problem
of social classes is looked at, since their existence and the class
struggle are conceded. While Communism offers the solution
of "the dictatorship of the proletariat," which means "the suppression of other classes by one class in a complete and
definitive fashion," Arab socialism calls for "a process of dissolving the contradictions of class in the framework of a
national union within which revolutionary interaction will
occur, the transformation of the society into a single class
within which individuals' positions will vary in accordance
with their work, totally devoid of any class barriers that
might arise to bar any individual's progress or block his road."

(2) This leads to a different way of looking at private
property: "Communism considers every owner an exploiter at
the same time"; Arab socialism believes that a distinction should
be made between two kinds of property: first, "property representing labor and that lies in an area that does not allow the
individual to exploit and dominate others . . . here we are
dealing with a right that must be broadened to reach the
greatest possible number of those who are deprived of it";

second, "the property of the exploiter, who must not be killed but who must simply be stripped of the weapons that enable him to exploit others, and then he will be admitted into the new society."

(3) While Communism believes in "expropriation," Arab socialism prefers "compensation" for nationalized properties. "Private property is a right, indeed an objective, provided that it be kept in a framework that prevents exploitation." And by way of illustration the measures of the summer and autumn of 1961 are cited, with emphasis on the very broad sector that remained in individual hands.

(4) Next comes the conception of the individual's function in society. "In a Communist society the state is the sole owner of all things, while the individual is a working tool that receives what it needs in order to meet its basic needs . . . The individual is a mere product of history." In the view of Arab socialism, "the individual represents the basis of the socialist structure . . . he is at once a product and a producer of history."

(5) In the period when Stalin was at the head of the Communist experiment, whole generations of men were sacrificed in order to attain high production. Arab socialism "is interested in the present, for if the present loses the concept of life, the future cannot create it out of nothing." That is why the UAR "does not overlook the immediate necessity of providing public services," housing, schools and hospitals, whereas, according to the author, nothing of this kind was done at the beginning of the Russian Revolution . . .

(6) Recalling the case of Tito, the author turns his attack on dogmatism: "Every Communist, even if he is dedicated to the principles of Marxist analysis, must remain within the broad outlines that have been drawn for him, the clearly marked paths, or he will be accused of deviationism." In contrast, "the Arab socialist feels that the whole cultural wealth of the world is at his disposal, that he can profit by it and explore its horizons and that in the end he can add his own contribution to it, that of his national experience, and take part in its enrichment thanks to his historic heritage."

(7) The final difference concerns the instrument of revolution: "Communism believes that the organization of political

8

activity should be kept in the hands of the Communist party alone . . . ; it would be impossible for any revolution to become legitimate unless the Communist party was its master and moving force." In contrast, "Arab socialism believes that the organization of political activity should extend to the entire nation and that development should take place within the framework of national unity in order to reach the next stage, that at which the nation gains its momentum . . ."[6]

Another, still more recent theoretical formulation, that of Ehsan Abdel Koddus in terms of his controversy with Kingsley Martin,[7] offers these clarifications: "Our socialism believes in God as well as in the materialist and spiritualist interpretation of history, of the future and the dignity of man. It believes in private ownership side by side with public ownership, provided that both be combined within a single, overall plan. It believes that personal motivation is a force of evolution along with collective motivation and that both should be directed toward a single objective. It believes that there are different levels—not classes—within a single society; the difference between level and class is that the former cannot be inherited, whereas exactly the opposite applies to class; that level is determined in terms of the individual's capacities, whereas class is based on birth, connection and ownership; there is always conflict among the various levels but this represents a conflict quite different from that in capitalist countries, for it becomes not an effort by class combinations to impose their domination but, rather, personal motivation and effort. Our socialism is based neither on dictatorship nor on bureaucracy. The first is not a system but a mentality that can infiltrate as far down as the level of the most unimportant functionaries and managers. At a time when many socialist states resort to methods that lead to despotism and the dictatorship of a single individual, our socialism is turning toward the application of decentralization, the strengthening of social control in all fields, as is attested by the participation of office and factory workers in boards of directors, as well as the National Union's control over the socialist tendency."

Minister Kamal Rifaat analyzed "the characteristics of Arab socialism." What it meant was not "a term in between Communism and capitalism, or an attempt to improve social conditions in our society," but rather a formal doctrine that owed its origin to "our intellectual and spiritual heritage, our national history and that of our civilization, as well as the very nature of the Arab people, which is distinguished by a number of characteristics, of which the most important are generosity, nobility and the love of the good." This was followed by a very close elaboration in thirteen points, the first four of which were of a theoretical order:

(1) "The humanist idea": the idea which "aims at serving all sections of society without trying to make socialist thought a means of serving only one element—for example, the state." The government's initiatives and experiences would not be capable of touching the essence of the socialist endeavor.

(2) This socialism "was not born of a rigid society," like European socialism, the product of capitalism; it "surged out of the social conscience of the movement of Arab nationalism."

(3) "Although we recognize the influence of physical and economic factors in the evolution of history and human societies, we believe as much in the influence of the ideal and spiritual factor."

(4) "Our socialism believes in the individual, on whom it is based and whose personality it sets free."

The practical aspects followed:

(5) Arab socialism, "grown out of the reality of the needs of our society . . . is a national socialism," but this does not prevent it from entering "into interaction with other socialist theories."

(6) The character of the state is that of the whole of the people, ". . . laborers, peasants, white-collar workers, intellectuals—whoever works for wages and takes part in social development." The nationalizations, "the first stage of the building of socialism," should be distinguished from those of the capitalist type, which benefit only the owners.

(7) Capital growth was no longer only for the capitalists or the state. That was why Arab socialism called for "the necessity of giving the workers—that is, the real producers—a part of the capital increase, which is profit, as compensation for their participation in production."

(8) "Centralist economic planning and decentralized execution . . . the state becoming a kind of socialist officer . . ."

(9) While democratic socialism rejects "democracy in the Western sense," it "compels social criticism, except what is directed against our own conception of socialism."

(10) There should be neither pluralism of parties nor a single party: "It is the masses of the people, not the party, that should play the leading part." There should be a "conscious vanguard," which, however, should "exert no influence of any sort, no domination in its own interests."

(11) "The right to private property" should not "make it a means of exploiting society and bringing about a rebirth of the capitalist system."

(12) "The right to inherit" was basic.

(13) The dialectic between the individual and society was resolved thus: "Organize social relations in such a way that there are no individual rights without obligations"; it was possible to accept "inequality among individuals to the extent inevitably required to allow for the motivation and competition that fulfill the interests of the socialist society . . ."[8]

The work of exploration on which *The Egyptian Political Science Review* embarked under the direction of Major Abdel Kader Hatem occasionally produced something worth preserving, including this from Abdalla Rabi'e: "Co-operativist democratic socialism is a political system which tends to stimulate a spirit of organized fraternity aimed at dissolving the differences between the classes in order to put an end to political struggle among popular powers. At the same time it takes a positive position in the global conflict, thus expressing the vigor of the lofty ideal that governs our contemporary society, surrounded by independent entities to which we are connected by bonds of ethnic unity and regional interests."[9]

Everyone on all levels had been talking of socialism since 1955–56. But the quotations that we have given, it seems, should cover the very wide range suggested by their authors, which is to be found in greater detail in the flood of publications of every kind that dealt with the new socialism.[10] There was hardly a day when the press did not publish editorials and studies on the new ideology, most often contrasting it to Communism and seeking its roots in the Islamic or Arab cultural heritage.

Occasionally a few lines struck an unexpected note in the midst of a rhetoric full of smugness and the joyous determination to reject any emulation, any dependence. Thus, deploring the theoretical confusion between "democratic and co-operativist socialism" and "Arab socialism," Professor Abdel Malek Auda stressed the necessity to compare current non-Marxist socialist experiments (Guinea, Mali, Yugoslavia, India), to clarify relations with Marxism and to formulate a policy with respect to the relationship between Arab socialism and religion.[11] To this Helmy el-Said, economic adviser to the President of the Republic and president of the Misr Agency, replied with an apologia full of sinuous and varied pragmatism that seemed simply unworthy of him . . . .[12]

The State and the Class Struggle

On the question of the relationship between democratic and co-operativist socialism and Marxism, we know what can be relied on. Clovis Maksud drew his Egyptian colleagues' attention to the imperative need of doctrinal clarity in the great ideological battle against Marxist Communism,[13] since that was indeed the crux of the ideological problem. The fact remains that in spite of a temporary moderation of language, the military rulers went on persecuting and suppressing the Marxist Left. This was a long way from Fidel Castro, who had been much admired before 1961.[14] But it was impossible to believe that socialism could be achieved without socialists, as Nasser intended. "There is the further obstacle," Fathi Ghanem said, "of finding genuine propagandists for co-operativist democratic socialism," the more so because they would run up against the skepticism of the peasants, inured for millennia to the lies of the state.[15] And the rest? The National Union included all the former personalities, especially at the village and provincial level, and Nasser himself conceded the setback, indeed the reactionary aspect of many quarters; whence the idea of the National Congress of Popular Forces at the end of 1961.[16] But then, how was socialism to be achieved without socialists? How could a new society be built, with its culture and ideology, without the collaboration of the intelligentsia?

The problems were many. The main one was the relationship between the state and the social classes.

In 1952–54 official doctrine had ignored the matter. Between 1954 and 1956 the tone was one of national unanimity; the favorite phrases then were of the type "the Arab *umma*," the "people's revolution," "the union of the people and the army," "the people's army," etc. The emphasis was naturally placed on the national content of the army movement. Suez, like the Bandung period, and other events gave a right of entry to projects of Marxist inspiration: it was no longer possible to evade the problems of class distinctions when it was time for nationalizations and state capitalism, but the officials continued to employ a unanimist nationalitarian vocabulary, accentuating its popular character (particularly in the two Constitutions of 1956 and 1958).

The Marxist analyses oscillated between branding the government the representative of the national middle class (this was the case with the DMNL and then the right wing of the Unified Egyptian Communist party, which was extended in the minority schism of the Egyptian Communist party during the autumn of 1958) or labeling it the instrument of the monopolist upper middle class (the organization known as the Egyptian Communist party's thesis before the merger). In the left center, the ECP's majority (particularly under the influence of the Workers' Vanguard, which became the Egyptian Communist party of Workers and Peasants before the merger) inclined toward a more subtle analysis, which began to make way for the idea of an alliance among various sectors of the Egyptian middle class under the leadership of big banking and monopoly capital (this was in 1958–59) and to take cognizance of a certain Egyptian individuality.[17] And it might be said that the repressions cut down the Marxist Left in full flight, at the very time when it was laboring to develop a close theoretical analysis of Egyptian society after the first outlines, duly censored, made by Ibrahim Amer, Shohdi Attia el-Shafei and Fawzi Guergues.

The controversy over the "crisis of the intellectuals" was to make it possible for some, notably Lutfi el-Kholy, to formulate the concept of the state as referee: "Inasmuch as the army revolution did not emanate from any of the political parties but was the expression and the realization of the will of the Free Officers under the leadership of Gamal Abdel Nasser, who maintained his movement independent of all the social and political forces in the collapsing society, it consequently erected a state whose authorities retain a subjective independence with respect to the social and political forces in existence today." The intellectuals, who had long believed that "the only possible way of changing the situation was that of the traditional popular revolution," had been paralyzed by the coup d'état (which the author, of course, calls "the revolution") of 1952; that was why "they had not studied it on the basis of objective physical conditions and the relations among the social forces, as a revolution working to build a new government for a new state, independent of social classes to a great extent, and having as its objective the development of a movement of industrialization and the smashing of imperialist dependency"; "a strong state power that expressed itself in its lack of political dependence on any given class, whether it be the landowners, the middle class or the workers, by reason of having made itself the judge among all these classes." World and local conditions "created an exceptional government on the historical level, that of a state generally independent of the interests of all classes in the political and social spheres."[18] Thus the military government was defined as an entity *sui generis*, transcending general history, the evolution of the national movement, and Egyptian society, hovering above the classes and the complex political interests that were intertwined and overlapped on the plane of real life. A "revealed" government, as it were . . .

In what way would this government be socialist? This was the heart of the new discussion of economic planning inaugurated by *al-Ahram* in May 1962. Once more, after the customary quibbles about semantics—planning, socialization, nationalization, etc.—the crux of the problem was approached. Dr. Ahmed Shukry Salem stressed certain truths: "There are various levels of planning; some can benefit the capitalist system, as was the case in Hitler's Germany at the time of the famous slogan 'guns or butter'; the Nazi party, which then dominated the state, began its planning in order to attain this objective, which was indeed one of aggression . . . There is also the Indian society, which has plans, but which it would be impossible to call socialist; during the first plan, the public sector represented 46 percent of the economy; it rose to 54 percent in the second five years; in spite of that, this was not socialist planning, even though it was oriented toward the interests of the broadest classes of the population."

Dr. Abdel Razek Hassan added that "as far as justice is concerned, the capitalist system stands for the same things as socialism; what matters is the execution." First of all, "total planning is contingent on the degree of the extension of public ownership as a basis for the economic system," since planning in itself is not socialism; "the purpose of socialist planning is to answer the growing cultural and material needs of every individual member of society to the greatest possible extent, by constantly increasing production, both quantitatively and qualitatively, through the use of the most advanced technology."[19]

Are we dealing, in the case of Egypt, with planning of the capitalist, the socialist or some intermediate type? We have seen that it was the intermediate type that had to be adopted. But it is understandable that for one segment of public opinion and leadership there were serious reservations regarding the label "socialist." That was why, one journalist was to say, "we need to stimulate the growth of what we call the national consciousness in the field of action, in socialist consciousness."[20] Born of the Egyptian economy's imperative needs but also of imperialist intervention, planning did not seem, in the view of many people, to have arisen out of a desire for socialism.

There was another problem: "the future of private property," the subject of a seminar organized by *Rose el-Yussef*, also in May 1962. Two tendencies emerged sharply. On the one side there were the champions of socialization, notably Major Kamal el-Hennawi, Kamel Zeheiry and Ahmed Fahim. Hennawi in particular, an influential member of the Free Officers, was most eloquent. "Experience," he said, "has demonstrated that the distribution of agrarian-reform land to the peasants and of houses to certain members of co-operative associations has alienated them from the socialist spirit . . . As the owner of a *feddan* or two, the peasant has joined the large landowners in his way of thinking, while houseowners have begun to turn to exploitation"; the inherent logic of industrial and commercial development will induce "small enterprises to join together as a large corporation, and this will force the state to intervene in order to prevent a monopoly."

But the discussions made it apparent that under the cover of "socialism," the liberal ideologists intended merely the development of the national economy. Rashed el-Barawi thought that "the textile industry in Egypt is the equivalent of heavy industry in England." Rifaat el-Mahgub asserted: "We transform those who have nothing into owners, and wage earners into owners, and this contradicts Marxist teaching." Galal Keshk, pointing out that "our socialism is that of an underdeveloped country," submitted that its purpose was "the increase of production."[21] In short, things were not far from "the Japanese road to development," which Baran had studied, and whose purpose was "the creation of a modern capitalist state,"[22] with the differences in internal and international context which we have pointed out and which brought about the emergence of intermediate economic and social forms.

The Sources of Egyptian Socialism

The problem of the ancestry of Egyptian socialism also had to be faced. Here again were the two component factors of ideological evolution: modernized Islam and na-tionalitarian technocracy.

But there was one other factor that must be underlined: the decisive influence of Nehru in this quest for a "national ideology" of socialist tendency which culminated in "co-op-erativist democratic socialism."

It was in 1958, in fact, that the two basic works in the area of the Indian Congress party's political ideology were published: "Congress Ideology and Program," by the philosopher Sampurnanand, and Nehru's "The Basic Approach."[23] Both articles, in particular Nehru's, recognized the value of the Communist experience, whose methods and revolutionary violence they rejected. "It is often said," Nehru wrote, "that there is a feeling of depression and frustration in India and that the spiritual strength of earlier times exists no longer at this time when we most need enthusiasm and serious effort . . . One of my former and honored colleagues [Dr. Sampurnanand] has said that this is because we do not have a philosophy of life . . . In our effort to assure the country's material prosperity we have not attached sufficient importance to the spiritual element in human nature. That is why, in order to provide the individual and the nation with the feeling of a goal to be attained, of something worth living for and, if necessary, dying for, we must have a rebirth of a philosophy of life and provide a background for our thinking in the broadest sense of the term."

What would the welfare state, democracy and socialism be like? "The law of life should be neither competition nor the acquisition of goods, but co-operation, the good of each contributing to the good of all. In this society, duties not rights will be emphasized; rights will follow the accomplishment of duties." The search for a better life does not in itself constitute a distinctive mark of the society's socialist character, for "every country, whether it be capitalist, socialist or Communist, in a certain sense accepts the ideal of the welfare state . . ."; generally speaking, "if the forces of a capitalist society are left to themselves, they tend to make the rich still richer and the poor poorer"; therefore they should be managed. "Planning is essential, for without it, we shall dissipate our resources, which are very limited . . . It is possible that India should encourage private enterprise in many sectors today, although this private enterprise should be set in the framework of national planning and be bound by necessary controls." Nehru emphasizes the essential purpose of agrarian reform, which is "to smash the stagnant society's old class structure." Finally, "although Marxist political economy is obsolete on many points, it throws light on the economic process."

These were the key ideas of Nasser's Arab socialism, and

all of the Indian Prime Minister's statement could be compared with the official doctrines advocated by the major Egyptian ideologists and officials, without revealing any new contribution from those sources.

Let us now look at the factors peculiar to Egypt.

For Islam, which, as Sheik Hassan el-Bakuri so well said,[24] "does not allow every individual to take part in setting the course of power," the problem was both to show that "co-operativist democratic socialism" was an outgrowth of Islam and to be prepared for the violent criticisms that came from certain Arab courts, contending that the military rulers were acting in violation of the spirit of the Koran.[25] The method was the same as Mohammed Abdu's: the return to the sources. The Islam of Mohammed and the early Caliphs contained the germ of socialist principles before the term was invented, particularly in Abu Bakr and Omar, the first two Caliphs of Islam. This was the theme of the Friday sermons in the mosques, of the statements by the Sheik of Al Azhar and the Grand Mufti,* of the proliferating works on the union between Islam and Arab socialism.[26]

It is impossible to apply the traditional patterns of medieval Orientalism and Islamology to twentieth-century Egyptian Islam. Maxime Rodinson has demonstrated this clearly: in the first centuries after the Hegira,† "Islam was as totalitarian as it was possible to be. In effect and in principle, it governed every act and every thought of its leaders . . . Now, Islam is in the process of losing this totalitarian aspect . . . The proof of this is the emergence of the problem of compatibility"; actually, "there is an implicit ideology of the current Moslem world"; "it is most important to emphasize that before the Moslem society had to take a stand regarding Communism, it had been . . . influenced by the scientific rationalism or liberal-humanitarian utopianism [that] had prepared the way for the 'reception' of Communism." Often "there have been reinterpre-

---

* The chief legal authority for Muslims.
† After fifteen years of meditation Mohammed had to escape from Mecca in 622, in face of the bitter opposition from its wealthy people, and went to Medina. This year marks the beginning of the Hegira, the Moslem calendar.

tations of Moslem concepts, ideas and symbols, by Moslems, as the equivalents of current Communist ideas or themes. The same operation is often performed by Communists who are driving toward an alliance . . ."[27]

This is an excellent appraisal of the compromise between Islam and Communism on the one side, and nationalist and pre-socialist reformism on the other, which has been customary in Egypt since 1945. It will be noted that Kamal Rifaat, who was virtually responsible for the ideological development within the governing circle, particularly in matters of Arab socialism, was entrusted with the responsibility of reforming Al Azhar at the same time that he was made Minister of Labor. Hassan Abbas Zaki, former Minister of the Treasury, tried to effectuate the theoretical conciliation between Islam and Arab socialism.[28] Examples on the political-leadership level could be listed in considerable number.

In any event, it was the nationalitarian technocrats who were to dictate the choice of sources.[29] The number of works in the social sciences (particularly politics, economics, sociology and history) rose substantially from 1960 on, in proportion to the ideological needs. In the field of social ideology, work progressed in two directions: one was inspired by American sociology, the other by liberalism and European social democracy.

"Quantitatively, the sociological research currently under way in the Middle East is dominated by Americans and Arabs trained in the American educational system or, to a lesser degree, in the English and French," Professor Lionel Armstrong of the American University in Beirut wrote in 1958. Among the Egyptian sociologists he listed Abbas Ammar and Hassan el-Saati, and he ridiculed the Sorbonne graduates. Out of a total of 1,115 sociological books and articles published in the Middle East between 1947 and 1957, only 375 meet serious scientific criteria. Armstrong was amazed at the proportions in the various sectors: 63.8 percent on ecology and demography, 54 percent on social psychology; then, after a very broad central group, only 7.5 percent on social problems and 3.8 percent on the refugee problems; this he finds "disappointing," because the Arabs refused to accept an accomplished fact . . .[30]

The United States had extraordinary resources at its disposal; in fact, the American University in Cairo was the only foreign institution of higher education allowed to function in Egypt after Suez, provided that an Egyptian co-president be appointed; in addition, the Franklin publishing and translation organization literally flooded the Egyptian and Arab market with handsomely produced reference books that assured the American authors of primacy in university reading and among the new intelligentsia lacking familiarity with traditional European culture and Marxism. From George Sarton to Pearl Buck, by way of Dale Carnegie, the theoreticians of the cold war and the American way of life, and from metaphysics to beauty care, there was a place and a public for everything. It is obvious what kind of socialism could be offered to Egyptian thinking by these groups, which, furthermore, reached a relatively broad and dynamic public.

Undoubtedly it was in order to mitigate the deficiency in socialist sources that the young theoreticians, particularly those around Kamal Rifaat, co-ordinated the government publishing company's output in the field of socialism. The list contained Harold Laski and Jules Moch, Bernard Shaw, André Philip, Hugh Gaitskell, Aneurin Bevan, Kardelj and Douglas Jay, along with many liberal representatives of English, French and German culture—K. Berger, John St. Loe Strachey, P. Ramadier, Adalbert Falk, I. Berlin, H. Clegh, W. Friedmann, M. Duverger . . . ;[31] Marx, Engels, Lenin, Gramsci, Mao Tsetung and the Marxist theorists and leaders were almost totally absent from the list of socialist authors; only Lenin's *Imperialism, the Higher Stage of Capitalism,* was reissued by its translator, Rashed el-Barawi.

There was much emphasis on the necessity for studying the experiments under way that called themselves socialist, notably Cuba (before Castro's conversion to Marxism-Leninism), Guinea, Mali, even India, and above all Yugoslavia. The countries of the socialist bloc were ignored, even China, Vietnam or Korea, though all were Asian states. Twelve university professors were appointed to develop syllabi for three new courses—Socialism, the July 23 Revolution and Arab Nationalism—to be compulsory in all faculties: no socialist professor, let alone Marxist, was mentioned, while there were several people known for their rightist opinions or their total lack of experience in problems of this kind.[32]

One qualified expert, Abdel Moghni Said, explained that "our Arab socialism does not consider collective ownership an objective, as European socialism does, but merely a means that it employs, to the extent that is desirable, in order to satisfy the interests of society."[33] In contrast to Fidel Castro, the Egyptian authorities refused to believe that "one of the most difficult tasks is to build socialism without socialists."

What the search for a national "socialist" ideology actually reveals is above all the need to provide an adequate answer to the complexity and urgency of the problems created by the precipitate development of Egyptian vitality.

It is interesting, in this connection, to consider the results of a recent sociological study dealing with the slogans of candidates in the 1957 elections, which was the period when positive neutralism and Arab nationalism emerged. Of 296 slogans used by candidates, 46.9 percent dealt with questions of domestic policy, 32.9 percent mentioned the candidate's personal and professional qualifications, and only 20.2 percent touched on foreign policy. These proportions were respectively 48.6, 29.2 and 22.2 percent among the seventy-two candidates who were actually elected to the Council of the Nation. Among the slogans on domestic matters the investigator distinguished between two categories: those dealing with general domestic policy and those bearing on economic and social questions; the first category comprised 79 slogans of candidates and 12 of elected deputies, while the second included 60 candidates' and 23 victors' slogans.

What this means is that within the main group of candidates concerned with domestic policy, it was those interested in economic and social questions—social justice, improvement of workers' conditions, increase in national income, notably—who were in fact elected by the people.[34] The story could not be told better.

At the heart of everything, then, there was the urgent need for "a vast economic and social transformation that would strengthen society and give it the capacity to carry the burden of the modern state—a necessary, if not adequate, condition for the establishment of a genuine democracy in the Middle East," as Charles P. Issawi rightly said.[35]

The modern state came into being in Egypt with the victory of the national-liberation movement, with the emergence and reinforcement of the socialist countries on a global scale. Therefore it would be built in the name of anti-imperialist nationalitarianism and—why not?—under the socialist label that attracted the popular masses and lent its authoritative aura to the growing intervention of the state in economic and social life.

There was no place for Communism here. Even worse, it threatened to overrun the work under way, to compromise the positions of the forces in power for the benefit of a future in which something quite different from mere "management" would be at issue. In 1956, in the midst of the Bandung period, Nasser told G. Sparrow: "Communism is dangerous only in the event that it is in a position to exploit mass nationalist opinion. There are almost five thousand Communists in Egypt, but we have stripped them of leadership in the nationalist movement." And in 1962 he gave the same reply to a question by Edouard Sablier: "It is class conflict that opens the door to Communism. In the UAR we have based our society on social justice, having nationalized banking and insurance and ninety percent of industry, limited landownership, distributed land to the peasants, and given the workers interest in industry. We intend to eliminate exploitation of one class by another. That is why Egypt is in no danger of Communism."[36]

So it was indeed a case, as Shafei liked to say in 1956–57, of "burning the slogans of popular democracy under our feet . . ." There was much talk of the "Arab road" to socialism. Some were uneasy, like Kamel Zeheiry, who wondered whether, since "the roads that lead to socialism differ, it may be legitimate to believe that socialism too can have different forms," to which he replied in the negative;[37] but in the spring of 1962 there were other avenues and other hopes.

Such, in short, was the situation on the ideological front on the eve of publication of the Charter of National Action.

TWO BOOKS

"What Is an Egyptian?"

From 1954 to 1959, while debate was raging and the new face of Egypt was becoming visible, a man was poring over seven thousand years of history.

"Let us be honest with ourselves and ask ourselves this question: At what point in my reading of Egyptian history have I felt that I was living among my own people, the sons of my fatherland of centuries gone by? For me, this happened when I began the history of the Mamelukes . . . The sentiments that I am voicing are my own, those of a Moslem of Cairo whose family has lived in Cairo since at least the seventeenth century, who was born in the Cairo quarter of Mo'ezz . . . The life that vibrates through the pages of [historians] Sheik Takieddine, of Abul Mahassen, of Siyuti and Ibn Iyas is indeed my life . . ."

Hussein Fawzi—physician, holder of the chair of oceanography at the science faculty of Alexandria University, later dean of that faculty and rector of the university, then Undersecretary of State in the Ministry of Culture during the Bandung period; author of several volumes of essays and journeys through history, and a musicologist—is one of the most authentic representatives of modernity—at the same time Egyptian, Mediterranean and rationalist—in the Egypt of our generation. This "Moslem of Cairo" presents us with "the epic of the Egyptian people"—himself profoundly Egyptian and, as such, aware of the centralism of millennia

("Cairo") and the depth of religious feeling ("Moslem"). His book, which was published in 1961, bore the exotic title *An Egyptian Sindbad.* In it he offered a conception of Egyptian culture at a time when minds were being recruited for the spiritual adventures that we have discussed. An outstanding work of historical learning, a work of art fashioned in an iridescent style, an act of faith, *Sindbad Misri* was greeted with enthusiasm by the cultivated élites and the mass public alike. And if use of the superlative had not gone out of fashion, we would say—properly—that this is the finest book to come out of contemporary Egypt.

Rather than a systematic history of the Egyptian character— although the author had devoted some thirty years to the personal investigation of an enormous bibliography—it is a study in depth of several typical episodes and problems. One, for instance, is "Holy Friday," *al-gomʿa al-ʾhazina,* the allegorical designation, in the Coptic era, of the sorrowful day in 1517 when Selim, Sultan of Turkey, invaded Egypt, put an end to a thousand years of autonomy by killing Tuman Bey, the leader of the Mamelukes, and systematically sacked the wealth, the arts and crafts, and the culture of medieval Egypt; these were indeed "the three or four blackest centuries in Egypt's long history, following the battles of Marg Dabek in Syria and Sabeil ʿEllan at the gates of Cairo."

Though the men of Cairo had not resisted Alexander, Julius Caesar and Augustus, the Arab commander Amr ibn-al-As, Genghis Khan's grandson Hulagu, the Crusaders, the Mohammedan Fatimites or the Ottomans, in 1777 they began to protest against the exactions of the Mamelukes, and later they rose to bar the way of Bonaparte's Christian forces; the movement continued, though it lacked bite. The whole of the nineteenth century, aside from Arabi's revolt, on which the author has virtually nothing to say, was a preparation for the modern period: "The dawn of Egyptian nationalism was to appear in 1919; the action of the Egyptian people in March of that year and the months that followed warrants the attention of historians, for it shows all the characteristics of mature nationalism, with no trace of religion or cult, never turning to the Caliphate of the Sublime Porte or to the occupant. Although it was a movement of liberation from alien dependency, this revolution carefully considered the foundations of Western culture, and rejected none. All were Egyptians first; they fought against the despoiler and demanded political independence, and economic and intellectual emancipation for their country. In other words, they attacked reaction in all its forms."

It was an exemplary national revolution, virtually as barren of pan-Islamic nationalism or pre-Wafdist opportunism as it was of the Arab nationalism of the next generation.

"I shall call the burning of Cairo the suicidal act of the Egyptian people, which had been conquered in its heart and whose faith in its representatives had been shattered"; it was the prelude to the army's action: "Who would have thought that the Egyptian people, which had launched its national movements with bludgeons . . . and the reading of Bukhari,* would entrust its liberation in the final analysis to its own sons bearing arms?"

The Mamelukes, the lords of Egypt before the Turks, had won back their lost ground little by little; we see them looting and killing again. But Hussein Fawzi also wishes to record their patronage of culture, the flowering of arts and crafts, the medical research. Ibn Iyas and Abdel Rahman el-Gabarti† provide the background for the analysis. Very well. "Whatever page of history is opened," says Fawzi, "science, study, books, rectitude, *fetwas*,‡ public readings are the companions of the Egyptians; war, brutality, betrayal, murder, attack, beheading, torture are always the work of the Mamelukes and the Ottomans." Captain Thurman, aide-de-camp to Bonaparte, reported what he saw, and his testimony accords well with the view of coeval chroniclers.

* Mohammed ibn-Ismail al-Bukhari (810–870) traveled throughout the Moslem world collecting traditions ('*hadiths*); out of 600,000 he selected 7,275 which he issued as *Sahih* ("sincere book"), a collection affording the basis of Mohammedan law and which is next to the Koran in canonical importance and in influence on the Moslem mind.

† The first modern Egyptian historian (1756–1825); wrote a remarkable social history of the country under Bonaparte and Mohammed Ali.

‡ A decision by a religious authority of national standing that used to have legal force, during the Moslem period.

Yet, from Mohammed Ali to Lord Cromer, Western civilization appears only in its material aspect: "In the areas of the mind and thought, Egypt made hardly any progress in comparison with the upheavals that European civilization brought to the state." Because we did not know that "the adoption of one element of a foreign civilization must entail its other elements as well if that civilization is to flourish," we found ourselves in a situation in which "the ways to spiritual reform had been lost, as well as the genuine bases for renascence . . . We have found ourselves incapable of progressing in a natural fashion by deriving a complete profit from that civilization, while the reactionaries have demonstrated their inability to do without the tools and material appurtenances of that civilization . . . The growing generation vacillated between an inveterate tradition of obsolete tendencies and practices on the one hand, and a science, and art and a civilization essential to its material and spiritual progress on the other."

There were three great periods in Egyptian history: the Pharaonic, the Coptic (Christian) and the Islamic. Now, there is a chasm in our national consciousness: this results both from the stretch of Egyptian history, the longest in the world, and from the diversity of the methods and languages required for its study.

Viewed historically, the Egyptians are of two kinds: "the Moslems, whose civilization goes back to the Arab invasion [A.D. 640], and the non-Moslems, who began theirs with the Apostle Mark, later rejoining their Moslem fellow citizens within their Arab culture." From the Persian invasion (525 B.C.) to the end of Byzantine era (A.D. 1453) we observe "the suppression of Egyptian nationhood." That is why Hussein Fawzi, "a Moslem of Cairo," reconstructs so forcefully the Coptic period, its Monophysism, "the expression of the spirit of national resistance, the same spirit which was responsible for the translation of the Gospels into the Coptic tongue, the ancient Egyptian language transliterated into Greek characters, and which has made them [the Copts] cling to the language of their fathers and forefathers a thousand years after Alexander's invasion and a thousand years after the Arab conquest"; he pays tribute to the great resistance figures, notably Pope Athanasius, Sawiris of Antioch, Pope Cyril I; the founders of the monastic system—Bulos, Antonios, Ammonius, Makarios, followed by Shenuda and Bakhum; the Coptic popular risings under San, Khrepta, Basta, Sanhur, Akhmim, and many others.

Next, three women, three queens—Shagaret el-Dorr, Cleopatra and the greatest of all, Hatshepsut; then a long and detailed exploration of the civilization of the Pharaohs; the Coptic historians' view of past eras; the destruction of monuments; the epic of Champollion's discovery of the Rosetta Stone; the birth of the Egyptian school of Egyptology; the unusual duration of the neolithic period, which lasted, concurrently with the copper age, until the advent of iron under the Lagides; the Egyptian sources of the Christian Trinity; the dearth of sources in the field of Pharaonic Egyptian literature. The whole book should really be cited . . .

A Single Industry: Civilization

It is the theoretical conclusions that demand our attention. In summary, they are as follows:

(1) "Seventy centuries of history (fifty by the most conservative estimates): 3,500 years of complete independence, 2,500 under the government of Egyptian dynasties and 1,000 under the rod of the foreigner."[1]

(2) This is indeed "the oldest and strongest unity that has ever been achieved by any nation on earth." This unity, "governed by the Nile and its silt, and animated by the dazzling sun," compelled the "civilized people—that people tilling the soil—to regulate its life by the rise and fall of the Nile, its calendar by the movement of the sun and the changing seasons, and to unite in order to derive the greatest possible benefit from the silt of the Nile and the sun of Egypt, to withstand the flooding and the perils of drought and disease when the river fell." Going back to the tale of the old Mary and Caliph Mamun, he drew from it the same conclusion as Wittfögel: "The beneficent power is the power that arms the Egyptians against the rise and fall of the Nile's

level. . . ." The master of the country is also the master of the waters and the representative of the gods.

(3) How is the Egyptian character to be defined? "Egyptian civilization in its successive forms reflects a people which is congenial and congruent in its origin, its source and its soul, a people which, though not large, foreshadows its strength by the creations of its splendid organizational genius, its forceful and tenacious art, its intellectual order, its belief in survival and its ideals of justice."

The first dimension of this unity of character lies in "the peasant's affinity . . . with the land, with irrigation, with culture," and in "his view of the *omdeh* and the sheik *el-balad* as the wielders of power." The second dimension, which is the product of political history, lies in "unity through suffering, born of exploitation." The third consists in "the Egyptians' preservation of their traditions of society and government and, what is more important, their beliefs . . . Art could not have survived through three thousand years if the Egyptian's eyes had not always turned toward his past." The fourth: "Egyptian spirituality has virtually no resemblance to Hindu spirituality, sealed off and lost in a maze of philosophical secrets; it is, rather, that of the man who strives to force the gate of the unknown or to explain it by means of physical representations." The fifth: the Egyptian's omnipresent allusive humor and the persistence of hope in the midst of anguish: *"Yeftah Allah"* (May God show you the way), to say that a price asked is too high: *"Salli 'ala l-Nabi"* (Pray invoking the Prophet's name), to propose that the bargaining begin; *"Alayya'l-Talak"* (May I be divorced), or: "Don't believe a word of it"; *"Ya Fattah, ya Alim"* (O you who have skill, you who know), meaning that "every word you say is a lie, God save us from your dirty work"; *"B'Ism'Illah"* (In God's name), which is an offer to divide one's own crust of bread, barely enough for one; *"Heleft 'aleik"* (I swear it on you), or: "You know exactly what I mean, sly one"; *"Etwakkel 'ala'Allah"* (rest with God), or: "Get out, out of my sight"; *"Dostur eh, ya'amm? Allah yekhallik"* (What, a constitution? Uncle, may God preserve you), or: "All right, let's stop the nonsense."

"I wanted this book to be the epic of the Egyptian people; but note how more than once it has been transformed into a long rhapsody on the duress that this people has endured through the ages. And here am I, who have vaunted this people's strength in resistance, in struggle and survival, who have cited the services it has rendered to civilization— here am I, turning for support to its sorrows and its defeats. Perhaps this has to do with one of the component meanings of the Egyptian soul, perhaps it is thus that I have expressed that melancholy soul, the soul of the Egyptian who laughs with his whole body and then suddenly exclaims: '*Allahumma ig'alhu kheir!*' (God, let it be for the best) . . . The most profound word that I have heard people say in the old quarters of Cairo is *al-farag* (Let the relief come!) . . ."

(4) Facing and fighting misery and hardship, the people of Egypt has "always flocked to its one industry—the shaping of civilization"—not only "that civilization which it has bequeathed to the world" but also "the civilization which it has imposed on its rulers." Otherwise, "let me inquire what explanation there is for that permanent characteristic of Egyptian history: the construction of *mastabas* (shrines), pyramids . . . , statues and tombs, churches and monasteries, schools, mosques, palaces, sanctuaries, the digging of canals and building of dams, the joining of the two seas, either through the Nile or directly between El Kolzom and El Ferma. And who made the famous vestments . . . ? Who decorated the mosques and their *minbars* (towers), the churches and their altars? Who painted popular images on wood to be placed later in the tombs at Faiyum and Bahnassa? Who conducted the school for the clergy at Heliopolis and established the Didascalia opposite the pagan school in Alexandria? Who founded Al-Azhar University?"

The people of Egypt, whose vocation and sole industry are civilization.

(5) In this industry of civilization a leading place, if not the first, is held by art—three thousand years of Egyptian art, and also the survival of common characteristics after the Arab conquest: "Neither great literature nor outstanding philosophy but rather—as in the past—mastery of the arts of

building and decoration, of the famous industries connected with them, the emergence of scholars and physicians, the effort given to religious studies and Arab studies as the sole means of understanding the religion."

(6) These factors of permanence entailed a fixation on the past that weighed heavily on future growth: "A cessation of growth in individuality and its sclerosis at the level of certain formulations that were barely altered throughout the thirty centuries of this civilization's life, and inadequacy in the realm of the pure thought and intellectual adventure which distinguished Greek and Indian civilization, since such changes as had occurred had not gone beyond the limits established by the beliefs rooted in Egyptian minds." The great spiritual adventure, however, was that of "man in quest of his creator, seeking to define his relationships to what is beyond the universe and nature, beyond life in this world." And it must be acknowledged that "the Pharaohs invented the principle of the divine right of kings and the principle of social co-operation."

(7) At the conclusion of this exploration it appears that Egypt, in spite of the deep break in her history, has remained unchanged in herself, in depth. But it is within the framework of the Arabic language and the mold of Islamic Arab culture that Egyptians view their present and past. Egypt—the center of the Arab and Islamic world by virtue of her ancestral historic being, her tradition of civilization, her old continous unity and her resources—is duty-bound to "effect a revival of this civilization in men's souls . . . , for it is the duty of a living people always to live in affective relation to its history." Students must learn about the most important dynasties of the three Kingdoms, and then about Coptic Egypt; after the Arab conquest there would be a detailed study of Moslem Egypt and her relations with the world of which she is the center. In every instance the writings and the works of art of Egypt must be given due prominence.

"The Arabic language is the pillar of our whole cultural structure . . . It could never be our excuse for not bringing back to life in our souls the history of our past civilization in an eloquent Arabic form. In fact, the Egyptian should mold his heart and mind by means of everything that is inspired in him by his whole cultural history. He should consider his whole civilization in its Arabic language as its framework. He should reinforce his mental and moral structure with everything that is Egyptian so that he may have a pure Egyptian character that will function in letters, in the arts and in the sciences."

There was certainly a popular heritage, but the prime Ariadne's thread was still "the history of civilization in its totality"; this alone would make it possible for the Egyptian to "arrive at the foundation and depth of his character so that he may be able to contribute something new to mankind . . ." Finally, there were some observations on method: "Revolutions and risings should not be the basis . . . , since Egyptians were the first to develop passive resistance"; in order to follow the winding course of the Egyptian character, study should be directed toward "the periods of governors dispatched here by the capitals of foreign empires," and then, "instead of Egypt's dissolution into her invaders, their dissolution into her"; no "miracles" in the field of civilization (the "Greek miracle"), but, rather, emphasis on a consecutive history of civilizations in which Egypt regains her chronological primacy and her essential place.

"Where can we find the Egyptian character that has been lost? Long centuries of occupation have dug an almost unbridgeable gulf between our minds and our emotions," a journalist wrote in 1954.[2]

Among the numerous functionaries who dedicated themselves to fabricating out of nothing a collection of ideas, precepts and aims, in all this confusion there stands this one pre-eminent work in which knowledge and the heart speak for Egypt.

The Thief and the Dogs

The odyssey of Said Mahran was very different. From his native village, dominated by the pyramid of the feudal pashas, the injustice of all the bureaucracies, the presence of the occupant, he remembered his friend Rauf Elwan, for Rauf went to school. And Rauf said to him, "Said, what does a young man need in our country?" Before Said could reply, Rauf did so: "A revolver and a book. A revolver to take care of the past and a book to build the future. Teach yourself and read! . . ."³ How many thousands and millions of adolescents spoke like that in febrile postwar Egypt?

So Said learned to read. Then he became a porter in the university dormitory in Cairo; he stole from rich men's sons, and Rauf, who was studying law, approved. For Said could not forget the day when his mother, who had just had a hemorrhage, went vainly knocking at the door of the luxurious hospital and crawled off to die in a wretched clinic. So Said was going to take it upon himself to hunt down injustice, to attack the rich, all alone. Gradually his reputation for banditry attracted a whole troop of young adventurers. Then, life being what it is, Said met Nabaweyya, as beautiful as the rising sun. After their marriage little Sana was born. Sentenced to prison, Said died a thousand deaths there. For in the meantime his wife divorced him in order to marry Eleish Sidra, one of his gang—the man, in fact, who had turned him in to the police.

Four years went by, and then one day Said returned to life. His daughter refused to have anything to do with him, Nabaweyya was not to be found, and his betrayer, surrounded by wealth and sycophants, protected by the police, defied him. Rauf himself, his old friend, had become a noted journalist gorged with riches, a traitor to himself and to their past.

So Said resumed his war, for "if life was to become pure again, criminal vices must be rooted out at the source." He tried to kill Eleish, but in the dark his shot killed an unfortunate workingman. Pursued by the police, he again killed the wrong man: it was Rauf's driver who fell to his bullets, while the master escaped death.

The police laid siege to the Abbassia quarter, where Said operated. Deserted by everyone, he had only one person who helped and protected him—Nur, a prostitute who had always loved him; one night he was sheltered by an old sheik absorbed in his own magic. With Nur the young bandit, whose childlike, loving heart had been so cruelly abused, found tenderness. But it was too late. Too many clues led the police to that lonely apartment to which he had fled, from which he could look out on the large cemeteries in the moonlight. And it was among the gravestones that Said perished under the volleys that crackled through the night.

One night, two days before his death, Said could no longer endure his solitude and took advantage of the dark to go in search of his friends in the coffee house. These hardened men were talking of peace, peace of mind:

> "The real trouble is that our enemy is also and at the same time our friend."
> "You mean our friend is our enemy . . ."
> "You should say we're cowards; why not admit it?"
> "Maybe. But how could we be brave in times like these?"
> "Bravery is bravery."
> "And death is also death."
> "Darkness and desert are both, at the same time!"

Thus ran the latest novel by Naguib Mahfuz, the outstanding Egyptian novelist today, the peer of the best. *The Thief and the Dogs* aroused amazement when it appeared in the spring of 1962. Why this penchant for gloom? Why this unprecedented subject in the master's work? What was the origin of the despair of this hero whom he depicted so movingly—the triumph of injustice, the irrationality, and this dog's world where hope wore a prostitute's face? The critics were embarrassed, though they hailed this book—of which I have given a bare skeletal outline—as a turning point in the work of Mahfuz, whose mastery no one challenged.[4]

Two books.

Why these two?

The first, the product of a labor of research and theoretical thought in depth, offers us the keys to Egyptian specificity. The other, a short novel, is as brutal as truth.

Each enjoyed a great success and created a great deal of discussion. And in spite of the difference in character and level, each is significant.

This is because the most important theoretical work of contemporary Egypt established the Egyptianity of Egypt in history and rigorous scholarship right at the time when a desire for Arabism was asserting itself. It re-established the proper dimension of Egypt's entrance into the Arab world and it laid the groundwork for the enrollment of the Egyptian desire to obtain truth and justice.

The work of fiction, on the other hand, slashed through the euphoria of the newspapers and their daily proclamations of victory in red-ink headlines. It portrayed the condition of man, who was still downtrodden. It rejected tranquillity and apathy, and through the story of a robber, it reiterated faith in the spirit of the people alone, and its contempt for the careerist "dogs" of the suffocating government apparatus.

Egypt's outstanding theoretical book today is Egyptian, not Arab.

The most successful novel by Egypt's best contemporary novelist concludes in crisis and drama, not with a happy ending.

And such is the road of Egypt's soul, in its depths.

CHAPTER 10

THE CHARTER OF
NATIONAL ACTION
AND ITS SEQUELS

THE CHARTER OF NATIONAL ACTION, proposed by President Nasser to the 1,750 members of the National Congress of Popular Forces on Monday, May 21, 1962 (which was the first day of work for this assembly), represented in all its aspects a doctrinal document, a program of major importance. The practical experience, whose stages we have analyzed, and the theoretical studies of this whole first decade came to maturity in it. This document marked a turning point; it presented the balance sheet of work done and efforts made, and laid down the "national action" to be followed by the nation as a whole.

Of its ten sections, only the last two dealt with "Arab unity" and "foreign policy"—the eight others were entirely devoted to domestic affairs and their problems, thus confirming the priority of the economic, social, ideological and political aspects inherent in today's Egyptian society.*

Tribute to the Egyptian People

In the first section, dedicated to an "overall view," Nasser paid tribute to the "Egyptian people." "This heroic

* Translation from the original Arabic text is the author's. There is no official English-language version.

people," he said, "began its Revolutionary march without having any political organization capable of meeting the problems of the battle, for the march itself was undertaken without a prior complete theory of revolutionary change." In 1952 the movement's leadership had simply six principles: "the destruction of imperialism and its traitorous Egyptian lackeys; the destruction of feudalism; the destruction of monopoly and of the domination of capital over government; the inauguration of social justice; the creation of a strong national army; and the construction of a sound democratic system."

It was by no means the military leadership but "this great people, this great master," that had schooled the Revolutionary leadership by "inspiring the elaboration of the six principles, endowing their movement with experience and practical application, by living interaction with the nation's history . . . in the direction of a detailed program that opened the Revolution's way to its limitless objectives," and then, in a second step, "by inspiring its Revolutionary vanguards with the secrets of its great hopes, by constantly reminding them of these hopes, by broadening their scope through the daily introduction of new elements capable of taking part in the development of its future."

It was not the illusory theory of "the union of all classes" on which the Egyptian people had based its revolutionary struggle against imperialism; on the contrary, it had "ousted from its ranks all those whose interests were linked to those of imperialism in order to prolong exploitation . . . ; it had struck at the local monopolies at the very moment when they might have thought that the people felt an urgent and important need for them simply by reason of the demands of development." The speaker was to come back to this point; but it might be helpful to point out this first confirmation of a change in attitude toward the capitalist ally before the summer of 1961.

Now the road had been cleared for a general revolution which would no longer be limited to the liberation of the national territory alone. The success scored thus far was the result of a combination of factors:

"(1) A will for revolutionary change that rejects any bond or limitation other than the rights and demands of the masses;

"(2) A revolutionary vanguard that the will for revolutionary change enabled to take over the power of the state in order to make it the servant of the interests of those having natural and legitimate rights, the interests of the masses, and no longer the servant of the former interests;

"(3) A profound consciousness of history and its influence on contemporary man on the one hand, and on the other, of the power man has to influence history;

"(4) A mind open to all human experience, drawing inspiration from it and contributing to it, a mind that should not allow itself to be diverted from such experience either by fanaticism or by [other political] groups;

"(5) An unshakable faith in God, in his prophets and in his chosen saints, whom he has sent as guides and bearers of truth to men at all times and in all places."

The Necessary Revolution

"On the Necessity for the Revolution"—this was the title of the second section. "Experience has proved, and continues to prove every day, that revolution is the sole avenue that will enable the Arab struggle to move from the past to the future."

Why? Because "the backwardness of the Arab Nation, the natural consequence of its subjugation and exploitation," was especially serious; because this was the only means of "standing up to the challenge" hurled by the advanced countries at the underdeveloped countries, since the gulf between the two groups could only increase.

In order to attain its three objectives—which were "freedom, socialism and unity," in that order—the Arab Nation should arm itself with three "faculties":

"(1) The consciousness that is created by scientific knowledge, the result of enlightened thought and free discussion which rebels against the whips of fanaticism and terror;

"(2) The quick and open removal of every barrier that the vicissitudes of the Arab struggle might entail, though such removal should respect the objectives and ideals of the struggle;

"(3) Clear perception of the objectives, continuous pursuit of them, and determined refusal to take secondary roads which would cause the national struggle to abandon its course and which would dissipate a large part of its resources."

President Nasser declared with vehemence what he was constantly to repeat throughout the Charter: that "it would be impossible for the Arab revolutionary experiment to copy the results at which others have arrived." But he quickly based this need for individuality on the common factors arising out of the changes in the world after 1945, of which he offered this account:

"(1) The increased power of the liberation movements in Asia, Africa and Latin America which has reached such a point that these movements have succeeded in waging many victorious battles against the imperialist forces . . . ;

"(2) The emergence of the Communist camp as a powerful force whose material and moral weight is growing from day to day in confrontation with the capitalist camp;

"(3) The tremendous scientific progress which, by causing a forward leap in productive forces, has opened unlimited horizons to the work of development . . . ;

"(4) The influence of all these factors in the sphere of international relations, particularly the strengthening of the influence of moral forces in the world, such as the UN, the uncommitted states and world public opinion. At the same time, imperialism has been compelled by the pressure of these circumstances to turn toward forms of indirect action through the invasion and subjugation of peoples from within, monopolist economic blocs and the cold war, which, among other things, seeks to make the small nations doubt their own capacities for self-development and for making adequate, positive contributions in the service of human society."

The combination of these factors "creates new circumstances for socialist experiments, circumstances that are totally different from those of the past." Similarly, "the experiences of German[1] and Italian unity" could not serve as models for Arab unity; to this, as well as to socialism, Gamal Abdel Nasser would return later in detail.

History Acknowledged at Last

The third section dealt with the "roots of the Egyptian struggle." This section very clearly repeats the thinking of *Sindbad Misri*, which at a certain point would be called on to make up for the Syrian defection: "Pharaonic history, the creator of Egyptian civilization and early mankind"; "the night of the Ottoman invasion"; popular resistance to the French expedition, which, however, enriched Egyptian thinking and imagination through its scholars and the reintroduction of the sciences; Mohammed Ali, who, in spite of his greatness, "had no faith in the popular movement that had paved the way for his accession to power in Egypt, but who regarded it only as a launching platform for his ambitions"; but Nasser said not a word of Coptic Egypt, whereas he gave full credit to the Greek-Roman period before going on to Islamic Egypt. Here and there certain ideas of Sobhi Wahida's emerged, notably on the "complexes" of growth.

It was Egypt's ill fortune that her period of decadence under the Turks coincided with the rise of imperialism, whose two chief undertakings were the Suez Canal and the transformation of Egypt into a cotton plantation. At the peak of the crisis and in spite of the national disaster, the dispatch of Egyptian scholarship students to Europe was to have fruitful repercussions. Soon Egypt became a haven for Arab liberals; a cultural impetus followed, serving as the background to Ahmed Arabi's revolt. Nasser paid tribute to Mustafa Kamel, Mohammed Abdu and Kassem Amine, and then—something new—to Saad Zaghlul, who "rode the new revolutionary wave," in 1919. For the first time he said, verbatim: "The revolution of the Egyptian people in 1919 warrants long study." He himself advanced three reasons to account for its failure:

"(1) The fact that the revolutionary leaderships were almost wholly ignorant of the exigencies of social change . . . , since the very nature of the historical phase then existing had made the class of rich landed proprietors the basis of the political parties that had assumed the leadership of the revolution . . . ,

"(2) The fact that the revolutionary leaders of those days had not been able to look farther than Sinai, that they had demonstrated their inability to define the Egyptian character or to learn from history that there was no contradiction between Egyptian patriotism and Arab nationalism . . . ;

"(3) The fact that the revolutionary leaders had not succeeded in carrying out the struggle with means comparable to the procedures of imperialism . . . , which had abandoned the saber for treachery, offering minor concessions that the revolutionary leaders quickly confused with the essential issues, the very logic of their class position making this all the easier for them . . ."

Some historians declare that "the Egyptian people differs from all other peoples in the world in that it never revolts except in times of prosperity." This is a fallacious notion which confuses the enrichment of a minority with the misery of the masses. The Anglo-Egyptian treaty of 1936 was to mark the climactic point of all the weaknesses.

On the Defeat of the Middle Class

On the basis of this analysis, Nasser then reviewed "the period of the great crisis"—from 1919 to 1952—in order to bring out "the lesson of the defeat," the subject of the fourth section.

This focused on a central thesis: the falsification of democracy—"confusionist democracy"—by the government, then in the hands of the king and the big landowners, in alliance and thorough agreement with imperialism. "Whoever monopolized the resources of the peasants and workers and dominated them was consequently in a position to monopolize their votes, to rule them, to dictate his will to them. The freedom of the crust of bread is the indispensable guarantee of the freedom of the ballot."

Out of those dark years Nasser recalled the tragedy that the Palestine war had represented for the Arab national consciousness; the creation of Israel had been sought by imperialism "to serve as a lash against the Arab struggle in the event that this might one day rise out of the rut of humiliation and acute crisis . . . , a division that would limit the expansion of Arab territory, that would separate the Orient (Mashrek) from the Maghreb . . . , a continuous dissipation of the personal effort of the Arab Nation, which was meant to halt its movement of positive development."[2] Thereafter "imperialism was not merely the pillage of the peoples' resources but rather an aggression against their dignity and their pride."

Previously "the Egyptian people had expressed its entity by firmly refusing to take part in the war [of 1939–45], which, in its view, was merely a battle for colonies and markets." After the Palestine defeat "the Egyptian people withdrew what confidence it still had in all those who had offered their hands to imperialism"; then "Egypt echoed with shots and grenade explosions while clandestine organizations of every tendency and every style multiplied;" then "peasants' rebellions came to armed clashes between those who were rising against slavery and the masters of the land"; then the fuse was lit for that "burning of Cairo which could have been quenched, whatever the preparations had been, but which, on the contrary, was fueled by the rebellious popular discontent."

Nasser admitted that "the Revolution did not occur on the night of July 23," but he asserted that "the way that led to it was opened during that great night." And the Revolution? "The nation's needs required a new structure resting on strong foundations, imposing and solid." Build the national state. By what means? The "six principles," of course; but, once again, Nasser paid tribute to "the Egyptian people, whose industry is civilization."

What Is Democracy?

The criticism of the "democracy of reaction" led logically to the definition—in the fifth section—of "healthy democracy." "Honest revolutionary action," Nasser said, has two characteristics: its "popular character" and its "progressivism." Sincerity is the basis of authenticity: "Political freedom—that is, democracy—does not lie in the imitation of formal constitutional trappings. By the same token, social freedom—that is, socialism—does not consist in the imposition of dogmatic theories that have not grown out of national practice and experience." Since "the political system in any given country is only the direct counterpart of the dominant economic situation," it must be obvious that because "economic power in Egypt [before 1952] was in the hands of a coalition between feudalism and exploiting capital," the result was quite naturally a thorough falsification of democracy—vote-buying, peasant illiteracy, financial discrimination to the advantage of rich candidates, etc.—and a real distortion of the public mind as well: "Successive generations of young Egyptians had been taught that their country did not lend itself to industrialization . . . ; they had learned their national history under a false light . . . ; and the purpose of this teaching was only to train functionaries to serve existing institutions and the laws or regulations that hardly concerned the interests of the people"; the combined pressure of the ruling classes on the intellectuals had forced them to choose between inescapable alternatives: "either yield to the temptation to pick up the crumbs of class privilege or vanish into isolation and oblivion."

What were the characteristics of the "democracy of the people"? "Of the people," not "popular." President Nasser listed six of them:

"(1) Political democracy is inseparable from social democracy; [it is essential that] the citizen enjoy three guarantees: freedom from exploitation of any kind; equal opportunity to a fair share of the national wealth; freedom from fear for the security of his future . . . ;

"(2) It is impossible to achieve political democracy where one class dominates all the others . . . It is impossible to either ignore or deny the necessary and natural conflict between classes, but it is essential that this struggle end in a peaceful solution within the framework of national unity and through the elimination of class distinctions . . . The way must then be opened for democratic interaction between the various elements of the working population: the peasants, the workers, the soldiers, the intellectuals and national capitalism. The alliance of these forces, representing the working population, is the legitimate successor to the alliance between feudalism and exploiting capital; this new alliance is tantamount to having substituted a healthy democracy for the reactionary democracy;

"(3) National unity, the result of the alliance between these forces representing the people, has the capacity to bolster the Arab Socialist Union . . . The political organization of the state requires a number of guarantees, which the Constitution will have to provide . . . : (a) the peasants and the workers should hold the majority of seats in all political and popular bodies at all levels . . . ; (b) the authority of the elected popular councils should always prevail over that of the state's executive bodies . . . ; (c) there is an urgent need to create a new political body within the Arab Socialist Union which will recruit suitable candidates for leadership . . . ; (d) the collective character of leadership must be guaranteed during the phase of revolutionary momentum . . . ;

"(4) Popular organizations—more specifically, the co-operative and trade union organizations—can play an influential and effective part in strengthening a healthy democracy . . . ; it is time to set up unions of farm workers . . . ;

"(5) Criticism and self-criticism represent two of the most important safeguards of freedom . . . ; the press, having become the property of the Arab Socialist Union, has been freed of the influence of the single ruling class . . . ;

"(6) The new Revolutionary concepts of healthy democracy should govern everything that can influence the training of the citizen, priority being given to education, legislation and administrative regulations . . . Democratic action in these areas will provide the opportunity for the development of a culture imbued with new values, endowed with a deep understanding of man's sensibilities, a culture that would express man's reality in a genuine way, that would illuminate the remote corners of his thinking and feelings, and stimulate the creative potentialities of his being . . ."

Socialism, "Inevitable" . . .

The sixth section—"On the Inevitability of the Socialist Solution"—brings us to the heart of the problem.[3]

We begin with the statement that "economic freedom," for

which the prerequisite is "the broadening of the base of the national wealth," cannot be accomplished in the capitalist mold; the reason is that in fact "experiments in development of the capitalist type were carried out in close collaboration with imperialism," the resources of the colonies serving the interests of the advanced economies; in addition, even if such an avenue were theoretically feasible, "it could only reinforce the political power of the class that owns and monopolizes the wealth." The Communist way? Nasser did not specifically mention it; at the same time, he said, "there are other experiments in progress that have achieved their objectives by intensifying the suffering of the working mass and exploiting it either for the advantage of capital or under the pressure of dogmatic methods that have extended to the complete sacrifice of generations of the living for the benefit of generations that have not yet been born."

For an underdeveloped country such as Egypt, "scientific socialism is the sole formula compatible with the discovery of a genuine method of progress." For "the gigantic growth of the international monopolies has now left only two possible ways open to national capital in the countries now developing: (a) national capital can no longer meet the competition unless it erects customs barriers for which the people must pay; (b) the only hope of growth for national capital is to harness itself to the movement of the international monopolies, to follow in their footsteps, to become their appendage and to lead its country behind it into this dangerous pit." In order to meet the challenge, three conditions must be fulfilled:

"(1) The consolidation of the national finances;

"(2) The dedication of all the resources of modern science to the task of making this capital profitable;

"(3) The inauguration of overall planning of the process of production."

"Efficient socialist planning" should be prepared to confront an extremely complex combination of needs: "How can we increase production? How can we at the same time increase the consumption of goods and services? How can we accomplish both these things while maintaining the rate of growth in savings with a view to new investments?" These problems of underdevelopment were unknown to the prosperous. These were everyday problems for two thirds of the world. Gamal Abdel Nasser clearly showed that it was the essential logic of the struggle against imperialism at the time of Suez that determined the substantial expansion of the public sector, as we have pointed out.

President Nasser offered no details on the "scientific socialism" in question. On the other hand, he presented a very detailed picture of the public sector as it was after the laws of the summer and autumn of 1961. The private sector was called upon to "restore its own vigor," for "it is no longer possible for it to shelter behind the high walls of customs protection paid for by the people." This sector would be able to undertake activities in the following spheres: a small part of heavy, medium and mineral industries; light industry; one fourth of foreign trade; three fourths of domestic commerce; land (within the framework of the new law on agrarian reform); residential building. Naturally, the public sector's supervision would extend into all these areas, especially in matters of industry, and of foreign and domestic trade.

Certainly the social reforms of 1961 represented "a decisive undertaking to eliminate the last traces of the era of feudalism, of reaction, of oppression, . . . but reaction continued to hold the sources of moral and material influence" that could lead it to act "in alliance with the reactionary remnants in the Arab world, supported by the forces of imperialism."

For the construction of the independent state's national economy from a starting point of underdevelopment, there was at that time no other solution apart from the extension of the collective sector directed by the state.

The Battle of Production

The seventh section was called "Production and Society." "The Arab will himself decide the destiny of his nation in its fertile fields, its huge factories, its high dams, through the use of its colossal energies that are the sources of its moving force." In order to cope with the population growth —"one of the most dangerous of the obstacles threatening the development of the Egyptian people"—recourse would have to be taken to "methods of organizing the family" (which of course simply meant birth control), but, above all, to increasing production.

It was industry that would have to furnish the bulk of the effort: "It should set itself a program of utilizing everything in the way of raw materials that lends itself to processing, either totally or partially." In this undertaking, industry should "familiarize itself with the newest achievements in science; ownership of advanced means of production not only gives us the proper point of departure but also provides a compensation for our backwardness." Of course "particular importance should be given to the heavy industries that are in a position to furnish the real foundation for the creation of modern industry", but "that should not delay progress in the field of consumer-goods industries, in view of the fact that deprivation among the masses of our people has gone on far too long . . . and that neglect of consumer industries violates our people's well-founded right to compensation." Among the various fields of industry President Nasser assigned special importance to mining and quarrying, shipbuilding,[4] communications and food.

Earlier he had dealt with agriculture; it is striking to note the extent to which he confused statist centralism and socialism: "Since very ancient times Egyptian agriculture has found genuine socialist solutions for the most complex problems that it has faced, in the primary area of which we must mention irrigation and drainage, which in Egypt today, as for centuries, are carried out as part of the public services . . ."

The hydraulic society, the foundation of Oriental despotism, was thus portrayed as authentic socialism—a perfect example of this kind of thinking. But there could be no question of collective ownership of the soil: "The revolutionary method of confronting the land problem in Egypt was to increase the number of landowners." The joint progress of co-operativism, reclamation of waste land, improvement of agricultural techniques and rural industrialization should assure the peasants' prosperity and contribute to the Ten-Year Plan.

President Nasser came back to the function assigned to private capital. The laws of July 1961, he said, had two objectives: "To create a kind of economic equilibrium among citizens that helps to achieve justice . . . and to increase the efficiency of the public sector, the property of the people . . . The achievement of these two objectives will remove the vestiges of the complexes due to imperialism, which rendered the function of the private sector suspect" by making it its ally and its tool.

It was then that the speaker turned to the question of "foreign capital," in which he differentiated between three elements: "foreign aid to which no conditions are attached" was the prime favorite; "loans to which no conditions are attached" ranked second; last place was given to "the participation of foreign capital in national activities," which implied "foreign participation in the management" of these affairs and "the export of part of the profits" to other countries. "Our people, which has learned the lesson of history, believes that states with imperialist pasts are under greater obligation than others to provide developing nations with part of what was earlier taken away from them."

After reviewing the government's concepts in the areas of "equal opportunity"—medical protection, education, employment, health and old-age insurance—child care, women's welfare ("their equality with men must be assured"), the family as the basis of society, the new ideals and national culture, and "freedom of religious belief," Gamal Adbel Nasser explained his concept of individual freedom, "the greatest possible incentive to struggle." The elimination of class distinctions made possible the diminution and elimination of class conflict. "Freedom of speech," which was manifested especially in freedom of the press, and "the rule of law" were the two component elements of individual freedom.

A final point: the armed forces. Their function was "to protect the process of constructing the society against foreign perils . . . and to be always ready to crush any reactionary imperialist attempt aimed at preventing the people from attaining its high hopes." It is significant to note that the new army was dealt with in the section on production and that its function was to protect economic activity and to be the state's main strength, both at home and abroad. Thus the continuity of Egyptian history was once more corroborated.

Some Ideological Problems

"With Socialist Execution and Its Problems"—the eighth section—showed the difficulties the military government was facing at that stage.

In the area of values, for example: "It is creative human labor that constitutes the only means by which society can realize its objectives. Labor is an honor, a right, a duty, life itself . . . Organized national labor, founded on scientific planning, represents the road of the future." In order to overcome resistance, reservations and ignorance on the part of the general public, particularly in rural areas, a theoretical foundation must be laid: "The written word must be encouraged so that it may provide the link between all who can still be saved for the future . . . Every holder of a responsible position in national action must be encouraged to set down his thoughts so that they may be accessible to other leaders when it is time for action."

Democracy became the chief urgency in development; whence the importance of the "elected popular councils," which would be defined later. For "many elements may hesitate to participate in national action; freedom is the sole means of doing away with their passivity and assuring their voluntary enlistment in the service of the goals of our struggle." This was in no sense a matter of principle, but, rather, the consequence of the rejection by a very large proportion of the educated, especially the intelligentsia; thus the enlargement of freedom seemed the result of a conflict between the military apparatus and the intellectuals in particular, backed by public opinion.

What was to be said of the "new leaderships" brought forward by "this fatherland, creator of civilization"? Nasser warned against the dangers of bureaucracy, "which, left to itself, might well become an insulating class that halts the drive of revolutionary labor and paralyzes the transfer of its achievements to all those who need them." "The new leaderships must clearly understand their social function, because what might be most dangerous of all for them would be to imagine that they constitute a new class which succeeded the old one and inherited its privileges."

The universities were given the function of "foremost vanguard exploring the way of life for the people . . . From now on we cannot hesitate a moment to enter the atomic age. In other times we missed the steam-engine age and the age of electricity; this backwardness, which was forced on us by reactionary imperialist oppression, has exacted a high price from us and continues to do so. Now that the atomic age is dawning on the world, it is our duty to rise at dawn with those who initiated it."

The Future of Arab Unity

The next section deals with "Arab Unity" in terms of the Syrian experience. Earlier, "at the stage of political revolution against imperialism," it was enough to "bring together the leaders of the Arab world . . . But the stage of social revolution has compelled an evolution in this superficial conception of Arab unity . . . and made unity of purpose the very essence of unity." Nasser emphasized that the "mere fact that differences exist [among the Arab countries] constitutes a proof of unity, for they arise out of the social conflict within Arab reality . . .

"Arab unity is not a single constitutional form that must invariably be imposed, but, rather, a long progression in which forms and stages can be many." Therefore, "any partial unity in the Arab world . . . represents an advance in the march toward unity."

Guarantees against a repetition of failure must be provided. First of all, "peaceful propaganda should be the premise." But above all "the work of unification . . . must be accompanied rigorously and in every way by practical efforts designed to fill the social and economic gaps created by the differences in degrees of social development among the peoples of the Arab Nation." The argument would justify holding aloof from states with semifeudal backward structures and also avoiding rash plunges into what now seemed to the military group a trap in the name of "Arab nationalism." "The road must also be cleared for new currents of thought so that they may act to counter efforts at disruption and overcome the current diffusions in thinking." In other words, no Arab unity until the ideology of Arab nationalism had eliminated all others.

The UAR "is under the obligation of propagating its message and its principles so that they may be available to every Arab citizen; not for one moment must it be stopped by the obsolete contention that such activity would amount to an interference by it in the internal affairs of others. While the UAR feels the definite obligation of supporting every popular national movement, that support must be contained within the limits of basic principles, leaving the management of the struggle itself in the hands of local elements"; the days were over when the Egyptian state snatched the Baath's chestnuts out of the fire . . .

The Arab League, then, could not perform the impossible. "Precisely because it is a league of governments, it can . . . make only one step along the road of the whole of our hopes," but under no pretext "should it become a means of infecting the present with inertia and thus impair the future."

Egypt and the World

The tenth and last section of the Charter was devoted to "foreign policy." President Nasser retraced the well-known ideas of positive neutralism and nonalignment; he mentioned Bandung and Belgrade; particular attention must be given to his description of the three lines of the UAR's foreign policy: "war against imperialism and domination," "work toward peace" and "international co-operation for prosperity."

It was this last aspect—directly linked to Egypt's urgent needs—that the President of the UAR considered especially applicable to the current phase. "Peace cannot be established in a world where there are appalling differences in the levels of the various peoples, on the brink of the deep gulf that separates the advanced nations from those on which backwardness was imposed. The foreseeable clash between the backward and the advanced is the second danger that threatens the peace of the world, the first being the danger that lies in the sudden launching of a nuclear war." International co-operation with a view to development included the following measures: "the availability of scientific secrets to all," the utilization of "the atom for peace," the reallocation "to the service of life" of the huge sums spent on nuclear weapons, and "resistance to the international economic blocs used by the powerful to smash the efforts of others who seek progress."

In conclusion Nasser stated the Egyptian credo in the realm of foreign policy:

"Our people is an Arab people, and its destiny is bound to that of the Arab world. Our people lives at the northeast gate of struggling Africa, from whose political, social and economic development it cannot remain aloof. Our people is part of the two continents where the greatest battles of national liberation are now being fought—the most striking characteristic of the twentieth century. Our people believes in peace as a principle and as a vital necessity; that is why it does not hesitate to work with all those who share this conviction with it. Our people believes in the mission of religions, for it lives in the region where the messages of heaven were received. Our people lives in combat for the high principles written with the blood of peoples in the Charter of the United Nations; many passages of that Charter were written in the blood of our people and other peoples."

The "three circles" (especially the "Islamic" circle) had been redrawn and at the same time greatly enlarged by the experience of these first ten years.

Attack from the Right

The great debate began the following day, not only in the official chamber but throughout the country. The state called meetings of the various professions, set up discussions in the press and in symposia, enlisted radio and television. But between May 26 and July 4, matters took an unanticipated turn. Too many forces were seething, or lay dormant. Let us take a closer look.

Under heavy questioning, the President stated clearly that essentially the problem was to ensure greater social justice:

"I did not say that we must eliminate the differences between individuals, only those between classes." And he castigated the "little men" who hoped to clamber up the ladder and become big landowners in their turn, those who were the new "class raiders." He placed emphasis on the reactionary danger.[5]

The real discussions erupted a day later. At the opening of the session President Nasser vehemently rejected all suggestions aimed at making him President for life: "If we elect someone, it is because we think he can follow the right road, and if he does not, we should remove him . . . the people should be able to choose the President of the Republic and to remove him as well." A prominent figure of Al Azhar, Sheik Mohammed el-Ghazali,[6] cutting across the ovations, attacked the secularizing tendencies of the Charter: "In order for freedom to triumph, our society must free itself from the vestiges of cultural and social imperialism, which has caused many complexes. The liberation of the country should be accompanied by the liberation of legislation . . . It is strange to see that Russia is governed by laws that accord with Communism, that the United States is governed by others inspired by the capitalist system, whereas our country, in the heart of the Arab world, is still governed by the foreign laws of France, England and other countries."[7] And he went on to attack the morals of Egyptian women and Western dress. On May 28 Ghazali returned to the assault, seeking an easy victory by a display of misogyny. He was immediately backed by Sheik Ahmed el-Shorabassi, who suggested "adding to the clause guaranteeing freedom of belief, another guaranteeing protection of the faith."

President Nasser retorted sharply: "Many Islamic states have signed treaties and aligned themselves with the West . . . We feel that there are efforts being made which are aimed at exploiting the Islamic religion for the benefit of a policy of alignment that contradicts our policy." And he defined "the crisis of mental growth" as one composed of "superficiality, fanaticism, terrorism and closed minds."[8]

It was then that Salah Jahine, the official cartoonist of *al-Ahram* and a talented folklore expert, assumed, in the euphoria of the general discussion, the duty of castigating Ghazali in a striking series of cartoons and ballads on May

29, 30 and 31, and June 1. Several of his colleagues echoed him. On May 30, speaking in the National Congress, Ghazali hurled a veritable indictment at the press, "which has been specializing in the publication of filth against men of religion." Anwar el-Sadate sought in vain to subdue the storm. On June 2 and 3, *al-Ahram's* management published two statements that amounted to apologies.

It was an excellent opportunity for the Right to form ranks behind the untouchable banner of religion. Several Congress speakers emphasized that the Charter should be amended to make Islam "the religion of the majority, that of the state"; their ranks included, particularly, Mrs. Soheir el-Kalamawi, professor of Arab literature at Cairo University, formerly esteemed for her liberal ideas.[10] Outside the hall, the *ulemas* of Al Azhar sounded the call to arms; five thousand delegates from the provinces gathered at the thousand-year-old mosque and heard the message of the Sheik of Al Azhar. "I call on the United Arab Republic," he cried, "to base its new Constitution —born of its Charter—on the principles of Islam and to proclaim openly that its official religion is Islam . . ."

Unanimously the *ulemas* adopted five resolutions to the same effect; they demanded that "Islam, as the official religion of the state, should illumine the laws of the land, its programs of education, its social customs, its policy regarding news media, its regulation of family life, and all the assistance given by the state to society and to individuals," and that "the paragraph of the Charter calling for equality between men and women be amplified with the words 'within the limits of Islamic religious law' . . ."[11] Within the Commission for the Drafting of the Charter there were stormy debates in which the champions of reaction emphasized the revolt of the *ulemas* and many other pressures.[12]

And who had applied these pressures? The former rich, who had progressively recaptured full use of their political rights once the main sources of economic power were safely in the hands of the state. After Khaled Mohammed Khaled's courageous campaign on behalf of the Left and the liberals, had not the Preparatory Committee in effect recommended limitations on the penalties of "political isolation"? As a consequence the

government had decided, in the interval between the Preparatory Committee's meeting and the Congress, to rescind these
measures with respect to 1,622 persons. Now only seven of the
total were of the Left (and non-Communist); all the others
were members of the old bourgeoisie . . .

These ex-grabbers, back on their feet, renewed their contacts
with officer groups of every tendency in protests against sequestrations (notably to Lutfi Waked, Wahid Ramadan, Daud
Eweiss, principal private secretary to the commander in chief,
Marshal Amer; Hamed el-Sakka; Abdel Ghani Shennawi, head
of the President's intelligence service, etc.), in demands for
removal of Mohammed Hassanein Heykal, a "secularist" of the
Right, and for curbs on the police machinery; and many of
them were irritated by the rise of the technocrats and the
reduction of the military's importance (particularly the group
around Lieutenant Colonel Abdel Kader Eid, head of operations at General Headquarters).

All in all it was only a very small group of officers—the figure
of fifty was mentioned—but it tended to increase after the
autumn of 1961. These officers looked for their doctrine—or,
rather, their shield—among the champions of Islam, the am-
nestied former officers of the Moslem Brotherhood, their spokesmen in the Congress and two members of the Council of State,
Sobky and Omar Marei. Only religious ideology seemed capable of allying men from such varying backgrounds, from
every point on the old Egyptian political scale. It is in this
perspective that we must understand the Drafting Commission's resolution, for "the concern that had given rise to the
stipulation in the Constitution of 1956 that the official religion
of the state be Islam and its language Arabic was the same
concern which in the Charter had given religion the place and
prestige it merited and which ought to make Islam the official
religion of the state in the future Constitution."[13]

At the same time the Right tried another breakthrough, this
time in order to ensure seats in all elective bodies to representatives of the former bourgeoisie, now jeopardized by the
proportion of 50 percent reserved to workers and peasants.
Professor Gaber Gad Abdel Rahman began by calling for the
pure and simple elimination of any allusion to the 50 percent,

since the "dynamic" nature of socialism was in itself an adequate guarantee to the workers.

On May 30, however, Nasser replied: "Our society includes classes that are in relations of contradiction, not of collision; it is essential that the state assure the people of the place which is its due and from which the ruling classes of the past threatened to evict it by all kinds of means. Thus far we have avoided a clash with reaction by peaceful means, whether these were political isolation or sequestration; if reaction persists in provoking clashes, it could be that peaceful means would no longer be adequate and that matters might come to violence . . . I want to repeat that we lived under the domination of one class for many hundreds of years and that we want to emerge into a government of the people, a democracy of the people, instead of the dictatorship of reaction."

The President then returned to his elaboration of his differences with Marxist-Leninist Communism; then, at the turn of a sentence, he said: "There are two types of differences [between classes] that should be eliminated: economic and material differences on the one hand, and differences in psychological consciousness on the other." In the opinion of the President of the UAR, the centuries of servitude had made the people incapable of freeing itself of acquired customs; it was the state that should act for it—quite properly, he thought —at the top.

Then, as if on signal, Anwar Salama, president of the trade unions, who had a quite different theme, read off the indictment of paternalism. "We must alter the policy under which certain managements make rules and decisions without consulting the workers; this policy must be eliminated and replaced by collective bargaining leading to agreement, in view of the fact that official rules and decisions sometimes become means of pressure on the workers."

The frontal attack having failed, the Right tried to blow up the basic concepts of "worker" and "peasant." The question was the inclusion of owners of businesses and former owners of large estates in these categories. This gave rise to discussions of terminology which might have been inspired by Koranic exegesis. More than five thousand motions and suggestions were presented to the secretariat of the National Congress, fifteen hundred of them by the trade unions alone; and it was learned that the majority of the proposals dealt with the definitions of "worker" and "peasant," while matters of trade union organization ranked second.[14]

The subcommittee on democracy suggested that "worker" should be defined as any person working for hire whose income did not exceed £E500 per year, while a person would no longer be considered a "peasant" if he owned more than twenty-five *feddans*; what was involved in this latter case was really farm hands, the landless, and small and even medium landowners.[15]

The others, meanwhile—those who were neither workers nor peasants and who were to share the remaining 50 percent in all future elected assemblies—defended their ground foot by foot. The most rabid, of course, were the different "Orders" that governed the professions, particularly the physicians, headed by Dr. Rashuan Fahmy. They tried to prevent an amalgamation with the trade unions in order to preserve their privileges, knowing that their small numbers would soon be swallowed up in the mass of workers.

As the discussions proceeded, many delegates to the Congress raised questions that were left unanswered. The former president of the Journalists' Union, Hussein Fahmy, pointed out that his group, "having got rid of the domination of private capital, had fallen under the yoke of the administrative agencies and the danger of bureaucracy; these agencies can now control advertising—that is, award it or refuse it to any newspaper, so that they have the power to dominate the thinking and opinions of these newspapers."[16] The next day a movie star, Magda, presented to the Congress a petition from a delegation of teachers of both sexes who complained that "their monthly salaries did not exceed £E3 . . ."[17]

Kamel Eddine Hussein, vice-chairman of the Congress, proposed that the debate be closed on Wednesday, June 6, and that the secretariat of the Congress appoint a special committee of one hundred members to complete the draft resolutions dealing with the amendment of the Charter. This committee, which was set up on June 6, was headed by the president of the University of Assiut, Dr. Soliman Hozayyen; six subcommittees were appointed: general questions under Dr. Lutfi Abul Nasr, 16 members; democracy under Dr. Teema el-Garf, 16 members; production under Dr. Mohammed Labib Shukeir, 20 members; socialism under Dr. Gaber Gad Abdel Rahman, 18 members; Arab unity under Dr. Khalafallah Ahmed, 7 members; and foreign policy under Mohammed Kamel Seddik, 9 members.[18]

The Problem of Political Leadership

It was then that the real problem came into view: political leadership. On June 5 Kamal Eddine Hussein had spoken of a body that he called the "political apparatus, a generator that will assume the task of disseminating political consciousness and political propaganda." The Congress adjourned until June 30 in order to give the delegates an opportunity to talk with the voters, and the government time to prepare a balanced solution in terms of the various pressures being exerted on it.

When the Congress reconvened it became clear that the work of the co-ordinating committee and its six subcommittees was in no way intended to change the original text of the Charter of National Action, though this had initially been presented as a "draft." In fact, the Congress was immediately presented with motions by 550 members calling for the immediate ratification of the Charter; this was done by unanimous vote. Dr. Hozayyen read his committee's report on ten subjects (the need for the Charter, its nature and its meaning; religion and society; democracy; socialism; production; science and the cultural revolution; women, the family and the young; Arab unity; foreign policy; the proclamation of the Charter); the Congress decided to annex this document to the Charter and publish both at the same time. Thus, for the first time, President Nasser found himself constrained to withdraw a measure that he himself had proposed, because Title II—"Religion and Society" —emphasized the determination to restore Islam to its political primacy. And it was impossible to hide the fact that this first retreat represented a gain for the Right.[19]

The Congress then took up the second item on the agenda, which was the plan for a political organization. Nasser stated his conception of it in his speech of July 2. The creation of this new entity had been made necessary by a number of factors: the prerevolutionary parties reflected "class interests and rested on an alliance between feudalism and exploiting capital, not on the people as a whole"; "in the majority of instances the political organizations that did not represent the interests of the ruling class were of only limited, indeed negative, effect . . . ; they were motivated by emotional considerations, or by forces outside the national territory, and in any case, they had not put out sufficiently deep roots to be able to face the inevitable social change."

The National Union, he continued, had been infiltrated by reactionary cells; hence it was necessary to create the Arab Socialist Union, with the following main features:

"(1) The ASU should constitute the overall political structure of the mass effort of the popular forces.

"(2) It embraced the Charter as its guide for action, shaped by experience and hope, and created by the free popular will.

"(3) It represents a structure democratically erected by the popular masses . . . the leadership organ of national action.

"(4) It incarnates the power of the people, which is paramount to all other powers, and guides it in all areas and at all levels.

"(5) The Union should be the shield that ensures healthy democracy. In the forefront of its guarantees are those ensuring the proportion of representation of workers and peasants, the strengthening of the co-operativist and trade union organizations, collective leadership, the right of criticism and self-criticism, and the tendency gradually to transfer the power of the state to the elected popular councils."[20]

On the following day President Nasser made an overall response to several dozen questions on the Arab Socialist Union's future. He disclosed that all members of the Congress[21] were appointed ex officio members of the ASU, that it would have a Provisional Executive Committee, that its Congress would not be held before the autumn, that its task would be to evolve means and methods for elections to the National

Assembly, which would give the country its Constitution. As for the "political organization"—the ASU's brain—it would be a secret agency, staffed by methods known only to the leaders; it would be both the mind and the eye of the government. Nasser added that the execution of this matter would be deferred, "until we have built up the Union. At that time," he explained, "there will be leader staffs within the Union; we shall see how they are composed and who the persons are who do the essential work."[22] (Previously the President of the UAR had made an appeal for unity addressed to the Algerian leadership group.)[23]

Waverings . . .

Something, however, seemed to be worrying the leaders: the disaffection of the intellectuals, which extended by now to those tolerated or appointed by the government itself. "A striking aspect of the Congress," Ehsan Abdel Koddus wrote, "was the fact that the class that we are accustomed to call the intelligentsia had less influence than we thought. The intellectuals were hardly heard from in the Congress. They were in attendance as professionals, as engineers, physicians, professors and teachers, rather than as intellectuals responsible in a general way for the society as a whole . . . Now, there can be no doubt that the President would have preferred that the Congress show some evidence of a better understanding of the Charter, that this or that member rise to challenge such and such a proposal . . ."

But not one of the intellectuals attending the Congress had done so. Yet there were many theoretical problems to be resolved: the difference between the state's property and the people's, between Arab socialism and the other forms of socialism, between the private sector and the public sector—and Koddus catalogued a whole list of them.[24]

As was fitting, Mohammed Hassanein Heykal provided a complete analysis of the concepts "at the top": he flayed the excesses of the superdemocrats and the ultrasocialists; he noted the silence of the landowners, the flabbiness of the business representatives of "national capital" preoccupied with finding a new designation in order to cater to prevailing tastes; he restated the imperative necessity of assuring the workers of half the national representation at this stage of social development. He insisted that "the contradiction between the people and the government has vanished of itself"; he pointed out that a great number of the critics did not even know the Charter and that "it was becoming necessary to revise our opinions as to the judgments made before the phase of ideological clarification marked by the Charter"; he indicated that the use of the word "freedom" should be viewed with mistrust in all kinds of old slogans; he drew a distinction between two kinds of Left, "the doctrinal Left and the natural Left" (the second being the good Left); and finally he warned the workers against the temptations of proletarian dictatorship, and the general public against the excessive demagogy.[25]

At the root of the intellectuals' disaffection, which was increasing and reaching into official circles, there was a lack of confidence and there was fear—the first resulting from the general apathy that had grafted itself on the old root of ancestral caution, the second exacerbated by the police state.

. . . and a New Direction

And what of the army?

The celebrations that marked the tenth anniversary of the government, from July 22 to 27, 1962, included the first Egyptian *Al-Kahir* (Victorious) rockets streaking 375 miles across the sky, as well as the proclamation of freedom of education at all levels.[26] A polite dispute with the Soviet press began, as well as another with the Italian Communist party—Italy was being drawn more and more into the Arab world—for both foreign opponents criticized the socialist pretensions of a system that persecuted the Left.[27] But the military parades afforded the occasion for the official definition of the army's function in the new society. At several points during the Congress, President Nasser had already turned back the arguments of those who called for the relegation of the army to purely military tasks. Once again it was Heykal who stated the official doctrine, which he described as a "new sociopolitical theory."

"Under the conditions that are typical of the class struggle in the underdeveloped countries, and bearing in mind the feeling of the general public that the leaders in power represent only interests which by their very nature are opposed to those of the masses, the popular revolutionary movement has no choice but to base itself on the army in order to pave the way for the revolution." According to the officers calling for a monopoly of power, the army should continue to be the chief force at the core of the state. But this was no longer the view of Gamal Abdel Nasser, mindful of the balance of power: "We want no politicians in the army. But the army as a whole represents a force within the national policy."[28] A few days earlier, in an order of the day to the army, Marshal Amer had voiced the army's gratitude to "the people that had created it and always made it capable of having the honor of fulfilling its duty in extremely difficult circumstances. Once again the armed forces swear before the people to be its shield, the instrument for the realization of its objectives, obedient to its orders and unsparing of their lives and blood in defending the honor and dignity of the fatherland."[29]

A new stage was thus defined, in which the army was designated as one of the ruling forces of Egypt and no longer as the sole important force. But it was a predominantly military apparatus which controlled the entire power structure and turned it toward the West, especially toward the United States.

Such was the meaning of the governmental changes of September 1962. The new Presidential Council comprised twelve members, ten of them officers (Ali Sabry and Kamal Rifaat thus being joined with the eight former members of the RCC) and two of them civilians (Dr. Nur Eddine Tarraf and Ahmed Abdu el-Shorabassi). And it was the man of the Washington dialogue, Ali Sabry—after all, an excellent administrator and a political thinker of distinction—who became chairman of the new Executive Council of twenty-five members. A change of "front"? In effect. In this case the front was a faithful portrait of the political direction.

The first move was a ban on controversy with the United States, even though Washington had just equipped the Israeli army with rockets . . .[30]

To Loosen the Vise

As we have seen, the year 1963 was marked by new waves of nationalizations and by the growing military commitment in Yemen.

At first sight the one has nothing in common with the other. Actually, this was not the case. For the installation of a huge bureaucratic apparatus crowned by technocracy and military leadership at the head of undertakings in the public sector was a costly enterprise that imposed an onerous burden on the investments projected for the ten-year development plan. Official estimates for 1960 had already painted a disturbing picture of employment in Egypt: at that time 77 percent of the population made up the potential labor force, while only 32.6 percent were in the actual labor force; this group, apart from agriculture, was concentrated in the tertiary sector: 54.3 percent in agriculture, 21.7 percent in the infrastructure and public services; 10.6 percent in commerce; 10.6 percent in industry; 2.8 percent in construction.[31] Two acute observers of the Egyptian economy, analyzing the figures of the Plan and those of the national treasury, arrived at virtually the same result. To Professor Charles P. Issawi of Columbia University, "the per capita increase in income in Egypt since 1952 has fallen below the world level."[32] But one must read the remarkable analysis by the Egyptian Marxist economist, Samir Amin, in *L'Egypte nassérienne* (*Nasserist Egypt*), which ends in this judgment: "It would seem that with the foreign aid it has obtained, the government could achieve investments in the neighborhood of £E200 million per year (approximately 17 or 18 percent of the gross national product), which, with allowance for a coefficient of 4.5 to 5 in total capital, could ensure an income growth of 3.5 to 4 percent per year.[33] Since the population increases at the rate of 2.5 percent per year, that would make it possible to raise the per capita income from 50 to 70 percent. This is far from the official goal of the current plan—to double the national income in ten years, i.e., to double per capita income in fifteen years."[34] A recent, remarkably detailed study by Dr. Patrick O'Brien of London

University, *The Revolution in Egypt's Economic System,* provides accurate evidence in every field about both the tremendous efforts to develop and advance, and the checks encountered—notably owing to the weight of the bureaucracy (which he does not, however, call by its name: the "new class"). It must be pointed out that no critical economic study has been offered by any official source to refute these conclusions. On the contrary, many indices point to the picture of what must indeed be called a welfare state aimed at consumption. One such is the investigation made by the large newspaper *al-Ahram,* which shows that consumption was increasing by £E50 million per year, rising from £E876 million in 1959 to £E1.05 billion in 1962.[35] And in the context of his own campaign in *Rose el-Yussef,* Ehsan Abdel Koddus added: "There are people who think of socialism in these terms: 'Why not sell the factory and buy a television set and a refrigerator for every worker instead?' Such people are dangerous and destructive!"[36]

This means that the situation was understood in high quarters; whence the ceaseless campaign against bureaucracy, which is the very type of society set up by the military government. Whence, too, the necessity, in order to put an end to it, of creating a genuine political party around an organization of socialist structure capable of mobilizing the masses—that is, to restore a direction to political activity.

It is also clear to what extent the Yemen campaign had demonstrated its wastefulness and become unpopular in Egypt. Yet, in order to go on, it was necessary to rely even more on foreign assistance, to increase the public burden, to sink in deeper.

Then it becomes easier to understand the counteroffensive of disengagement that was carried on in 1963–64, toward France, China and the Soviet Union.

Diplomatic relations with France were resumed in April 1963. Everything was made ready on the Egyptian side to seek support in Gaullist diplomacy and to arouse the interest of business circles.

From December 14 to 21, Premier Chou En-lai of China was in Egypt. He was warmly welcomed, but it appeared that the effort to enlist Egypt in Chinese concepts, even if only in the Afro-Asian sphere, was marking time.

Nothing of that kind happened during Nikita Khrushchev's visit to Egypt from May 9 to 25, 1964. This was indeed a popular triumph; never before had the people of Egypt hailed a foreign visitor with so much fervor and enthusiasm. Here was a visitor in whom the Egyptian people saw the standard bearer of socialism, the representative of the state that had halted the aggressor at Suez and done everything to ensure the success of the Aswan High Dam. Besides, the public discussion that took place between the head of the Soviet government and President Nasser on the subject of the popular element in the Arab unity movement stirred the people's interest.[37] The communiqué that was issued at the end of the visit indicated that the USSR would take part in the second Five-Year Plan on all levels and in all areas and would give the UAR a supplemental loan of 250 million rubles.

The Liberalization of the Spring of 1964

On March 24, 1964, a Constitutional Proclamation was issued. It contained 169 articles. "The United Arab Republic is a socialist democratic state based on the alliance of the active forces of the people. The Egyptian people is part of the Arab Nation" (Article 1); "property will have three forms: (1) state property, which means the people's property, through the creation of a strong and capable public sector in a position to guide progress in all areas and to carry the chief responsibility for the realization of the development plan; (2) co-operative property, which means the property of all those who participate in a co-operative organization; (3) private property, a private sector that will participate in development within the framework of the comprehensive plan, but without exploitation. The people's control will extend to all three sectors and will govern them completely" (Article 13).

This proclamation was accompanied by the creation of new institutions: the committees of the Arab Socialist Union (the 7,000 committees with 4,310,851 members, of whom a majority of 57 percent of workers and peasants had been elected to posts of responsibility in December 1962); the abolition of the Presidential Council and the appointment of a new additional Council of Ministers, as well as the designation of six Vice-Presidents of the Republic;[38] and, finally, the election of the Council of the Nation (National Assembly), with a majority of worker and peasant delegates (March 21).

It was also accompanied by the release of all Communist political prisoners interned in concentration camps (March and April 1964); then, on the eve of Khrushchev's arrival, the release of all Communist political prisoners serving prison terms.

On March 24, the day after the abolition of martial law, however, Law No. 119 of 1964 was promulgated. It gave the President of the Republic the right to order the arrest of any person who had been named in any order of detention or sequestration between 1952 and 1964, and to have him brought before an extraordinary tribunal. In one blow, the liberal measures were stabbed in the back: the state of emergency was continued in legal fashion, just as menacing because of the suffocating impact of the police apparatus.

part four

The Value of the Egyptian Experiment

His is the valley who can slake its drought
And make its barrenness a harvest-rout.
Each thing belongs to him who makes it more.

—BERTHOLT BRECHT, *The Caucasian Chalk Circle*

CHAPTER 11

ON SPECIFICITY . . .

FIFTEEN YEARS of changes, of experiments, of efforts, of sufferings. Fifteen years of inching progress. A question arises after all the analysis: Does an "Egyptian way" to the conquest of independence exist, to the construction of the national state, to victory over underdevelopment? In other words: Does the Egyptian experience have value as an example for the Afro-Asian world, more specifically for the African continent and the Arab world?

One is tempted to go back to the title of Croce's book on Hegelian philosophy, *What Is Living and What Is Dead*, though not without substituting "what is Egyptian" for "what is living"—which is specific and not susceptible to generalization.

We come back now to the analysis of the essential character of Egyptian economic history, on which we have placed so much emphasis, particularly when we were examining the Agrarian Reform.

From the earliest dynasties to Mohammed Ali and even to the British occupation, the principal basis of economic wealth —the land—was the property of the sovereign. Only 3 percent of the area of modern Egypt is fertile; and this narrow green strip through which the Nile runs is surrounded on all sides by deserts, drought, burning sun. These arable lands parsimoniously doled out to the peasant must still be provided with regular irrigation, since rain is more than rare. Hence a whole system of water storage, distribution and drainage has been developed. Only a powerful and continuous central authority can carry this burden: here individualism is a synonym for anarchy and disintegration; for no great lord, no provincial governor could assure his subjects what only the capital is in a position to provide: water, the source of life.

It is in this fact above all others that the deep-lying reason must be sought for Egyptian national unity, the oldest unity in the world, the only unity, too, to persist as such, through multiple occupations, for seventy centuries. It is this fact too that gives the central authority its crushing, abnormal power: the state is indeed the determinant, the master of life and death, in the day-to-day life of Egypt as it has been through the ages.

The tendency to unity, to centralism, to concentration, to pyramidal hierarchy spares no domain. The government, the master of the waters, is the master of the land as well, and now and then condescends to let it out in tenancy to those whom it wishes to privilege. The central state brooks no provincialism, no feudalism; the Mamelukes themselves, once they had seized power in Cairo, hurried to name the strongest among them Sultan or Emir; in other words, they held him answerable for the proper functioning of what the Egyptian state could neglect only at the cost of the sources of its life: water.

Even heaven could not escape the universal tendency: as early as the Old Kingdom, all the deities of the two Egypts were combined in the god Amen-Ra; the trinity of Isis-Hathor-Osiris set the pattern for the Christian Trinity. Thus Egyptian unity established itself—more symbiosis than syncretism—from the furrow in the earth to the heights of Parnassus, from the *gamuss** to life eternal, from the peasant to the god. It is a unity that for Egypt and in the farthest depth of the Egyptian's being is fundamental, essential, constituent; it is a premise and he in no way sees it as a conclusion. Everything emanates from the center and is related to it; nothing is valid if it causes the collapse of what nature has cemented.

The state, the master of political power, whose head is the

* Egyptian cow.

incarnation or the representative of divinity, has in its hands the economic life, of which it was the sole owner throughout history until the irruption of capitalism three quarters of a century ago.

For the second time, geography was to impose its rhythm. For Egypt, the junction point of three continents, the chosen land of civilization, attracts conquerors and inspires adventures. So the state turned its efforts toward the creation of a powerful and well-equipped army, the key component in the machinery, for it is concerned with maintaining and organizing the home front (economy and administration) as well as with protecting the borders and occasionally launching imperial offensives in order to prevent the creation of another powerful and rival state in the region.

There are many climaxes in this dialectic whose two terms are, on the one hand, the fertile, salutary earth, as long as it is watered by the Nile, and on the other, the man in power who depends on it and exploits it without respite.

It was Ahmose, founder of the Eighteenth Dynasty (1575–1550 B.C.) and liberator of Egypt from the yoke of the Hyksos, who apparently created the first Egyptian national army. Thutmose III (?–1447) continued the struggle and gave Egypt her empire in Africa and Asia in sixteen splendid campaigns. Finally there was Ramses II (1292–1225), strategist and politician, preserver of the empire, exponent of *Realpolitik* before the word existed. In order to assure themselves of the unfailing loyalty of the military corps, the Pharaohs conferred land on its leaders and endowed the priests. This was the great epoch of Pharaonic Egypt: the power of the state, the creation of the empire, prosperity in the economy, the flowering of the arts.

Henceforth the fortunes of the army were bound to the country's social and economic destiny. The denationalization of the Egyptian army under Psamtik (663–609 B.C.) was the prelude to the great invasions—Persian, Greek, Roman. The Byzantine army of occupation busied itself with policing a country which was cut up into five "duchies"—Augustamnichia,

Arcadia, the Thebaid, Libya and Egypt—and which in the seventh century A.D. hailed commander Amr's soldiers as liberators. In 1097 the First Crusade attacked Syria. The Ayubite dynasty (1171–1250) marked the beginning of the army's return to power. Saladin, in particular, took care to surround his Turks and Kurds with popular backing. Egypt entered the military period: on her borders and even as far as Damietta the Crusades raged until 1291; the Mongols reached Asia Minor in the thirteenth century and threatened Syria in the fifteenth; Circassians, Greeks, Albanians, Slavs and Serbs fell back before the Mongols and found in Egypt a refuge and good positions. The Mameluke corps that was to rule Egypt from 1250 to 1517 was formed. A select force, the Mameluke army gradually grew rich in land given in fief, though it could not be inherited, to officers of every rank, from *atabek el-'assakir* (commander of the army) to *dawadar* (corporal). "They abandoned themselves," the great Moslem historian Maqrizi tells us, "to such excesses as the Franks, had they been the masters of the country, could not have equaled." Around them Egypt lived a strange, confused life, "a society dominated by the idea of war: war by Moslems against Christians, war by Mongols against Moslems, war by Mamelukes among themselves, and all in a barbarity for which there are no words . . ."[1]

A feudalism on the Oriental model was established, but it led to slackness and disaffection among the military, thus opening the way to Selim I in 1517. Then desolation was everywhere. Cairo, "the metropolis of the universe, the garden of the world, the ant hill of the human race, the porch of Islam, the throne of royalty," as Ibn Khaldun loved to call it, was emptied of its artisans and teachers; the Egyptian population dropped from 8,000,000 to 2,500,000 between the fourteenth and eighteenth centuries; destitution was sovereign everywhere. The Turks looted the country and established a military condition of a military feudalism without a center and without traditions. Yet the bond persisted between the land and the power of arms. And the military paid in ever-increasing ineffectiveness for Oriental feudalism, for the scattering of the national patrimony into the hands of foreign mercenaries.

With Bonaparte, Cairo became once more the center of everything: a Council composed of leading Egyptians had its seat there; finally the people became aware of a foreign presence that was no longer Moslem but European and Christian. Two insurrections against the French expeditionary corps broke out (October 1798, and March and April 1800), and General Kléber was assassinated. "The inhabitants of Cairo," Gabarti tells us, "even the poor, began to sell their clothes and go into debt in order to buy arms and defend themselves." The leaders who rallied around Omar Makram were played off by Mohammed Ali against the Mamelukes, and through the former he became *Wali* (Viceroy) on May 13, 1805.

For Mohammed Ali the army was neither the instrument of power nor an element, not even a prime element of the state, nor a department of the government: it was the center of everything, the pivot of national life. Under his reign the Egyptian army became not only the amazingly effective instrument of the reconstruction of the Egyptian empire in Asia and Africa and even in the Mediterranean, but also the instigator of and the pretext for the industrialization of the country, the reshaping of the administration, the rebirth of culture and education. With the army as his starting point Mohammed Ali constructed a state and restored strength and life to millennia-old Egypt.[2] From 1811 to 1815 Mohammed Ali strove to subdue the Wahhabites—stern, purist, backward-looking, active in the Arabian peninsula—in order to win favor with his suzerain; during that period the idea to found an Arab empire came to Ibrahim, who had demonstrated his qualities as a leader. In 1820 Colonel Seves reorganized the Egyptian army, which very quickly became one of the best of its time. While Egyptians could not rise above the rank of captain, Turks and old Mamelukes held the grades of higher officers and generals: the pay was alluring, but there was also land, in fee or in life tenure; thus a new warrior and feudal aristocracy was created, the origin of many of the prominent Egyptian families of the pashas.

Ibrahim's victories between 1820 and 1839, notably over Turkey, infused the hinterlands, which provided the soldiers, with a feeling of national pride. What for Mohammed Ali was only a move on the chessboard of power within the Ottoman Empire became in the eyes of Egyptians a national movement aimed against the Turkish occupant, the most hated of all. There were distinct echoes of this in Colonel Arabi's revolt in 1882. It was not in the name of the Islamic *umma* or Turkish legitimacy that Mohammed Ali made war, but rather in the name of the glory of Egypt—and in reality his own. Thanks to Sheik Omar Makram's sacrifice and the Viceroy's victories, the Egyptian nation was launched on a new cycle of life.

Highly centralized and led by a military chief who was also an adroit politician, in the center of a predominantly feudal social system in which, however, the rudiments of an Egyptian bourgeoisie were taking shape, the state subordinated everything to the army. One third of the *diwans* (ministries) was concerned with war; the state established educational institutions of all sorts—from the Military School to the School of Languages and the Polytechnic School—designed to endow the army with the modern experts that it so badly needed and, as a by-product, to provide the country with the specialists required for the smooth functioning of the economy and the administrative machinery that backed up the victorious endeavors of Ibrahim and his generals. The state also imposed a monopoly on commerce and industry, centralized in Mohammed Ali's hands; having effected the ruin of a large number of small artisan industries, he replaced them with a whole network of military and medium-sized processing industries (textiles, iron ore, copper, etc.) The state also sent several hundred students on scholarships to Europe, especially to France, most of whom were destined for careers in the army and the military industries; among them was Rifaa Rafe' el-Tahtawi, the founder of the Egyptian cultural renascence.

It must be emphasized that the new class of big landowners —Mohammed Ali's colonels and generals, as well as the high dignitaries—was originally a class of foreigners who owed their wealth to the master of the country and who always regarded the Egyptian as an inferior, a subordinate; in spite of their increasing alliances with the great Egyptian families of the sheiks and other notables, the masters of the army and the land would still, in the middle of the twentieth century, be the descendants of the occupants of the past . . .

In a period of independence, of the conquest of independence and expansion, the army played a prominent national part in Egyptian society; such was the case under the Old Kingdom, the Middle Kingdom and Mohammed Ali. On the other hand, it was relegated to the function of an internal police force whenever Egypt was the prey of a foreign conqueror: from the last of the Ptolemeis to the Arab conquest, and then especially under the British occupation.

It was this third, specifically Egyptian aspect of the army's function in the life of the nation that was dramatically illustrated by the revolt of the colonels and then by the revolution of 1882 under Arabi. The incidents that triggered these events—especially the dissension between the Egyptian officer corps and the Circassian and Turkish high command—should not obscure the deeper character of the movement; it followed the thinking of the national demands as these were defined in the National party's program of 1879: the end of foreign control, the Egyptianization of the state and the army, an elected parliament, etc. And the mass rising of the Sharqiya peasants, in particular, to support the army and bar the invader's road to Cairo, made the military corps the spearhead of Egyptian patriotism and was a portent of 1952. Lord Cromer understood it clearly. "The soldiers," he said, "did not mutiny against their officers; it was the officers who mutinied against the Khedive, carrying the soldiers with them. And it might be said that the army went into the rebellion virtually *en bloc* . . . It represented, or at the very least it wanted to represent, the forces of indignant patriotism . . . , defending the soil of the fatherland against the enemy. Its cause was the cause of Islam against the Christians, of the autochthonous Egyptians against the supporters of Turkish tyranny." This national union was underscored by the National party's manifesto of December 18, 1881, signed by Sheik Mohammed Abdu, Colonel

Ahmed Arabi and the great poet Mahmud Sami el-Barudi, among others.

Six days after Tell el-Kebir, Khedive Tewfik issued a decree: "The Egyptian army is dissolved." Lord Dufferin, more shrewdly, declared that "Egypt had had enough of the Mamelukes and their like," and called for the creation of an army "composed essentially of autochthonous Egyptians" under English command in order to "prevent the Bedouins from making trouble along the whole length of the desert border, [and] to put down small local risings."[3] In other words, a police force, a show army meticulously purged of all officers suspected of nationalism. This was when the humiliation of the general officers, who came from the Turkish aristocracy, reached its height; and now General Mohammed Sultan Pasha, the same man who had stabbed Arabi's army in the back, "regretted the position that he had taken during Arabi's war and the support that he had given the English in their penetration of the country; crushed by the contempt that was heaped on him, he fell ill and died . . ."[4]

Thenceforth the army grew at the same pace as the national movement. A British protectorate in 1914, Egypt provided 1,170,000 men as soldiers or members of the Labour & Camel Corps. The 1919 revolution, the accession of the Wafd, the agitation of 1930–35, the uprising of 1935–36, the Anglo-Egyptian treaty of 1936, and the return of the Wafd finally opened the doors of the Military Academy to young men of the middle classes, the bearers of hope, harshly humiliated by February 4, 1942, and the Palestine war.

Thus seven thousand years of history within an immovable geographical structure formed the foundations of Egypt's threefold individuality on the level that concerns us: the state as master of the waters was at the heart of economic life, the essentials of which were in its hands; the army, the drive shaft in the machinery of the state, and also its sword and its shield, formed an integral part of the economic and social structure and activity; it was also a component part of the vanguard of the national movement.

.   .   .

This triple combination was to serve as a justification to the theoreticians of military government in Egypt: national development in independence should be primarily the work of the unifying and centralized state, not of the political parties, which were sowers of discord; political action should be conceived as the task of a single organization closely bound to the government, because party conflict could only delay and undermine the future; the army, the officer corps, made it possible to guarantee stability to the government, to assure the defense of the country and to furnish effective leadership for economic activity and the whole life of the society, much better than these tasks could be performed by any of the social classes in conflict with one another.

The example was followed in part by other parallel experiments in Pakistan, in Iraq and especially in Burma. But China, Cuba, India and Indonesia, Ceylon and Algeria provided diverse models. The very nature of the single ruling party in Guinea, Cuba, or Mali, for example, was quite different from the National Union in the areas of social recruiting, ideology, methods of operation. Multiplicity of parties had hardly paralyzed either progress or independence in India, Indonesia and Ceylon. The Iraqi example was one of confusion ripening into civil commotion. On the other hand, the rejection of the Egyptian concepts by many states in Black Africa was hardly a sign of their genuine independence—far from it.

This was because the essence was to be found in the substance, not the formal appearance, of the program, the ideology, the organization and the methods in force in each Afro-Asian country. The substance was the character of the society that these political factors advocated and intended to build, the mission actually assigned to the people, to the various social classes and categories, in rural areas and in cities, the extent to which they could take initiatives, their participation in political decisions, the accomplishment and then the supervision of what had been decided. In short, the essential criterion was the genuinely popular character of the work undertaken.

Strength, unity and efficiency are only three factors among others, all of which should be strictly subordinated to the will and the interests of the popular masses.

To acknowledge its specific Egyptian character and to view the domination of the military in terms of history and overruling geography is not to deprecate its value, for all the black that must be set off against the white. It is simply to recognize that what could be done in Egypt does not on that account stand as an example for other areas and countries that differ in their historical evolution, national traditions and developmental needs.

In other words, it is not in the primacy of the army, or in the crushing monolithic state as the source of all initiative, but in other spheres that the universal interest of the Egyptian experiment lies. For all that, it is no less important on its own scale, which is also that of the two thirds of the world —the "Three Continents"—being brought back to life.

CHAPTER 12

NATIONALITARIAN CONSTRUCTION OR SOCIALISM?

WAS THIS SOCIALISM? The question arose in earnest with the laws of the summer of 1961, although the first references to "co-operativist democratic socialism" go back to 1956–57.

Nationalization of the bank of issue, of the monopoly complexes, of heavy industries and basic sectors (insurance, mining, transportation, foreign trade in particular) can be found in many countries in a public sector that has its place in the general structure of an economy of the capitalist type.

But in the case of Egypt these measures of statist nationalization affected a substantially broader range: all the commercial banks, the greater part of heavy and basic industries, transportation and the greater part of foreign trade were nationalized. The state set up a mixed sector, embracing what remained in the hands of private capital in the fields of heavy industry, industrial and commercial companies of medium size and a certain number of light industries in which the state owned either half the stock or a certain surplus, occasionally considerable, in excess of the ceiling deemed sufficient for private capital.

The private sector continued to exist: some heavy industries, a large part of the medium industries and businesses, light industries and businesses, one fourth of foreign trade,[1] three fourths of domestic commerce and, above all, the vast majority of land after the two agrarian reforms, and a similar majority of estates. Aside from the former royal family, no owner was dispossessed, and payments for property provided handsome sums to the capitalists, until then the only masters on board, enabling them to buy without limit into the corporations of every kind that were springing up and adding to their incomes.[2]

There has long been a lack of precise figures on which to judge the scope of the new surge of the middle classes, and its limitations. But Dr. Gamal Said summed up the situation for the Preparatory Committee of the NCPF: 1,779 large landowners were affected by the Agrarian Reform of 1952, and 2,936 by that of 1961; the July 1961 laws affected 1,148 big capitalists, of whom 8.8 percent owned stocks totaling more than £E100,000 per person and thus controlled 60 percent of the wealth in circulation.[3]

The whole of these three sectors, which intermingled here and there (notably the public and mixed sectors on the one hand, and the mixed and private sectors on the other), was put to work for the Plan for Economic and Social Development, conceived with the fundamental purpose of carrying out the "national action"—that is, doubling the national income in ten years. The appointment of new political, economic and social management groups, selected among the technocrats and the qualified officers, assured the decisive reduction of the political power of the landed, mercantile, industrial and financial upper bourgeoisie of the past; the first category was the hardest hit. The social advancement of the workers, especially in the cities and the industrial sector, the participation of factory and office workers in the fruits of their labor, the determination to associate them more actively with the exercise of the power of decision under the terms of the new Charter—all these were steps that tended to ensure improved social justice, to reduce glaring inequalities and the better to mobilize the popular masses for national development.

Between the prevailing type of state capitalism and the

Egyptian experiment, then, there was a substantial difference. What were the reasons for it?

First of all, it is worth noting that the Egyptian public sector had come into being as a victory over the national-liberation movement, as a retort, in a sense, to the Suez affair and the attack in October 1956. It was the West that drove the Egyptian state in the direction of nationalization. A political means of asserting national sovereignty, the work of the public sector, followed by the success of the Economic Agency, was in turn to raise a question: Why not take over the basic economic units, all the more since big capital seemed either unwilling or unable to break the pattern set by the agonizing population problem and to go in the direction fixed by the political authorities under military leadership?[4]

This second phase in the evolution of the public sector, though predominantly economic, retained nonetheless a political character. Obviously the movement had far outstripped the example of state capitalism in European countries because of the imperatives of the struggle for national independence and for the development of the economy and the social system. Here, let us note, was a primary difference.

There was another: the general orientation of the process of evolution thus set in motion. Whatever the name adopted, it was clear that the Egyptian government had been induced to opt for a progressive but uninterrupted accentuation of the tendency to make the state, viewed as the representative of all "popular forces," the owner or, more often, the director and guide of the national economy, notably in the key sectors of industry and finance. The question therefore was not one of limiting the losses after the unavoidable but "so deplorable" nationalizations, as was the case in Europe, but rather of extending the field of operations of the public sector, defined as the possessor of the basic economic power and the spearhead of the development of the entire country.

All of this notwithstanding, was it socialism?
The basic rebuttal is both theoretical and practical in nature.

Essentially, we know, it lies in the autocratic, paternalistic, statist character of the process initiated in 1961.

At no time was there any thought of allowing the urban and rural workers to make their political desires known directly, or to organize themselves into parties, to work for the achievement of a program of their own within the framework of "national action" supposedly open to all, to act as conscious masters and sovereigns of their own destinies.

The long antidemocratic tradition, which had produced the leaders of the military apparatus, had conditioned them to reject vehemently the very idea of a plurality of political parties in a country with a social structure as diversified as Egypt's in 1952–67, at the time when their great Asiatic allies —notably India and Indonesia—were rejecting the idea of a single party, and at the time when that idea, adopted in Cuba in the sense of a genuine fusion of autonomous revolutionary forces endowed with their own leaderships, was being employed in many countries of Africa for the purpose of eliminating competitive democratic forces.

The Charter of National Action, however, formally renounced other concepts that had seemed to be constituent parts of the system until very recently in the past: the primacy of the state over the political action of the masses during the period of construction; the emergence of the army movement *ex nihilo*, hesitantly viewed in relation to a past that was still largely skeletal; the essentially Arab character and mission of Egypt, now restored to her own problems and personality; the function of the laboring mass, now the master of thought and the guide in the field of action, the army having been assigned to the tasks of vigilance and protection; the increased importance of the trade unions and co-operatives, and indeed the promised creation of agricultural trade unions, without which it would be impossible to mobilize all the national forces; the recognition of the necessity to restore a certain freedom in order to enable the "uncommitted," especially among the intellectuals, to emerge from their silence; and still others.

All that survived intact was the thesis of the single party:

the Liberation Rally, which, after it had become the National Union, was to turn into the Arab Socialist Union.

The reason was that the concept of the single party was the sole foundation for the predominance of the military apparatus which had successfully carried out the coup d'état of July 23, 1952. Unquestionably that apparatus had since been enriched by the adherence of Egyptian technocracy and burdened down by the thousands of renegades and opportunists of every color who clung to its coattails. But the only possible justification (possible but neither adequate nor necessary) for the thesis of the single party—namely, the need to guarantee continuation in power to the political organization that had led the Revolutionary movement of national liberation to its victorious conclusion—did not exist. What happened on July 23, 1952—Gamal Abdel Nasser himself admitted this in the Charter—was not a revolution but a coup d'état led by a group of military conspirators. The main forces of the national movement, employed one after another as need dictated, had been eliminated or smashed. And it was the state, ruled henceforth by the military apparatus, which determined the objectives and modes of national action: the task of the people was to supply the manpower. And this was a people which, when the defections began under the impact of the 1956 and 1967 attacks, had risen as a single mass united around its national government and its leader in spite of all its wounds.

Between 1952 and 1967 the single-party method put the men of the old order back into power in all areas. A devouring bureaucracy was let loose with the immunity of autocracy. That is why it has thus far been so difficult to understand fully the deep nature of the popular reactions in the face of this "socialism" imposed by a state that in everyone's view is still the military apparatus. There is virtually no way of knowing whether the general principles of this economic and social policy satisfy the wishes of the various popular classes, how these classes conceive the socialism that they would have liked to see as a replacement of the old order, indeed the period of military dictatorship itself, nor in what way this massive body of new measures has succeeded in altering the daily life of the masses, although, on this point, observers seem to agree that there has been improvement in the cities.[5] The only point of reference is the testimony of Egyptian and foreign observers: the latter agree that the figure of 50 percent for the "uncommitted," as published by the semiofficial *Rose el-Yussef,* is considerably short of the truth.

A second observation warrants study: planning and statism are absolutely not synonymous with socialism. For in fact its projected goal, i.e., increase in national income and the modification of social structures—from anachronism to modernity—can very well be accomplished to the benefit of the national bourgeoisie as a whole.[6] The evidence adduced is that of Japan in the nineteenth century. Nasser himself had it in mind when he said in the Charter that had it not been for imperialist intervention, Egypt today would have come up to Japan's level, since both nations began their rebirth at the same time and with the same handicap.

But even though the share of the state apparatus—not only the army but also the various security and police forces and the mushrooming economic bureaucracy—is truly gigantic and a number of the old rich are still where they were, even if under another name, the fact remains nonetheless that the major beneficiary of the development now under way is the national economy as a whole, in whose progress the workers have been given an "interest," either directly (profit sharing, bonuses, etc.) or indirectly (social services, education, insurance, public health, etc.). Certainly the proportions are different from what they are in the socialist countries; but already they have ceased to be like those in underdeveloped countries of the traditional capitalist type.

This analysis was confirmed by the proposed budget for the fiscal year 1962–63. It was a record budget, amounting to £E2.135 billion, against £E235 million in 1952. This is because the figure included the budgets for the companies in the public sector, which amounted to £E889 million. There remained £E1.462 billion, of which £E502 million was for social services, £E138 million for administration and £E821 million for current operations (notably the various economic sectors). The gross national product for the new fiscal year was estimated at £E3.255 billion, of which £E1.9359 billion would come from the private sector and £E1.3191 billion from the public sector; thus the private sector owned 60 percent of the production facilities, in spite of the "socialization" laws. The same trend appeared in the national income: £E1.6338 billion, with £E1.0745 billion for the private sector and only £E559.3 million for the public sector.[7]

There is a third and final objection, this one ideological in nature: the group in power has no socialist roots in its thinking; it resorts to quasi-socialist schemes and formulas in order to attract the masses, which are deeply angered by the dictatorship, and it uses them to cloak what in reality is planning and statism. It is impossible to build socialism by keeping the Left under the threat of Draconian emergency legislation, which points to a revival of concentration camps, or to create a classless society by denying the historic and authentic advocates of Egyptian socialism all participation, all autonomous expression and existence, and by establishing this enormous bureaucratic and security apparatus with all its privileges.

Actually, we have before us an experiment in national, or, better, *nationalitarian* development, which has been led by world conditions on the one hand, and by the inordinately acute nature of Egyptian human needs on the other, to choose the path of a statist planning that takes its inspiration from the advanced forms of the welfare state.

This state planning, as we have shown, is the result of an alliance between the military apparatus and the technocrats. And Samir Amin is right in insisting on the lower-middle-class social recruiting of this power élite: "The contemporary history of Egypt is marked by the rise of the lower middle class, certain groups of which have become the ruling class since the military coup d'état of 1952 and have gradually been transformed into a bourgeoisie of a new type, a state bourgeoisie, which has replaced the old ruling class, the middle-class aristocracy."[8]

To go back to the Japanese example, cited by the chief of state himself, it would have been inconceivable for it to take so harsh a statist form and especially for it to be expressed in a socialist vocabulary.

That is because the world in this second half of the twentieth century is no longer what it was at the time of the Japanese development: the powerful bloc of socialist states, constantly increasing, has made a basic change in the world scene. And the emergence of dozens of new independent states in Asia and Africa, the assertion of independence by other nations in Latin America appear concurrently with this surge of socialism as a world force; one indication after another warrants us to consider this socialism as the source of unlimited dynamism, the key to the future. Particularly in theoretical matters, the movements of national liberation have been brought willy-nilly by their own experience to the confirmation of the Marxist-Leninist theories of imperialism, social evolution, the nature of the state, social stratification, relations between socioeconomic infrastructure and ideology. They have taken cognizance of the very high rate of growth in countries such as the USSR and China, which also started from the degrading gutter of underdevelopment; they have seen that Vietnam and Cuba have conquered illiteracy, standing indomitably face-to-face with the most powerful imperialism in world history, and they have envied the efficiency of action of the Communist political apparatus in the peoples' democracies, especially in those where the socialist government represents the achievement of a genuine national revolutionary struggle. In the case of Egypt these elements have acquired increased importance because of the predominant influence of Marxists in the spheres of culture and public opinion until they were eliminated in 1959, and also through the Yugoslav influence, both socialist and nationalitarian, which has apparently had useful examples to offer, at least to the radical wing of the state apparatus.

The combination of these factors has led the Egyptian military rulers to place even more emphasis on the state's grip of all economic and social life, in a country whose tradition of thousands of years takes exactly this direction of a syncretism of state, economy and religion, the army emerging as the instrument of choice for effecting the merger of politics and economics.[9]

This is nationalitarian building at a time when socialism is successful in two fifths of the world, when the 2,000,000,000 inhabitants of the underdeveloped countries are coming back to life; the Egyptian experiment, which began in the battle against imperialism and the old reactionary landed aristocracy, and which was persuaded by circumstances that we have examined to extirpate imperialist influence and undermine the economic influences and state power of the landed aristocracy and the *comprador* bourgeoisie, has thus adopted an orientation that creates the conditions necessary to a future development in the direction of socialism.

The erection of an advanced industrial economy, the creation of a nucleus of technicians within an ever more numerous mass of industrial workers, the extension of agricultural co-operativism in the rural areas, generalized planning, the privileged place reserved for labor in the new scale of values, the propagation of slogans, tenets and analyses of a socialist type, even if reinterpreted in a nationalitarian sense, an anti-imperialist and neutralist foreign policy, broadened co-operation with the socialist countries in the field of economic development, particularly in long-range projects, the progress of socialism in the ambient environment of underdevelopment, from China to Cuba via Vietnam, the destitution of the great Egyptian monopoly groups—all these are factors making the current stage, in spite of the hand outstretched to the new forces of capitalist penetration (especially the United States and West Germany), an *objectively* valid point of departure for a future development in the direction of socialism, in spite of the growing burden of state capitalism's managers and functionaries.

It is from this point of view, I believe, that the "socialist" process now under way should be judged.

CHAPTER 13

WHAT IS LIVING . . .

IN ORDER TO UNDERSTAND clearly the Egyptian contribution to the common fund of decolonization and re-conquest of identity beyond regained independence, it is necessary to go back to the efforts that had been made in this area before 1952.

China and North Vietnam chose the socialist course. Elsewhere the habits of the imperial past, or, more simply, the rejection of this continuity, did not create any coherent policy.

In addition, from 1952 to 1954 Egypt was marking time. It literally became necessary for the West to back her against the wall so that her leaders could no longer evade the real issue. Suez and Port Said marked the beginning of what became the essential contribution of the Egyptian military government to decolonization: the thorough extirpation of the imperialist grip and its influences.

It was no longer a matter of bases or garrisons, or even of restricting foreign penetration of the economic sector. The Eyptianization and nationalization measures stripped the large foreign financial interests and monopolies of all their resources and, consequently, of all their means of influence in Egypt. Certainly Gamal Abdel Nasser was inspired by Dr. Mossadegh's undertaking, but the takeover of the Egyptian economy was accompanied by the complete evacuation of the national soil and, above all, by economic planning. The influence of the Egyptian Left in the direction of planning acted to reinforce Egypt's pyramidal tradition; quite naturally, so to speak, the state proceeded to make itself the centralizer of all energies after having liberated the nation's strength.

Before Suez, the positive neutralism inspired by the five principles of Pancha Sila adopted by Nehru and Chou En-lai in 1954 offered a sort of charter of principles. It was Egypt that gave it substance, dramatically breaking her traditional ties of dependence with the Western powers, taking the initiative of dialogue with the socialist countries, from which she requested weapons and factories—in other words, the tools of independence and power.

What was at stake here was the power of decision: more precisely, the reconquest of the rights and the power of decision; the concrete assertion of sovereign autonomy; the end of the "dialogue" between the former imperial power and the former colony, which dialogue had been considered the sole possible means for the growth of the new independent state; and its replacement by a polyphonic chorus that gave everyone a voice, in conformance with the attitude and peaceful contribution of each to the development of the new state's independent personality.[1]

This is precisely what the West could not forgive in Nasser's Egypt, for it rightly feared the force of her example and the contamination or overthrow of the docile groups in office virtually everywhere.

With Suez as the springboard, and in spite of the liquidation of the first phase of positive neutralism in favor of nonalignment, Egypt, having represented Africa at Bandung, where the Afro-Asian world held its sessions in 1955, renewed Afro-Asianism quite in spite of herself at the Cairo Conference and then, in Belgrade, undertook in conjunction with Yugoslavia to knock on the door of Latin America. It was a search for alliances, of course, and it was bargaining as well—what policy is innocent of it? The essential matter was still that sustained, even angry determination to strip herself of all dependency, to be herself. And on a realistic level, we have seen how much the Egyptian state profited by it.

Bandung, Cairo, Casablanca, Conakry, Belgrade—each was a milestone on the road of neutralism. The disciples multiplied, and Suez took on the value of a symbol.

But there was something else: the West could no longer refuse to admit that it was no longer at the helm of the old European colonial empire. The United States first, and then Great Britain (this order was reversed after June 1967), recognized de facto the legitimacy of the Egyptian experiment. Neutralism gained status in diplomacy and even in international policy. The two blocs, which continued to hold the means of life and death, were no longer facing each other alone. And in order to win supporters among their former subjects, the Western powers multiplied their overtures. The reconquest of autonomy was going to make it possible to erect the national state in proportion to the nation's needs.

Certain maneuvers tended to block the movement, to taint the anti-imperialist orientation of the neutralist wave; it seemed nevertheless extremely difficult, not to say impossible, to reverse the engines completely. The West—notably the United States and West Germany and, to a lesser degree, Italy and Japan—made major efforts to obtain a foothold on Egyptian soil and counterbalance the socialist bloc's influence; competitive bidding led these powers, moreover, to further their game by offering to participate substantially in Egypt's Ten-Year Development Plan instead of merely, as before, selling her surpluses and food stocks.

In spite of the poor harvest and the repression of the Left, the military regime, which had entered the ring and mastered the art of feinting, could expect that henceforth nothing could compel it again to accept the universally hated dependence.

This first lesson in antihegemony was augmented by the fruit of protracted groping in the field of economic development: in order to struggle out of the rut of underdevelopment, only the state was capable of setting the new pace for the predominantly agrarian and *comprador* colonial economies.

The scale could range from economic planning in the structure of an economy of the capitalist type, with a state sector of variable magnitude, to Cuban socialism, passing by way of experiments of intermediate type as in India and Egypt. What crumbled in the uproar of the general crisis of imperialism

was the false concepts that the professional magicians had
never stopped flashing in the eyes of those who were embraced
in the scornful term "the underdeveloped": private capital was
eager to take up the tasks of the great leap forward; the former
colonial countries had hardly any need for heavy industry
because they could always turn to Big Brother; economic planning and state intervention in economic life were synonymous
with chaos, paralyzing bureaucracy, frustration, etc.

Objectively, even if private ownership were preserved in
a more or less widespread sector of production, capitalism
seemed incapable by itself to provide satisfactory answers to
the questions that were raised by the resurgence of the forgotten continents. The national collective was persuaded to
intervene, to organize activity, to limit the privileges of the
rich, to distribute the meager national income better, and to
proclaim a new standard of values in which labor took the
place of wealth and the common good that of the profit motive.

There was no socialism here, but it was already no longer
the traditional capitalism. Objectively, the Egyptian experiment
contributed to the defeat of capitalism in the eyes of the Arab
and African masses, who had nothing to lose, even though—
as we have shown—what was actually taking place was a com-
posite experiment in which a large private capitalist sector
remained.

A third lesson: the right of every nation to choose for
itself the avenues of its development, a right made complete
by the duty of every people to restore its deepest self to life.

It is easy to find agreement in acknowledging the exceptional character of the Egyptian experiment. That is because
the exceptional character of every instance is quickly glossed
over: Is Cuba part of the classic patterns of political science?
How is one to account for the exceptional maturity of the
Algerian people? The evolution of Guinea and Mali, the ce-
menting of the states of Black Africa into a single community
that gives first place to the old dominant nation (France), the
two Koreas, the two Vietnams, the underdeveloped areas of
Europe, the modulations of South American nationalism, and,

above all, the heroic war of national liberation of the people of Vietnam, rising high above any other feat in the history of peoples' struggle for their liberty, dignity and existence— nothing could be left out—are not all of them "exceptional" in one way or another?

Actually, what is exceptional in this second half of the twentieth century is the idea that patterns born of an evolution peculiar to Europe and North America should mandatorily remain valid for the world that is coming to the surface. Stubborn and often even virulent, the illusions of "Eurocentrism" infect yesterday's masters and some of today's élites with alienation and distort their analyses.

Undeniably Egypt has an impressive, even a unique past, large areas of which are well known and survive vigorously as part of the daily life of the masses. The search for authenticity, as we have seen, often gives an appearance of exclusivity to ways that are nevertheless fundamental, and occasionally it assumes the aspect of rejection of others. Only those who have never known the humiliation of living as strangers in their own country, in the depths of their own being, or those who have forced that experience on others, can take offense at this. For those who believe in the future this is only a first stage of necessary negation and surgery, which, together, are the preludes to the richest exchanges between true peoples.

What was positive in the Egyptian experiment and could serve as an example for Asia and Africa as a whole was seized upon by the leaders of the military regime with the intention of offering it as their own creation, owing nothing to the past!

Thus they were led to shatter the continuity of Egyptian history in favor of nothing but the only links of which they wished to be the preservers. Pharaonic Egypt, Coptic Egypt, modernist and liberal Egypt from Bonaparte to Mustafa el-Nahas were deliberately minimized. All that stood out was Islamic Egypt, from the Arab conquest to the end of the eighteenth century, the incidental islet of Arabi's revolt, and military Egypt since July 23. Thus the government could confer on itself a patent of nobility in the hierarchy of the Islamic and Arab world, deny any passage to the currents of democracy and pluralism, and make the people the attentive but, in the last analysis, passive spectator of what took place at the summit. Thus mutilating Egypt's history, it declared the people under age and appointed a guardian for it. Here again the Charter marked a desire for reappraisal.[2]

The same procedure was applied to everything that, in the current world situation, had made it possible for Egypt thus to free herself without any mortal danger. Hence it became possible to present the national effort as a reality *sui generis* which quite naturally evolved out of the very type of government set up in Egypt after 1952; foreign influences and support were blacked out, most of the time, as well as the fact that this experiment would have been inconceivable one or two generations earlier, before the emergence of a second bloc: the socialist powers opposed to the imperialists, the bloc that from 1955 on, but above all at the time of Suez and after, gave the Egyptian state and people the decisive help that has become history. And so the myth of the military regime and its leader was created.[3]

It is these things that have given the Egyptian experiment the strange aspect and offensive tone which often disguise its achievement.

CHAPTER 14

AN EVOLUTION
IN CRISIS

YET THE LEADERS of the military government themselves did not try to ignore the fact that they were encountering a "noncommitment" in certain quarters which refused to support the state's activities. The crisis, as we know, was labeled "crisis of the intellectuals," whereas it was, in fact, the crisis of the general process of evolution then under way.

We have emphasized the positive aspect of this evolution enough for us to come back to it once again. It is important to define clearly the nature of the obstacle that made everything more difficult, for the leadership as well as for the masses. This, in my opinion, was a paralysis in social dialectic.

It was not only socialism that was supposed to be built without socialists. From one end of the social scale to the other —from the economic to the ideological—the military authority categorically refused to allow any dialectical confrontation of opposites, and it imposed by force—artificially—the modes and pace of the evolution.

We have seen how the landed aristocracy's refusal to work with industrialization brought on its downfall, and how the new nationalitarian, bureaucratic and military technocracy had substituted state capitalism and the welfare state for the anachronism of underdevelopment. With regard to the industrial upper bourgeoisie, eliminated from everything after the nationalizations of 1961, a spoliation followed for which there was no justification—an evolution, so to speak, that was not the natural product of interactions taking place at the very core of the new economy. The heads of medium-sized enterprises, who also were affected in the manner described earlier, could not understand why they had first been urged to plunge into the adventure, to become "entrepreneurs," only to be ousted later. At once their co-operation and their experience were withheld.

The evolution into socialism was supposed to occur without class conflict. Immediately the class-struggle organizations of the working class and peasants were destroyed: there was neither a Communist party nor trade unions created and led by the workers themselves. The Left was enjoined to fuse itself into the single party, by way of the concentration camps; and the dissolved trade unions were reorganized by the state in the form of a single union for each craft or profession, their leaders were selected and appointed by the government, their function was conceived to be essentially that of supplying the government with a task force to be maneuvered against imperialism, not against the class in power. Earlier the Agrarian Reform, which was imposed from the top, had neutralized the direct action of the peasants.

The effects of this paralysis were especially damaging on the cultural front. The leashing of the universities, the "positive" censorship of the press, the suffocation of any thinking except the government's brought on the "crisis of the intellectuals," which was made public because it threatened to compromise the construction of the new state. Symptoms of the disease were visible here and there: the Minister of Higher Education declared that the universities had become factories for the sale of diplomas, a kind of secondary-school network in professorial guise; the official ideologists whipped the thinkers who balked at disgorging a philosophy for the new system; the poor sale of state-published books was conceded by everyone, as was their mediocre quality; conformism was stifling originality—these and dozens of others were the complaints that were made.

But the search for causes encountered invisible barriers. And night and day the voices chattered of "socialism," though not once, in all the prattle of the apprentice ideologists, penitent careerists and sophists, was there a single Marxist voice that could call itself such and take part, independently, in socialist development in the name of revolutionary Marxism.

As a result of the military rulers' arbitrariness, the official picture of Egyptian society fifteen years after the seizure of power was a series of fruitful accomplishments interspersed with anomalies.

The destruction of the semicolonial state had a counterpart —the destruction of the political parties; the construction of an industrial economy was accompanied by the negation of class conflict, "interaction" alone being recognized; the advance to national socialism progressed over the destruction of the Marxist socialist wing of the national movement; the reconquest of independence on the world stage put up with the constantly growing harshness of domestic autocracy; the rebirth of the Egyptian state hid the crisis of the intellectuals; new strength was infused into the economy and the military while the hopes of internal democracy vanished; the completion of one new school every second day could not hide the deterioration in scholastic achievements; the will for anti-imperialist Arab nationalism was expressed in an unmistakably imperial style. The list could be continued indefinitely . . .

Before the burning of Cairo, a deep-rooted evolution of Egyptian society was in progress on all levels, within the framework of a national front in which the major influences were those of the Wafd and the Left. Because of the historical formation of each of these forces, and in spite of their definite weaknesses, it was to be expected that this evolution would progress in a national democratic direction with a socialist orientation of the Indian type, but more radical. But the disintegration of the Wafd, the divisions within the Left, and the extreme strategic and political importance of Egypt made it possible for the organization of the Free Officers to take over through an adroit maneuver after six months of spasms in which the old reactionary middle class had shown itself impotent to manage the state's affairs once the national front had been eliminated.

What the military group has done since is history.

It has reversed the engine, set up a totalitarian technocratic national state in Egypt and industrialized the country, which has become the leading industrial basis in Africa and the Middle East, asserted the determination to preserve autonomy in the world, assured national independence, created a military power and put Egypt at the head of the Afro-Asian world.

It could have done much more, much more quickly, and above all without so deeply mutilating the nascent democracy. But the ideological and historical training of the officer corps, its distrust of political parties, its aversion to Marxist internationalism and European culture, which it branded imperialist and cosmopolitan, its determination to remain the sole holder of power in the sense of being the center and launching platform of the Arab collectivity—all these factors impressed on the movement the stamp of an autocratic tendency that has steadily been accentuated.

Since then the pace of progress has been the pace of the destruction of freedoms. Crises have erupted in many quarters. Monolithism stifles dialectic. The pyramidal tradition crushes liberty.

And yet the advance goes on.

In spite of sufferings and crises, Egypt definitively regained her dignity. Humiliation no longer existed, not before June 5, 1967.

The advance goes on.

Certainly it takes neither the avenues nor the aspect that were envisaged after the Second World War by the excited groups which stimulated the appetites and plans of those who would enslave Egypt, the groups that designed the future and invested the passion of their youth in the timeless soil of their abased country. The ways and the aspect are others. Others too are the protagonists, at least those who hold the center of the stage.

For in reality what is impressive here is to see how far the growth of Egypt exceeds the plans of the military rulers: geographical imperatives set the pace of planning; the history of Egyptian society, and especially that of the bourgeoisie, accelerated the establishment of state capitalism, of planning with a presocialist trend; imperialist humiliation, grafted on four centuries of disasters, incited the resurgence of the state and the army; the workers' movement forced the welfare state; the traditions of the national movement were the root of neutralism; the influence of the Left drew the outline for the cultural renewal. But it must also be remembered that the ancestral tradition of bureaucratic centralism snuffed out freedoms and oppressed minds.

The advance goes on—no matter what those who yearn for servitude may say of it.

For the moment it is the peaks of the crises that are visible. But the elements foreshadowing the future are there: independence, reconquest of identity, increase in economic and state potential, growth of the working class, quest for national personality, autonomy of will, emergence of the technocrats, primacy of the social body and its values in the name of socialism. Other elements still lie crushed, with the social dialectic.

But for how long?

Already one can see the outlines of the different aspects of the basic contradiction that is Egypt today: on the one hand between the new, technically advanced working class, heir to a long past of political and trade union battles, destined for the leading ranks, and on the other, the brutal, all-powerful machine; on one side between the army officers—the "new class"—who thus far have taken the country as their fief and intend to "preserve" the positions that they have gained, and on the other, the technicians, to whom more and more of the command posts in the economic, social and cultural sectors are being entrusted and who have won substantial representation in the new political apparatus; between the bureaucrats and the police on one side, and on the other, the Egyptian intellectuals, the guardians of revolutionary traditions, the motivating, fecundating elements of the social dynamic for a century. And the peasants—the central force in the Egypt to come —still sealed within their primitive life, are awakening.

The basic exigencies of economic and social development will *compel* a confrontation, meanwhile strengthening a little more every day the function and possibilities of action of the positive elements: proletariat, intelligentsia, technocrats— above all, the peasants. Here, unremittingly, time is on the side of the resurgence of the social dialectic.

Inexorably too, because it must, the necessity of freedom will take shape.

Then Didi, the magician, appeared before King Khofu (Khefren). The king said:

"Why, O Didi, is it that I have not seen thy face before this moment?"

Didi answered: "We go to those who summon us. The king summoned me, I answered his call."

The king said: "Is it true, as they tell it, that thou hast the power to replace a head that has been cut off from a body?"

Didi answered: "Yea, O my lord the king, this lieth in my power."

The king said: "Let a prisoner be brought, that he may be beheaded at once."

Then Didi recovered himself and said: "No, O my lord! I do not work my magic on men. Would it not be more fitting for us to make such an experiment on animals?"

Then a goose was brought, that he might work his magic upon it.

(From the tale of *Khofu and the Magicians*)

Source Notes

THE TITLES of the publications most frequently cited have been abbreviated as follows:

A   *al-Ahram* (daily newspaper)
AI   *al-Ahram al-Iktissadi* (bimonthly magazine)
AK   *al-Katib* (monthly)
CBE Econ. Rev. *Central Bank of Egypt: Economic Review* (quarterly)
COC   *Cahiers de l'Orient contemporain* (quarterly; Paris)
EC   *L'Egypt contemporaine* (quarterly)
EI   *L'Egypte Industrielle* (bimonthly)
EPSR   *Egyptian Political Science Review* (monthly; publication stopped)
G   *al-Gumhuriyya* (daily newspaper)
MEJ   *The Middle East Journal* (quarterly; New York)
MENA   *Middle East News Agency*
M   *al-Missa* (daily newspaper)
NBE Econ. Bull. *National Bank of Egypt Economic Bulletin* (quarterly)
RY   *Rose el-Yussef* (weekly)

PREFACE

1. Written by Nagib Mahfuz as he was finishing his latest novel, *Miramar* (Cairo, 1967), a work of rare insight.

2. Also, it was often: "No Zakaria! No dollar!," the general feeling being at the time that Vice-President Zakaria Mohieddine would be more amenable to Western overtures. Cf. Eric Rouleau and J.-F. Held, *Israël et les arabes, le troisième combat* (Paris, Le Seuil, 1967).

3. "On the Israeli-Arab War," *New Left Review*, No. 44 (July-August 1967), pp. 30–45.

4. Detailed analysis and references first given in my essay, "Nasserism and Socialism," *The Socialist Register 1964* (London, The Merlin Press, 1964), pp. 38–55.

5. Cf. my two essays "Le Rôle de l'armée dans la vie politique en République Arabe Unie," *Le Mois en Afrique*, No. 14, (February 1967), pp. 58–73, and "Crisis in Nasser's Egypt," *New Left Review*, No. 45 (September-October 1967), pp. 67–81.

6. From the point of view of scientific sociological analysis, the only contemporary society which can be described technically as a "military society" *stricto sensu* is the Israeli society. The best study available is S. N. Eisenstadt, *Israeli Society* (London, 1968).

7. I owe it to C. Wright Mill's memory to mention the following fact: I did not read his *Sociological Imagination* until 1965, i.e., three full years after the first draft of my book was written. It confirmed, strengthened and enriched my thought and vision, as it has done with a great many sociologists around the world. On the methodological aspect, cf. my paper "Sociology and Economic History: An Essay on Mediation," at the Conference on the Economic History of the Middle East, School of Oriental and African Studies, University of London (July 4–6, 1967). Early 1968 publication.

8. Further elaborated in "Introduction à la pensée arabe contemporaine," in *Anthologie de la littérature arabe contemporaine, II: les Essais* (Paris, Le Seuil, 1965), pp. 9–33; "Problématique du socialisme dans le monde arabe," *L'Homme et la société*, No. 2 (October-December 1966), pp. 125–48; "Robespierre, le Jacobinisme et la conscience nationale égyptienne," in *Actes du colloque Roberspierre* (Vienna, 1965; Paris, Société des études Robespierristes, 1967), pp. 283–303; "Esquisse d'une typologie des formations nationales dans les Trois Continents," *Cahiers Internationaux de Sociologie*, XLII (1967), pp. 49–57; "Sociologie du développement national: problèmes de conceptualisation, quelques remarques introductoires," *Revue de l'Institut de Sociologie*, No. 2–3 (Brussels, 1967), pp. 249–64; and, in Arabic, *Dirassat fi'l-thakafa al-wataniyya* (Studies in National Culture), Dar al-Tali'a, (Beirut, 1967).

9. As interpreted in my "L'Orientalisme en crise," *Diogène*, No. 44 (October-December 1963), pp. 109–42.

PART I

1. *Al-Mussawar* (1953), quoted by Ibrahim Amer in *Thawrat Misr al-kawmiyya* (Egypt's National Revolution), p. 43. Cairo, 1957.

2. The non-Egyptian reader will find an interesting description in Jean and Simone Lacouture's book, *L'Egypte en mouvement*, 2nd ed. (Paris, 1962), pp. 98–115 (English translation: *Egypt in Transition*, London, 1958, Methuen—Criterion Books, New York, pp. 105–122). A curious document on *Une nouvelle convulsion du mouvement panarabe: l'insurrection du 26 janvier 1952 au Caire* (A New Convulsion of the Pan-Arab Movement: the Insurrection of January 26, 1952 in Cairo), published by the Central Committee of Overseas France, Vol. 3 (Paris, 1952), professes to see in it "analogies with prerevolutionary Russia"; "a short time earlier, the Soviet fishing fleet had been hailed at Port Said . . ." (p. 5). From sardines to the burning of the capital, so to speak.

3. "Min agl 'huriyyati wa 'huriyyat biladi" (For My Liberty and My Country's Liberty), *M*, December 2, 1958.

4. "Bayya' wa mudmin kira'a" (A Salesman Crazy about Reading), *M*, November 13, 1958.

5. "Kissat al-taalim ma kanetchi 'ala'l-bal" (The Question of Education Was Not on the Books), *M*, November 30, 1958.

6. *A*, January 8, 1960.

7. *A*, January 22, 1960.

8. *A*, September 17, 1961.

9. All Egyptian historians admit the valuable contribution of the scientific mission that accompanied Bonaparte. Emphasis is put at the same time on the persistence of Egyptian culture in spite of the Turkish occupation and on the national resistance of the Egyptian people. Shafik Ghorbal, Abdel Rahman el-Rafei, Mohammed Anis and Hussein Mo'nes, among others, point to this. There is a convincing demonstration of it in *Fi ussul al-mas'ala al-misriyya* (On the Principles of the Egyptian Question), by Sobhi Wahida (Cairo, 1950); in *Sindbad Misri* (An Egyptian Sindbad), by Hussein Fawzi (Cairo, 1961); and in Mohammed Fuad Shukry's monumental work *Al-'hamla al-Françiyya wa-khurug al-Françiyyin min Misr* (The French Expedition and the French withdrawal from Egypt), Cairo, 1962.

10. Fawzi Guergues, *Dirassat fi tarikh Misr al-siyassi munzu'l-'asr al-Mamluki* (Studies in the Political History of Egypt since the Mameluk Era), pp. 36–7 (Cairo, 1958).

11. Ibrahim Amer, *Al-ard wa'l-fellah, al-mas'ala al-zira'iyya fi Misr* (The Land and the Fellah: The Agrarian Problem in Egypt), pp. 81–2. Cairo, 1938.

12. *Rapport de Lord Cromer sur l'Egypte et le Soudan pour l'année 1905* (*Lord Cromer's Report on Egypt and the Sudan for the Year 1905*), p. 117. French translation published in Cairo, 1906; detailed list by E. Burns, *British Imperialism in Egypt* (London, 1928).

13. Amer, *Thawrat Misr, op. cit.*, pp. 16–17; NBE, *Al-Bank al-*

Ahli al-Misri 1898–1948 (The National Bank of Egypt 1898–1948). Cairo, 1948.

14. A. E. Crouchley, *The Investment of Foreign Capital in Egyptian Companies and Public Debt* (Cairo, 1936), pp. 58 ff.; Mohammed Fahmy Leheita, *Tarikh Misr al-iktissadi fi'l-'ussur al-haditha* (The Economic History of Egypt in Modern Times), p. 476 (Cairo, 1944); *Al-kitab al-sanawi li Ittihad al-Sina'at al-Misriyya 1957–1958* (EFI Yearbook 1957–1958), p. 247 (Cairo, 1958).

15. Shohdi Attia el-Shafei, *Tatawwor al-'haraka al-wataniyya al-misriyya 1882–1956* (The Evolution of the Egyptian National Movement), p. 12, (Cairo, 1957); Charles P. Issawi, *Egypt at Mid-Century* (Oxford U. Press, 1954), p. 36. Also, see chapter on the agrarian question.

16. Issawi, *op. cit.*, pp. 40–1. Shohdi A. el-Shafei points out that the National Spinning Co. of Alexandria had 260 workers, the fez factory had 180 of both sexes and the Cairo brick factory had 150 (*op. cit.*, p. 29). Cf. E. H. Mulock, *Report on the Economic and Financial Situation of Egypt for 1919* (London, 1920).

17. Guergues, *op. cit.*, p. 131.

18. "Bank Misr fi khidmat al-iktissad al-kawmi 1920–1960" (Bank Misr in the Service of National Economy 1920–1960), *A*, October 26, 1961.

19. Quoted in Shafei, *op. cit.*, p. 50.

20. Guergues, *op. cit.*, pp. 139–40.

21. M. K. Issa speaks of "the end of the British monopoly [of Egyptian foreign trade] and the beginnings of the Anglo-American monopoly in 1921," in "Anglo-American Rivalry in Egypt between the Two World Wars," *Review of Economic, Political and Business Studies V*, No. 2 (Cairo, 1957), pp. 43–4.

22. This tendency is recognized by all: Ibrahim Amer and Fawzi Guergues, but also Rashed el-Barawi in *The Military Coup in Egypt* (Cairo, 1952), pp. 58, 70–1; K. Grunwald and J. O. Ronald, *Industrialization in the Middle East* (New York, 1960), pp. 182–205; Y. Durelle, "Structure et développement de l'économie égyptienne," *Economie et Politique*, No. 72 (July-August 1960), pp. 36–53; etc.

23. Former Undersecretary of Commerce and Industry Abdallah Fikry Abaza, *La Part des capitaux étrangers dans l'économie nationale* (The Share of Foreign Capital in the National Economy), Cairo, 1951, quoted in Amer, *Thawrat Misr, op. cit.*, p. 56.

24. *EFI Yearbook* (Cairo, 1948); Amer, *Thawrat Misr, op. cit.*, pp. 68–9.

25. At the time when the French Chamber of Deputies was studying the Montreux agreements for the elimination of the Capitulations, the Foreign Affairs Committee's report showed that although the overall total of capital in circulation in Egypt in

1938 was 55 billion francs, foreign investment amounted to 50 billion, of which 30 billion represented French investments (*A*, July 10, 1938).

26. Statistics taken from Abaza, *op. cit.*

27. Barawi, *op. cit.*, p. 66.

28. United Nations, *Economic Evolution in the Middle East, 1945–1954* (New York, 1955); but, mainly, M. M. Hamdi, *A Statistical Survey of the Development of Capital Investment in Egypt since 1880*. Unpublished Ph.D. thesis (London, 1943), pp. 1–51, 251–322.

29. Issawi, *op. cit.*, p. 90; *Kitab al-Maglis al-Da'em li Tanmiyat al-Intag al-Kawmi* (The Book of the Permanent Council for the Development of National Production), Cairo, 1955.

30. Eva Garzuzi, *Old Ills and New Remedies in Egypt* (Cairo, c. 1959), p. 15.

31. High Committee of Agrarian Reform, *Haza al-fellah wa usrat Mohammed Ali* (This Fellah and Mohammed Ali's Dynasty), Cairo, c. 1952; Amer, *Thawrat Misr, op. cit.*, pp. 41–3.

32. Taha Hussein, the dean of Arab letters, has set forth his philosophy of Egyptian culture in an important work, *Mustakbal al-thakafa fi Misr* (The Future of Culture in Egypt), Cairo, 1936, in which he affirms Egypt's Mediterranean destiny.

33. On this legislation, cf., among others, Zaki Badawi, *Les Problèmes du travail et les organisations ouvrières en Egypte* (The Problems of Labor and Workers' Organizations in Egypt), French translation, Alexandria, 1948; Mohammed Fahim Amin, *Tarikh al-'haraka al-nikabiyya wa tashri'at al-'amal fi Misr* (History of the Trade Union Movement and of the Labor Legislation in Egypt), Cairo, 1961.

34. "The landed aristocracy had more than one means of assuring the permanence of its legislative and executive powers . . . Direct universal suffrage, even though it was democratic, kept this class of society in power." Adel Amer, *La Faillite du système constitutionnel égyptien* (The Bankruptcy of the Egyptian Constitutional System). Unpublished thesis in law (Paris, 1955), p. 413. Cf. the recent general survey of Zaher Masood Quraishi, *Liberal Nationalism in Egypt: Rise and Fall of the Wafd Party* (Allahabad, 1967).

35. This period, which gave birth to the Free Officers, among other groups, has been very little examined. Some sources are: Abdel Rahman el-Rafei, *Fi a 'kab al-thawra al-Misriyya*, II (In the Footsteps of the Egyptian Revolution), pp. 191–221 (Cairo, 1959), and *Mukaddimat thawrat thalatha wa ishrin yolyo 1952* (Prolegomena to the July 23 Revolution), Cairo, 1957; Amer, *Thawrat Misr, op. cit.*, pp. 66–75; Shafei, *op. cit.*, pp. 80–6; Guergues, *op. cit.*, pp. 172–8; Ahmed Baha'Eddine, *Faruk malikan*

1936–1952 (King Faruk 1936–1952), Cairo, 1952; the collective dossier "Asalib al-nidal al-Miçri min harb al-tahrir didd al-ghazw al-Frinçi ila'l-mouqawama al-sha'biyya didd al-'oudwan al-thoulathi" (The Methods of the Egyptian Struggle, from the War of Liberation against the French Invasion to the Popular Resistance against the Tripartite Aggression), *al-Tali'a*, III, No. 12 (1967), p. 7–55.

36. Ahmed Hussein published his credo, *Imani* (My Faith), Cairo, 1936, a sort of Egyptian *Mein Kampf*. It was then that the young Gamal Abdel Nasser joined the ranks of Misr al-Fatat, in which he remained for two years.

37. Sadek Saad, *Ma'sat al-tamwin* (The Tragedy of Supply [literally, of Food]). Cairo, 1945.

38. In his testimony at the trial of the murderer of Amin Osman Pasha, Mustafa el-Nahas raised the possibility of an infiltration by British provocators . . .

39. On the history of the intellectual movements of the time, cf. R. Makarius, *La Jeunesse intellectuelle d'Egypte au lendemain de la deuxième guerre mondiale* (The Intellectual Youth of Egypt after the Second World War), Paris-The Hague, 1960. The often quoted works of Shohdi A. el-Shafei, Fawzi Guergues and Ibrahim Amer have been thoroughly mutilated by the censor. The story told by W. Z. Laqueur in his *Communism and Nationalism in the Middle East*, (London, 1957), pp. 31–62, is secondhand and, what is more, riddled with lacunae. A certain number of very richly documented publications bearing on the history of Egyptian Communism from 1939 to 1958 appeared clandestinely, beginning in 1947. It is not improbable that the greater part has been irreparably destroyed.

40. Shafei, *op. cit.*, p. 95.

41. Rafei, *Fi a'kab, op. cit.*, III (Cairo, 1951), pp. 178–9.

42. Cf. Shafei, *op. cit.*, pp. 98–9; but the censor has greatly slashed the text.

43. From 1945 to 1949 the following held power: Mahmud Fahmy el-Nokrashy (February 24, 1945); Ismail Sidky (February 17, 1946); Nokrashy (December 9, 1946); Ibrahim Abdel Hadi (December 28, 1948); Hussein Sirry (November 3, 1949).

44. The result was the first "great Communist trial" after the war: twenty party leaders were indicted; they were acquitted February 24, 1955. Cf. A, July 10–17, 1946.

45. And yet a pro-Arab English professor, A. J. M. Craig, confines himself to a psycho-social description of the student circles in which he lived: *"The Egyptian Students,"* MEJ, VII, No. 3 (1955), pp. 293–9.

46. Rafei, *Fi a'kab, op. cit.*, III, pp. 262–72; Barawi, *op. cit.*, pp. 161–3.

47. Quoted in Shafei, *op. cit.*, p. 112.

48. A National Front committee held a meeting in Sept. 1951;

the participants included Fathi Raduan, Ahmed Hussein and Ahmed Kamel Kotb representing the Peasant Socialist Party, and Yussef Helmy, secretary-general of the Peace Movement. *Al-Malayin,* No. 19 (September 2, 1951).

49. Even *Akhbar el-Yom* admitted it; cf. Shafei, *op. cit.,* p. 118.

50. The *Times* of London, December 26, 1951.

51. Shafei, *op. cit.,* p. 116.

52. *Ibid.,* p. 120.

53. *Ibid.,* p. 121.

54. Reflecting on "the epic of the Egyptian people," Hussein Fawzi was to say quite rightly: "January 1952, or what I shall call the suicidal act of a people conquered within itself, having lost all faith in its representatives." (*Op. cit.,* p. 56.)

55. Cf. the January-July 1952 volume of the weekly *Actualité:* it contains a rich survey called a "digest of the Arab press," as well as analyses that I contributed under the pseudonym of "Ebn el-Nil." The volume can be found in the National Library in Cairo under "Per. 1628, 1629." A survey of available sources and "acceptable" hypotheses can be found in Abdel Rahman el-Rafei's last volume in his history of the national movement: *Mukaddimat thawrat, op. cit.,* pp. 113–49.

56. UN, *op. cit.,* pp. 33–46.

57. This last document, "EFI Report for the Year 1952," is in *EI,* XXIX, No. 6 (1953), pp. 21–34. It is shocking to observe that no authors except Shafei, *op. cit.,* pp. 136–8, and Guergues, *op. cit.,* pp. 215–7, cite these documents.

58. Especially P. W. Taylor, the minister in charge of commercial questions at the British embassy in Cairo: *Economic and Commercial Conditions in Egypt* (London, November 1947), p. 4.

59. Dr. Sobhi Wahida, an economist educated in Italy, and secretary-general of the Egyptian Federation of Industries after the war, was one of the most intelligent representatives of the rising new technocracy. He was the victim of an assassin in 1956. Cf. my article in *M,* January 8, 1959.

60. Sources to be consulted on this period include: Barawi, *op. cit.;* Anwar el-Sadate, *Kissat al-thawra al-Misriyya* (The Complete Story of the Revolution), Cairo, 1957—American edition (New York, 1957) entitled *Revolt on the Nile;* also by Sadate: *Asrar al-thawra al-Misriyya* (The Secrets of the Egyptian Revolution), Cairo, 1957; Rafei, *Mukaddimat thawrat, op. cit.;* interesting accounts in Lacouture, *op. cit.,* and in Tom Little's *Egypt* (New York, 1958). The book by Andrew Tully, *CIA—The Inside Story* (New York, 1962), confirms the existence of close ties between that agency and the Free Officers: at the time of the burning of Cairo, Tully says, "CIA and British Intelligence began casting about for somebody to take over. General Walter Bedell Smith was director of CIA, but much of the planning for the Egyptian

intelligence campaign was put in the hands of Allen Dulles, then Smith's No. 2 man. At first a survey was made of Egypt's Wafd Party, but the verdict was that the only potential leaders either were as corrupt as Faruk or too weak to stand up to him. With no great enthusiasm CIA turned to the Army . . . CIA agents and British intelligence operators were close to these young reformers at the time and correctly gauged their strength . . . Naguib was CIA's man . . . As late as a few days before the Free Officers' coup which unseated Faruk [whom the author calls 'Faruk the swine, an absolute and degenerate monarch'], Nasser's plan called for the assassination of thirty military and political leaders, including the King. CIA heard of this and an agent hurried to Nasser to present a horrified dissent to this blood bath. Nasser was told, in effect: 'Look, it's no good killing a lot of people without any assurance that the killing will change the system . . .' The Brotherhood, of course, was spurring Nasser on, but he made no move until he had consulted people he considered more expert on such matters as military coups. This was CIA, which had sent a number of its skilled operatives to Cairo to keep a close watch on the weakening Faruk regime. Among these operatives were former Army intelligence officers who had spent most of their careers in the Middle East and with whom Nasser felt at home. CIA gave the word late in July 1952, and Nasser's Free Officers Corps swung into action . . . CIA suggested that Naguib present Faruk with a demand that he renounce his power to dissolve Parliament and appoint prime ministers . . . Nasser remained in the background, a shadowy figure the CIA suspected of biding his time for a seizure of power. At this time, a CIA appraisal reaching Washington described Nasser thus: 'His vices are vanity, obstinacy, suspicion, avidity for power. His strengths are complete self-confidence, great resilience, courage and nervous control, willingness to take great risks, great tactical skill and stubborn attachment to initial aims. He gets boyish pleasure out of conspiratorial doings. Has a real streak of self-pity. While a patient, subtle organizer, he can lose his head.' . . . By early 1954 . . . [a] CIA report . . . said it was 'obvious' Nasser would unseat Naguib . . . This was followed by the CIA's 'contempt' because it thought that Nasser would yield in 1956." (Pp. 102–12.) It is difficult to establish the facts, but in the period 1952–54 the Free Officers did in fact enjoy excellent relations with the United States; Minister Ali Sabry was personally entrusted with Egyptian-American relations.

PART II

1. The Land Problem

1. This chapter draws in part on two earlier studies: "La reforma agraria en Egito," in *Combate*, IV, No. 20 (Costa Rica, 1962), pp. 24–32, and "La Question agraire en Egypte et la réforme de 1952," in *Tiers-Monde*, III, Nos. 9–10 (1962), pp. 181–216.

2. Amer, *Al-ard, op. cit.* This book, as well as the works of Shohdi A. el-Shafei, Fawzi Guergues and Ibrahim Amer, was published by Lutfallah Soliman. It was he who introduced in Egypt the ideas of K. Wittfögel, the author of the celebrated *Oriental Despotism* (New Haven, 1957), on the hydraulic society, ideas that are encountered again at the core of the book by Ibrahim Amer that we discuss.

3. Amer, *Al-ard, op. cit.*, p. 53. Baron Jechereau de St. Denis, in his *Histoire de l'empire ottoman (1792–1894)*, said: "It seems, on the basis of a few documents which history has handed down to us, that from the time of the Pharaohs the ownership of the soil inhered in the sovereign and that it was according to this principle, slightly modified, that the country was ruled by the kings of the Ptolemaic dynasty and by the Romans." Quoted by Yacub Artin, *La Propriété foncière en Egypte* (Land Ownership in Egypt), p. 72, Cairo, 1883. (There is a good thesis by R. F. Bastouly: *Le Régime foncier en Egypte depuis l'époque grec jusqu'au X° siècle de notre ère*—The Land System in Egypt from the Greek Period to the Tenth Century A.D. Unpublished M.S., Paris, 1962.)

4. Mohammed Kamel Mursy, *"L'Evolution historique du droit de propriété foncière en Egypte"* (The Historical Evolution of the Right to Landownership in Egypt), in *EC* (1935), p. 288; this is the introduction to his thesis, *Al-milkiyya al-ʿakariyya fi Misr wa tatawworiha al-tarikhi min ʿahd al-Pharaʿina hattaʾl-an* (Landownership in Egypt and Its Historical Evolution from the Times of the Pharaohs until Today), Cairo, n.d., c. 1940.

5. Rushton Coulborn, ed., *Feudalism in History* (Princeton, 1956). There is a much more detailed explanation in *La Civilisation égyptienne*, by A. Ermann and H. Ranke (French translation, Paris, 1952), pp. 111–34, 578–600. Also, François Daumas, *La civilisation de l'Egypte Pharaonique*, (Paris, 1965), p. 215–46. It is from this period, it seems, that we should date the so-called code of Bosheris, a king of the Twenty-fifth Dynasty, which recognized the *jus abutendi*. (Mursy, "L'Evolution historique," *op. cit.*, p. 290)

6. *Ibid.*, p. 293.

7. Artin, *op. cit.*, pp. 69, 77, 78–81.

8. *Ibid.*, p. 86.

9. Amer, *Al-ard, op. cit.*, p. 64.

10. The text of this exchange will be found in Karl Marx-Friedrich Engels, *On Colonialism* (Moscow, n.d.), pp. 277–8; French translation in *Molitor*, III (Paris, 1931), pp. 216–26. Maxime Rodinson has drawn my attention to two works published in East Berlin that provide important critical developments of these theses. One is the German edition of Karl Marx, *Grundrisse der Kritik der politischen Ökonomie, Rohentwurf, 1857–8* (Outline of the Criticism of Political Economy, First Draft, 1857–8), Berlin, 1953; the other is E. C. Weiskopf, *Die Produktionsverhältnisse im alten Orient und in der griechisch-römischen Antike. Ein Diskussionsbeitrag* (Production Relationships in the Ancient Orient and in Greek and Roman Antiquity: A Contribtuion to a Discussion), Berlin, 1957. E. E. Leach, "Hydraulic Society in Ceylon," in *Past and Present*, No. 15 (April 1959), pp. 2–29, contains a Marxian criticism of Wittfögel's theses.

11. Amer, *Al-ard, op. cit.*, p. 69.

12. Artin, *op. cit.*, pp. 95–6.

13. Amer, *Al-ard, op. cit.*, pp. 79–97.

14. Rashed el-Barawi and Mohammed Hamza Eleish, *Al-tatawwor al-iktissadi fi Misr fi'l-'asr al-hadith* (Economic Evolution in Egypt during the Modern Era), 4th ed. (Cairo, 1949), pp. 59–65. On the life of the peasant, the classic works of P. H. Ayrout, *Moeurs et coutumes des fellahs* (Manners and Customs of the Fellahs), Paris, 1938, and J. Berque, *Histoire sociale d'un village égyptien au XX° siècle* (Social History of an Egyptian Village in the Twentieth Century), Paris-The Hague, 1957, among others.

15. The census of 1821 gave the following figures: 5,532,000 inhabitants and 2,231,915 *feddans*. Abdel Rahman el-Gabarti, as well as Amin Sami, Yacub Artin and the *Journal Officiel*, provides background of the impressive account given by Mohammed Sobeih in *Kissat al-ard fi iklim Misr* (The Story of Land in the Egyptian Region), pp. 22–45 (Cairo, 1960).

16. Amer, *Al-ard, op. cit.*, pp. 81–2.

17. Ismail accomplished the establishment of the landed aristocracy; see the list of donations to the members of the dynasty and the prominent men of the kingdom, *Al-aradi allati sara ihabuha wa i'hsanuha bi amr fakhametlu al-khidiwi Ismail pasha* (The Lands That Were Permitted and Distributed by Order of His Highness Khedive Ismail Pasha), discovered in the archives of Abdin Palace, in Sobeih, *op. cit.*, pp. 51–8.

18. Cf. Gabriel Baer's important book, *A History of Landownership in Modern Egypt, 1800–1950* (London-New York, Oxford U. Press, 1962).

19. High Committee on Agrarian Reform's *Haza al-fellah (op. cit.)*, quoted by Amer, *Thawrat Misr, op. cit.*, pp. 41–3.

20. Amer, *Al-ard, op. cit.*, pp. 91–2.

21. This word, borrowed from the Chinese Marxists, has since been naturalized in French; in the *Grand Larousse Encyclopédique* it is defined thus: "a native who is the required intermediary for trade between colonial companies and those populations whose governments forbid them all relations with foreigners." In political terminology the word is synonymous with "parasite"; it designates that sector of the middle class in colonized countries, especially the merchants, which grows rich by trading with the colonial power.

22. There is a good description of this method of exploitation in Samir Saffa, *Exploitation économique et agricole d'un domaine rural égyptien* (Economic and Agricultural Exploitation of a Rural Egyptian Estate), thesis in law (Paris, 1948). Also J. Anhury, "Les Grandes Lignes de l'économie agricole de l'Egypte," (Broad Outlines of the Agricultural Economy of Egypt), in *EC*, No. 199 (1941), pp. 570–81.

23. P. Fromont, *Cours d'économie rurale—le progrès agricole au XX⁰ siècle en France et en Egypte* (Course of Rural Economy—Agricultural Progress in the Twentieth Century in France and Egypt), p. 87 (Paris, 1954).

24. See especially Mohammed Hussein, *Al-ittigahat al-wataniyya fi'l-adab al-mu'asser* (Patriotic Trends in Contemporary Literature), II (Cairo, 1956); Shawki Deif, *Al-adab al-'Arabi al-mu'asser fi Misr 1850–1950* (Contemporary Arabic Literature in Egypt 1850–1950), Cairo, 1957; Mustafa M. Musharrafa, *Cultural Survey of Modern Egypt*, two volumes (London, 1948); a good sociological description by H. Ammar, *Growing Up in an Egyptian Village* (London, 1954).

25. "Pression démographique et stratification sociale dans les campagnes égyptiennes" (Population Pressure and Social Stratification in Egyptian Rural Areas), by a study group of the IEDES, in its publication, *Tiers-Monde*, I, No. 2 (1960), pp. 319–20.

26. There are good studies on the history of banks in Egypt, notably Professor Fuad Mursi, *Al-nukud wa'l-bunuk fi'l-bilad al-'Arabiyya: (1) Misr wa'l-Sudan* (Coins and Banks in Arab Countries: (1) Egypt and the Sudan), Cairo, 1955, followed by *Al-nukud wa'l-bunuk* (Coins and Banks), Cairo, 1958; Ali el-Gereitly, *Tatawwor al-nizan al-masrafi fi Misr* (The Evolution of the Banking System in Egypt), Cairo, 1961; Ali Abdel Rassul, *Al-bunuk al-tugariyya fi Misr* (The Commercial Banks in Egypt), Cairo, 1961.

27. Ahmed Rushdi Saleh, editor in chief of *al-Fagr al-Gadid* in 1945–46, is the author of a very important book on popular literature, *Al-adab al-shaabi* (Popular Literature), Cairo, 1950 and 1955, followed by *Funun al-adab al-shaabi* (The Arts of Popular Literature), two volumes (Cairo, 1957). Director of the Center of

Popular Arts in the Ministry of Culture, he headed its magazine, *Folklore*. All of this offers an abundant harvest to the future historians of the peasant movement.

28. On the treachery of the Bedouins and Mohammed Sultan Pasha there are contemporary reports, notably those of John Ninet, of the lawyer Broadley, of W. S. Blunt, the *muzakkarat* (memoirs) of Ahmed Arabi and Mohammed Abdu, the works of Rafei. Until there is a systematic search of the Abdin archives, see R. L. Tignor, "Some Materials for a History of the Arabi Revolution: A Bibliographical Survey," in *MEJ*, XVI, No. 2 (1962), pp. 239–48.

29. Mohammed Khattab frequented the Dar al-Abhath al-Ilmiyya group at that time, when its leaders, Shohdi Attia el-Shafei and Abdel Maabud el-Gibeili, published their programatic book, *Ahdafuna al-wataniyya* (Our National Aspirations). Cairo, 1945.

30. Sadek Saad, *Mushkelat al-fellah* (The Fellah Problem), pp. 7–8, 61–9 (Cairo, n.d., c. 1945).

31. Speech to the Senate, in *A*, July 16, 1946.

32. From the French translation of the text published in 1945 under the title "Un programme de réforme agraire pour l'Egypte" (A Program of Agrarian Reform for Egypt), in *EC*, Vol. 38 (1947), pp. 1–66.

33. Sayed Kotb, *Al-Islam wa'l-ra'smaliyya* (Islam and Capitalism), Cairo, 1951. On the detailed programs of political parties and groups, see Gabriel Baer, "Egyptian Attitudes Towards Land Reform (1922–1955)," in W. Z. Laqueur, *The Middle East in Transition* (London, 1958), pp. 80–99, reprinted in Baer, *A History of Landownership, op. cit.*, pp. 201–19.

34. Texts emphasized by Amer, *Al-ard, op. cit.*, pp. 136–7; the following documents are involved: UN, *Land Reform, Defects in Agrarian Structure as Obstacles to Economic Development* (New York, 1952); U.S. State Department, *Land Reform, A World Challenge* (Washington, 1952); Gordon Gray, *Report to the President on Foreign Economic Policies* (Washington, 1952); *Report of the International Development Advisory Board to the President* (Washington, 1951).

35. Both at the beginning of Marei's book, *Al-isla'h al-zira'i fi Misr* (Agrarian Reform in Egypt), Cairo, 1957, and in *Al-kitab al-sanawi li'l-Gumhuriyya al-Arabiyya al-Muttahida, 1959*, (UAR Yearbook for 1959), p. 442.

36. Aziz Khanki, "Hawadeth al-ightiyal fi'l-aryaf," (Murder in the Countryside), *A*, October 23, 1944.

37. Ten days after the coup d'état, the editorial in *Actualité*, signed "Ebn el-Nil," was the only one in the Egyptian press to define July 23, 1952, as "a coup d'état, not a revolution."

38. The official version was given by General Mohammed Naguib in *Egypt's Destiny* (London, 1955), pp. 172–4: 29 persons belonging to the Democratic Movement of National Liberation

(DMNL) were accused of having started the trouble, causing the deaths of 9 persons (including 1 policeman and 2 soldiers) and the wounding of 23 others (including 7 policemen); 13 of the accused were sentenced to prison terms ranging from five to fifteen years, 15 were acquitted and 2 were condemned to death and executed.

39. Marei, *op. cit.*; also *UAR Yearbook for 1959, loc. cit.* In 1962 Galal Keshk admitted that the Agrarian Reform of 1952, "more than anything else, created the popular base that has surrounded the socialist state with its allegience, the state that gave the land to the peasants . . ." (discussion of "Mustakbal al-milkiyya al-fardiyya" (The Future of Private Ownership), in *RY*, No. 1769 (May 7, 1962). The state of those days hardly spoke of "socialism."

40. On the law of 1952, see Mohammed Ali Arafa, *Shar'h kanun al-isla'h al-zira'i* (Explanation of the Law on Agrarian Reform). Cairo, 1959.

41. Fromont, *op. cit.*, p. 125. The figures are those of Minister A. M. Nur, in his press conference on the tenth anniversary of the Agrarian Reform, in *A*, September 9, 1962.

42. *UAR Yearbook for 1959, op. cit.*, pp. 469–70.

43. Doreen Warriner, *Land and Poverty in the Middle East* (London, 1948); *Land Reform and Economic Development* (London, 1955); *Land Reform and Development in the Middle East* (London, 1957; 2nd ed. 1962). Gabriel S. Saab's well-documented *The Egyptian Agrarian Reform 1952–1962* (Oxford U. Press, London, 1967) stresses the inefficient results of this altogether very timid "revolution," and subtly puts forth the theses of private landowners.

44. Ali el-Shalakani, "Mushkelat igarat al-aradi al-zira'iyya wa kanun al-isla'h" (The Problem of Renting the Farmland and the Agrarian Reform Law), then "Hal yadfaa al-fellah aksatan za'ida?" (Is the Fellah Paying Excessive Instalments?), in *M*, August 8 and September 25, 1958.

45. *G*, September 17, 1958.

46. Amer, *Al-ard, op. cit.*, p. 153.

47. An American observer quoted the following figures furnished by a high official of the agrarian-reform agency for January 1959:

Land requisitioned	240,000	*feddans*
Land confiscated from the Mohammed Ali family	180,000	
Land sold by former owners	145,000	
	565,000	*feddans*
Land retained by the agency	130,247	*feddans*

Keith Wheelock, *Nasser's New Egypt*, (New York-London, 1960), p. 81.

48. *UAR Yearbook for 1959, op. cit.*, pp. 467–8.

49. *L'Egypte entreprend sa réforme agraire* (Egypt Begins Her Agrarian Reform), in *Croissance des jeunes nations* (Growth of the New Nations), No. 23 (June-July 1963), p. 14.

50. *I'hsa' al-nikabat wa'l-itti'hadat al-'ummaliyya fi Gumhuriyyat Misr* (Statistics of the Trade Unions and the Trade Union Federations in the Republic of Egypt). Cairo, 1956.

51. Ali el-Shalakani, "Al-taadil al-akhir fi kanun al-isla'h al-zira'i" (The Latest Modification in the Agrarian Reform Law) and *"Min al-ussus al-iktissadiyya li thawrat al-isla'h al-zira'i"* (On the Economic Foundations of the Agrarian Reform Revolution), in *M*, August 29 and October 2, 1958. On the general situation, cf. M.E.A. Abu Hindia, *Irrigation in Modern Egypt: A Study in Economic Geography.* Unpublished Ph.D. thesis, London, 1955.

52. See the note explaining the Order in Council in *A*, July 26, 1961; also Warriner, *Land Reform and Development, op. cit.*, 2nd ed., pp. 191–229.

53. Statements of the "provincial" minister, Hassan Boghdadi, in *A*, July 30, 1961.

54. On this matter, see the Aziz Wafa'i trial and the defense of Sayed Marei in *AK*, January 9 and 11, 1962. In the first case the accused was acquitted, and Sayed Marei was received by the President (*A*, April 11 and 16, 1962); the final verdict acquitted all the high officials and convicted four civilians (*A*, June 1, 1962).

55. Ministerial decrees, in *A*, November 2, 1961.

56. *M*, September 9, 1958. However, *UAR Yearbook for 1959, op. cit.*, gives the figures of £E29,760,594 for 1959 (p. 511); and Garzuzi says that the number of farm co-operatives rose from 1,689 in 1952 to 1,917 in 1955 (*op. cit.*, p. 43).

57. *UAR Yearbook for 1962*, pp. 270–4, Nur speech, *A*, September 9, 1962.

58. *UAR Yearbook for 1959, op. cit.*, p. 457.

59. Statements by Sayed Marei to *A*, February 17, 1960.

60. *A*, January 23, 1960.

61. "Agrarian Reform in Egypt," in *NBE Econ. Bull.*, V, No. 3 (1952), p. 167.

62. "EFI Report . . . 1952," *op. cit.*, p. 22.

63. Marei, *Al-isla'h, op. cit.*

64. *EFI Yearbook 1955–1956* (Cairo, 1957), p. 18.

65. "Absenteeism is most widespread among the very smallest proprietors of less than one *feddan* (in 1950 there were 1,981,000 owners of less than one *feddan* but only 214,300 worked their land. In 1956, out of a total of 2,985,400 owners of less than one *feddan*, 405,200 worked their land)." Gabriel Saab, *Motorisation de l'agriculture et développement agricole au Proche-Orient* (Motorization of Agriculture and Agricultural Development in the Near East), p. 309, Note 1. (Paris, 1960).

66. Sayed Marei stated in 1957: "The system of ownership under agrarian reform is one of limited ownership for each individual, with the organization of agricultural exploitation in the hands of a general co-operative system . . . The basis of the farm under reform is individual ownership. Each man has his parcel of land, the product of which belongs to him personally. The reform co-operative society facilitates the means of this exploitation for him." Quoted in Saab, *Motorisation, op. cit.,* p. 312, Note 1.

67. Durelle, *op. cit.,* pp. 45–6.

68. *Political and Economic Planning: World Population and Resources,* (London, 1955), pp. 127–8.

69. UN, *Economic Evolution, op. cit.,* p. 136.

70. Saab, *Motorisation, op. cit.,* pp. 317–22. Cf. also the same author's already mentioned detailed survey, from a capitalistic point of view, *The Egyptian Agrarian Reform 1952–1962,* to be contrasted, *inter alia,* with Dr. Hazem el-Beblaui, *L'Interrelation agriculture-industrie et le développement économique, étude de l'interdépendance de production au cours du développement économique appliquée à l'exemple égyptien* (Paris, 1966), and A. Abdel-Malek, "La Réforme agraire en Egypte (RAU): problèmes et perspectives," *Développement et Civilisations,* No. 22 (June 1965), pp. 19–27.

71. Cf. the analysis of the first results of the 1959–60 census, in *A,* October 24 and 25, 1960. Cf. W. Cleland, *The Population Problem in Egypt* (Lancaster, Pa., 1936), especially pp. 69–107.

72. Here is the IEDES analysis by the Egyptian economist Samir Amin: "How is this system to be described? As precapitalist, most assuredly, to the extent that capitalism can be defined as the concentration of ownership of capital (and its intensive use), and this likewise presupposes the intensive use of paid labor. Here, on the contrary, the use of capital is very little developed, there is no paid labor, each peasant family of tenants contributes not only its work but the primitive working tools and the livestock necessary for cultivation. Precapitalist, too, in the sense that the rural economy of land tenures and estates is virtually closed, even though part of the product is delivered to the estate (and then to the big owners) and in this way feeds the cities. To describe this precapitalist system as 'feudal,' however, seems dangerous if one wishes to preserve a precise meaning for the idea of 'feudalism.' Nothing is gained by the use of ambiguous terms, and one can rightfully be satisfied to define the elements of this precapitalist system *sui generis.*" (*Tiers-Monde, op. cit.,* p. 334.) There seems to be some confusion between "precapitalism," a concept that is quite properly applied to the European economies of the Renaissance, and "backward capitalism of a colonial type, predominantly agrarian," a concept directly born out of the experience of the imperialist stage.

A precise official explanation of the agrarian policy appears in "The Egyptian Economy during the Fifties: IV. Agriculture," *NBE Econ. Bull.*, XV, No. 1 (1962), pp. 13–27.

2. The Army and the Industrial Revolution

1. "EFI Report . . . 1952," *op. cit.*, p. 21.
2. A. J. Dorra, "L'Industrie égyptienne et ses possibilités de développement" (Egyptian Industry and Its Developmental Possibilities), *EC*, XXXIV, No. 214 (1943), p. 481.
3. Text in Barawi, *The Military Coup, op. cit.*, pp. 226–7.
4. "La Loi sur les investissements de capitaux étrangers" (The Law Governing Foreign Capital Investments), *EC* (April 1953), p. 21; also "La Collaboration des capitaux étrangers" (The Collaboration of Foreign Capital), *EI* (May, 1953), pp. 19–21.
5. Introduction to *EFI Yearbook 1953–1954*, in *EI* (November 1954), p. 21.
6. "The Investment Effects of the Land Reform in Egypt," *EC*, Vol. 45 No. 278 (1954), pp. 1–15.
7. Little, *op. cit.*, pp. 219–20.
8. Lacouture, *op. cit.*, 1st ed. (French), p. 348.
9. Barawi, *The Military Coup, op. cit.*, pp. 205–6.
10. See the account of this given by Ahmed Abul Fath, *L'Affaire Nasser* (Paris, 1962), pp. 53–5.
11. Text in *Journal d'Egypte*, Sept. 10, 1952; also Barawi, *op. cit.*, pp. 252–6.
12. P. J. Vatikiotis, *The Egyptian Army in Politics* (Indiana U. Press, 1961), p. 283.
13. Naguib, *op. cit.*, pp. 176–7.
14. *Ibid.*, pp. 176–8.
15. Quoted in *ibid.*, pp. 184–5.
16. Vatikiotis, (*op. cit.*, pp. 48–9), however, does not mention Hussein el-Shafei; on relations between the MB and the Free Officers, see especially Anwar el-Sadate, *Kissat, op. cit.*, and the English version, *Revolt on the Nile* (New York, 1957); and Fath, *op. cit.*, pp. 174–9.
17. A good description in *ibid.*, pp. 113–99.
18. Speech by Gamal Abdel Nasser to the Co-operative Conference, June 1, 1956, in *Thawratuna al-igtima'iyya* (Our Social Revolution), pp. 5–74. (Cairo, n.d., c. 1958.)
19. Naguib, *op. cit.*, pp. 209, 215, 236.
20. No Egyptian source exists, the censorship having meanwhile obliterated it; cf. Laqueur, *Communism, op. cit.*, p. 48; the figures were given by *MENA*, August 28, 1954.
21. Wheelock, *op. cit.*, pp. 99–100.

22. On Anglo-Egyptian negotiations between 1950 and 1954, see Farag Mussa, *Les Négociations anglo-égyptiennes de 1950 à 1951 sur Suez et le Soudan* (Paris, 1955); Egyptian International Law Society, *The Regional Defence Pacts* (Cairo, 1952); and *Documents on the Sudan, 1899–1953* (Cairo, 1954).

23. Little, *op. cit.*, pp. 242–6. John S. Badeau (American ambassador in Cairo) and R. H. Nolte state the West's hopes well: "For England and the West, this agreement removed the major obstacle to Egyptian participation in a treaty for the defense of the Middle East," in *The Emergence of Modern Egypt* (New York, 1953), p. 62.

24. Introduction to "EFI Report for the Year 1953," in *EI*, XXX, No. 5 (1954), p. 18.

25. "The Egyptian Economy during the Fifties: I," *NBE Econ. Bull.*, XIV, No. 1 (1961), pp. 19, 40, 44–5.

26. "Indices of Industrial Production," in *EI*, XXVI, No. 7 (1960), p. 46.

27. *EFI Yearbook . . . 1957–58, op. cit.*, tables p. 313.

28. Rassul, *Al-bunuk, op. cit.*, pp. 76–81.

29. Introduction to "EFI Report for the Year 1952–1953," in *EI* (November 1953), p. 17.

30. *Bourse Egyptienne* (published daily), June 10, 1954.

31. *Financing Economic Development in Egypt* (Cairo, 1955), p. 28.

32. *NBE Econ. Bull.*, I, No. 1 (1956), p. 20. S. Sitton, in *Aspects et problèmes du financement interne en Egypte* (Aspects and Problems of Internal Financing in Egypt), in the IEDES' *Tiers-Monde*, No. 53 (April 1957), p. 36, estimates that "in order to obtain a 2 percent increase in income, investment would have to represent 8 percent of the national income."

33. *Ibid.*, p. 30.

34. Dr. Zaki Saad, "La Situation en Egypte," *Bulletin de la Banque belge et internationale en Egypte* (April 1956), p. 9.

35. *NBE Econ. Bull.*, I, No. 2 (1956), p. 109.

36. The *New York Times*, October 14, 1955.

37. On the context and the Egyptian official records of the matter, cf. Dr. Mustafa el-Hefnawi, *Les Problèmes contemporains posés par le Canal de Suez* (Contemporary Problems Raised by the Suez Canal), Paris, 1951; Ibrahim Amer, *Ta'amim al-kanal* (The Nationalization of the Canal), Cairo, 1956; H. Mo'nes, A. K. Hatem, M. Abu Nosseir, A. Amer, et al., *The Suez Canal, Facts and Documents* (Cairo, n.d., c. 1957); Dr. B. Butros-Ghali and Y. Shlala, *Le Canal de Suez* (Cairo, 1958). There exists a wealth of literature on this question. Everyone is silent, however, on the fact that the Egyptian Communist party, alone among all the parties of the period, had mentioned "the nationalization of the

Suez Canal" in its program ("Communist Party of Egypt, Some Ambitious Aims," in *The Egyptian Gazette*, March 3, 1924).

38. The only book that not only recounts all the facts but also analyzes the question of Egyptian relations with the West in an objective spirit is E. Childers, *The Suez War* (London, 1962); the reader in search of truth is referred to it. On the organization of internal resistance, cf. Ahmed Rifaʻi and Abdel Moneim Shatla, *Ayyam al-intissar* (Days of Victory). Cairo, 1957.

39. Rassul, *op. cit.*, pp. 84–102. The problem was to put an end to the semicolonial period, the impact of which was discussed by Dr. Samir Amin in his distinguished thesis, *Les Effets structurels de l'intégration internationale des économies précapitalistes* (The Structural Effects of International Integration of Precapitalist Economies). Unpublished M.S., (Paris, 1957).

40. *COC*, XIV, No. 35 (1957), p. 48; statements by Ali el-Shafei, vice-president of the Union of Egyptian Chambers of Commerce (A, May 18, 1960); report by Dr. Kayssuni to the Central Economic Committee on the Egyptianization of foreign insurance companies (A, March 5, 1961).

41. On the history of planning since 1952, see *UAR Yearbook for 1961*, pp. 255–82; on the revision, A, October 13, 1962.

42. UAR, *Résumé—le Plan Quinquennal pour le développement économique et social 1960–1965* (Summary—The Five-Year Plan for Economic and Social Development), pp. 3–4, 7 (Cairo, n.d.)

43. E. Garzuzi shows that in the single area of the creation of industrial corporations during the years 1954, 1955 and 1956, the state held £E11.6 million out of a total of £E26.6 million invested, or 45.1 percent (*op. cit.*, p. 58).

44. Cf. special issue on the EA and the banks: *AI*, No. 140 (June 15, 1961); also No. 143 (August 1, 1961); reports by Dr. Kayssuni, A, (May 7 and July 13, 1961); Rassul, *op. cit.*, pp. 90–4.

45. "Company Finances in the UAR Southern Region 1956–57 and 1957–58," *NBE Econ. Bull.*, XII, No. 2 (1959), pp. 85–104.

46. "Company Finances in 1958–59—UAR Southern Region," *NBE Econ. Bull.*, XIII, No. 3–4 (1960), pp. 264–86.

47. Here is the list of the twenty-seven companies in the Misr complex: Misr Press (founded in 1922, current capital £E50,000); Misr Paper Manufacturing Co. (1924, liquidated in 1927); Misr Cotton-Ginning Co. (1924, £E250,000); Misr Transport and Navigation Co. (1925, £E1 million); Misr Theater and Cinema Co. (1925, £E1 million); Misr Fisheries Co. (1927, £E75,000); Misr Flax Co. (1927, liquidated in 1956); Misr Silk-Weaving Co. of Heluan (1927, £E1 million); Misr Spinning & Weaving Co. of Mahalla el-Kubra (1927, £E4 million); Misr Cotton Export Co. (1929, £E400,000); Misr Airways (1932, £E500,000); Misr Insurance Co. (1934, £E500,000); Misr Maritime Navigation

Co. (1934, £E750,000); Misr Tourism Co. (1934, £E100,000); Misr Tobacco & Cigarette Co. (1936, liquidated in 1940); Misr Spinning & Fine Weaving Co. of Kafr el-Dawwar (1937, £E2 million); Misr Beyda Dyers Co. (1937, £E1 million); Misr Vegetable Oils Co. (1938, £E75,000); Misr Tanning Co. (1938, liquidated in 1940); Misr Reinforced Concrete Construction Co. (1938, £E100,000); Misr Mining & Quarrying Co. (1939, £E100,-000); Misr Sales Co. for Egyptian Manufactures (1940, £E500,-000); Misr Pharmaceuticals Co. (1940, £E300,000); Misr Rayon Co. (1946, £E3 million); Misr Foreign Trade Co. (1953, £E500,-000); Misr Domestic Trading Co. (1953, £E500,000); Misr Hotels Co. (1954, £E2 million); Misr Food Products and Dairy Co. (1954, £E500,000); and Misr Chemical Products Co. (1957, £E2 million). Taken from Rassul, *op. cit.*, pp. 262–3.

48. A, October 26, 1961.

49. On Talaat Harb, see C. Issawi, "The Entrepreneur Class," in S. N. Fisher, *Social Forces in the Middle East* (New York, 1955), pp. 125–7; F. Harbison and Ibrahim Abdel Kader Ibrahim, *Human Resources for Egyptian Enterprise* (New York, 1958), pp. 44–5.

50. On this question and on the history of capitalism in Egypt, see the excellent thesis by Dr. Ali el-Gereitly, "The Structure of Modern Industry in Egypt," in *EC* (1948), and Hussein Khallaf, *Al-tagdid fi'l-iktissad al-Misri al-'hadith* (Renovation in Egypt's Modern Economy), Cairo, 1962.

51. Gereitly, "The Structure," *op. cit.*, pp. 433–45.

52. Rassul, *op. cit.*, pp. 352–63.

53. Harbison and Ibrahim, *op. cit.*, pp. 46–53.

54. G, February 20, 1960.

55. Harbison and Ibrahim, *op. cit.*, pp. 40–44.

56. *COC*, XIV, No. 35 (1957), p. 50.

57. *Al-Shaab*, November 2, 1957.

58. A, January 29, 1958.

59. Mohammed Hassanein Heykal, *Maza gara fi Suriya?* (What Happened in Syria?). Cairo, 1962.

60. A, June 1, 1957; up to December 1958, the total volume of credit reached £E430.5 million, of which only £E172 million (28.3 percent) went to industry; commerce received 59.8 percent of the total figure (NBE, *Credit and Banking Developments in 1958* (Cairo, 1958), p. 73.

61. "Supplément relatif à la nouvelle législation sur l'organisation et l'encouragement de l'industrie dans la province égyptienne" (Supplement Concerning the New Legislation for the Organization and Encouragement of Industry in the Egyptian Region), in *EI* (June 1958).

62. "La Nouvelle Composition des conseils d'administration de

la Fédération des Industries et des Chambres industrielles" (The New Composition of the Boards of Directors of the Federation of Industries and the Industrial Chambers), in *EI*, XXVI, No. 5 (1960), pp. 5–8; the new board of directors, wholly Egyptian (and Moslem), was well laced with technocrats and former magnates, to the profit of the former.

63. Cf. A. Jacoviello, "Verso la creazione in Egitto di un unico partito comunista" (Toward the Creation of a Single Communist Party in Egypt), in *L'Unità* May 14, 1957. Only the parties concerned know all the details.

64. Cf. *Afro-Asian Peoples' Solidarity Conference—Inaugural Addresses, Resolutions, Closing Addresses,* published in Arabic, French and English by the permanent secretariat (Cairo, 1958).

65. *A*, December 24, 1958.

66. On the repressions, a good source is the bound volumes of the Beirut weeklies, *al-Akhbar* and *al-Nida* (1959–61); also those of the bulletin *Solidarité,* published in Paris from 1955 to 1960; two studies by Adel Montasser, "La Répression anti-democratique en Egypte" (Anti-Democratic Repression in Egypt) and "La Répression anti-démocratique en RAU" (Anti-Democratic Repression in the UAR), in *Les Temps Modernes,* XVI (1960), pp. 418–41, and XVII (1961), pp. 184–92; bound volumes of *World Marxist Review* (London, 1960 and 1961) .

67. *A*, December 23, 1959.

68. Press conference by Mahmud Yunes on the fifth anniversary of the withdrawal of foreign Suez Canal pilots, in *A*, September 15, 1961.

69. "Stock Exchange," in *NBE Econ. Bull.*, XIV, No. 1 (1961), p. 546.

70. Wheelock, *op. cit.*, pp. 149–56.

71. "Forming the Future Society," in *President Gamal Abdel Nasser's Speeches and Press Interviews 1958* (Cairo, n.d.), pp. 289–326. It is interesting to note that the predominant concern in Dr. Kayssuni's thesis was the prevention of a new crisis; to this end he called for state planning (*Monetary Policy in Agricultural Raw Material Producing Countries with Special Reference to Egypt*). Unpublished Ph.D. thesis (London, 1942), pp. 1–11, 78–211, 212–38.

72. I. H. Abdel Rahman, *Al-takhtit al-kawmi* (National Planning), p. 30 (Cairo, 1961). The basic study is still the thesis of Mahmud Amin Anis, "A Study of the National Income of Egypt," in *EC*, No. 261–2 (1950), pp. 659–924; also "The National Income of Egypt, 1950," in *EC* XLIX, No. 271 (1953): it informs us that the national income, which was £E170 million in 1939, reached £E855 million in 1950 (p. 22).

73. "Les Projets du 1er plan quinquennal dont l'inauguration est prévue en 1960" (The Projects of the First Five-Year Plan,

Scheduled to Begin in 1960), in *EI*, XXVI, No. 6 (1960), pp. 3–7; "Les Projets du second plan quinquennal 1960–1965" (The Projects of the Second Five-Year Plan 1960–1965), *ibid.*, pp. 8–17; *UAR Yearbook for 1962, op. cit.*, pp. 78–94; *COC*, XVII, No. 49 (1960), pp. 422–8.

74. UAR, *Résumé, op. cit.*, pp. 9–10.

75. Interview in *RY*, No. 1644 (December 14, 1959).

76. "Layssa hunaka ittigah 'am li'l-ta'mim." (There Is No General Tendency to Nationalization), in *A*, March 6, 1960.

77. "Da'haya al-irhab al-damawi fi Misr" (The Victims of the Bloody Repression in Egypt), in *al-Akhbar* (Beirut), August 13, 1961. Two other prisoners died in the spring of 1962 as a result of lack of medical care, including Shaaban Hafez Rabbat, a veteran of the Communist party of 1924. The complete record was released in January 1962 by the League of Egyptian Progressives Abroad—*Al-garima al-Kubra didd al-shaab al-Misri* (The Greatest Crime against the Egyptian People), multigraphed (p. 114). Later two other important figures, Fathi Khalil, a member of the staff of *RY*, and Nabil el-Hilaly, a member of the Cairo Bar, were reported to be in very serious condition. Cf. appeal by Egyptian political prisoners at the oasis of Wadi al-Ghedid, in *Comment* (August 31, 1963), pp. 554–5.

78. Abu Seif Yussef, professor of philosophy, author of *Hawla'l-falsafa al-marxiyya* (On Marxist Philosophy), Cairo, 1945, translator of D. Guest's *Dialectical Materialism* (London, 1945) and editor of *al-Fagr al-Gadid;* Ismail el-Mahdawy, professor of philosophy, literary critic of *al-Missa* (1957–58) and translator of G. Politzer's *Principles of Philosophy* (1958); Ahmed Salem, former vice-president of the Textile Workers' Trade Union at Shubra el-Kheima. Cf. the French text in *Les Temps Modernes*, XVII (1961), pp. 187–90, and *Esprit*, XXIX (1961), pp. 157–60.

79. Text in *La Gazette fiscale, commerciale et industrielle* (April 1959); commentary by N. Tomiche, "Aperçu sur le nouveau code de travail de la RAU (Summary of the New Labor Code of the UAR), in *COC*, XVI, No. 40 (1959), pp. 160–71.

80. Excellent facts in W. A. Beling, *Pan-Arabism and Labor* (Harvard, 1960): of the 1,249 trade unions in 1958, 70 had more than 1,000 members each and 8 had more than 5,000 each; Major Toeima, under orders to discipline the union movement along the lines laid down by Anwar el-Sadate in "Tanzim al-'haraka al-'ummaliyya ta'hta ishraf al-Ittihad al-Kawmi" (The Organization of the Workers' Movement under the Control of the National Union), in *Akhbar el-Ummal*, May 8, 1958, was thwarted by Anwar Salama. The staff of the Federation of Egyptian Trade Unions, elected on January 1, 1961, by the representatives of twenty-four unions, was composed of Anwar Salama, president; Ahmed Fahim and Abdel Rehim Ezzeddine, vice-presidents; Fathi Foda, treasurer,

and Abdel Meghid Shedid, secretary-general; cf. A, May 6 and June 1, 1960, and January 2, 1961.

81. "Foreign Trade 1960," in *NBE Econ. Bull.*, No. 1 (1961), pp. 61–4.

82. According to the table in A, March 18, 1962.

83. Remarks by Sir Harold Beeley (once again British ambassador in Cairo as of December 1967) after the presentation of his diplomatic credentials (A, March 30, 1961); Egyptian reservations were voiced, especially in Mohammed Hassanein Heykal, "Bayna dukhan al-'itr wa dukhan al-barud" (Between the Scent of Perfume and the Smoke of Cannon), in A, March 17, 1961, and the interview given by the ambassador in London, Mohammed Awad el-Kony (A, February 12, 1962). There were, however, 700 Egyptian students in Great Britain. Cf. Board of Trade, *Report of the United Kingdom Trade Mission to the Egyptian Region of the UAR* (London, March 1960), which pointed up the official optimism on both sides.

84. A, March 31 and May 11, 1961.

85. "From 1954 to 1959 the profits recorded by the owners of food industries increased by more than 37 percent, those of textile industries by 14 percent and those in the construction industry by more than 30 percent, whereas wages rose only 3 percent in the same period," *RY* reported (No. 1706, February 1961).

86. "New Capital Issues," in *NBE Econ. Bull.*, XIV, No. 1 (1961), pp. 56–7.

87. Sidky's thesis, *Da'm al-nizam al-masrafi li'l-nuhud bi'l-sinaa* (The Strengthening of the Banking System for the Promotion of Industry), Cairo U., June 1958; Rassul, *op. cit.*, pp. 341–51; and Gereitly, *Tatawwor, op. cit.*, p. 450.

88. G, January 12 and 14, 1959.

89. NBE, *Credit and Banking, op. cit.*, pp. 17–8.

90. Speech by Dr. Kayssuni during the discussion held on March 5, 1960, in the faculty of commerce of Ain Shams University (A, March 6, 1960).

91. Here are the successive eight-column headlines in *al-Ahram* on February 13, 1960:

SECRETS OF THE NATIONALIZATION DECISION

WHY WAS THE DECISION TO NATIONALIZE THE
NATIONAL BANK OF EGYPT AND THE MISR
BANK INEVITABLE?

FIRST, FOR POLITICAL AND SOCIAL REASONS;

SECOND, FOR ECONOMIC AND FINANCIAL REASONS

92. A, February 13, 1960.

93. A, February 20 and 22, 1961.

94. A, April 10, 1960.

95. See the roster of the boards of directors in *A*, December 21, 1960.

96. *A*, April 28, 1961.

97. *AI*, July 15, 1960.

98. *Al-Wihda* (Damascus), July 30, 1960.

99. *A*, April 16 and 19, 1961.

100. *A*, May 21, 1961.

101. "Al-petrol al-'arabi wa Isra'il" (Arab Oil and Israel), in *A*, May 10, 1961.

102. See the list of deputies in *A*, July 19, 1960; for the regulations of the National Assembly, see *UAR Yearbook for 1961, op. cit.,* pp. 86–120.

103. The speech (*A*, July 22, 1961) was followed by a report of the debates (twelve lines blanked out by the censor). There is hardly any accurate information on the composition of the National Assembly; however, an American investigator, Leonard Binder, began research on the matter in February 1961 (*A*, March 9, 1961).

104. French translation of the decree in *COC*, XVII, No. 43 (1960), pp. 200–1.

105. *A*, May 30, 1960. The exegesis was provided by M. H. Heykal in his series entitled *Al-sahafa* (The Press), in *A*, May 28, June 1 and 3, 1961, on the theme that "the press has not been nationalized; it has been handed back to the people."

106. *A*, February 9, 1961.

107. *A*, March 27, 1960.

108. *A*, August 31, 1961.

109. The list of governors (*muhafiz*) appeared in *A*, September 12, 1960; see the criticism by the Syrian Left in "Hawla kanun al-'hokm al-'ma'halli fi'l'Arabiyya al-Mutta'hida" (On the Regional Government Law in the UAR), in *al-Akhbar* (Beirut), May 1, 1960.

110. *A*, October 8, 1958, and September 21, 1960.

3. Dismantling of the Old Bourgeoisie

1. It is therefore incorrect to say that "as the result of schematicism in its social conceptions, and also because it was afraid of providing ammunition for the theoreticians of colonialism, the Egyptian Left, Marxist or sympathetic to Marxism, refused to take the population problem into consideration." "La Société urbaine égyptienne" (Egyptian Urban Society), by a study group of the IEDES, in *Tiers-Monde*, II, No. 6 (1961), pp. 189–90. From its side, the government encouraged birth control—cf. the work of the International Family-Planning Congress in Cairo (*A*, May 24–26, 1962), and the abortion investigation, *Hurriyet el-ighad*

(The Freedom of Abortion), in *RY*, No. 1774 (June 11, 1962); the government established birth-control clinics at Kafr Abu-Gomaa and Kom Eshfin, near Cairo, while a large center was created in Alexandria (*A*, June 9 and 12, 1962); and contraceptive pills were put on sale as early as the summer of 1962 (*A*, August 23, 1962).

2. "A Socialist Pattern of Society," in *NBE Econ. Bull.*, XIV, No. 3 (1961), p. 274.

3. An interesting commentary by Gamal el-Oteifi, "Al-ishti-rakiyya fi tawzi' arba'h al-sharikat" (Socialism in the Distribution of Company Profits), in *A*, July 6, 1961; on May 12 and 16, 1962, the government decided to expand the distribution of the 10 percent of profits to the workers in five thousand establishments and then to apply part of the 10 percent reserved for social benefits to the workers in corporations whose profits had not been sufficient (*A*, May 17, 1962).

4. These figures, as well as the list of companies affected, are taken from *NBE Econ. Bull.*, XIV, No. 3 (1961), pp. 326–32. But *A*, which gives a fuller list, since it takes both regions of the UAR into consideration, has the following figures: 149 companies wholly nationalized, 91 companies owned 50 percent by the state, 159 companies in the third group (issue of July 21, 1961).

5. "New Legislation," in *NBE Econ. Bull.*, supra, p. 322.

6. Press conference of July 20, 1961, in *A*, July 21, 1961.

7. See the detailed catalogue of these maneuvers according to the accounts of Zakaria Mohieddine, Vice-President of the Republic for production agencies, in Adli Galal's article in *A*, December 8, 1961.

8. M. H. Heykal, "Al-Suez al-igtima'iyya" (The Economic Suez) and "Al-su'al al-sabe'" (The Seventh Question), in *A*, July 28 and August 18, 1961.

9. *A*, July 24 and 27, 1961.

10. *Al-sharika al-khumassiyya*, with a capital of 4 million Syrian pounds, the central group of the Syrian-Lebanese financial middle class, closely linked to Ma'mun el-Kuzbari, Premier of Syria after the collapse of the merger with Egypt, notably through Adel el-Khoja.

11. *A*, August 17, 1961.

12. The development of the tactic of the President of the UAR may be followed by studying his speeches in *A* of September 29 and 30, and October 6, 1961.

13. This was particularly the case of the Italian Communist party.

14. *A*, October 17, 1961. A self-criticism that was to be elaborated by M. H. Heykal in the series of editorials collected under the title *Maza gara, op. cit.* The best Syrian analysis, heavily documented and detailed, is that of General Afif el-Bizry, former

Chief of Staff of the Syrian army, in *al-Akhbar* (Beirut), June 14 and 17, and July 8 and 13, 1962.

15. *A*, October 19, 1961.

16. Cf. text of statement by Zakaria Mohieddine and the lists, in *A*, October 22, 1961.

17. Fathi Nawwar's article on the different kinds of sequestration (emergency, security, Belgian, English, French, Third Reich, Palestine war), in *A*, November 15, 1961.

M. H. Heykal, however, reassured the rich families: the sequestration decree, he said, provided for the creation of commissions "that will have to study each individual case and make their decisions on the basis of the interest of the people, but above all, to preserve the revolutionary impulse untainted by the desire for vengeance, which is alien to the religious, moral and historical characteristics of the people of the UAR. These commissions will take many factors into account, including the necessity of providing the opportunity, for all who seek it, to work for their own and their families' benefit within the framework of the national interest and without the inherited privileges of class that have been imposed on society, and of doing so without punishing the children for the sins of the parents, as well as the necessity of helping the children to liberate themselves from the inevitable exploitation and monopoly, to give them the awareness of their allegiance to the masses as well as the heartfelt conviction that their own interests can be served only within the framework of the higher interest of the people." "Ma hua al-maydan al-'hakiki li'l-thawra al-igtima'iyya?" (What Is the Real Field for Social Revolution?), in *A*, November 7, 1961).

18. E. Halim Saab, "En Egypte, le conseil de la révolution reprend les rênes du pouvoir" (The Revolutionary Council Regains the Reins of Power in Egypt), in *Le Monde*, October 25, 1961. In London there was talk of the arrests of 150 officers, all for opposition to the "socialization" laws, and, in Amman, of fifteen executions. *COC*, XVIII, No. 47 (1961), p. 402.

19. *A*, February 13, 1962.

20. On the revocation of the sequestration orders, cf. *AK* of January 9, 1962; *A*, throughout March, especially on the 18th and 22nd, gave prominence to the exemption of the former notables of the middle class from the so-called "isolation" measure; on the Abbud trial, cf. *AK* of December 22, 1961, and the *Times* of London, January 5, 1962.

21. M. H. Heykal, "Al-thawra al-igtima'iyya fi yad al-shaab" (The Social Revolution in the Hands of the People), in *A*, November 6, 1961.

22. Here is the table of landholdings by foreigners in Egypt, mostly in the province of Beheira:

	1951		1959	
NUMBER OF		NUMBER OF		NUMBER OF
FEDDANS	AREA	OWNERS	AREA	OWNERS
−1	446	1,198	328	777
1–10	3,284	894	2,598	675
10–50	15,076	644	17,458	701
50–100	13,813	204	11,744	166
100+	130,499	325	109,023	295
TOTAL	163,118	3,265	141,151	2,614

The reference to Durrell was made in terms of a literary document typical of those decadent circles (familiar to the author), which were full of *compradores* and agents. Alexandria and its people are complete strangers to this talented stylist in the tradition of decadent estheticism, nostalgic for the *imperium,* and well known for his right-wing positions, courted by sections of the "Left."

23. "Suwar al-mugtama' al-misri 'ala 'hakikatihi" (A Picture of Egyptian Society As It Is), in *A,* October 23–31 and November 1, 1961.

4. Anatomy of the New Class

1. *NBE Econ. Bull.,* XIV, No. 4 (1961), pp. 441–4.
2. "The Reorganization of the Public Sector," *ibid.,* pp. 387–8. See also the opinions of four presidents of public agencies—Dr. Hussein Khallaf (banking), Ali Shalaby (savings), Ahmed Shawki el-Hakim (insurance) and Nur Eddine Korra (commerce)—on the relations between their agencies and the ministries charged with counseling them in questions of general policy, in *A,* January 17, 1962.
3. "Maza yuridu mumathilu al-ra'smaliyya al-wataniyya mina'l-mithak al-watani?" (What Do the Representatives of the National Capitalism Want from the Charter?), in *A,* March 11, 1962.
4. On the establishment of categories before sequestration, cf. Gamal el-Oteifi, "Nazara fi kanun al-sharikat 'ala daw' al-tashri'at al-ishtirakiyya al-akhira" (A Look at Company Law in the Light of the Latest Socialist Laws), in *AI,* No. 149 (November 1, 1961), pp. 10–11.
5. Report on the stock exchanges, in *AI,* No. 156 (February 15, 1962), pp. 218–9; see the text of the application of Law No. 118/1961 covering companies in the second category, in *A,* July 26, 1961. On the stimulation of small savings accounts, cf. the interpretation by Nabil el-Sabbagh in *AI,* No. 155 (February 1, 1962), p. 52.
6. Gamal el-Oteifi, "Al-kuwwa al-gadida al-mutaganissa fi idarat

al-sharikat" (The New Integrated Forces in the Directorship of Societies), in *A*, August 24, 1961.

7. "Al-borsa fi nizamina al-ishtiraki" (The Stock Exhange in Our Socialist Order), in *AI*, No. 158 (March 15, 1962), p. 4.

8. The anonymous author of the previously quoted study by the IEDES on "La Société urbaine égyptienne" provides the following table on social categories in the cities:

	POPULATION (thousands)	%	TOTAL INCOME (£E in millions)	PER CAPITA INCOME (£E)
0. No work listed	2,988	37	—	—
1. Servants	934	12	20	21.4
2. *Lumpenproletariat*	186	2	5	26.8
3. Regular wage earners	400	5	16	40
4. Proletariat	790	10	48	60.8
5. Subordinate office workers	1,117	14	118	105.6
6. Regular self-employed	736	9	94	127.7
7. Middle managerial, etc.	614	8	83	133.5
8. Middle class and aristocracy	240	3	203	845.8
TOTAL	8,000	100	587	73.4

The author correctly points out that "the 'popular masses' constitute only categories o through 3 . . . The proletariat, under these conditions, constitutes a class apart in Egypt, differing in its political and social attitudes from the most underprivileged classes of the urban population. Categories 5 through 7 . . . have been combined under the general term 'lower middle class.' " (*Tiers-Monde, op. cit.*, pp. 186–7.)

9. *AI*, No. 152 (December 15, 1961), p. 18.

10. M. Berger, *Bureaucracy and Society in Modern Egypt* (Princeton, 1957), has a good description of the corps of high officials in 1954–55. Cf. also the daily series of biographies in *A*, "Lama'hat shakhsiyya" (Personal Insights), beginning in January 1962. This is the analysis of university people in the summer of 1961:

(a) Students in the four universities (exclusive of Al Azhar): 77,000;

(b) Holders of bachelor's and advanced degrees from the various faculties since the foundation of Cairo University in 1908:

medicine, 8,000; pharmacy, 2,000; engineering, 10,000; agriculture, 9,000; sciences, 5,000; literature, 18,000; law, 17,000; business administration, 15,000;

(c) Between 1931 and 1961 the following doctorates were conferred: literature, 168; law, 104; business administration, 11; sciences, 196; medicine, 202; pharmacy, 18; engineering, 27; agriculture, 22; veterinary medicine, 30. To these should be added several hundred doctorates conferred by foreign universities ("Altaalim al-ali" [Higher Education], in *A*, August 22, 1961). At the end of 1962 it was expected that there would be 170 new doctorates from abroad, to be followed by 1,050 more during the next three years (*A*, March 18, 1962); the number of Egyptian students abroad rose from 1,656 in 1957 (including 281 on state scholarships) to 5,670 (including 2,395 on scholarships) in 1962 (*A*, September 20, 1962).

11. Dr. Mohammed Said Abdel Fattah, "Hazihi hia khuttat i'dad al-khubara' al-idariyyin" (This Is the Plan for the Formation of Administrative Experts), in *A*, March 8, 1960; the seminar "Man hom agdar bi idarat al-sharikat?" (Who Are Those Most Fit to Manage Societies?), in *AI*, No. 152 (December 15, 1961), pp. 18–23; Helmy el-Said, economic adviser to the President, was appointed to head the National Institute of Higher Administration in order to prevent any surprise (*A*, May 30, 1962).

12. Table derived from data in the special issue of *Dalil al-mu'assassat* (The guide to public companies [societies]), in *AI*, No. 160 (April 15, 1962), p. 66; completed with new data, *A*, May 25, 1962.

13. *A*, April 18 and 21, 1962.

14. See the rules of this school, in *A*, September 11, 1961, and May 31, 1962.

15. *A*, August 9 and October 15, 1960, and June 13, 1961. On public education under the new government, cf. Mohammed Khayri and el-Sayed Mohammed el-Azzawi, *Education in Egypt (UAR) in the Twentieth Century* (Cairo, 1960).

16. *A*, February 17, 1962.

17. "Numuw magmu'at al-mudirin al-fanniyyin wa'l-takaddom al-iktissadi" (The Growth of the Technical Managers Corps and Economic Progress), in *A*, April 1, 1961.

18. *A*, April 6 and 19, 1960.

19. "Al-ikta'iyyun wa'l-ra'smaliyyun wa'l-muthakkafun" (Feudalists, Capitalists and Intellectuals), in *RY*, No. 1353 (May 17, 1954).

20. "Azmat al-muthakkafin" (The Crisis of the Intellectuals), in *A*, June 2, 1961.

21. Sadate, *Kissat, op. cit.*, pp. 124–5.

22. Republic of Egypt, *Goals of the Egyptian Revolution* (Cairo, n.d.), p. 73.

23. M. Berger, *Military Elite and Social Change—Egypt Since Napoleon* (Princeton, 1960). An interesting analysis of several subjects, especially the time of Mohammed Ali and the historical training of the officer corps. But the author approves the lack of democracy and refuses to admit the religious bias of at least one area of ideology inspired by the Moslem Brotherhood.

24. Text of the Presidential declaration, in *A*, November 5, 1961.

25. According to the text of the decree establishing it, published in *A*, November 19, 1961; the internal regulations were published in the issue of November 30.

26. *A*, November 30, 1961. The complete texts of the Preparatory Committee's work have been published in a bound volume, *Al-tarik ila'l-dimokratiyya* (The Path to Democracy), Cairo, 1962; this debate is reported there on pp. 191–215 and 262–80.

Fathy Ghanem tried to make the questioner appear a religious idealist in "Difa' 'an a'hlam Khaled wa mu'arada fi tatbik al-a'hlam" (A Defense of Khaled's Dreams and an Opposition to the Application of Those Dreams), in *Sabah el-Kheir*, No. 309 (November 7, 1961).

27. *A*, November 27, 1961.

28. Preparatory Committee, *op. cit.*, pp. 362–4.

29. On the Communist party's different conceptions of labor, cf. Ahmed Baha'Eddine, "Hazihi al-dunya" (This World), in *Akhbar el-Yom*, December 23, 1961.

30. These were the members of the subcommittee: Dr. Ahmed el-Sayed Darwish, Shiek Ahmed el-Shorabassi, Ahmed Baha'Eddine, Dr. Hamdy el-Hakim, Dr. Gaber Gad, Dr. Gamal Eddine Said, Hassan Himam, Dr. Rifaat el-Mahgub, Abdel Meguid Amer, Kamal el-Hennawi, Dr. Lutfi Abul Nasr, Fathi Foda, Dr. Labib Shukeir, Mohammed Fuad Galal, Mrs. Mufida Abdel Rahman, Yussef Morcos Hanna, Mrs. Karima el-Said, Hussein Mahmud, Abdel Rehim Ezzeddine, Mohammed Ezzat Kotb and Helmy el-Said (*A*, December 7, 1961). Five special subcommittees were elected for different social categories: national capitalism (chairman, Dr. Gamal Said); workers (Khaled Fawzi); peasants (Dr. Osman Khalil Osman); university graduates and students (Dr. Mohammed Labib Shukeir); the professions, state officials and women (Dr. Hussein Khallaf); cf. *AK*, December 20, 1961.

31. Much effort has been devoted to looking for the foreign models for the political structuration of the "popular forces." Let us remember that in 1945–47, Nasser saw much of his Marxist friends in the "army" section of two Communist organizations, Iskra and the Egyptian Movement of National Liberation (which were merged into the Democratic Movement of National Liberation in 1947); it was at that time that the mistaken thesis of "feudal Egypt" served as the foundation for the so-called thesis of the "party of national and democratic forces," conceived as a coalition

of autonomous sectors representing the different social categories; the battle against these theses, led by "Soliman," "Seif" and "Adel," brought about the collapse of the DMNL, the Egyptianization of the leadership, and the decisive allegiance to the concept of the Communist party as a working-class party. It seems reasonable to assume that Nasser might have remembered these disputes and chosen the solution best suited to discourage a class struggle that would benefit the proletariat.

32. Based on the tables and statistics supplied in Preparatory Committee, *op. cit.*, pp. 592 and 727–30. A gives the final results as follows: professional associations, functionaries, women, 461; peasants, 379; workers, 300; university graduates and students, 210; national capitalists, 150 (issue of February 25 1962).

33. Complete text of the subcommittee's report, in Preparatory Committee, pp. 586–9.

34. The record shows the amendment proposed by Professor Aisha Abdel Rahman, alias Bent el-Shati, who demanded that those subject to "isolation" be "interned in concentration camps," and who criticized the minister concerned, Zakaria Mohieddine, for not having thought of this earlier . . .

PART III

5. The Crisis of the Intellectuals

1. "Azmat al-muthakkafin" (Crisis of the Intellectuals), II, in *A*, June 16, 1961.

2. All these documents were brought together by Heykal into a book, *Azmat al-muthakkafin* (Cairo, 1961); he claimed to have received fifty thousand letters from readers on the subjects discussed (*A*, July 21, 1961).

3. "They have," he said, "an ambivalent nature: on the one hand they constitute a unit by reason of their common mental work; on the other, and at the same time, they are in competition because of the variances in their social status." (*A*, March 12, 1961.) But this applies equally to capitalist business owners, political leaders, etc. This is not the essential. In my study of 1958, "Al-muthakka-fun wa'l-thakafa" (Intellectuals and Culture), published in *M* (November 25, 1958), I made a distinction between the *muthakkifun*, the creators and distributors of culture, and the *muthakkafun*, the intellectual consumers of that culture, from the point of view of Gramsci. It has now been included in my recent volume *Dirassat fi'l-thakafa al-wataniyya* (Studies in National Culture), pp. 200–5 (Beirut, 1967).

4. Currently head of the research department in the Industrial

Bank, author of several works, notably *Azmatuna al-iktissadiyya* (Our Economic Crisis), Cairo, 1956, and former economic contributor to *M*.

5. Assistant professor in the new faculty of economic and political sciences and the author of a number of interesting works.

6. Quoted in *A*, May 31, 1961.

7. Professor of English literature at Cairo University until 1954, a delegate to the UN, one of the leading intellectuals of contemporary Egypt, the author of literary and philosophical studies: *Plutoland wa kassaed ukhra* (Plutoland and Other Poems; 1947), *Studies in Literature* (1954), *Fi'l-adah al-ingilizi al-hadith* (On Modern English Literature; 1950), *The Alchemist in English Literature* (1951), *The Essential Prometheus* (1953), *Al masra'h al-Misri* (Egyptian Theater; 1953), *Dirassat fi adabina al-hadith* (Studies in Our Modern Literature; 1961), *Al-muatharat al-agnabiyya fi'l-adab al-'arabi al-hadith* (Foreign Influences of Modern Arabic Literature) 2 vols. (1962/63), *Al-raheb* (The Monk; 1962), etc.; after the repression of 1959, he contributed to *G* and then to *A* and became co-editor of the projected *Arab Encyclopedia*. in his latest book, *Al-'anqa' aw tarikh Hassan Muftah* (The Wonder Bird, or the Story of Hassan Muftah), Beirut, 1966, the author launches a virulent frontal attack on the honor of Egyptian Communism, both in his theoretical preface and in the novel itself.

8. One of the Baath party's theoreticians of Arab nationalism, the author of several books, notably *Na'hw ishtirakiyya 'Arabiyya* (Towards an Arab Socialism), Beirut, 1957, and *Azmat al-yassar al-'Arabi* (The Crisis of the Arab Left), Beirut, 1960; Arab League representative in India until 1966.

9. Assistant professor of English literature at Cairo University, author of several works in the English language, contributor to *A* and *AI*.

10. *A*, June 10, 1961.

11. "Azmat al-muthakkafin" (Crisis of the Intellectuals), IV, in *A*, June 30, 1961.

12. *RY*, No. 1344, March 15, 1954.

13. "Al-hiyad harakaton wa gihad" (Neutralism as Movement and Struggle), in *RY*, No. 1334 (January 5, 1954). What is more, President Nasser did not boggle at admitting it: "Nine years ago we had no line. There were six basic principles—among them the destruction of imperialism, feudalism and exploitation by capital, and the accomplishment of social justice—principles that we keep constantly and permanently before our eyes; day after day and month after month, and, on the basis of our national experience, we have taken the decisions that opened the way to the realization of these principles" (Columbia Broadcasting System interview reported in *A*, August 26, 1961).

14. Gamal Eddine el-Shayyal's book, *Rifaa Rafe' el-Tahtawi* (Cairo, 1958), constitutes the start of a systematic study of this man who left his mark on the whole Egyptian cultural life from Mohammed Ali to this day.

15. There is a major bibliography devoted to Mohammed Abdu. The foreign reader can consult, in particular: C.C. Adams, *Islam and Modernism in Egypt* (London, 1933); Osman Amin's thesis *Muhamad 'Abduh, essai sur ses idées philosophiques et religieuses* (Mohammed Abdu, Essays on His Philosophical and Religious Ideas), Cairo, 1944; J.M. Ahmed, *The Intellectual Origins of Egyptian Nationalism* (Oxford, 1960); and Malcom Kerr's percep- tive *Islamic Reform: The Political and Legal Theories of Muham- med Abdu and Rashid Rida* (U. of Calif. Press, Berkeley, 1967), which establishes the connection between Islamic reformism and the army movement.

16. A second doctoral thesis, under completion, *La Pensée sociale dans la renaissance nationale de l'Egypte (1805–1892)*, should provide a systematic analysis of this virtually unchartered field. Cf. also my *Dirassat*, Part III: "Azmat al-fikr fi Miçr" (The Crisis of Thought in Egypt), pp. 327–409, and my *Anthologie de la littérature arabe contemporaine, Vol. II: les Essais* (Le Seuil, Paris, 1965), especially the Introduction and the Egyptian texts. N. Safran's *Egypt in Search of Political Community* (Harvard, 1961), dealt with the evolution of political thinking in a superficial, sketchy fashion.

17. *Akher Saa*, July 23, 1958.

18. G. Vaucher, *Gamal Abdel-Nasser et son équipe* (Gamal Abdel Nasser and His Group), I (Paris, 1959), pp. 71–3, 94–104.

19. Works already quoted; Nasser wrote an introduction to *Asrar al-thawra*; in August 1957, Dar al-Hilal published a special issue, *Al-Mussawar yukaddem Gamal Abdel-Nasser* (Al-Mussawar Presents Gamal Abdel Nasser), which contains a wealth of histori- cal documents and photographs on the President's life, as well as the history of the relations between the Left and the Free Officers since 1942, as told by Khaled Mohieddine (pp. 62–5); on this subject as viewed from abroad, see R. Vailland's *Choses vues en Egypte* (Things Seen in Egypt), Paris, 1952. An interesting biog- raphy is R. St. John's *The Boss* (New York, 1960); a superficial study is J. Joesten's *Nasser: The Rise to Power* (London, 1960); Nasser's conversations with D. Wynne-Morgan appeared under the title *My Revolutionary Life—President Nasser's Own Story*, in the (London) *Sunday Times* (June 17 and 24 and July 1, 1962), giving much detail: "During the two years that followed the demonstration in Alexandria [1935], I was a member of Misr al-Fatat [Ahmed Hussein's party]"; the coup d'état of July 23 was the work of "some ninety officers"; from 1948 on, Nasser carefully

read Laski, Nehru and even Bevan; on January 26, 1952, the date of the burning of Cairo, "the day began with a violent demonstration by Misr al-Fatat."

20. "Maza hadatha laylat 23 yolyo?" (What Happened During the Night of July 23, 1952?), in *A*, July 23, 1960. It will be noted that the author dates the formal establishment of the Free Officers between the end of the Palestine war and 1950, while Anwar el-Sadate implies that it goes back to 1938, the time of the first meeting of Nasser and his companions in the Mankabad garrison. Rashed el-Barawi, on the other hand, mentions 1945.

21. Vatikiotis, *op. cit.*, pp. 44–68. The relationship between Gamal Abdel Nasser and Kamal Rifaat is not mentioned there.

22. *President Gamal Abdel Nasser's Speeches . . . 1958, op. cit.*, pp. 336–8; cf. my article "Gami 'at al-Kahira fi 'idiha al-khamssini" (Cairo University on Its Fiftieth Anniversary), in *M*, December 21, 1958.

23. *Khutab al-Ra'is Gamal Abdel-Nasser fi i'htifalat al-'id al-sabe' li'l-thawra, 23 yolyo 1959* (Speeches by President Gamal Abdel Nasser during the Seventh Anniversary of the Revolution, July 23, 1959), pp. 107–13 (Cairo, n.d., c. 1959).

24. Questioned about his reading, he voiced his preference for "news and Arab nationalism." *A*, March 9, 1960.

25. *A*, January 21, 1960.

26. *A*, February 27, 1960.

27. *A*, April 23, 1961.

28. *A*, April 7 and 15, 1961; *RY*, No. 1658, March 21, 1961.

29. *A*, June 7, 1960.

30. *A*, April 29 and July 1, 1960.

31. *A*, April 18 and 19, 1962, August 8, 1961, June 26, 1962.

32. Texts, particularly in *A*, June 23, September 11 and October 7, 1961.

33. *A*, January 16, 1961.

34. *A*, November 10 and 22, 1961.

35. *A*, January 1, 1960.

36. *A*, March 1, 1960.

37. *A*, January 24, 1960.

38. *A*, November 23, 1961.

39. *Bourse Egyptienne*, September 16, 1954; a good summary in *COC*, XI, No. 30 (1954), pp. 146–7.

40. *A*, November 25, 1960, and January 27, 1961. These were the figures on student exchanges: 114 sent from Al Azhar to Asia, 63 to Africa, 1 to Europe, 6 to North America; there were 3,000 foreign students at Al Azhar, from 60 countries; 1,879 scholarships were offered for foreign students in 1962 by the religious university, and 2,400 by the High Council for Islamic Affairs (*A*, June 20, 1962). The figures are increasing steadily.

6. The Stages of Neutralism

1. In 1954, Abdel Rahman Azzam, secretary-general of the Arab League, wrote: "It would be impossible for Egypt to survive without an attitude in accord with her needs and with her anger against her own and the Arabs' attackers. That attitude consists in refusal to co-operate with the aggressors, and in co-operation with those who are in agreement with her . . . a positive attitude . . . : allegiance where it pleases her to give it and enmity on the same basis." "Al-'hiyad al-tam" (Total Neutralism), in *RY*, No. 1335 (January 11, 1954).

2. A detailed and accurate exposition of the evolution in the relations between Egypt and the Western powers before Suez can be found in Wheelock, *op. cit.*, pp. 206–76; also in the books by Lacouture, *op. cit.*, and Little *op. cit.*, A. Jacoviello, "L'Europa a Suez" (Europe at Suez) in *La coesistenza difficile* (Difficult Coexistence), pp. 75–89 (Milan, 1961).

3. The *New York Times*, April 20, 1954.

4. *MENA*, February 14, 1954, quoted in Wheelock, *op. cit.*, p. 216.

5. The testimony of Henry Byroade, then American ambassador in Cairo, the chronology of the *New York Times* for the previous month, and the reports of the UN's mixed armistice commission are unanimous in failing to confirm the Israeli allegations to the effect that the operation had been made necessary by the actions of the *fida'iyyin*; cf. *Hearings before the Committee on Foreign Relations and the Committee on Armed Services*, U.S. Senate, 85th Cong., 1st sess. H. J. Res. 19, H. J. Res. 117 (January and February 1957, Washington, 1957, pp. 746–7), and *Hearings*, House of Representatives (p. 395), in Wheelock, *op. cit.*, pp. 222–3.

6. *Ibid.*, pp. 228–9.

7. U.S. Senate *Hearings*, 85th Cong., Part II, p. 783; Part I, p. 438. *Ibid.*, p. 228.

8. *MENA*, October 11, 1952.

9. *MENA*, November 8, 1952.

10. Wheelock, *op. cit.*, p. 215.

11. The *New York Times*, June 25, 1953.

12. R. K. Karanjia, *Arab Dawn* (Bombay, 1958), p. 187.

13. Tanyug News Agency, July 19, 1956.

14. On this first period, see my study, "De Bandoeng à Accra" (From Bandung to Accra), in *Horizons*, VII (1958), pp. 14–8; G. C. Stevens, "Arab Neutralism and Bandung," in *MEJ*, XI, No. 2 (1957), pp. 139–52.

15. J. Marlowe, *Arab Nationalism and British Imperialism*, (London, 1961), p. 85. The Lacoutures' appraisal, according to

which "positive neutralism is only a cloak for anti-Westernism" ("Dix Ans de nassérisme"—Ten Years of Nasserism—in *Esprit*, No. 303, February 1962, p. 297), confuses "Westernism" and "imperialism."

16. There is an excellent elaboration of it in Khaled Mohieddine's report to the Afro-Asian Conference of Cairo, summarized in "Le Neutralisme positif," *Horizons*, VII, No. 82 (1958), pp. 52–6; especially: "There is no connection between the policy of positive neutralism and an internal Communist system. Objectively, we are in a historical period in which the nation's capital wealth must be reinforced . . . There is no objective basis [in Egypt and Syria] on which to build socialism or Communism. Positive neutralism is the policy followed by the newly independent states that want to work toward the development of their economies." The studies and articles by Aziz Fahmy, Abdel Azim Anis, Taher Abdel Hakim, etc., must also be cited, as well as my 1958 study on the peace movement as an anti-imperialist campaign in the Afro-Asian countries.

17. In 1960–61 Egypt had sent 782 professors to 6 African countries, 631 of them to the Sudan (*UAR Yearbook for 1961*, *op. cit.*, p. 584); in 1962 some 500 African students from 17 countries were studying there (*AK*, March 10, 1962) out of a total of 15,683 foreign students, including 2,868 on scholarships. *UAR Yearbook for 1962*, pp. 178–9.

18. *Ibid.*, . . . *1961*, pp. 1004–5; "Helm Ifrikiya allazi ya'ishu fi'l-Kahira" (The African Dream That Lives in Cairo), in *A*, February 24, 1960; "Sharaf al-kalima" (The Crisis of African Studies), in *A*, July 1, 1960; the decisions of the First African Radio & Television Congress, in *A*, April 28, 1961; Dr. Hassan Ahmed Mahmud, "Azmat al-dirassat al-ifrikiyya" (The Crisis of African Studies), in *A*, May 2, 1962. The monthly magazine *Nahdat Ifrikiya* should also be consulted.

19. *President Gamal Abdel Nasser's Speeches . . . 1958*, *op. cit.*, pp. 152–86.

20. Speech on May 16, 1958, *ibid.*, pp. 187–99. Wilton Wynn, long the chief correspondent for The Associated Press in Cairo, explained the American attitude: "Except for an understanding with Nasser, what alternative is there? . . . The classic bromide is called 'economic assistance.'" From *Nasser of Egypt, the Search for Dignity* (Cambridge, Mass., 1959), p. 208. Earlier John S. Badeau had acted as intercessor: "A Role in Search of a Hero: A Brief Study of the Egyptian Revolution," in *MEJ*, IX, No. 4 (1955), pp. 373–84.

21. This was the exact language of M. H. Heykal, *A*, June 15, 1958. A detailed picture of Egyptian foreign trade appears in "The Egyptian Economy in the Fifties: II," in *NBE Econ. Bull.*, XIV, No. 2 (1961), pp. 146–7.

22. On the Egyptian view of the UN at this period, see *Egypt and the United Nations*, by a study group of the International Law Society (New York, 1957): "For the man in the street the UN is an American institution working for American diplomacy. [There is] considerable confusion between the United Nations and the United States . . ."

23. Butros Butros-Ghali, *Dirassat fi'l-siyassa al-dawliyya* (Studies in International Politics), pp. 13–38 (Cairo, 1961).

24. Interviews on January 27, 1958, with American newspaper publishers and editorial writers, in *President Gamal Abdel Nasser's Speeches . . . 1958, op. cit.*, pp. 361–77.

25. CBS interview of April 7, 1958, *ibid.*, pp. 378–88.

26. Akram el-Hurani, leader of the Baath and former Vice-President of the UAR, makes much of the existence of a report sent by the American ambassador in Cairo to his government, in which he said that at that time (1958) the UAR was scrupulously carrying out the American plan in the region, notably in Syria; the USSR's discovery of Egypt's double game was supposed to be at the root of this controversy. *Al-Akhbar* (Beirut), June 3, 17 and 24, July 8 and August 26, 1962.

27. Statements to the Regional Congress of the National Union in Assiut, in *A*, June 7, 1961; cf. the particulars in the Syrian public prosecutor's indictment of Helu's assassins, in *al-Akhbar* (Beirut), August 19, 1962.

28. *A*, June 6, 1961. Fikry Abaza, having published an article in *al-Mussawar* calling for peace with Israel, was stripped of his post as president of the Dar el-Hilal group (*A*, August 18, 1961). After a burlesque self-criticism (*A*, September 25), he was restored to grace.

29. "Igtimaa rua'ssa' al-duwal ghayra'l-munhaza" (The Meeting of the Chiefs of State of the Nonaligned States), in *A*, May 26, 1961.

30. The "twenty-five" were Afghanistan, Algeria, Burma, Cambodia, Ceylon, the Congo, Cuba, Cyprus, Ethiopia, Ghana, Guinea, India, Indonesia, Iraq, Lebanon, Mali, Morocco, Nepal, Saudi Arabia, Somalia, the Sudan, Tunisia, the UAR, Yugoslavia and Yemen. Cf. resolutions, in *A*, September 7, 1961.

31. "We can in no way—even if we wished to do so—remain isolated from the bloody and terrible struggle that is raging today in the depths of Africa between 5,000,000 whites and 200,000,000 Africans. We cannot do so for a very simple reason: we are Africans. The peoples of this continent will continue to look toward us, who hold the northern gate of the continent and who are its link with the entire outside world. We cannot, whatever the circumstances, slough off our responsibilities, which are to provide as much help as we can in spreading enlightenment and civilization to the farthest depths of the virgin forest. There is another im-

portant reason: the fact that the Nile, the lifeline of our country, receives its waters from the heart of the continent. And there is also the fact that the frontiers of the Sudan—our beloved brother —reach into the depths of Africa . . ." (Nasser, *Philosophy of the Revolution,* Cairo).

32. The African general public will long remember the editorial in *Le Monde* at the time of the Congolese Premier's arrest: "The first reaction that the arrest of M. Lumumba by his opponents aroused was relief . . ." (December 4, 1960). On the UAR's policy in the Congo, see *A* (December 13, 1960, January 15 and February 14 and 16, 1961); M. H. Heykal's embarrassed apology (February 17); the decision to withdraw the battalion (September 13, 1960); and Nasser's telegram to Tshombe (August 12, 1960). On American policy, cf. the "Bulletin d'information" of *L'Express,* by P.-M. de la Gorce (supplement to No. 501 of January 19, 1961). Serge Michel's *Uhuru Lumumba!* (Paris, 1962) and M. Merlier's *Le Congo, de la domination belge à l'indépendance* (The Congo, from Belgian Domination to Independence), Paris, 1962, tell the story from the victims' side. Since then a considerable number of works has laid bare the truth of the drama, which is still going on . . .

33. Cf., among others, "Hakikat al-tassallol al-Isra'ili fi Ifrikiya" (The Truth about Israeli Infiltration in Africa), in *A,* November 3, 1960; Yussef el-Sherif, "Al-tassallol al-sahyuni dahkel Ifrikiya" (The Zionist Infiltration Inside Africa), in *RY,* No. 1768 (April 30, 1962); in the UN, Israel indicated that she had sent out 600 experts and received 1,600 students, most of them Africans, in *Le Monde* (October 11, 1962). A major work on this problem from the Egyptian side is Ahmed Baha' Eddine's *Isra'iliyyat wa ma ba'd al-'oudwan* (Israeliana, and the Aftermath of Aggression), Cairo, 1967. Much work is now in progress, at the university level, on this problem.

34. *A,* December 10, 1960.

35. Complete text of the decisions in *A;* a good summary in French in *COC,* XVIII, No. 45 (1961), pp. 1–2.

36. *A,* January 16, and February 4, 19 and 25, 1961.

37. Mahmud el-Maraghi, "Tarik al-shimal wa'l-da'ira al-sakhina" (The Northern Path and the Hot Circle), in *RY,* No. 1768 (April 30, 1962).—The facts completely knocked down the traditional Western argument: "Through his break with the West, which alone was in a position to give him grants and long-term credits, Colonel Nasser has imposed a heavy handicap on the future of the Egyptian economy." G. Rousseau, "La Politique du colonel Abd al-Nasser et l'économie l'égyptienne" (Colonel Abdel-Nasser's Policy and the Egyptian Economy), in *Orient,* No. 1 (January 1957), pp. 17–35.

38. Speech in Moscow, in *A,* December 3, 1960. On the Soviet

theory of aid to the Arab countries, cf. S. Skatchkov, Distinterested Soviet Aid to the Countries of Asia and Africa," Arabic text in *Ittihad al-Shaab* (Baghdad, April 5, 1960). Also W. Z. Laqueur, *The Soviet Union and the Middle East* (London, 1959), pp. 136–358; B. Kerblay, "La pénétration économique des pays du bloc soviétique au Moyen-Orient" (Economic Penetration of the Middle East by Soviet-Bloc Countries), in *Orient*, No. 13 (1960), pp. 169–74; V. Alkhimov, "Co-operation between the USSR and the Underdeveloped Countries," in *Voprossy Ekonomiki*, No. 6, 1957 (English translation). Tadros A. A. Malek draws an accurate balance sheet of the advantages gained by Egypt in his *Some Aspects of the Control of Egypt's Foreign Trade Since 1945*. Unpublished Ph.D. thesis (London, 1961), especially pp. 158–213.

39. "Inside Egypt (II): Egypt in Blinkers," January 10, 1962. This was an extension of the policy of the Middle East Supply Center; cf. S. Argov, *American Policy in the Near East 1941–1945*. Unpublished M.Sc. in economics thesis (London, 1954), pp. 105–145.

40. Mahmud el Maraghi, "Al-'hiyad yakifu 'ala riglayhi" (Neutralism Stands on Its Feet), in *RY*, No. 1759 (February 26, 1962).

41. *A*, April 30, and May 5 and 6, 1962; *Le Monde*, May 14 and 23, 1962. "Egypt has become closely dependent on American aid, which mainly takes the form of wheat surpluses up to a value of £60 million sterling per year. If the Egyptian army relies on Russian arms, the Egyptian people, at the present moment, relies no less urgently on American food products." "Socialism on the Nile," in *The Economist*, No. 6193 (May 5, 1962), pp. 457–8. According to Senator J. William Fulbright, chairman of the Senate Foreign Relations Committee, the United States gave Israel assistance amounting to ten to twenty times the maximum accorded to any Arab country (*A*, quoting The Associated Press, May 4, 1962). "The entire world should study the Charter of National Action with the closest attention," declared Dr. Jacobsson, head of the IBRD's mission in Cairo (*A*, May 25, 1962).

42. Dr. Abdel-Razek Hassan, "Al-'alakat al-iktissadiyya maa Almanya al-Gharbiyya" (Economic Relations with East Germany), in *A*, May 22, 1961.

43. *A*, June 29 and July 7, 1961. A curious work, *Behind the Egyptian Sphinx—Prelude to World War III?*, by I. Sedar and H. Greenberg (Philadelphia, 1960), teems with information on a so-called Hitlerian-Communist conspiracy to build an Arab power that could turn the West's flank in the next world war; unfortunately the array of names and events is presented without any indication of sources or references. On German-Egyptian relations, cf. my essay "Almanya al-Gharbiyya wa'l-Shark al-Awssat" (West Germany and the Middle East), in *M*, January 24, 1959; but particularly the records of the Leipzig colloquium headed by Professor

W. Markov: *Probleme des Neokolonialismus und die Politik der beiden deutschen Staaten gegenüber dem nationalen Befreiungskampf der Völker*, Band I (Problems of Neocolonialism and the Policies of the Two German States Toward the Peoples' National-Liberation Movements, Vol. I), Leipzig, 1961. Also J. Joesten's *The Germans and Col. Nasser—West and East German Relations with Cairo 1958–1959* (mimeographed, Hartsville, Mass., 1959); contains useful economic information; among the Nazis sheltered in Egypt he lists Dr. Hans Eisele, Dr. Johannes v. Leers and Hermann Zind (pp. 16–7).

44. *"Les Rapports économiques et commerciaux de l'Italie avec le continent africain"* (Italy's Economic and Trade Relations with the African Continent), in *Notes et Etudes Documentaires*, No. 2858 (March 1962); "Italia wa'l-petrol al-'Arabi" (Italy and Arab Oil), in *AI*, No. 167 (August 13, 1962).

45. "Limaza mada safiruna fi London thalathat shuhur fi'l-Kahira?" (Why Has Our Ambassador to London Spent Three Months in Cairo?) and "Al-'arsh al-Saudi wa'l-mukhabarat al-britaniyya" (The Saudi Throne and the British Intelligence Service), in *RY*, No. 1768 (April 30, 1962). On what British control had been before 1952 and who held "the power of decision," cf. Gad Labib, *La Structure économique en Égypte et les relations monétaires anglo-égyptiennes depuis 1931* (Economic Structure in Egypt and Anglo-Egyptian Currency Relations since 1931). Cairo, 1952.

46. In May the Egyptian press gave prominent display to offers by French firms, notably Cofrédi, running as high as £E65 million (*A*, May 4, 1962). The Egyptian press announced the end of broadcasts by Radio Free Egypt (*A*, May 25, 1962). This was the state of Egyptian-Western economic relations in the spring of 1962: the West accounted for 43 percent of Egyptian foreign trade, and the United States, Great Britain and West Germany together provided 40 percent of Egypt's imports; the United States represented 14 percent of Egyptian trade but took no part in the Five-Year Plan's projects; however, Egypt showed a deficit of £E76 million in her trade balance for 1961; most of this was accounted for by the credit facilities that enabled her to meet her needs in foodstuffs. Mahmud el-Maraghi, "Al-ghadibun fi'l-shimal" (The Irate Ones in the North), in *RY*, No. 1769 (May 7, 1962).

47. The president of the IBRD in person, Eugene Black, furnished the theory for it in his work *The Diplomacy of Economic Development*, with a preface by former Secretary of State Christian Herter (Harvard, 1960). In the face of "the revolution of rising hopes," it must be recognized that "the governments of these countries are the chief agents of change within societies in which very many persons are opposed to change . . . This is a question not so much of ideology as of necessity. The politician and the

bureaucrat in these countries are literally rulers at the same time as governors" (pp. 6, 12). It was up to the West to propose "an alternative course [to Communism] that would succeed in approaching the rate of growth under Communism without having to pay the terrible price in human terms that the latter imposes." And he remarks that the underdeveloped countries "do not see how . . ." (pp. 15–6).

7. Egyptian Problems of Arab Nationalism

1. Lack of space prevents a presentation of the historical background. Two detailed bibliographies (up to 1959) can be found under the headings of *Kifa'h al-Arab fi sabil al-'huriyya wa'l-wi'hda* (The Arabs' Struggle for Liberty and Unity) and *Al-kawmiyya al-'arabiyya* (Arab Nationalism), National Library, Cairo, 1959.

2. Zaghlul's famous remark is often quoted, to the effect that if the Arab states united, they would never total more than zero; cf. Salah Abdel Sabbur, "Innaha thawrat al-'Arab gami 'an" (This Is the Revolution of All the Arabs), in *RY*, No. 1625 (August 3, 1959). On the genesis of Arab nationalism, cf. H. Z. Nuseibeh, *The Ideas of Arab Nationalism* (Cornell, 1956): F. A. Sayegh, *Arab Unity* (New York, 1956); Mohammed Ezzat Darwaza, *Al-wi'hda al-'Arabiyya* (Arab Unity), Beirut, 1957. On the Egyptian attitude, cf. Anis Sayegh, *Al-fikra al-'Arabiyya fi Misr* (The Arab Idea in Egypt), Beirut, 1959.

3. "Al-Misriyyun 'Arab" (Egyptians Are Arabs), in *al-Hilal* (April 1939), special issue on *Al-'Arab wa'l-Islam fi'l'asr al-hadith* (Arabs and Islam in the Modern Era).

4. On the League's history, see the series of articles entitled "Mafhuman li'l-tadamun al-'Arabi" (Two Conceptions of Arab Solidarity), in *Ittihad al-Shaab* (Baghdad, August 20–24, 1960), which contains much material not available elsewhere; B. Butros-Ghali, *Arab League Bibliography* (Cairo, 1955).

5. There is a great wealth of literature on the practical aspects of the merger; I should like to mention particularly M. A. Darwaza, *Hawla al-'haraka al-'Arabiyya al-haditha* (On the Modern Arab Movement), Sidon, 1950; A. Nassif, "Traités et accords de fraternité entre les pays arabes" (Treaties and Brotherhood Agreements between Arab Countries), in *Revue Egyptienne de Droit International* (Cairo, 1949); Mahmud Kamel, *Al-dawla al-'Arabiyya al-Kubra* (The Greatest Arab State), Cairo, 1958; M. Anis and H. A. Mahmud, "Yakzat al-'Arab al-haditha wa kifa'huhom" (Modern Arab Awakening and Struggle), in S. Ashur, ed., *Dirassat fi'l-mugtama' al-'Arabi* (Studies in Arab Society), pp. 87–167 (Cairo, 1961); Fathi el-Tubgy, *Harakat al-wi'hda fi'l-watan al-'Arabi* (The Unity Movement in the Arab Fatherland), Cairo, 1962; M. A. G. Yehia, *The Pan-Arab Movement in Theory and*

Practice, unpublished Ph.D. thesis (London, 1950); the collectively written volume by A. K. Hatem, Y. Eweiss, M. M. Ata, H. Jamati, et al., with a preface by Nasser, *Al-kawmiyya al-'Arabiyya wa'l-Isti'mar* (Arab Nationalism and Imperialism), Cairo, c. 1956; "Mahader galasat moubahathat al-wi'hda, mars–april 1963" (Minutes of the Negotiations on Unity, March–April 1963), in *Koutoub Qawmiyyah* (Patriotic Books), Cairo, 1963; Monte Palmer, "The United Arab Republic: An Assessment of Its Failure," in *MEJ*, XX, No. 1 (1966), pp. 50–67; etc.

6. Azzam is quoted in Sate el-Hossari, *Al-'Uruba awwalan*, (Arabism First), p. 121; Talaat Harb, *Khutab* (Speeches), Vol. I (Beirut, n.d.), p. 140.

7. Cf. Shafei and Gibeili, *Ahdafuna*, *op. cit.*, and the bound volumes of *al-Fagr al-Gadid* (1945–56), *al-Gamahir* (1947–48) and *al-Malayin* (1951).

8. A very violent criticism of the Syrian-Lebanese extreme left in Yussef Khattar el-Helu, "Al-wi'hda al-iktissadiyya al-'Arabiyya fi daw' al-wake' wa'l-tagriba" (Arab Economic Unity in the Light of Reality and Experience), in *al-Akhbar* (Beirut), May 27, 1962.

9. Kamel, *op. cit.*, pp. 580–6. The statement recalls those of Antun Saade's Syrian Popular party, which was implicated in a number of armed conspiracies against Lebanon's integrity; Akram el-Hurani, moreover, was supposed to have been one of the prominent party leaders just after the Second World War and before he set up his Arab Socialist party. Mamduh Reda, "Al-mawkef fi Suriya," (The Situation in Syria), in *RY*, No. 1769 (May 7, 1962).

10. Beling, *op. cit.*, pp. 13–21, 99–112; G. Lenczowski, *Oil and State in the Middle East* (New York, 1960), pp. 281–93 and 319–350; W. A. Leeman, *The Price of Middle East Oil* (Cornell, 1961).

11. Beling, *op. cit.*, observes that the relations between the Arab trade union movement and the World Federation of Trade Unions improved, while the discord with the International Federation of Free Trade Unions increased; he quotes Fathi Kamel: "our eastern comrades support us completely in our objectives . . ." (pp. 81–4 and 124).

12. According to Kingsley Martin, Arab nationalism "is more like nineteenth-century pan-Germanism, when all the German-speaking peoples were at once irritated and attracted by Prussia's aspirations to power . . . It might be said that Prussia and Austria were then in the same position with respect to the members of the German confederation as Egypt and Iraq today with respect to the other members of the Arab League" ("Arab Nationalism," in *New Statesman*, No. 1615, February 23, 1962).

13. An editorial by Ehsan Abdel Koddus is a good illustration of the problem: "Our attention [before 1952] was concentrated chiefly on internal problems: corruption in the government, the evacuation of the English, the mobilization of opinion behind the

Revolution, etc. . . . The Arab problem is not specialization but, rather, knowing to what extent it is possible to arouse the reader's interest. The ordinary reader, in fact, can maintain all this enthusiasm and understanding for all Arab problems taken as a whole, arising out of the same general source. But it is difficult for him to continue to be interested in the details pertaining to each problem separately . . . The struggle for the determination of a destiny should always remain within the framework of the people of the region itself. All that the [Egyptian] Arab general public can do is protect the region against foreign aggression and against the efforts of imperialists within it . . ." "Na'hnu wa'l-kadaya al-'Arabiyya" (We and Arab Issues), in *RY*, No. 1630, September 7, 1959. Cf. Anouar Abdel-Malek, "Esquisse d'une typologie des formations nationales dans les Trois Continents" (Outline of a Typology of the National Formations on the Three Continents), in *Cahiers Internationaux de Sociologie*, XLII (1967), pp. 49–57.

14. On the theoretical development during the 1956–58 period, see N. Rezhwan, "Arab Nationalism in Search of an Ideology," in W. Z. Laqueur, ed., *The Middle East, op. cit.*, pp. 145–65; and T. J. Le Gassick, *Studies in Contemporary Arab Nationalist Literature*. Unpublished Ph.D. thesis (London, 1960), pp. 246–312.

15. Michel Aflak's latest book is *Maarakat al-massir al-wa'hed* (The Struggle for a Unified Destiny), Beirut, 1958; in addition to his doctrinal writings, Clovis Maksud has recently made interesting contributions, especially to *A* and *RY*.

16. This is discussed in the first point in the Arab Cultural Unity Agreement between Egypt, Syria and Jordan (1957) and in the Charter of Arab Cultural Unity between the UAR and Iraq (1958); it was repeated by the Fourth Arab Cultural Congress (1959).

17. "Arab unity is above all a problem in the Syria of today; tomorrow, perhaps, it will be that of the Arabian peninsula. There too the same situation is found: an Arab sentiment to which no counterweight is afforded by territorial patriotism and, consequently, the existence of artificial political units in the true sense of the term" (Professor Albert Hourani, "The Middle East and the Crisis of 1956," in *St. Antony's Papers, Middle Eastern Affairs*, No. 1, Oxford, 1958, p. 37); cf. C. Ernest Dawn, "The Rise of Arabism in Syria," in *MEJ*, XVI, No. 2 (1962), pp. 145–68, and the remarkable and decisive synthesis provided by Professor Hourani in his *Arabic Thought in the Liberal Age, 1798–1939* (Oxford U. Press, 1962), pp. 260–323.

18. Texts in *President Gamal Abdel Nasser's Speeches . . . 1958, op. cit.*

19. *A*, September 28, 1960. However, the President of the UAR never missed an opportunity to harangue the crowd in the vernacular, in that Egyptian dialect which is so much more percussive than the written language . . .

20. Mahmud Kamal, *Athar hadarat al-Phara 'ina fi Misr al-yawm* (The Traces of Pharaonic Civilization in Today's Egypt). Cairo, 1956.

21. Dr. Ali Ahmed Issa, "Madda gadida tadkhol ru'uss al-sha-bab" (A New Subject Enters the Minds of the Youth), in *A*, August 24, 1960.

22. *Na'hwa ideolozhiyya 'Arabiyya gadida* (Toward a New Arab Ideology). Cairo, 1957.

23. Let us note, among others, two group works: A. F. Ashur, ed., *Dirassat fi'l-mugtama' al-'Arabi*, already cited, and B. Butros-Ghali, M. K. Ismail and A. M. Awda, *Al-mugtama' al-'Arabi* (The Arab Society), Cairo, 1960; the books by Ali el-Kharbotly, Mo-hammed Abdalla el-Arabi, Mohammed M. Ata, et al.; the work of the Jordanian Abdallah el-Rimawi, published in Cairo (1961–62). A curious investigation undertaken by Ahmed Y. Awni, professor of hematology at Ain Shams University, starting with the blood of the Nubians, sought to "establish that the Arabs share a common origin, that they constitute a single people scattered throughout the Middle East" (*A*, April 30, 1960).

24. On the devastation perpetrated by this group, cf. Hosny Labib, "Wake' al-ta'lim fi Misr" (The Reality of Education in Egypt), in *al-Akhbar* (Beirut), September 24 and October 13, 1961.

25. "Yesterday was the twenty-fourth anniversary of the death of Saad Zaghlul"—this was all that *A* of August 24, 1961, had to say on this subject, on page 12, in the gossip column. Likewise: "Forty-three years yesterday since the 1919 revolution," *A*, March 10, 1962.

26. *A*, July 29 and August 5, 1960.

27. Thus Faruk Khorshid, a young critic and an ardent disciple of Islamic Arab nationalism, declares: "The Arab field in our studies remains unplowed . . . We want to know whether we pos-sess what is generaly called a national heritage, whether our Arab literature, our Arab culture and our Arab thought form a cultural whole that can serve as a basis for our vital affirmation today with respect to Arab existence and Arab nationalism." "Al-thawra al-fikriyya" (The Revolution in Thought), in *A*, July 14, 1961; Hassan Abbas Zaki, the minister, attempted to arrive at this in "Mukawwemat al-baka' fi'l-mugtama' al-'Arabi" (The Foun-dations of Permanence in Arab Society), in *A*, January 5, 1960.

28. *'Uruba wa din* (Arabism and Religion), p. 63 (Cairo, n.d., c. 1959). Bakuri was evicted from his post in 1959, having been implicated in a scandal. He is now Rector of Al Azhar.

29. Speech by Gamal Abdel Nasser to the Association for the Protection of Islam in Lahore, in *A*, April 16, 1960.

30. Fathi Ghanem, "Maza nuridu min'al-tadamum al-'Arabi?" (What Do We Want from Arab Solidarity?), in *RY*, No. 1637,

September 28, 1959; Salah Abdel Sabbur, article cited; C. Maksud, "Man huwa al-'Arabi?" (Who Is an Arab?), in *RY*, No. 1643, December 7, 1959; M. Arcash, "Tarikh al-'Arab wa tabi'at biladihem (The History of the Arabs and the Nature of Their Countries), in *A*, April 4, 1960; etc.

31. Shafei, *Tatawwor al-haraka, op. cit.*, pp. 162–3; A. G. Shezhne observed that Egyptian public consciousness became impregnated with Arabism only under the new government, in "Egyptian Attitudes towards Pan-Arabism," in *MEJ*, XI, No. 3 (1957), pp. 253–68.

32. See bound volumes of *M* for 1957 and 1958; one of its contributors, Gamil Abdel Shafie, made Salama Mussa, even though he was a fierce partisan of Pharaonic Egypt, into an "Arab Egyptian from the day of his birth to the day of his death . . ." (*M*, August 8, 1958).

33. On leftwing publishing houses of this period, see "Al-ma'raka wa harakat al-nashr fi Misr" (The Battle and the Publication Movement in Egypt), in *al-Thakafa al-Wataniyya* (Beirut), VI, No. 1 (1957), pp. 60–1.

34. *Ibid.*, special issue, No. 64 (1954), especially pp. 44–50.

35. *Al-Adab* (Beirut), special issue, IV, No. 10 (1956), notably pp. 97–100.

36. On the part played by Yussef el-Seba'i in the eviction of the leftist writers before the Congress, cf. "La irhab fi'l-thakafa" (No Terror in Culture), in *al-Thakafa al-Wataniyya*, V, No. 9 (1956), p. 56; on the Third Congress, cf. the special issue of *al-Adab*, VI, No. 1 (1958); and my essay entitled "Khutwa gadida fi tarik nahdatina al-thakafiyya" (A New Step in the Path of Our Cultural Renaissance), in *al-Thakafa al-Wataniyya*, VII, No. 2 (1958), pp. 7–10.

37. On the Fourth Congress and the text of the Iraqi delegation's protest, cf. *ibid.*, VIII, No. 2 (1959), pp. 69–71.

38. *L'Unità*, May 14, 1957; French version in *Bulletin édité par la section de politique extérieure du C.C. du P.C. Français* (*Bulletin Published by the Foreign-Policy Section of the Central Committee of the French Communist Party*), No. 28 (Paris, July 1957), pp. 40–3.

39. According to El-Hakam Darwaza, *Al-shuyu'iyya al-ma'halliyya fi ma'arakat al-'Arab al-kawmiyya* (Local Communism in the Arab National Struggle), pp. 157–9 (Beirut, 1961).

40. *Bayan min al-Hizb al-Shuyu'i al-Misri 'an al-wi'hda al-Suriyya al-Misriyya* (Proclamation from the Egyptian Communist Party on the Syrian-Egyptian Unity), quoted *ibid.*, pp. 187–9.

41. *Takaddamu al-suffuf al-wataniyya fi ma'raket al-wi'hda al-Arabiyya!* (Stand in the Front Ranks of the National Ranks in the Struggle for Arab Unity!), quoted *ibid.*, pp. 189–90.

42. *Bayan ila'l-shaab 'an al-wi'hda al-Misriyya al-Suriyya* (Proc-

lamation to the People on Egyptian-Syrian Unity), quoted *ibid.*, pp. 183–4.

43. *Ashat al-Gumhuriyya al-'Arabiyya al-Muttahidat!* (Long Live the United Arab Republic!), quoted *ibid.*, pp. 184–5.

44. Quoted from *Ittihad al-Shaab* (Cairo), No. 1 (February 1958), p. 5. *Ibid.*, p. 186.

45. Quoted from *Ittihad al-Shaab*, No. 3 (March 15, 1958). *Ibid.*, p. 199.

46. Quoted from *Ittihad al-Shaab*, No. 9 (April 1958). *Ibid.*, p. 200. Beling points out that "an almost psychopathic fear of Communist infiltration of the working-class movement was one of the chief factors behind the government's reactionary attitude" (*op. cit.*, p. 106).

47. *Hawla al-wi'hda maa'l-Gumhuriyya al-'Arabiyya al-Mutta-'hida wa'l-Yaman* (On the Unity with the UAR and Yemen), in Darwaza, *op. cit.*, pp. 206–14; on the attitude of the Syrian Communist party, cf. *al-Nida* and *al-Akhbar* (Beirut) for the years of 1958–62.

48. *Baad al-tatawwurat al-akhira fi'l-Shark al-'Arabi* (After the Recent Developments in the Arab East), in Darwaza, *op. cit.*, pp. 217–8.

49. It is interesting to observe that in spite of everything, this group stopped short of the extreme positions taken in certain Syrian-Lebanese leftist circles. Thus, having published *Kadiyyat al-Gazair wa'l-tadamun al-'Arabi* (The Algerian Problem and Arab Solidarity) in 1957, Ahmed Rifa'i, one of the leaders of the Egyptian minority group, was castigated by the critic on *al-Thakafa al-Wataniyya* for having spoken of an Algerian nation: "We are opposed to the idea that there should be an Algerian nation, for we believe that the Algerian people is a part of the Arab nation, etc." (VI, No. 11, 1957, pp. 63–4).

50. *A*, August 14, 1961.

51. "Hugum al-rabie allazi naga'ha fi'l-kharif" (The Spring Offensive That Succeeded in the Autumn), in *A*, October 6, 1961.

52. Heykal, *Maza gara, op. cit.*

53. *A*, September 30, 1961.

54. *A*, December 24, 1961.

55. M. H. Heykal, "La nuridu an natadaman" (We Do Not Want to Solidarize Ourselves), in *A*, March 9, 1962.

56. See the version given by Heykal on the contacts between the higher Syrian officers and Gamal Abdel Nasser after the separation, in *A*, April 20 and 27, 1962.

57. "Hal na'hnu 'ala isti'dad li tagribat wi'hda gadida?" (Are We Prepared to Experiment with a New Unity?), in *A*, June 11, 1962. A few weeks earlier G. Keshk had made a very violent attack on the "Arab youth" staff of the magazine *al-Huriyya*, even though it was pro-Nasser, for having published a book contending

that basic unity did not preclude the possibility of adopting different paths; only one road was possible, he said in substance— Gamal Abdel Nasser's ("Wi'hdat al-uslub hia wi'hdat al-hadaf" (Unity of Method Is Unity of Aim), in *RY*, No. 1770, May 14, 1962).

58. "La wi'hda bi dun dimokratiyya" (No Unity without Democracy), in *al-Akhbar* (Beirut), June 24, 1962.

59. *A*, June 22, 1962.

60. M. H. Heykal, "Fi zikra 15 mayo 1948" (On the Anniversary of May 15, 1948), in *A*, May 18, 1962.

61. *A*, June 27, 1962.

62. Nasser, *My Revolutionary Life, op. cit.*, (3), "My Aims for the New Egypt," in the (London) *Sunday Times*, July 1, 1962.

63. The complete text of the Syrian statement, in *al-Akhbar* (Beirut), emphasized a document emanating from the office of "the technical and administrative department of the Ministry of Foreign Affairs" in Cairo, No. 27/1961, dated August 10, 1961; in it General Mohammed Hafez Ismail, Undersecretary of State, advised the heads of diplomatic missions "as much as possible to avoid discussing the problem of the Palestinian refugees . . . in order to facilitate the negotiations now under way, calmly and through diplomatic channels, between our government and the American government . . ." (*al-Akhbar,* September 2, 1962). The Egyptian reply took, in particular, the form of the publication of the Kennedy–Nasser correspondence (May 11–August 18, 1961) in *A*, September 21, 1962; also the texts of the speeches of the Egyptian delegation (composed of former Syrian ministers), in *A*, August 27 and 28, 1962.

64. *Le Coup d'état syrien* (Cairo, October 8, 1961). This unsigned document spoke on behalf of the "Egyptian Communists." It should be pointed out that as early as 1959 the Syrian Communist party was talking of "pharaonic imperialism," whereas the unification was indeed effected in the name of an Arabism tinged with Islamism, and the Marxist advocates of Egyptian individuality were persecuted for their thesis in opposition to the unification . . . A very important text by Nasser, his preface to *Misr wa rissalatuha* (Egypt and Its Mission), by Dr. Hussein Mo'nes (Cairo, n.d., c. 1956), spoke of Egypt in this fashion: "The Egypt that made her personality felt when history was still in confusion . . . the Egypt that had her own independent personality, her individual character, her emancipated entity throughout all the stages of history, is still the Egypt of today and will be that of tomorrow, whence come her independence in planning, the individuality of her policies, her distinct character: she is that great force which could not be permeated by imperialism even at the paroxysm of its drive and the peak of its power, and which has retained her own character, her own characteristics and her own existence . . ." (p. *v*).

This text should be compared with the earlier one by the former president of the Liberal-Constitutional party, Dr. Mohammed Hussein Heykal, which is part of his preface to Vol. I of *Al-siyassa wa'l-stratezhiyya fi'l-Shark al-Awsat* (Politics and Strategy in the Middle East), by Dr. Hussein F. el-Naggar (Cairo, 1953): "It is striking to observe that Egypt, alone among all the African peoples, falls within the structure of the Middle East, alone among all the African states . . . Egypt, alone among the states of the Arab League, is an African state . . . The destiny of Egypt has been linked more closely to Syria's and Iraq's than to the Sudan's and Libya's . . ."

8. What Is "Co-operativist Democratic Socialism"?

1. *A*, July 10, 1960.
2. *A*, July 17, 1960; *UAR Yearbook for 1961, op. cit.*, pp. 51–80. The chairman of this committee was Ali Sabry.
3. Tom Little, *Modern Egypt* (New York, 1967), pp. 218–20. Formerly entitled *Egypt* (*op. cit.*).
4. Cf. the "Central Bank's Report for the Year 1961," in *A*, April 14, 1962.
5. Version given by M. H. Heykal in *A*, June 9, 1961. This phrasing of Khrushchev's remarks has been challenged by the Lebanese Communist organs, *al-Nida* and *al-Akhbar*.
6. "Na'hnu wa'l-shuyu'iyya" (We and Communism), in *A*, August 4, 1961.
7. The latter had contended that "the essential institutions [for socialism] do not exist. In Egypt the proletariat is minuscule, the middle class is not sufficiently large, knowledgeable or sufficiently honest, and the peasantry is illiterate in the majority." "Arab Socialism," in *New Statesman*, No. 1614 (February 16, 1962), pp. 218–20. The article by Koddus, "Ishtirakiyyatuna wa'l-shuyu'iyya" (Our Socialism and Communism), in *RY*, No. 1759, (March 5, 1962).
8. "Khassa'ess al-ishtirakiyya al-'Arabiyya" (Characteristics of Arab Socialism), in *AK*, March 18, 1962. See also Rifaat's essay "Al-dimokratiyya," in *RY*, No. 1658 (February 21, 1960), and his preface to Mustafa el-Mestekawi's book *Ma'alem al-tarik fi'l-tatbik al-ishtiraki* (Landmarks in the Path to the Application of Socialism). Cairo, 1962.
9. "Al-falsafa al-dimokratiyya al-ishtirakiyya al-ta'awuniyya fi mu'hit al-mazaheb al-siyassiyya al-mu'assira" (The Democratic Socialist Co-operativist Philosophy in the Framework of Contemporary Political Doctrines), in *EPSR*, No. 12 (1962), pp. 57–8.
10. Books by M. K. el-Abd, A. E. Khalafallah, A. M. Shemeiss and Kamal Rifaat; Ali Sabry's "Al-tatbik al-'amali li'l-ishtirakiyya al-dimokratiyya al-ta'awonniyya" (The Practical Application of

Democratic Co-operativist Socialism), in *RY*, No. 1680–2 (August 22 and 29, and Septmber 5, 1960); A. R. Nosseir, etc.; there was not a week without a new book on Arab "socialism." See also the magazines *Bina' al-watan* and, especially, *EPSR*, as well as the other periodicals cited. Saad Afra, *Al-ta'awon fi mogtama'ina al-ishtiraki* (Co-operation in our Socialist Society), (Cairo, 1959); ex-Minister A. K. Hatem, *Hawla'l-nazariyya al-ishtirakiyya* (On the Socialist Theory), (Cairo, 1959)—the latter book makes a violent racial attack on "Marx, a Jew by birth," and is meant to redeem from their errors "those who contend that Marx was the founder of socialism" (p. 9); the special issue of *AK* (March 1962); "Le Socialisme arabe, expérience-pilote pour les jeunes nations (Arab Socialism, Pilot Experiment for the New Nations), in *Scribe*, IV, No. 5 (1962), and M. H. Kerr, "The Emergence of a Socialist Ideology in Egypt," in *MEJ*, XVI, No. 2 (1962), pp. 127–44. This should be contrasted with the serious theoretical work expounded by the Marxist groups in *al-Tali'a*, since December 1965, and in *al-Katib*, and, especially, the collective volume *La Voie égyptienne vers le socialisme* (Cairo, 1967).

11. "Munakashat mabadi al-mithak" (Discussion of the Principles of the Charter), in *A*, April 22, 1962.

12. *RY*, No. 1767 (April 23, 1962).

13. "Nura'hheb bi'l-'hiwar wa nastanker al-tahaggom" (We Welcome Discussion and Deny Contempt), in *A*, June 8, 1961.

14. Later Castro took a position: "What do I think of the Communist party militants? That they deserve respect; and I think that while for a long time they were misunderstood, attacked, shut out, cast aside as if they were parasites, barred from any outlet in the newspapers, we ought to recognize that they have merit, a great merit, in being Communists." F. Castro, "Je suis marxiste-léniniste," in *Partisans*, No. 4 (1962), p. 14.

15. "Dimokratiyyat al-ishtirakiyya" (The Democracy of Socialism), in *RY*, October 26, 1959.

16. On disaffection with respect to the government, see the results of the survey "Ayna yakef al-ra'y al-'am?" (Where Does Public Opinion Stand?), in *RY*, No. 1770 (May 14, 1962): "More than half of the people have reservations about the new political experiment . . ."

17. In the spring of 1959 the Egyptian Communist party's Central Committee published an important sixty-page study that analyzed Egyptian society under the signature "Abbas" (its secretary-general). A little earlier a study of *L'Idéologie sociale de la révolution égyptienne* (The Social Ideology of the Egyptian Revolution) had stated in all seriousness: "There are no classes, properly speaking, in Egypt, and still less is there a class struggle . . ." F. Berthier in *Orient*, II, No. 6 (1958), p. 56, Note 16. The controversy inside the concentration camps seems to have changed the

relation of forces and hardened the extremes: while the majority preferred a harsher description of the government, a substantial minority apparently supported the plan for the dissolution of the Egyptian Communist party and its merger into the Arab Socialist Union. The center group (Abu Seif Yussef, Fuad Mursi, Mahmud el-Alem, Ismail Sabri Abdallah, et al.) worked toward unity and made a more finely shaded analysis.

18. A, March 12, June 13, and July 2 and 31, 1961.

19. "Al-takhtit fi waki'ina" (Planning in Our Concrete Reality), in A, May 19, 20, 21 and 24, 1962. Dr. Ahmed Shukry Salem, former lecturer in the faculty of sciences at Cairo University, and director of Dar al-Abhath al-Ilmiyya and later of the Popular University, was a particular victim of repression under Faruk; a doctor of science, he is one of the finest of the progressive intellectuals and is now one of the leading experts at the head of Planning.

20. F. Ghanem, "Al-daawa ila damir ishtiraki" (The Call for a Socialist Moral Consciousness), in RY, October 19, 1959.

21. Keshk, "Mustakbal," article cited; Mohammed Auda and Ahmed Baha'Eddine developed the same ideas as the proto-socialist wing in the AK seminar. Galal Keshk made anti-Communism his specialty in the series of articles published in RY in April, May and June of 1962: "Our socialism represents a philosophical and political challenge to Marxism. The success of our experiment and its transformation into a world force of orientation that illuminates the path for the peoples of Asia, Africa and Latin America means the end of the age of Marxist-Leninist thought. Such is the authentic and direct meaning of the slogan: our socialism arises out of our reality itself . . ." "Al-ard li'l-fellah" (Land for the Fellah), in RY, No. 1775 (June 18, 1962).

22. P. A. Baran, The Political Economy of Growth (London, 1957), pp. 221–2; on the "Japanese road," see G. C. Allen, A Short Economic History of Modern Japan (London, 1962).

23. In AICC Economic Review, X, No. 7 (1958), pp. 7–9, and Nos. 8–9, respectively; also the symposium "The Party in Power," in Seminar, Bombay, I, No. 1 (1959). The similarity is striking. Nasser himself acknowledged the decisive influence of Nehru on the development of his political thinking, in My Revolutionary Life, op. cit., in the (London) Sunday Times, June 17, 1962, whereas he barely mentioned Tito. An important doctrinal work by Sampurnanand is Indian Socialism (London, 1962), immediately translated into Arabic and put on sale on September 20.

24. RY, No. 1345 (March 22, 1954); on his return from China, however, the former Minister of Wakfs had said: "I have seen Islam in China . . ."

25. "Islam was the first revolution that proclaimed socialist principles in matters of justice and equality" (Gamal Abdel Nas-

ser, in speech commemorating Syrian-Egyptian unity, in *A*, February 23, 1962); also Marshal Amer's speech at promotion ceremonies for air force officers (*A*, April 24, 1962); etc.

26. *Ishtirakiyyat al-Islam* (The Socialism of Islam), by Mustafa el-Seba'i (Cairo, 1961), supposedly sold 120,000 copies during the first four months (*AK*, March 23, 1962). Other books that must be cited: A. Farag, *Al-Islam din al-ishtirakiyya* (Islam as the Religion of Socialism); Abdel Rahman el-Sharkawi, *Mohammed, rassul al-horriyya* (Mohammed, Prophet of Liberty), Cairo, 1962; the books by I. Mazhar, M. A. el-Arabi, H. Abd Rabbo, Mohammed el-Ghazali, Sayed Kotb, I. M. el-Barayri, et al. Here too the flood poured on. But attention must be called to "Al-ishtirakiyya wa'l-Islam" (Socialism and Islam), by Sheik Mahmud Shaltut, in *G*, December 22, 1960. A thesis, required reading thereafter, provided the co-ordinates: Mohammed Shawki Zaki's *Al-Ikhwan al-Muslimun wa'l-mugtama' al-Misri* (The Moslem Brothers and Egyptian Society), Cairo, 1954.

27. Maxime Rodinson, *Problématique de l'étude des rapports entre Islam et communisme* (Problems of the Study of Relations between Islam and Communism—symposium on "Moslem sociology"), Brussels (1961), pp. 10–21; *Mouvements politiques et mythes: l'exemple du nationalisme arabe* (Political Movements and Myths: the Example of Arab Nationalism)—Cerisy discussions on "myths in political life," 1962. He correctly points out that "most often the authors who deal with this subject either do not know Islam or do not know Communism. Quite often, in fact, they know neither the one nor the other . . ." The book contains a detailed bibliography of previous publications on these questions.

28. H. A. Zaki, "Al-sira' al-fikry" (The Struggle of Ideas), (*A*, December 13, 1959), and "Mukawwemat," already cited.

29. State publishing was then centralized in two bodies. One was the Egyptian Public Agency for Editing, Translating, Printing and Publishing, headed by Professor Mahdi Allam, who was assisted by Ibrahim Z. Khurshid, Abdel Razek Hassan, Salah Abdel Sabbur and two other eminent men. The other body was the Egyptian Public Agency for Information, Publishing, Distribution and Printing, headed by the Minister of State, Abdel Kader Hatem, assisted by the directors of broadcasting and information. It was in fact he who, after October 1961, directed the combination of information and culture, the only man in the new Cabinet to hold two portfolios at the same time. The new cabinet of Sidky Soliman (September 1962) marked the ousting of Hatem, and his network of public-relations playboyish propagandists which lowered Egyptian cultural work to a hitherto unheard-of level. Culture was entrusted to Col. Dr. Sarwat Okasha, and publishing to Mahmud el-Alem, followed by Dr. Abdel Azim Anis, now in charge.

30. L. Armstrong, "American Sociology in the Middle East,"

in *Sociology and Social Research,* XLII, No. 3 (1958), pp. 176–84.

31. *A,* May 4, 1962; scheduled for publication late in 1962, Hobson's *Imperialism,* Panikkar's *Asia and Western Dominance,* a book by H. Kabir, another by Arnold Toynbee. This double list confirms the fact that what was of interest was books on the construction of the modern independent state, not those of specifically socialist turn.

32. *AK,* February 19, 1962.

33. "Al-milkiyya al-ʿamma wassila la hadaf" (Public Property: A Means, Not an End), in *A,* August 16, 1961; A. M. Said was arrested later, during the autumn of 1961.

34. Mohammed F. el-Khatib, "Appeals to the Voters in Egypt's General Elections," in *Review of Economic, Political and Business Studies,* Cairo, V, No. 2 (1957), pp. 57–73.

35. "Economic and Social Foundations of Democracy in the Middle East," in *International Affairs,* XXXII, No. 1 (1956), pp. 40–1.

36. G. Sparrow, *The Sphinx Awakes* (London, 1956), p. 60; E. Sablier, "Mon Entretien avec Nasser" (My Talk with Nasser), in *Candide,* No. 56 (May 24–31, 1962). Little by little a distinction was arrived at between "existence of classes" and "class struggle," as was done by Ehsan Abdel Koddus in "Tabakat bila siraʿ" (Classes without Struggle), in *RY,* No. 1774 (June 11, 1962).

37. "Tayyarat ishtirakiyya" (Socialist Currents), in *RY,* No. 1767 (April 24, 1962); also, by Lutfi el-Kholy, "Hadith sari'h fi'l-ishtirakiyya" (An Open Speech on Socialism), in *A,* May 5, 7, 8, 9 and 10, 1962).

9. Two Books

1. The great Belgian historian H. Pirenne has often maintained the same thesis, showing, for instance, that the Pyramids were the product of a collective drive, not of slavery. There are many similar indications, in A. Erman, A. Gardiner, etc. H. Fawzi, in resuscitating the cultural history of the Egyptian people, deserves the credit for demonstrating the falsity of the myth of the "seven thousand years of slavery."

2. Ehsan Abdel Koddus, in *RY,* No. 1350 (April 26, 1954).

3. This is the author's view of the "revolutionaries" of the time before 1952. But no leftist movement is based specifically on these symbols.

4. In 1962 the author published a new novel, *Al-samman wa'l-kharif* (The Quail and the Springtime). In this book the burning of Cairo serves as the background to the drama of a young Wafdist politician who feels condemned, by the fall of the old order, to loneliness in a world that he refuses to see and understand. Cogitation on the other life—"the better life," as Chekhov called

it—brings the hero to a shattering encounter, in the final chapter, with "a young revolutionary" who follows his road with courage, in spite of prisons and camps and incessant ordeals . . . The face of hope, then, is indeed that of the crucified hero.

10. The Charter of National Action and Its Sequels

1. A few days earlier, Hamdy Hafez cited German unification as an example in his book *Taw'hid Almanya* (The Unification of Germany), brought out by the government publishing house.

2. Fifty-one Israeli spies were arrested and tried on Egyptian soil between 1952 and 1961 (*A*, February 20, 1962); later there were two new trials.

3. Two days before, on Saturday, May 19, Khrushchev made a major speech in Sofia: "Many leaders of countries that have gained their national independence," he said in particular, "attempt to carry out some vague policy, an intermediate policy, that they describe as being 'outside classes.' Thus they ignore the class struggle and the social structure that exist in their countries. Now only the class struggle can gain the victory for socialism. Many countries of Africa and Asia now say that they are building socialism. But what socialism are they talking about? What is meant by the word? Those leaders who are really concerned with the interests of the people will sooner or later have to understand that it is only by basing themselves on the working class, the most stable class, united with the peasantry and supported by all progressive forces, that they can win the victory and arrive at a just solution of basic social problems" (*Le Monde*, May 22, 1962).

4. The Egyptian merchant fleet, which then comprised 24 freighters, 7 tankers and 4 passenger vessels, was soon enlarged by 38 new freighters, 12 tankers and 18 cruise ships (*A*, February 17, 1962).

5. *A*, May 27, 1962.

6. One of the most prolific authors of the Islamic renaissance, closely allied to the Moslem Brotherhood; principal works: *Al-Islam wa'l-awda' al-iktissadiyya* (Islam and the Economic Situation), *Kholk al-muslim* (The Character of the Muslim), *Al-Islam wa'l manahig al-ishtirakiyya* (Islam and the Socialist Ways), *Al-Islam al-mufatara 'alayhi* (Islam, the Denigrated Religion), *'Akidat al-muslim* (The Faith of the Muslim), *Fi mawkeh al-daawa* [dealing with the MB phase], (On the Spot of the Predication), *Al-Islam wa'l-takat l-mu'attala* (Islam and the Unemployed Potential), *Kayfa nafham al-Islam?* (How to Understand Islam?), *Nazarat fi'l-Kor'an* (Views on the Koran), etc.

7. *A*, May 28, 1962.

8. *A*, May 29, 1962.

9. *A*, May 29 to June 3, 1962.

10. *A*, June 7, 1962.

11. *A*, June 14, 1962.

12. Complete lists of members elected, in *A* (February 7, 12–15, 17, 18, 20, 21 and 25, 1962).

13. *A*, June 27–8, 1962.

14. *A*, May 31, 1962.

15. *A*, June 20, 1962.

16. On the discussions in the trade unions, cf. *A* (March 14, and June 11, 14 and 16, 1962); on the peasants, cf. symposium, "As'hab al-gallalih" (Those Who Wear the Gallabieh [the fellah's simple skirt]), in *RY*, No. 1772 (May 28, 1962).

17. *A*, March 10, May 29, and June 2 and 7, 1962. Among the speeches in the Congress, one by Dr. Apollos Bulos should be mentioned: "Fifty percent of Egyptian children die before the age of fifteen," while cancer of the intestines, brought on by schistosomiasis and pellagra, attacks 2,250,000 persons. Mustafa el-Baradei, president of the Bar Association, won committee approval for his plan for a "consitutional court" to curb despotism. Sheik Sayed Sabek denounced the practice of secret files and "the administrative spy hanging like the sword of Damocles over the heads of government employees." (*A*, May 31, June 25, March 12, 1962).

18. *A*, March 11, 1962. The team of Kamal Eddine Hussein and Soliman Hozayyen, oriented to the past, drew up resolutions most of which were pushed aside by Nasser. See also the complete list of Congress members in *A*, as cited in Note 12 *supra*.

19. *A*, March 13, 1962.

20. *A*, March 12, 1962.

21. *A*, June 3, 1962.

22. *A*, June 4, 1962.

23. *A*, June 7 and 11, 1962.

24. E. Abdel Koddus, "Mak'ad fi'l-mu'tamar" (A Seat in Congress), in *RY*, No. 1773 (June 1962).

25. M. H. Heykal, "Hal yakdar al-fallahun wa'l-'ummal 'ala ta'hammol mas'uliyyatihem al-gadida?" (Can the Peasants and Workers Assume Their New Responsibilities?); "Hadith 'an al-akhta' wa 'an al-'huriyya" (A Talk on Mistakes and on Liberty); "Naga'h al-mithak yartabet bi shay'en wa'hed: mumarassat al-'huriyya" (The Success of the Charter Is Conditioned by One Thing: the Use of Liberty), in *A*, June 1, 8 and 29, 1962). An interesting study of the Charter by Lutfi el-Kholy from the point of view of the official "Left," "Ab'ad al-sura allati yarsimuha al-mithak" (The Scope of the Picture Drawn by the Charter), in *A*, June 11, 12, 14 and 20, 1962), elaborated in his book *Al-Mithak al-watani* (The National Charter), Cairo, 1962.

26. M. H. Heykal, "Al-gaysh wa'l-thawra" (The Army and the Revolution), in *A* (July 27, 1962).

27. *Pravda*, reprinted in *A* (August 5, 1962), from the full text

published in *al-Akhbar* (Beirut), July 20, 1962; interview with P. Satiukov and A. Adzhubei, in *A* (July 30, 1962); etc.

28. *A*, July 23–7, 1962.

29. *A*, July 24, 1962. Several studies marked the tenth anniversary; let us mention among others the special issues of *AI*, No. 166 (July 15, 1962), and *EPSR* (July 1962); the semiofficial group work *'Ashr sanawat magida* (Ten Glorious Years); Dr. G. E. Ramadi, *Min thamarat al-thawra fi'ashr sanawat* (From the Fruits of the Revolution after Ten Years); A. M. Shemeiss, *'Ashr sanawat fi mashrek al-shams* (Ten Years in the Rising Sun of the Revolution); the special issue of *al-Magalla*, VI, No. 66 (1962); etc.

30. *A*, September 25 and 27, and October 1, 1962; the (London) *Times* (September 28 and October 1) pointed out that the "Presidential Council" included five vice-chairmen, in this order: Abdel Latif el-Boghdadi, Zakaria Mohieddine, Hussein el-Shafei, Kamal Eddine Hussein and Abdel Hakim Amer. Of the twenty-five ministers, only ten kept their posts; among the significant appointments these must be noted: A. M. Kayssuni, Treasury and the Plan; Abdel Kader Hatem, Culture and National Guidance, and also Information (two separate ministries), thus removing Sarwat Okasha from cultural matters; General Abdel Azim Fahmy (formerly head of the political police), Interior; Sidky Soliman, High Dam; Anwar Salama (the first worker to reach the Cabinet), Labor; Dr. Hekmat Abu Zeid, a woman professor, Social Affairs.

A "Council of Defense," headed by Nasser, had twenty members, comprising fifteen ministers and the four Chiefs of Staff; it was under the jurisdiction of a "Permanent Defense Committee" whose only members were Abdel Hakim Amer, Abdel Latif el-Boghdadi, Zakaria Mohieddine and Kamal Eddine Hussein. On the American rockets, cf. "Hugga Kadima makshufa" (The Old Pretext Uncovered), in *A*, September 28, 1962.

31. "Population and Manpower," in *NBE Econ. Bull.*, XVI, Nos. 1–2 (1963), pp. 5–16.

32. Charles P. Issawi, *Egypt in Revolution: An Economic Analysis* (Oxford U. Press, 1963), p. 47, Note 3.

33. The author adds in a note: "An official document (Hansen, *The Growth of National Income in the UAR*, Cairo, 1963) estimates the rate of growth for the 1952–62 period at 4.4% to 4.8%. This estimate, with allowance for the fact that the growth of income in terms of constant prices was 6% (official figures for 1952: £E790 million; for 1962: £E1.411 billion), would suppose that prices had risen by only 12–16% during this decade, which is manifestly false. This correction in prices having been made on the bases of price indices [which are no longer published], we find an actual rate of 3–3.2%." Hassan Riad, *L'Egypte nassérienne* (Paris, 1964).

34. *Ibid*, pp. 190–1. Pages 9–191 must be studied with all the attention that they deserve: they represent the best study of the Egyptian bourgeoisie now available.

35. *A*, August 1, 2, 3, 4, 1963.

36. *RY*, No. 1843 (October 7, 1963). The best analysis, by any standard, is the comprehensive textbook by B. Hansen and G. A. Marzouk, *Development and Economic Policy in the UAR (Egypt)* (Amsterdam, 1965), which should be used by serious students and specialists because of its technical character.

37. All the officiating members of the old Revolutionary Command Council became Vice-Presidents of the Republic, except Abdel Latif el-Boghdadi and Kamal Eddine Hussein, who were removed because of their rightist opposition—Hussein turned openly for support to the Moslem Brotherhood—and Anwar el-Sadate, who became president of the National Assembly. The government comprised 11 Vice-Premiers and 22 ministers. The eleven were Dr. Nur Eddine Taraf (Ministries of Justice, Labor and Youth); Mohammed Abdu el-Shorabassi (*Wakfs* and Al Azhar University); Kamal Eddine Rifaat (Higher Education anl Scientific Research); Dr. Mahmud Fawzi (Foreign Affairs and Foreign Cultural Relations); Dr. Abdel Moneim el-Kayssuni (Finance, Economy and Foreign Trade); Dr. Kamal Ramzi Stino (Supply and Internal Trade); Dr. Aziz Sidky (Heavy Industry, Electricity and Mineral Resources); Dr. Mustafa Khalil (Transportation and Post Office, Telephone and Telegraph); Abbas Raduan (Health, Education, Social Affairs, Housing and Public Services); Dr. Abdel Kader Hatem (Culture and National Guidance); Abdel Mohsen Abul Nur (Agriculture, Agrarian Reform and Irrigation).

38. Even just before the visit, M. H. Heykal hurled an indictment at the Arab Communist parties: "Arab-Soviet relations have undergone a severe test at the end of 1958 and the beginning of 1959. The Arab Communist parties will long have to bear the responsibility for that ordeal: in every way they have paid a heavy price for it. The Arab Communist parties made three mistakes: (1) They were incapable of seeing that there was a third path of progress, the one offered by the prototype of the national revolution and its social revolution; from the start these parties demonstrated their incapacity to recognize the potentialities and possibilities of the Revolution of July 23, 1952. (2) They were incapable of recognizing the national reality with its wealth of possibilities for unity, and all they saw in unity was an attempt by Arab capitalism to extend its markets, thus robbing the unity movement of any possibility of having a progressive content. (3) They were incapable of recognizing the function of Egypt in the Arab zone both as an indispensable base and as a vanguard forged by historic circumstances of vast scope" (*A*, May 8, 1964).

PART IV

11. On Specificity . . .

1. Wahida, *op. cit.*, p. 57. "Social changes were substantial within the limits of the military society. Outside that society they were negligible." D. Ayalon, *Gunpowder and Finances in the Mameluk Kingdom* (London, 1956), p. xv, Note 1.

2. In the very plentiful bibliography on Mohammed Ali, I should like to mention especially the following works: Dr. M. Fahmy's quick survey, *La Révolution de l'industrie en Egypte et ses conséquences au XIX° siècle: 1800–1950* (The Industrial Revolution in Egypt and Its Consequences in the Nineteenth Century: 1800–1950), Leyden, 1960; Leheita, *op. cit.*, pp. 79–193; both these books deal with the economic aspect; on the army, cf. A. R. el-Rafei, *'Asr Mohammed Ali* (The Era of Mohammed Ali), 3rd ed. (Cairo, 1951), pp. 372–463; Berger's study, *Military Elite, op. cit.*

3. Earl Cromer, *Modern Egypt*, Vol II (London, 1908), pp. 473–7.

4. Shafei, *Tatawwor, op. cit.*, p. 14.

12. Nationalitarian Construction or Socialism?

1. An authorized spokesman pointed out that the private sector did in fact provide 25 percent of the foreign trade, particularly 40 percent of the cotton, 50 percent of the onions, potatoes and garlic, 40 percent of the citrus fruits, and a high proportion of other vegetables and fruits; copper, wood, glass, plastic and metal products, medicinal plants and travel services (*A*, May 23, 1962).

2. The total sum of investments in the private sector after the 1961 laws was reported to have reached £E30 million (*A*, May 10, 1962); there is a detailed collection of statistics on the economic situation at the end of this first decade in *NBE Econ. Bull.*, XV, No. 1 (1962), pp. 75–102.

3. Preparatory Committee, *op. cit.*, pp. 669–70.

4. Mohammed el-Khafif, "Al-kita' al-'am kabla kawanin yolyo wa ba'daha" (The Public Sector Before the July Legislation, and After), in *A*, March 8, 1962.

5. In mid-April the Minister of Industry, Aziz Sidky, rendered the accounting of nine months of nationalizations: 28,000 new jobs for workers, a production increase of £E22 million (*A*, April 15, 1962). The process of concentration gathered speed: during the second half of 1961 the number of industrial firms employing more than 500 persons was 123, against 105 during the corresponding period in 1960; salaried personnel increased 16 percent and production 10 percent ("Tatawwor al-intag al-sina'i"—

Evolution of Industrial Production—in *A*, February 18, 1962); salaries rose from £E20.1 million to £E23.7 million (*A*, March 31, 1962). In the Congress he announced the establishment of a minimum wage of 25 piasters per day in 4,469 private firms with capital of more than £E1,000, employing 413,000 workers; at the end of May, £E3.75 million in profits was distributed to the employees of 33 companies; production by companies in the public sector rose by 15.3 percent in one year (*A*, May 30 and June 1, 1962); all state functionaries and workers received a bonus of ten days' pay up to a maximum of £E25 in order to match nongovernmental salaries (*A*, May 11, 1962). "In Egypt the rich are under pressure, though not painfully so (except the unfortunate sequestered families). The lower middle classes are gradually becoming stronger . . . Working-class children in Cairo seem merrier and in better health than four years ago. In the villages, hard times continue as before . . ." ("Socialism on the Nile," *loc. cit.*)

6. The Audit Commissioner's report covering statements for the year 1961–62 indicated that virtually all corporations in the public sector had earned profits higher than those of the period before their integration, thanks to the efficient utilization of the collective resources of the national economy and a more judicious employment of reserves (*RY*, No. 1774, June 11, 1962); cf., among others, the analysis of the statements of seventy-six industrial corporations in *A*, June 1, 1962. This was indeed the thinking of Nasser himself, who told the Congress: "We must speak of the middle class . . . which includes national capitalism . . . , merchants, those who work in their own businesses with their children and others . . . We are telling this middle class frankly that its interests are bound to those of the people, the workers and the peasants more than to those of the feudal and capitalist class . . ." (Preparatory Committee, *op. cit.*, pp. 248–9).

7. *A*, June 30, 1962.

8. Riad, *op. cit.*, p. 8. Despite the difference in terminology, the analogy is visibly the same.

9. A semiofficial booklet of political economy, *Al-iktissad al-siyassi* (Political Economy), by A. M. Abdel Khalek (Cairo, Cultural Library No. 13, 1961), is an apologia for Nazism and fascism assimilated into "socialism" . . .

Elsewhere a symposium on freedom enabled Taher Abu Zeid to call for "the restoration of due process," and Sheik Ahmed el-Shorabassi to voice the hope that "the day may come when the Ministry of the Interior can no longer intern anyone without a court order," while Dr. Omar Shahine declared that "emergency measures are one of the sources of fear . . ." "Mugtama' bila Khawf" (A Society without Fear), in *RY*, No. 1774 (June 11, 1962).

13. What Is Living . . .

1. Cf. my first sketch, "La Vision du problème colonial par le monde afro-asiatique" (The Vision of the Colonial Problem by the Afro-Asian World), *Cahiers Internationaux de Sociologie*, XXXV (1963), pp. 145–56.

2. *Rose el-Yussef*, especially, scented something in the wind and organized a great national discussion on the failure of the 1919 revolution, beginning in its issue No. 1782, August 6, 1962.

3. M. H. Heykal, "Al-umma, dawruba fi san' el-batal wa dawr al-batal fi 'hayatiha" (The Nation: Its Role in the Formation of the Present, and the Role of the Hero in the Nation's Life), in *A*, May 25, 1962, presents the military view of the hero.

Bibliography

(A supplement to the detailed bibliographical references provided in the Source Notes which might be useful for further reading and research)

I. Bibliographical Guides

A Cumulation of Selected and Annotated Bibliography of Economic Literature on the Arabic-Speaking Countries of the Middle East 1938–1960 (London, G. K. Hall, 1967).

Dagher, Joseph A., *Al-dimoqratiyyah fi'l-maktaba al-'Arabiyya* (Democracy in Arabic Literature), short bibliography (Beirut, 1959).

Ljunggren, Florence, and Geddes, Charles L., *An International Directory of Institutes and Societies Interested in the Middle East* (Amsterdam, Djambatan, 1962).

O'Brien, Patrick, *The Revolution in Egypt's Economic System, from Private Enterprise to Socialism 1952–1965* (London, Oxford U. Press, 1966), pp. 338–43. Bibliography of statistical and official publications (economic) sources.

Pearson, J. D., *Index Islamicus* (Cambridge, Heffer, 1958).

———, *Index Islamicus Supplement 1956–1960* (Cambridge, Heffer, 1962).

Soliman, Salah Mohammed Ahmad, *Dalil al-maçader al ihça'iyya fi'il-Gumhuriyya al-'Arabiyya al-Muttahida* (Guide to the Statistical Sources in the UAR). Sirs el-Layan, 1959.

II. Readers, Anthologies, etc.

Abdel-Malek, Anouar, *Anthologie de la littérature arabe con-temporaine, II: les Essais* (Paris, Le Seuil, 1965).

Daumal, J., and Leroy, M., *Gamal Abdel-Nasser avec ses textes essentiels* (Seghers, 1967).

Issawi, Charles, *The Economic History of the Middle East 1800–1914* (Chicago, U. of Chicago Press, 1966). A highly provocative pre-Revolution guide. For details and comparative history of the Egyptian economy, see pp. 517–24.

Karpat, Kemal, *Political and Social Thought in the Contemporary Middle East* (New York, Praeger, 1967).

Khalil, Muhammad, *The Arab States and the Arab League: A Documentary Record*, 2 vols. (Beirut, Khayats, 1952).

Le Monde arabe cherche les leçons politiques de la défaite. Special issue of *Démocratie Nouvelle*, XXI (February-March 1968).

Rivlin, Benjamin, and Szyliowicz, Joseph S., eds., *The Contemporary Middle East, Tradition and Innovation* (New York, Random House, 1965).

III. Periodical Publications

1) EGYPTIAN:
al-Mussawar (weekly)
al-Tali'a (monthly)
al-Ishtirakiyya (monthly)
al-Fikr al-Mou'açer (monthly)
al-Magalla (monthly)
al-Hilal (monthly)
al-Siyassa al-Dawliyya (monthly)

2) ARABIC:
Dirassat 'Arabiyya (monthly; Beirut)
al-Adab (monthly; Beirut)

3) FOREIGN:
Egyptian affairs are best followed up in *Le Monde*, the London *Times*, *L'Unità*, the *New York Times*, the Sunday *Times*, the *Observer*, *The Economist*, etc.
International Socialist Review (quarterly; Rome)
The Journal of Asian and African Studies (quarterly; Toronto-Leiden)
Middle Eastern Studies (quarterly; London)
Mizan (bimonthly; London)
Orient (quarterly; Paris)
Tiers-Monde (quarterly; Paris)
World Marxist Review (monthly; Prague)

IV. Official Publications

All ministries issue more than one periodical and several series, giving official statistical and documentary information; the list runs to several hundred titles, available on demand from each ministry.

1) *The Republic of Egypt (later: the UAR) Yearbook,* 1953–
2) Central Agency for Mobilization and Statistics: *Statistical Yearbook;* and all publications of a general nature.
3) The Presidency of the Republic: official documents and speeches by President Gamal Abdel Nasser.
4) The Arab Socialist Union General Secretariat: publications, documents, statistics, etc.
5) The League of Arab States General Secretariat: publications, documents, statistics, etc.

Index

ANOUAR ABDEL-MALEK was born, in 1924, into a long-established Coptic Cairo family of intellectuals, state officials and businessmen. He was educated at the French Jesuit College in Cairo, the British Institute, and Ain Shams University, where he studied philosophy. Dr. Abdel-Malek also received a doctorate in sociology from the Sorbonne (1964).

From 1940 to 1959, he was deeply involved in the national movement as a Marxist. During these years, he was also at different times a social theorist, bank clerk, philosophy teacher, and a writer and prominent journalist.

In 1959, because of the repression in Egypt of the Left, Abdel-Malek left for France. He has lived in Paris ever since. Since 1960, he has been on the staff of the Centre National de la Recherche Scientifique, where he is at present research lecturer in the sociology division. He is also a lecturer on the sociology of national movements at the Ecole Pratique des Hautes Etudes (sixth section).

His books include *Peuples d'Afrique; Anthologie de la littérature arabe contemporaine: les Essais;* and *Studies in National Culture* (published in Arabic). Dr. Anouar Abdel-Malek has published in journals in France, Italy, England, Belgium, Egypt, Lebanon, Poland, Turkey and Latin America, and is at work on books on the ideology of the Egyptian renaissance; Egypt's future; the role of the army in Asia, Africa and Latin America; and comparative sociology of civilizations.